𝕿𝖍𝖊 𝕹𝖊𝖜 𝖄𝖔𝖗𝖐 𝕿𝖎𝖒𝖊𝖘

MANUAL OF STYLE
AND USAGE

The New York Times

MANUAL OF STYLE AND USAGE

REVISED AND EXPANDED EDITION

ALLAN M. SIEGAL
Assistant Managing Editor
AND
WILLIAM G. CONNOLLY
Senior Editor

THREE RIVERS PRESS

NEW YORK

Published by Three Rivers Press, New York, New York.
Member of the Crown Publishing Group.

Random House, Inc. New York, Toronto, London, Sydney, Auckland
www.randomhouse.com

THREE RIVERS PRESS is a registered trademark and the Three Rivers Press
colophon is a trademark of Random House, Inc.

Originally published in hardcover by Times Books in 1999.

Printed in the United States of America

Library of Congress Cataloging-in-Publication Data
Siegal, Allan M.
The New York times manual of style and usage, revised and expanded edition
by Allan M. Siegal and William G. Connolly. — 1st ed.
1. Journalism—Style manuals.   I. Connolly, William G.
II. New York times.   III. Title.
PN4783.S57   1999
808'.027—dc21   99-10630

ISBN 0-8129-6389-X

10 9 8 7 6

First Paperback Edition

FOREWORD

There is Style, and then there is style. This book will traffic in the second kind, but must reach its territory by way of homage to the first. Style, with a capital S, achieves what a rule book never can: it lights the page, draws readers, earns their delight, makes them gasp or weep and sometimes captures a place in memory.

Writerly style (even without the illicit capital S) is a set of tools and tricks, a tone of voice. Or rather it is the tone of many voices. At its best, edited with restraint, style is the ingredient that enables any single issue of The New York Times to supply the minimum daily requirement of crisis and struggle and triumph without homogenizing the insights and wit of scores of individual writers.

The best of style relies on reporters' ears and eyesight, and on simplicity—the unpretentious language of a letter to an urbane and literate friend. In that setting, the sudden glimmer of an unusual word, a syncopation or a swerve in logic lets the reader know that here is something richer than an hourly bulletin:

> Like clockwork, the caseworker visited the mother in her spotless apartment in the Bronx. Twice a month, she checked on the young children who had been abused by their mother but had recently returned home from foster care. And when the mother was charged with killing her 5-year-old son last spring, city officials mourned the boy's death but commended the worker's vigilance.   *Rachel L. Swarns*

> OMIYA, Japan
>
> From the time they invaded northeast China in 1931 and the rest of China in 1937, through World War II, Japanese troops massacred civilians, tortured captives and raped young girls almost everywhere they went, and yet those same men—now graying at the temples, raising wrinkled hands to the ear—are unfailingly courteous, gentle and honest.
>
> They are deeply respected in their communities, and everyone knows they would never think of cheating anybody or losing their tempers. Yet they collectively killed 20 million or 30 million people.   *Nicholas D. Kristof*

A single image can elevate a few hundred words, even for readers who may never have expected to read eagerly about Afghanistan:

> Mirbacacot, Afghanistan
> With gunfire snapping in the wind and artillery blasts punctuating his sentences, the commander of the Taliban's front-line forces was in a boastful, triumphant mood today.
>
> He removed his artificial leg, sat comfortably on a blanket in his small brick fortress and pointed a few hundred yards to the north where, lodged in the foothills, was the last bastion of what was once grandly called the Northern Alliance.
>
> "We are giving the enemy 10 days, so that anybody who wants to get out can get out," said the commander, Hajji Mulla Abdus Sattar. "Then, by the will of God, we will crush the life from anyone who remains behind."
> *Barry Bearak*

Style can take the form of humor and surprise:

> If the heavens cooperate tonight, two teams will gather on a swath of Queens County grass to demonstrate how the game of baseball has particularly blessed New York City this year with talent and character. An umpire will shout a familiar demand, the Mets' Al Leiter will fire a baseball to the Yankees' Chuck Knoblauch, and all will be right in one corner of an ever-churning metropolis.
>
> As they say from Queens Boulevard to the Bronx River Parkway: Yeah, right. If you want "Field of Dreams" fantasies, it would be best to go chase flies in some sandlot.
> *Dan Barry*

> Moscow
> In a season of crashing banks, plunging rubles, bouncing paychecks, failing crops and rotating governments, maybe it is not the ultimate insult. But the nation that bore Tolstoy and Chekhov and still regards a well-written letter as a labor of love is buckling a little this week, because it can no longer wish good health to Baba Anya in Omsk.
>
> The Post Office is broke.
> *Michael Wines*

Notice, in that last example, how shrewdly the writer has redeployed an incongruous idea: what have Tolstoy and Chekhov to do with a currency crisis? And in this example from a magazine article, an import from theater, applied to environmentalism, supplies the twist:

> For most of this century, the Hudson has been the John Barrymore of rivers, noble in profile but a sorry wreck. Decades of bingeing on toxic chemicals gradually took a toll,

and although the river's grandeur could not be denied, most people, looking at the Hudson, could only shake their heads in sorrow. The mighty river, once home to porpoises and even reportedly a whale, had entered the final stages of decline, fit habitat only for a few funky fish.   *William Grimes*

Look back, now, at all the examples. Verbs work hardest, and adjectives little: the welfare worker *checked*; the gunfire *snapped*; the pitcher was ready to *fire* a ball. Sentences are nearly all short; exceptions are rare, purposeful and easily navigated. And what is missing? Not one example speaks of *implementing* anything, or *funding* an *ongoing* program. Nothing is *prior to* something else, or *hitherto*. No sentence creaks under the tread of bureaucracy or recycles prefabricated originality: no one gets a *wake-up call* or puts anything *on hold*. No one is *in-your-face*. The word choices break ground: who ever heard of a *funky* fish?

———

If that first kind of style is a form of painting, the second kind—stylebook style—is framing and canvas. Its structure of spelling, grammar and punctuation supports and protects the writer's craft. The rules avert missteps that could keep the reporter from holding the exacting reader. As the previous edition of this book noted, there is little difference between a Martini and a martini, but a rule can shield against untidiness in detail that might make readers doubt large facts.

This manual traces its roots at least to 1895; The Times's archives show that a version existed then, but the earliest one still accessible dates from 1923. It consisted of 40 pages, set in the same agate type as the classified ads. With its pasteboard cover, it slid easily into a letter envelope. It prescribed the credit for an overseas dispatch: *By Wireless to The New York Times*. (The paper dropped the hyphen from *New-York* in December 1896.) The 1923 booklet cautioned printers that in following copy, they must make allowance "for the intelligence (or lack of intelligence)" of the advertiser. It listed *pasha*, *pigmy* and *seraglio* among "Words Frequently Misspelled" (raising a question: What were they doing in The Times at all, not to mention frequently?).

Between 1923 and the latest previous edition of this book, in 1976, rule inflation set in: that volume ran to 231 pages, in book-size 11-point type. Its preamble quoted, in turn, from the 1962 revision: "Style rules should be extensive enough to establish the desired system of style, but not so extensive as to inhibit the writer or the editor. The rules should encourage thinking, not discourage it. A single rule might suffice: 'The rule of common sense will prevail at all times.' "

Common sense, in today's newsroom, should mean that this book—aside from its guidance about vulgarity and slurs—does not serve as a catalog of bans on words or phrases. Indeed, few notions can curdle the joy of journalism more quickly than the idea that rules outweigh the freshness a writer may infuse into a phrase usually considered irregular or shopworn. So if the manual seems to lean on qualifiers like "normally" and "ordinarily," it is to remind writers and editors that one measure of skill is exceptions, not rules.

———

In approaching the mechanics of usage and grammar, this manual reflects The Times's impression of its educated and sophisticated readership—traditional but not tradition-bound. In several entries on evolving usage (CONTACT, DATA and SPLIT INFINITIVE, for example) the manual abandons the most conservative standard but alerts writers that a minority of readers may differ. In a few notable cases (BLAME; HOPEFULLY; LIKE; MEDIA; and WHO, WHOM), the manual hews to a traditional course while acknowledging the change that is unfolding elsewhere. Many entries also offer examples of rephrasing to avoid stodginess.

Throughout, the goal is a fluid style, easygoing but not slangy and only occasionally colloquial. Newcomers will find that while The Times favors terseness (as in the entries on BOARD OF DIRECTORS and ONE OF THE), it uses fewer abbreviations than the news agencies or most other papers. The aim is to avoid a telegraphic staccato: even a terse newspaper can usually spare a word or two to say, for example, *critics of the tax* rather than the compressed *tax critics* (are those like music critics?).

Nowadays any style manual must grapple with the vocabulary of social issues. This one counsels respect for the group sensibilities and preferences that have made themselves heard in the last two or three decades—concerns, for example, of women, minorities and those with disabilities. The manual favors constructions that keep language neutral, a crystalline medium through which journalists report ideas without proclaiming stances. That advice takes its most explicit form in the entry on MEN AND WOMEN. (It is worth recalling that in 1976, a more limited entry was called simply "women." Sexual equality had yet to be elevated, at least by The Times, to an agenda for society over all.)

At many points, the manual tries to explain its choices: note, for example, the discussion of apostrophes in the entry on PLURALS, and the comments on AMERICAN INDIAN(S). Although a stylebook cannot also be a journalism text or a policy handbook, readers will find a window into The Times's character in the entries on ANONYMITY; ATTRIBUTION; CORRECTIONS; DATELINE INTEGRITY; EDITORS' NOTES; FAIRNESS AND IMPARTIALITY; OBITUARIES; OBSCENITY, VULGARITY, PROFANITY; and QUOTATIONS. The newspaper's preferred tone is addressed in many entries, notably COLLOQUIALISMS and SLANG.

———

Finally a word about using the manual. It is self-indexing. A word that appears in bold-face without discussion should be spelled and capitalized or lowercased as shown. Cross-references are shown in SMALL CAPITALS. Many compound words are listed in the entries for their prefixes or suffixes. The authority for spelling any word not found here, and for the word's usage, is the most recent printing of Webster's New World College Dictionary (IDG Books Worldwide). For place names, foreign and domestic, other backup authorities apply. They are shown in the manual's entries on SPELLING and GEOGRAPHIC NAMES.

ACKNOWLEDGMENTS

The creation of this expanded and overhauled volume began on the day in 1976 that the first copies of The New York Times Manual of Style and Usage arrived in the newsroom. Since then, scores of staff members in many departments have offered suggestions, pleas and drafts for additions and changes. Specialized writers in fields like finance, science, religion and the arts volunteered time, expertise and a capacity to suffer philistines. The contributions of editors, particularly in the manuscript checking phase, were indispensable. The Times's research librarians exceeded even their wondrous everyday energy and inventiveness. And the newsroom systems staff tamed the database, more than once wresting whole chapters back from digital oblivion.

The manual owes its structure to Lewis Jordan, news editor of The Times, who died in 1983. As editor of the 1962 and 1976 editions, he left his mark on numerous entries, but his central legacy was the self-indexing format, since adopted by many other news organizations for their stylebooks.

Two contributors to this edition defy submersion in the "too numerous" category. Barbara Oliver, now research editor of The St. Petersburg Times in Florida, transmuted the project from the index-card world of 1976 to the era of Word and the Web, checking every fact, date, name and merger along the way. And Merrill Perlman, the editors' editor, took on the role of burnisher, skeptic and goad. Her mission was thankless, until this moment.

A. M. S.
W. G. C.

The New York Times

MANUAL OF STYLE
AND USAGE

A

a, an, the. Use the article *a* before a word beginning with a consonant sound, including the aspirate *h*: *a car; a hotel; a historical*. Also use it before words like *union, euphonious* and *unit*. Use *an* before a word beginning with a vowel sound: *onion; uncle; honor*. The choice of article before an abbreviation, a numeral or a symbol depends upon the likely pronunciation: *an N.Y.U. student; a C.I.A. officer; an 11-year-old girl*.

Avoid the journalese practice of dropping *A* or *The* at the beginning of a sentence. If several consecutive sentences or paragraphs begin with the same article, recast some to break the monotony.

An article should appear before each parallel noun in a series or a pair: *The ambulance carried a nurse, a paramedic and a doctor; The hero and the heroine received medals.* Make an exception if the nouns convey a single idea: *a bow and arrow; a hook and eye.*

In the title of a literary, artistic or musical work—in English or a foreign language—omit the opening word *a, an* or *the* when it follows an adjective: *That dreadful "Old Curiosity Shop" character.* Similarly, omit the opening article when it follows another article: *An "Old Curiosity Shop" character.* The article can also be omitted to avoid awkwardness after a possessive. Thus: *"A Tale of Two Cities," by Dickens,* but *Dickens's "Tale of Two Cities."* If the opening article in a title is necessary information, rephrase the surrounding sentence to avoid direct juxtaposition with a possessive, an adjective or a second article.

If a foreign-language expression begins with an article and appears in an English-language passage, translate the article: *at the Arc de Triomphe.* But if the article forms part of a title, uppercase it, untranslated: *Le Monde; La Scala.*

Also see THE.

A.A. for Alcoholics Anonymous.

AAA (without periods). The former American Automobile Association has adopted the initials as its full official name.

A.&P. for the Great Atlantic and Pacific Tea Company, the supermarket chain. In a headline, insert a thin space after the ampersand, to balance the appearance of the preceding period.

AARP, an association of middle-aged and older Americans, was the American Association of Retired Persons until 1998. The newer name, written without periods, is officially considered neither an abbreviation nor an acronym.

A.B. or **B.A.** for Bachelor of Arts. Also: *a bachelor's degree.*

A.B.A. It can stand for the *American Banking Association*, the *American Bar Association* or the *American Booksellers Association.* In headlines, abbreviate only when the context is unmistakable.

abbreviations. Commonly used abbreviations are listed separately. In general, spell out the names of government bureaus and agencies, well-known organizations, companies, etc., on first reference. In later references, use short forms like *the agency* or *the company* when possible because handfuls of initials make for mottled typography and choppy prose. Here is an example of what *not* to do: *The U.A.W. and the U.M.W. supported the complaints made by the W.H.O., Unicef and the F.A.O., but A.F.L.-C.I.O. leaders did not.*

When abbreviations are highly familiar, though, long or cumbersome expressions may be shortened even on first reference, and especially afterward. Examples include *A.F.L.-C.I.O.* and *F.B.I.* If the article deals centrally with such an organization, the full name should appear somewhere in the copy.

Abbreviations may be used more freely in headlines. A title that would be spelled out in copy may be shortened with a surname in a headline: *Gen. Barany*; *Gov. Lamb*; *Rep. Berenich* (but not *Sen.*, even in a headline). Place designations and company terms may also be abbreviated in headlines: *Fifth Ave.* (or *5th Ave.*); *Fordham Rd.*; *Patchin Pl.*; *Brooklyn Hts.*; *Warner Bros.*; *Acme Co.*; *News Corp.* And *Department* may be abbreviated in a headline as part of a name (*State Dept.*).

Even freer use of abbreviations is permitted in charts, listings and tables to conserve space. All standard abbreviations may be used, as well as coined contractions, so long as they are understandable. In all types of copy, avoid unfamiliar or specialized short forms like *N.R.D.G.A.* (National Retail Dry Goods Association).

Ordinarily use periods in abbreviations when the letters stand for separate words: *F.C.C.*; *I.B.M.*; *N.R.A.* Use no spaces after the periods within an abbreviation. (But use thin spaces between personal initials, even those forming part of a company or organizational name: *J. C. Penney.*)

In an acronym—an abbreviation pronounced as a word—omit periods. Ordinarily uppercase such an expression if it is up to four letters long: *NATO*; *CUNY*; *AIDS*; *SALT.* Acronyms of five or more letters are upper-and-lowercased: *Unicef*; *Unesco*; *Alcoa*; *Awacs.* (Lowercased exceptions exist, and the dictionary is the guide: *modem*; *radar*; *sonar.*)

If a corporation legally adopts a former abbreviation or other cluster of letters as its full name, without periods, follow that style: *the AT&T Corporation*; *ITT Industries.*

When letters within a single word are extracted for use as an abbreviation, they are capitalized without periods: *DDT; TV; TB.* (By contrast, *V.D.* requires the periods because it stands for two words.)

For consistency in references to broadcasting services, networks and stations, omit periods in all their abbreviations, and in call letters (*CBS, CNN, PBS, NPR, WNBC, KPFA*).

Also see ACRONYMS; COMPANY AND CORPORATION NAMES; DEPARTMENT; STATE ABBREVIATIONS; SUBWAY LINES; TELEVISION NETWORKS.

ABC for the former American Broadcasting Companies, now a subsidiary of the Walt Disney Company. ABC operates the *ABC Television Network. ABC News* and *ABC Sports* are divisions of the network, which also owns and operates 10 television stations, among them *WABC-TV.* Any of these names, as well as *ABC,* may be used in a first reference. (Do not attribute an ABC News production to ABC Television.) *ABC* may stand alone in later references and should stand alone when several networks are mentioned together: *ABC, CBS, CNN and NBC will televise the news conference.*

A B C's (the alphabet or the basics). Use thin spaces between the letters.

able-bodied.

ABM('s) for antiballistic missile(s).

A-bomb may be used in articles or in headlines, but *atomic bomb* or *atom bomb* is preferred. In cap-and-lowercase headlines: *A-Bomb.*

abortion. The political and emotional heat surrounding abortion gives rise to a range of polemical language. For the sake of neutrality, avoid *pro-life* and *pro-choice* except in quotations from others. Impartial terms include *abortion rights advocate* and *anti-abortion campaigner* (or, in either case, *campaign, group* or *rally*). *Anti-abortion* is an undisputed modifier, but *pro-abortion* raises objections when applied to people who say they do not advocate *having* abortions. *Abortionist* carries overtones of stealth and illegality. In copy about abortion, *woman* and *fetus* are more neutral terms than *mother* (for a pregnant woman) and *baby* (for a fetus).

absence. *See* LACK.

absolutely necessary. A redundancy.

Abstract Expressionism. Capitalize when referring to the postwar American art movement. Recognized Abstract Expressionists include Willem de Kooning, Robert Motherwell, Jackson Pollock and Mark Rothko. *See* ARTS TERMINOLOGY.

A.C. for an athletic club after first reference and in headlines: *the Downtown Athletic Club; Downtown A.C.*

academic degrees and titles. *See* separate entries, and DR. and PROF.

academic departments. Lowercase *history department, English literature department,* etc. (school, college or university). That wording is preferred, but style also permits *department of natural history; department of English literature.*

academy. Lowercase in later references to the French Academy and the National Academy of Sciences. For the United States Military, Naval, Coast Guard and Air Force Academies, on later references make it *the Air Force Academy* or *the academy*.

Academy Award(s); *the award(s);* *the Oscar(s).* Articles dealing centrally with the awards should mention that they are presented by the Academy of Motion Picture Arts and Sciences. In brief or passing references, *Oscar* can stand alone, without explanation. *Also see* Emmy Award(s); Grammy Award(s); Tony Award(s).

a cappella.

accent marks are used for French, Italian, Spanish, Portuguese and German words and names. For simplicity, use the marks uniformly with uppercase and lowercase letters, despite conventions that treat certain uppercase accents as optional. Do not use accents in words or names from other languages (Slavic and Scandinavian ones, for example), which are less familiar to most American writers, editors and readers; such marks would be prone to error, and type fonts often lack characters necessary for consistency.

Some foreign words that enter the English language keep their accent marks (*protégé, résumé*); others lose them (*cafe, facade*). The dictionary governs spellings, except for those shown in this manual.

In the name of a United States resident, use or omit accents as the bearer does; when in doubt, omit them. (Exception: Use accents in Spanish names of Puerto Rico residents.)

Times style calls for six marks:

é   The *acute accent* on an *e* in French signifies an "ay" sound (*communiqué*). In Spanish or Portuguese it denotes an irregularly placed syllable stress (*Lázaro; simpático*).

à   The *grave accent* alters various vowel sounds in French (*frère; voilà*) and occasionally in Portuguese. In Italian it marks an irregularly placed syllable stress (*Pietà; tiramisù*). In Italian and French it sometimes distinguishes between similar-looking words (*où* and *ou; la* and *là*).

ô   The *circumflex*, in French, may modify vowel sounds (*Rhône*) or signify the evolutionary disappearance of an *s* that existed in Latin (*hôtel*). In Portuguese the circumflex usually marks syllable stress (*Antônio*).

ç   The *cedilla* beneath a *c*, in French or Portuguese, produces the soft sound of *s* in front of certain vowels that would otherwise dictate a hard *k* sound (*garçon; français*).

ñ   The *tilde*, in Spanish, produces a *y* sound after *n* (*mañana*). In Portuguese it denotes a nasal vowel sound (*São Paulo*).

ü   The *umlaut* modifies vowel sounds in German (*Götterdämmerung; Düsseldorf*). Some news wires replace the umlaut with an *e* after the affected vowel. Normally undo that spelling, but check before altering a personal name; some individual Germans use the *e* form. In the Latin languages, the umlaut is known as a *dieresis*. It denotes separated pronunciation of two adjacent vowels (*naïve; Citroën; Noël*), or signals pronunciation of a normally silent final consonant (*Saint-Saëns; Perrier-Jouët*).

Two Spanish punctuation marks—¿ and ¡—are available for special effects. But ordinarily punctuate Spanish questions and exclamations in English style.

access. Use it only as a noun; as a verb it is technical jargon. Conversational substitutes abound: *look up, retrieve, find, connect, enter* and even *gain access*.

accommodate.

accouterment.

accused. Just as an *accused* stockbroker is a stockbroker, an *accused* forger is some type of forger. Avoid any construction that implies guilt on the part of someone merely *accused, charged* or *suspected. Also see* ALLEGEDLY.

Achilles' heel (not *Achilles heel* or *Achilles's*). The exceptional style is customary for the possessive of a classical name.

acknowledgment.

acre. An *acre* equals 43,560 square feet or 4,840 square yards or 4,047 square meters. The metric *hectare* equals 10,000 square meters or 2.47 acres. In copy, generally convert hectares into acres; if the hectare figure is a round number, round the acres as well.

acronyms. An acronym is a word formed from the first letter (or letters) of each word in a series: *NATO* from North Atlantic Treaty Organization; *radar* from *radio detection and ranging*. (Unless pronounced as a word, an abbreviation is not an acronym.) When an acronym serves as a proper name and exceeds four letters, capitalize only the first letter: *Unesco; Unicef. Also see* ABBREVIATIONS and COMPANY AND CORPORATION NAMES.

across from. Often *opposite* is smoother: *The shop was across from the school.* In that sentence, *across* seems to need an object. Make it *The shop was across 50th Street from the school*, or *The shop was opposite the school*.

acting. Uppercase only when it modifies an uppercased title: *Acting Attorney General Hilary B. Miel; the acting attorney general; the acting secretary of state; the acting secretary; the acting chairwoman of the committee.* Generally move a long title after the name, to avoid this awkwardness: *Acting Secretary of Health, Education and Welfare Hilary B. Miel*.

activist. The expression is not always neutral: sometimes it seems to cloak a cause in nobility, and sometimes it implies militancy when involvement in a cause is no more than routine. Terms like *advocate* and *campaigner* may be more precise.

actor, actress. While *actor* can refer to a woman as well as to a man, *actress* remains widely used and seems exempt from most objections to grafted feminine endings. *See* MEN AND WOMEN.

acts, amendments, bills and laws. Capitalize the name of an act or law when using the full title or a commonly known shorter form: *Sherman Antitrust Act; Social Security Act; Taft-Hartley Act; Multiple Dwelling Law;* etc. But lowercase *act* when it stands alone or in a general description: *the antitrust act; the housing act.*

A draft measure is *a bill* until it is enacted; then it becomes *an act* or *a law.* Lowercase the names of bills and proposed constitutional amendments not yet enacted into law (*housing bill; food stamp bill*) except for proper names occurring in the description (*Baranek-Lamm bill*).

A ratified amendment to the United States Constitution is capitalized in a reference to its formal title (including the number): *the Fifth Amendment; the 18th Amendment.* But lowercase an informal title (*the income tax amendment*), except words that are capitalized in their own right (*the Prohibition amendment*).

Act Up. Upper-and-lowercase the name of the protest group concerned with AIDS issues. (It is not an advocacy group.) Its full name is the AIDS Coalition to Unleash Power.

acute accent. *See* ACCENT MARKS.

A.D. for anno Domini. Since it means *in the year of the Lord* (or *of our Lord*), place the abbreviation ahead of the numerals: *The town was founded in A.D. 73.* In a reference to a century, though, the number comes first: *fourth century A.D.*

B.C., for before Christ, always follows the date: *founded in 128 B.C.* or *The town dates from the second century B.C.*

ad can substitute for *advertisement* in light or colloquial contexts and in all headlines. *Want ad* is acceptable in most contexts because replacements tend to be stilted.

adage. The word means an old saying. So *old adage* is redundant.

addresses. For the names of streets, avenues, etc., in ordinary copy, spell out and capitalize ordinal numbers: *First* through *Ninth.* Also spell out and capitalize *Avenue, Street, West, East,* etc.: *First Avenue; Fifth Avenue; Park Avenue; East Ninth Street.* Use figures for *10th* and above: *10th Avenue; West 14th Street; 42nd Street; West 113th Street.* When an address includes a compass point, abbreviate it without periods: *818 C Street SE; 1627 I Street NW.*

Use the plural (*Streets* or *Avenues*) when *and* appears in a location: *between 43rd and 44th Streets.* But use the singular in a *to* phrase: *along Fifth Avenue, from 43rd to 44th Street.* For "decades" of numbered streets, use figures: *the 60's; the East 60's; the West 80's; the 130's;* etc.

Avenue, Street, Road and the like may be abbreviated with a name (*Ave.; St.; Rd.*) in headlines, charts, maps, lists and tables, but not in ordinary copy. In headlines, figures may also be used for the ordinal numbers through *9th* in the designations of streets and avenues. But avoid *1st*.

Use figures for all building numbers: *1 Fifth Avenue*; *510 Broadway*; *893 12th Avenue*. When numbers exceed three digits, omit commas: *1135 11th Avenue*. Omit *No.* before a building number except in a phrase like *at 510 Broadway, but not at No. 512*.

House numbers in Queens often take hyphens: *107-71 111th Street*.

When mentioning an address on a major thoroughfare in New York City, ordinarily specify the nearest cross street. In an address on a cross street, the nearest avenue may be specified when useful. If a street or avenue has both a commemorative name and an original one, use the better-known address in routine references: *West 43rd Street*, not *Adolph S. Ochs Street*. When a special context warrants the newer name, also provide a graceful translation: *the block of West 43rd Street known as Adolph S. Ochs Street*.

Generally give specific addresses for places in the New York metropolitan area. But in writing about a person whose family might face harassment or harm, consider a general neighborhood reference instead. If an exact address seems newsworthy because of a crime or other visible event, carefully consider the potential for harm before publishing it.

Foreign addresses may be punctuated and capitalized in the local style (*3, rue Scribe*, etc.), but a simple reference to a foreign street should be capitalized in American style: *the Rue de l'Odéon*. Also, for the French municipal districts: *Ninth Arrondissement*; *10th Arrondissement*.

Also see AVENUE OF THE AMERICAS and ZIP CODE.

Adelphi University (in Garden City, N.Y.).

adjutant. An officer overseeing administration in a military unit. The expression denotes an assignment, not a rank. So it is not abbreviated and is separated from the name by a comma.

adjutant general. The officer (often a colonel or a general) in charge of administration in a major military headquarters. In most American states, the term is also applied to the commander of the National Guard. The plural is *adjutants general*. The term denotes an assignment, not a rank, so it is not abbreviated and is separated from the name by a comma.

Adm. *Lynn A. Karitsa*; *Admiral Karitsa*; *the admiral*.

administration. Lowercase in all governmental references, federal, state or local, foreign or domestic: *the Cordeiro administration*; *the administration*. But uppercase when it is part of an agency name: *Social Security Administration*.

administrative law judge. Lowercase it after the name: *Stacy N. Lamm, administrative law judge*. In later references: *Judge Lamm*; *the judge*. In the federal system, this title has replaced hearing examiner. But many states have *hearing examiners* and *hearing officers.*

Administrator *Lee D. Barany* (for the head of a governmental agency who bears that title); *Administrator Barany; the administrator; Mr.* (or *Ms., Mrs.* or *Miss*) *Barany.*

Admiral of the Fleet *Morgan T. Kuzu; Admiral Kuzu; the admiral of the fleet.* In foreign navies that have the rank, it is often honorary or ceremonial. Note, too, that the title differs from *Fleet Admiral.*

admissible.

admitted homosexual. Avoid this term, which suggests criminality or shame. Make it *acknowledged* or *declared homosexual, openly gay* or *openly lesbian* if a modifier is indeed necessary. *Also see* GAY; LESBIAN; SEXUAL ORIENTATION.

adoption. Adoptive status, as child or parent, should be mentioned only when it is pertinent and when its pertinence is made clear. In this context, avoid terms like *natural parents* and *real parents*, which seem to downgrade adoptive status. Use *biological parents* or *birth parents* instead.

Adrenalin, adrenaline. Use *adrenaline* (or a synonym, *epinephrine*) in references to the hormone produced by the adrenal gland, or in idioms: *A good fight made their adrenaline flow.* Uppercase the trademark *Adrenalin* in references to a synthetic or chemically extracted product.

adult. An *adult* novel or movie is one intended for grown-ups. It need not be pornographic. Avoid *adult* as a euphemism for sex-related.

adverb placement. In fluid writing, an adverb used with a compound verb should normally be placed between parts of the verb (the way *normally* is, a few words back in this sentence, and the way *usually* is, in the next example): *He will usually take the opposing side.* A similar rule applies when a verb like *is* links a noun to its modifier: *Refundable fares are often expensive* (not *often are expensive*). *Also see* SPLIT INFINITIVES, a different matter.

adverse (opposed or unfavorable); **averse** (unwilling or reluctant). Example: *Ms. Lamm was averse to going to court because she thought the ruling would be adverse.*

adviser.

Aer Lingus (the Irish national airline).

Aeroflot (the Russian airline).

Aerolíneas Argentinas (the Argentine airline).

Aeroméxico (the Mexican airline).

Aeroperu (the Peruvian airline).

aesthetic (not *esthetic*).

affect, effect. The verb *affect* means influence or change (*Her attitude affected the outcome*), stir emotions (*His departure affected the staff*), enjoy using (*He affected cowboy boots, spurs and a fedora*) or feign (*She affects an unlikely expertise*). The verb *effect* means accomplish or carry out (*They effected changes in the rules*).

The noun used more often is *effect*, meaning a result or a consequence (*One effect of the protest was new legislation*). The rarely used noun *affect* means an emotional response or feeling.

affirmative action is defined by the United States Commission on Civil Rights as "active efforts that take race, sex and national origin into account for the purpose of remedying discrimination" in fields like employment, education and government contracting. Society remains divided on many aspects of such programs, and news articles should detail the provisions in question when reporting on the argument. Do not use partisan terms like *reverse discrimination* except in quoting the debaters. Note that in 1978 the Supreme Court outlawed the use of numerical quotas in any such program with government backing. Permissible techniques include goals and timetables, as well as preferences for women or minority candidates. *Also see* PREFERENCES; QUOTAS; SET-ASIDES.

afflicted. Generally use less emotional language in citing disabilities. *She has cancer*, not *She is afflicted with cancer. Also see* DISABILITY, DISABLED; SUFFER; VICTIM.

affordable (as a description of housing) often occurs in government jargon and is imprecise. It is more useful to give the price range or the qualifying income.

Afghan, afghani. The people of Afghanistan are *Afghan*. The currency is the *afghani*.

aficionado(s).

A.F.L.-C.I.O. for the American Federation of Labor and Congress of Industrial Organizations, the umbrella organization of the labor movement. Use the abbreviation for almost all first references, and usually the full name can be omitted altogether (especially in a short article). For later references, an expression like *the federation* can serve in place of a spattering of initials.

African-American, black. Try to determine and use the term preferred by the group or person being described. When no preference is known, the writer should choose. But use *black* when the reference is not only to people of African descent but also to those whose more immediate roots are in the Caribbean or South America. Use more specific terms—*Nigerian-American*; *Jamaican-American*—when they are appropriate. *Also see* ETHNICITY and HISTORICALLY BLACK.

African Methodist Episcopal Church. *See* A.M.E.

African Methodist Episcopal Zion Church. *See* A.M.E. ZION.

Afro(-). In most contexts, use *African* rather than the prefix *Afro*. Thus, in references to international or intercontinental relations: *African and Asian* or *African-Asian*, not *Afro-Asian*; *African-Chinese*, not *Afro-Chinese*. In direct quotations or in the names of organizations and publications, *Afro-American* is acceptable. *Afro-Cuban* is an established description of a musical style. *Afro-centric* and *Afrocentrism* refer to cultural and educational programs that focus on African heritage. An *Afro* is a hairstyle. *Also see* AFRICAN-AMERICAN, BLACK and ETHNICITY.

after(-). Most but not all compounds formed with *after* are one word: afterbeat, afterbirth, afterburner, afterdeck, after-dinner (adj.), aftereffect, after-hours, afterlife, aftermarket, aftermath, after-shave, aftershock, aftertaste, after-theater (adj.), afterthought, afterworld.

after is less stilted than *following*, and preferred, in this construction: *He went home after the game.*

afterward (not *afterwards*).

Aftra for the American Federation of Television and Radio Artists.

Agana, the capital of Guam, has been renamed *Hagatna.*

Agence France-Presse. In news copy, it is *Agence France-Presse*, without *the* or *L'*. Ordinarily no translation or explanation is necessary. In later references, it is *the agency*. In direct quotations, A.F.P. may be used. In datelines: *BEIJING, June 10 (Agence France-Presse)* — etc. Use this credit on undatelined articles:

By Agence France-Presse

agent (intelligence). Experts confine the term to someone, usually a foreigner, who has been recruited or suborned to work on behalf of an intelligence service. Use *officer* instead for the service's staff employees, even those working under cover abroad. An *officer* recruits *agents.*

ages and eras of history. Capitalize *Stone Age, Bronze Age, Iron Age, Dark Ages, Middle Ages, Age of Discovery, Christian Era, Renaissance*, etc. But: *ice age.* Also: *atomic age, missile age, space age.*

ages of people and animals should be given in figures: *Terry M. Daan, 25; a 7-year-old boy; 3-month-old daughter; 4½-year-old son; a race for 2-year-olds.* Omit *years old* if the context is clear. Specify ages only when they are useful or relevant.

In giving ages of inanimate objects or other things, spell out through nine and use figures for 10 or above: *a two-year fight; a house eight and a half years old; a 10-month vacation; a wine 20 years old.* Use numerals for decades of age: *people in their 60's.* (Exception: *in their teens.*)

aggravate. It means make worse, not anger or irritate.

aging.

A.I.D. for the Agency for International Development. But after the full title has appeared in an article, *the aid agency* or *the agency* can serve in place of initials.

Aida. Use quotation marks for the title, not for the name of the character; neither includes a dieresis (*ï*).

aide. An *aide* is an assistant. Except in military contexts, the word is overused, probably because it is short. Resist it except in confined headlines.

aide(s)-de-camp. The term for a personal assistant sounds archaic except in military contexts.

AIDS for acquired immune deficiency syndrome. *Also see* H.I.V.

AIDS advocate. The term is illogical; no one advocates AIDS. Make it *advocate for AIDS research* or *advocate for AIDS patients,* or otherwise specify the cause.

AIDS victim. *See* AFFLICTED; STRICKEN; SUFFER; VICTIM.

air (v.). Reserve the verb to mean ventilate a room, freshen bedding or voice griev-ances. As used in the broadcast business (*they aired the program; the movie airs Thursday*), the verb is jargon. Replace it with phrases like *they showed the program* and *it goes on the air.* And except in direct quotations, change *an on-air mistake* to *a mistake on the air.*

air(-). Some compounds formed with *air* are one word, some are hyphenated and some are two words: air bag, air ball, air base, airborne, air brake, airbrush, airbus, air-condition, air-conditioned, air-conditioner, air-conditioning, air-cooled, aircrew, airdrop, air express, airfield, airfoil, airframe, airfreight, air gun, air lane, airlift (n., v., adj.), airline, airmail (n., v., adj.), airman, airplane, air raid (n.), air-raid (adj.), air rifle, air shaft, airship, airsick, airspace, airspeed, airstrike, airstrip, airtight, airwaves, airworthy. *Also see* AIR FORCE.

air base, Air Force base. The United States uses *air base* for overseas bases and *Air Force base* for bases in the United States and its possessions. *See* MILITARY BASES.

Air Canada.

Air Chief Marshal *Alex L. Miel; the air chief marshal.* Like other titles in the air forces of countries with British-influenced systems, this one cannot properly be shortened.

aircraft names are printed in roman type without quotation marks: *Air Force One* (the president's plane); *the Spirit of St. Louis; Concorde; Boeing 747; DC-9; F-15 Eagle; F-22 Raptor; MIG-23.* The standard source for names and model numbers is Jane's All the World's Aircraft. For a plural, use the apostrophe: *MD-80's; F-117's; B-52's; VC-10's.* Use a hyphen before the numeral, but not after it: *747B; F-117.* An ex-ception: *Airbus A320; Airbus A340.* In first references, the model number or name of a well-known aircraft can appear without the name of its manufacturer or de-signer: *DC-10; MIG-29; L-1011.* In some cases, Western military authorities apply their own designations to Eastern European aircraft: *Backfire* (for the TU-22M); *Foxbat* (for the MIG-25). When using such names, attribute them. But resist them if the overtones seem sinister or disparaging.

Air Force. Capitalize in *United States Air Force, Royal Air Force,* etc. It is *the Air Force* in later references to the United States service, and *Air Force* for United States Air Force Academy sports teams. But lowercase later references to any foreign air force; many of them do not formally use *air force* as part of their names.

In historical references, use whichever name applied at the time: The United States Air Force was established in 1947. It succeeded the Army Air Corps, which existed from 1926 until 1947, and the Army Air Forces, which existed from 1941 to 1947. (From 1941 to 1947 the Air Corps was a subordinate element of the Army Air Forces.)

Air Force bases are not the same as air bases: the United States uses Air Force base for operations in the United States and its possessions and air base for overseas bases. See MILITARY BASES.

Air Force Academy; the academy.

Air Force base, air base. The United States uses Air Force base for bases in the United States and its possessions and air base for overseas bases. See MILITARY BASES.

Air Force One (the president's plane).

Air Force ranks (United States), in descending order, and their abbreviations:

COMMISSIONED OFFICERS

Gen. Stacy T. Milori; General Milori; the general. (A general wears four stars.)

Lt. Gen. Dana L. Cordeiro; General Cordeiro; the general. (A lieutenant general wears three stars.)

Maj. Gen. Lindsay M. Karitsa; General Karitsa; the general. (A major general wears two stars.)

Brig. Gen. Lee A. Agnello; General Agnello; the general. (A brigadier general wears one star.)

Col. Merrill H. Kuzu; Colonel Kuzu; the colonel.

Lt. Col. Lee R. Agneau; Colonel Agneau; the colonel.

Maj. Stacy D. Miel; Major Miel; the major.

Capt. Hilary L. Daan; Captain Daan; the captain.

First Lt. Theo D. Barany; Lieutenant Barany; the lieutenant.

Second Lt. Alex C. Lam; Lieutenant Lam; the lieutenant.

NONCOMMISSIONED OFFICERS

(Enlisted supervisors.)

chief master sergeant of the Air Force. Do not use this title before a name, do not capitalize it and do not abbreviate it. Make it Hollis M. Bildots, the chief master sergeant of the Air Force. In later references: Sergeant Bildots; the sergeant. The title is held by only one person at a time, the highest-ranking enlisted member of the Air Force. It usually requires explanation.

Chief Master Sgt. Lauren T. Kikondoo; Sergeant Kikondoo; the sergeant.

Senior Master Sgt. Lee S. Miel; Sergeant Miel; the sergeant.

Tech. Sgt. Dana D. Kuzu; Sergeant Kuzu; the sergeant.

Staff Sgt. Ashley C. Lam; Sergeant Lam; the sergeant.

Sgt. Terry A. Agnello; Sergeant Agnello; the sergeant.

OTHER ENLISTED PERSONNEL

Senior Airman *Hilary M. Arniotis*; *Airman Arniotis*; *the airman* (male or female).

Airman First Class *Chris T. Berenich*; *Airman Berenich*; *the airman* (male or female).

Airman *Alex H. Cordero*; *Airman Cordero*; *the airman* (male or female).

Also see RETIRED.

Air Force Two (the vice president's plane).

Air France.

Air-India.

AirLanka (the Sri Lankan airline).

airline(s). That is the usual spelling, but follow each line's own style in a proper name: *American Airlines*; *Delta Air Lines*. The major lines are listed separately.

Airman *Alex H. Cordero*; *Airman Cordero*; *the airman* (for a man or a woman). Also: *Airman First Class Alex H. Cordero*; *Airman Cordero*.

Air National Guard.

airplane names. Use without quotation marks. *Also see* AIRCRAFT NAMES.

Air South Airlines (the discount airline).

AirTran Airlines (formerly ValuJet Airlines).

Air Vice Marshal *Robin S. Berenich*; *the air vice marshal*. Like other titles in the air forces of countries with British-influenced systems, this one cannot properly be shortened.

a k a, for *also known as*. Use thin spaces between the letters.

AK-47 for the ubiquitous 7.62-millimeter military rifle. *Also see* BULLET; CARTRIDGE; HANDGUNS; RIFLES; SHELL; SHOTGUNS.

akvavit. Use *aquavit* instead.

Alabama. Abbreviate it as *Ala.* after the names of cities, towns and counties.

à la carte.

à la mode.

Alaska. Do not abbreviate after the names of cities, towns and boroughs, even in datelines.

Alaska Airlines.

Alberta (Canadian province). Do not abbreviate after the names of cities and towns, even in datelines.

Alcan Aluminium Ltd. With a second *i*. But the company's United States subsidiary is *the Alcan Aluminum Corporation*.

Alcoa for the Aluminum Company of America.

alcoholic beverages. When alcohol figures significantly in an article — about its marketing, profitability or taxation, for example, or about traffic laws or health effects—draw distinctions among beverages: *beer*, which is fermented from grain, using yeast; *wine*, which is fermented from fruit, usually grapes; and *spirits* or *liquors*, which are made by distillation. Alcohol content differs by beverage and is expressed in *proof*. In the American system, the proof equals twice the alcohol percentage; a *100-proof* liquor is *50 percent* alcohol. *Also see* WHISKEY(S) and WINES AND SPIRITS.

Alcoholics Anonymous (A.A.). A related but separate organization, *Al-Anon*, provides help to the families of alcoholics.

Al Fatah, the Palestinian guerrilla organization. Omit *Al* when the name is preceded by *a* or *the*: *a Fatah leader*. In headlines: *Fatah*.

alfresco.

alibi. Use the word with care. Colloquially it suggests not merely an excuse but an excuse contrived to evade responsibility. In law, it means a claim to have been elsewhere when a crime was committed.

Alice Tully Hall (at Lincoln Center).

alien. As a term for a foreigner or an immigrant, while technically correct, it often conveys overtones of menace or strangeness. Resist its use except when unavoidable in a headline, or when quoting others. The preferred term for those who enter a country in violation of the law is *illegal immigrants*.

Alitalia Airlines.

Allah is the Muslim name for God. Lowercase *he, him, his, thee, thou, who* and *whom* in references to the deity of any faith.

all-American (n. and adj.).

all-around (adj.). Not *all-round*. Also see ROUND.

Allegany is the spelling for a county in New York; a town, an Indian reservation and a state park in Cattaraugus County, N.Y.; a county in Maryland; a town in Coos County, Ore.; and a township in Potter County, Pa. *Also see* ALLEGHANY and AL-LEGHENY.

allegedly. *Alleged* and *allegedly* are police-blotter jargon, best rephrased into conversational English: *accused of, charged with* or *suspected of*. If legal concerns leave no choice, apply the modifier to the offense, not the suspect: *alleged theft*, not *alleged thief*. Do not confuse *allegedly* with this more suitable modifier, for a phrase that is *not* an accusation: *She was defeated by three ostensibly neutral referees. Also see* ACCUSED.

Alleghany is the spelling for a town in Sierra County, Calif.; a county in North Carolina; a township in Davidson County, N.C.; a township in Ransom County, N.D.; a town in Loudon County, Tenn.; and both a county in Virginia and a town within it. *Also see* ALLEGANY and ALLEGHENY.

Alleghany Corporation is an insurance and financial services company.

Allegheny is the spelling for a town in Madison County, N.C.; a college, a county, a national forest and six townships in Pennsylvania; rivers in New York and Pennsylvania; tunnels in Pennsylvania, Virginia and West Virginia; and the mountain range in Maryland, Pennsylvania, Virginia and West Virginia. The plural for the mountains is *Alleghenies*, an exception to the rule that, for example, makes *Germanys* the plural of *Germany*. *Also see* ALLEGANY and ALLEGHANY.

Allegheny Ludlum Corporation is the nation's largest producer of stainless steel.

AlliedSignal Inc. was merged into Honeywell Inc. in 1999.

allies. Do not capitalize *allies* or *allied* except in proper names or in references to World War I and World War II alliances.

All Nippon Airways.

allot, allotted, allotting.

all right (never *alright*).

all-time. Applied to sports, weather and other records, the adjective is imprecise, superfluous and a cliché.

allude, refer. *Allude* means speak of something without direct mention; *refer* means mention it directly.

almanacs. Use their titles without quotation marks; capitalize the principal words.

along with is not the grammatical equivalent of *and*. *Along with six others, she was cited for contempt* is properly singular. But: *She and six others were cited for contempt.*

alphabetical (not *alphabetic*).

alphabetizing names and titles. When dealing with *Mc* or *Mac*, alphabetize as if all the letters were lowercase: *Mabley, MacAdam, Maynard, McNeil.* In a listing, if family names are printed before given names, place *Jr.* or *Sr.* or *III* or *3rd* last: *BERENICH, Lauren Jr.,* not *BERENICH Jr., Lauren.*

In listing titles (of literary or artistic works, for example), alphabetize by the first principal word: "Les Misérables" under *M* and "A Tale of Two Cities" under *T*.

alphanumeric (not *alphanumerical*). Consisting of letters and numbers.

also-ran (n.).

alternate, alternative. As an adjective, *alternate* can mean every second one: *Our club meets on alternate Wednesdays* (not *alternative*). As adjectives, both *alternate* and *alternative* can refer to a choice between two things or among more than two: *We have to choose an alternate* (or *alternative*) *route.* As a noun, *alternative*, long restricted to choices between only two options, has come to mean one among several: *There are six alternatives.*

aluminum (not *aluminium*, except in proper names).

Aluminum Company of America (Alcoa).

alumna (fem.), **alumnae** (fem. pl.), **alumnus** (masc.), **alumni** (masc. pl., or a mixed group). For general references, and for passages about mixed groups, *graduate(s)* is conveniently neutral.

a.m. (time). Lowercase: *10:30 a.m. yesterday*. Avoid this redundancy: *10:30 a.m. yesterday morning*. Also: *10 a.m.*, not *10:00 a.m.* In a headline, uppercase both letters. *Also see* TIME.

A.M.A. for the American Medical Association.

Amazon.com (the Internet bookseller).

Ambassador *Morgan E. Lamb; Morgan E. Lamb, ambassador to France; the ambassador; Mr.* (or *Ms., Mrs.* or *Miss*) *Lamb.* The title may be applied to the head of an embassy or to a bearer of the personal rank whose assignment is outside an embassy—the chief representative to an international organization, for example (*ambassador to the United Nations*), or a diplomat on a special mission. Lowercase *ambassadorial* in all contexts. *Also see* CHIEF DELEGATE; CHIEF REPRESENTATIVE; DELEGATE; HIGH COMMISSIONER; REPRESENTATIVE; TITLES.

Ambassador at Large *Hollis T. Agneau* (no hyphens); *Ambassador Agneau; the ambassador at large; the ambassador.*

ambassador to Britain, not *Great Britain.* Another title, *ambassador to the Court of St. James's,* may also be used, but reserve it for contexts that warrant a ceremonial flavor.

ambience. The adjective is *ambient.*

A.M.E. for the African Methodist Episcopal Church, an independent black Protestant denomination formed in 1821 in reaction to racial barriers in the Methodist Episcopal Church. The name should usually be abbreviated even in first references, but in any article dealing centrally with the church, spell it out at some point. When using the abbreviation, make the context clear with a phrase like *A.M.E. congregation, A.M.E. minister,* etc. *Also see* A.M.E. ZION.

amendments, legislative. *See* ACTS, AMENDMENTS, BILLS AND LAWS.

amendments to the Constitution. Capitalize when referring to a specific one: *the Fifth Amendment.* Spell out ordinals through the ninth and use figures for 10th and above: *First Amendment; 14th Amendment.* Lowercase general descriptions of amendments, except for proper names occurring within them: *income tax amendment; Prohibition amendment. Also see* ACTS, AMENDMENTS, BILLS AND LAWS.

America. The terms *America, American(s)* and *Americas* refer not only to the United States but to all of North America and South America. They may be used in any of their senses, including references to just the United States, if the context is clear. The countries of the Western Hemisphere are collectively *the Americas.*

America Online (AOL).

America West Airlines.

(-)American. Hyphenate *Italian-American, Japanese-American, Irish-American, Polish-American, Asian-American* and similar phrases denoting foreign heritage. Though some idioms (like *Korean grocery* and *Irish Catholic*) seem entrenched in the language, many members of such groups demand the addition of *-American* to acknowledge their full membership in this society. Usage does not call for the hyphen in religious references like *Jewish American* or in *French Canadian, English Canadian* or *Latin American. Also see* AFRICAN-AMERICAN, BLACK; ASIAN-AMERICAN; ETHNICITY; HISPANIC.

American Airlines.

American Baptist Churches in the U.S.A. This group of Northern Baptists split from the Southern Baptists in 1845 over the issue of whether slaveholders could be missionaries.

American Broadcasting Companies (former name). *See* ABC.

American Federation of Labor and Congress of Industrial Organizations. *See* A.F.L.-C.I.O.

American Federation of State, County and Municipal Employees. Do not abbreviate. *District Council 37* is the local council that represents most municipal employees in New York City.

American Indian(s) remains the most widely used term for the native people of North America and the term recognizable to most readers. Use it for individuals and groups who prefer it and in proper names and general references. In later references and in headlines: *Indian(s).* The alternative term *Native American(s)* is rejected by some Indians because government programs extend it to others (Eskimos, Aleuts, Native Hawaiians and Pacific Islanders) along with them. But use *Native American(s)* in specific references to individuals and groups who prefer it and in proper names that call for it.

American President Lines (the ocean carrier).

American Revolution, the. Also: *the Revolutionary War; the Revolution.*

American Stock Exchange. In later references: *the American Exchange; the exchange* and (especially in headlines) *Amex.*

American Telephone and Telegraph Company officially changed its name in 1994 to the AT&T Corporation.

America's Cup (yachting), **Americas Cup** (golf).

Ameritech (the regional telephone company primarily serving Illinois, Indiana, Michigan, Ohio and Wisconsin). In 1998, it announced an agreement to merge with SBC Communications.

Amex, or *the American Exchange,* in later references to the American Stock Exchange. *Amex* may also be used in later references and in headlines for *American Express,* if the context is unmistakable.

A.M.E. Zion for the African Methodist Episcopal Zion Church, a Protestant denomination formed in 1821 by black Methodist Episcopal churches in the New York area. The name should usually be abbreviated even in first references, but in any article dealing centrally with the church, spell it out at some point. When the abbreviation is used, make the context clear with phrases like *A.M.E. Zion congregation*, *A.M.E. Zion minister*, etc. *Also see* A.M.E.

amicus curiae (friend of the court) is the legal term for an outside party who submits a brief to advise or influence the judge or judges on the issues in a case. In later references, if the technical term is necessary and the context clear, *amicus* may stand alone. (The plural, even more daunting to readers, is *amici curiae*.) Lay terms, like *supporting brief*, are usually preferable. On occasion, *"friend of the court"* may also be useful, in quotation marks and without hyphens.

amid (not *amidst*).

amidships.

Amish. They are members of a Christian sect that separated from the MENNONITES in the 17th century. They refuse military service, favor plain dress and shun modern technology.

amnesty, clemency, pardon. A *pardon* is a release from punishment or forgiveness of an offense, granted to an individual. An *amnesty* is a general pardon, usually for political offenses, granted to a group. *Clemency* is leniency or mercy shown by someone in power, who does not necessarily forgive the offense. *Also see* PAROLE, PROBATION.

Amoco Corporation merged with the British Petroleum Company in 1998 to form *BP Amoco*.

among (not *amongst*).

among, between. In general, *between* applies to two things, and *among* to more than two. But *between* is correct in reference to more than two when the items are related individually as well as severally: *Trade between the United States, Canada and Mexico has grown under Nafta.* Each country trades with each of the others, rather than with all simultaneously. When more than two things are related in a purely collective and vague way, use *among*.

amount applies to quantities in mass or bulk but not to things that can be counted. *The hermit had a great amount of money,* but *the hermit had a great number* (not *amount*) *of $100 bills; the cook prepared a large amount of rice in a small number of bowls.*

amp for ampere, the unit for measuring the strength of an electric current.

ampersand (&). In company and corporation names, substitute an ampersand for *and* between personal names (*the Procter & Gamble Company*) and in phrases like *& Company, & Brothers, & Sons* or *& Associates: J. P. Morgan & Company; Harris & Brothers.* Also: *Ringling Brothers and Barnum & Bailey Circus.*

Use the ampersand when personal names compose the titles of partnerships, law firms, accounting firms or brokerage firms: *Paul, Weiss, Rifkind, Wharton & Garrison*; *Stroock & Stroock & Lavan*.

Certain railroad names and other company names, though not derived from personal names, also require ampersands; they are listed separately. Also keep the symbol when it is part of a periodical's title. This rule applies to some section names in The Times: *Arts & Leisure*; *Money & Business*; *House & Home*.

Do not otherwise substitute & for *and* in copy, in tables or in headlines.

Also see COMPANY AND CORPORATION NAMES.

Amtrak is a synonym for *the National Railroad Passenger Corporation*. Use the shorter term in all references.

Amvets for American Veterans of World War II, Korea and Vietnam.

an. *See* A, AN, THE.

analog, analogue. *Analog*, an adjective, denotes a system of recording or measuring data in an unbroken stream, the way sound is captured on a long-playing record, for example, or the way time is shown by the movement of clock hands. (Most often, these days, such a system is contrasted with *digital* recording or measurement.) *Analogue*, a noun, means a counterpart or an equivalent.

anchor is the preferred term for the chief reporter on a news broadcast. *Anchorman* and *anchorwoman* are acceptable, especially in direct quotations. Do not use *anchorperson*.

and. Use the ampersand (&) instead in company and firm names composed of personal names (*Brown & Williamson*) and in phrases like *& Company*, *& Brothers*, etc. *See* AMPERSAND and COMPANY AND CORPORATION NAMES.

Do not use *and* to link unrelated matters. *The senator, a Democrat and an avid golfer, was born in Idaho* suggests a relationship between party membership and golf. Make it *who is an avid golfer*.

and/or is stilted. Except in a quotation, phrase it *apples or oranges, or both*.

anemia, anemic.

anesthetic.

Angeleno(s) for a person or people of Los Angeles. Not *Los Angeleno(s)*.

Angkor for the Khmer ruins in Cambodia. *Angkor Wat* is a temple within the complex.

Anglican Church may be used in later references to the CHURCH OF ENGLAND, but *the church* is almost always enough.

Anglican Communion. It comprises the Church of England and Episcopal churches that are informally related to that church in doctrine and ritual. The association includes not only independent churches in Britain but also the Anglican Church of Canada, the Episcopal Church in the United States and others elsewhere. The administrative arm is the Anglican Consultative Council. Every 10 years the bishops of the Anglican Communion gather for the Lambeth Conference. *Also see* CHURCH OF ENGLAND and EPISCOPAL CHURCH.

Anglo (n. and adj.) originated in the Southwest as a term for a non-Hispanic white American. While its use is spreading, the word remains most suitable for articles about people in the Southwest and the West, or articles reflecting their points of view. *Also see* LATINO.

Anglo(-). *Anglo-Catholic*; *Anglo-Saxon*. But: *Anglophile*; *Anglophobe*. In compound modifiers referring to two countries, ordinarily use *English-* or *British-*: *British-French trade*; *English-Irish cultural rivalry* (not *Anglo-French* or *Anglo-Irish*).

angstrom, a length measurement in the sciences. It is lowercased, though it is named for the physicist Anders Jonas Angstrom.

animals. Call an animal *it*, not *he* or *she*, unless its sex has been mentioned or it has been personalized with a name: *The dog was lost; it howled. Marmaduke was lost; he howled. The dog, which was lost, howled. Adelaide, who was lost, howled. The bull tossed his horns.* Use figures for ages of animals: *a race for 3-year-olds.*

Annapolis (the site and informal name of the United States Naval Academy, in Maryland).

anonymity is a last resort, for situations in which the newspaper could not otherwise print information it considers newsworthy and reliable. Reporters should not offer a news source anonymity without first pressing to use a name or other helpful identification. *See* ATTRIBUTION.

If concealment proves necessary, writers should avoid automatic references to sources who "insisted on anonymity" or "demanded anonymity"; rote phrases offer the reader no help. When possible, though, articles should tersely explain what kind of understanding was actually reached by reporter and source, and should shed light on the reasons. Anonymity should not shield a press officer whose job is to be publicly accountable. And, given the requirements of newsworthiness and substance, it should not be invoked for a trivial comment: *"The party ended after midnight," said a doorman who demanded anonymity.* (If the doorman simply refused to give his name, that is a less grandiose matter, and the article should just say so.)

Anonymity must not become a cloak for attacks on people, institutions or policies. If pejorative remarks are worth reporting and cannot be specifically attributed, they may be paraphrased or described after thorough discussion between writer and editor. The vivid language of direct quotation confers an unfair advantage on a speaker or writer who hides behind the newspaper, and turns of phrase are valueless to a reader who cannot assess the source.

antagonist, protagonist. An *antagonist* is an adversary, competitor or opponent. One person can have many antagonists. A *protagonist* is the central character in a drama or novel. One drama or novel can have only one protagonist.

Antarctic (n., adj.). *Antarctic Circle; Antarctic continent; Antarctica.*

ante(-). Except before a proper name, compounds beginning with *ante* are not hyphenated: *antebellum; antechamber; antedate; antediluvian; anteroom.* But use a hyphen if the second part of the term is capitalized: *ante-Victorian.*

antecedents. *See* PRONOUNS AND ANTECEDENTS.

antelope(s).

antennas (not *antennae*).

anthems. Use quotation marks around their titles: *"The Star-Spangled Banner."* Lowercase *the national anthem. Also see* SONGS.

anti(-). Hyphenate compounds beginning with *anti* if they would otherwise be hard to understand (*anti-abortion, anti-bias, anti-rejection, anti-vice*), if the second element begins with the letter *i* (*anti-inflation, anti-intellectual*) or if the second element is capitalized (*anti-American, anti-Communist, anti-Semite*). An exception: *Antichrist.* Other *anti* words are solid: *antiaircraft, antibiotic, antibody, anticancer, anticlimax, antidrug, antifreeze, antimagnetic, antimissile, antislavery, antismoking, antisocial, antiterror, antitrust, antiwar.*

anticipate. It means foresee and prepare, not merely expect.

Anti-Defamation League (a division of B'nai B'rith).

antitrust division (of the Justice Department).

anxious means uneasy or worried. Avoid the less precise sense, as a synonym for *eager.*

any(-). Most compounds formed with *any* are one word: anybody (pron.), anyhow, any more (something additional), anymore (adv.), anyone (pron.), any way (in any manner), anyway (in any event), anywhere.

But if the emphasis is on singling out an individual in a group, use two words: *Any one of them may win.*

anybody, anyone, everybody, everyone, no one, someone. Each of these pronouns is singular and requires *he* or *she* (never *they*) on further reference: *Has anybody lost his ticket?* To avoid assuming maleness or femaleness in a general reference, rephrase: *Has everyone bought a ticket?* Often a plural construction will serve: *Have people all bought tickets?* As a last resort, the awkward *his or her* is tolerable; a plural pronoun with a singular antecedent is not.

anywhere. This word is often superfluous, as in *The roadster's top speed is anywhere between 100 and 120 miles an hour.*

apogee. It is the highest altitude of an orbiting object in relation to Earth. The word also has the general meaning of highest or farthest point. Its opposite is *perigee*, the lowest or nearest point.

apostle(s). Capitalize in proper names (*the Apostle Thomas; the Apostles' Creed*), but generally lowercase (*the apostles of Jesus; an apostle*). An exception: *the Twelve Apostles.*

apostolic delegate. *Bishop* (or *Archbishop*) *Lee S. Agneau; the apostolic delegate; the delegate.* An apostolic delegate is a Roman Catholic diplomat designated by the pope as his envoy to the church in a foreign country with which the Vatican does not have formal diplomatic relations. He is not a PAPAL NUNCIO (or a nuncio), an envoy accredited to a foreign government with which the Vatican has a treaty.

apostrophe. Use it to create the possessive form of a noun (*man's*) and to denote a contraction or omission of letters or numerals (*it's* for *it is*; *'94* for *1994*).

Also use the apostrophe for plurals formed from letters or numerals (*p's and q's; size 7's; B-52's*) and terms like *PC's, TV's* and *VCR's*. While many authorities prefer to omit the apostrophe in these cases, it is necessary for clarity in all-uppercase headlines. Therefore use it in other kinds of copy also, for consistency.

Form the singular possessive with *'s* (*boy's coat*) and the plural with *s'* (*girls' coats; reporters' computers*).

For a plural that does not end in *s* (*women; children*), the possessive is formed with *'s*: *women's; children's*.

Sometimes a singular idea is expressed in words that are technically plural; in such a case, use the plural form of the possessive: *United States'; General Motors'.* Never *United States's*, etc.

Almost all singular words ending in *s* require a second *s* as well as the apostrophe to form the possessive: *James's; Chris's; The Times's*. But omit the *s* after the apostrophe when a word ends in two sibilant sounds (the *ch, j, s, sh, ts* or *z* sounds) separated only by a vowel sound: *Kansas' Governor; Texas' population; Moses' behalf*. The possessive *s* is also traditionally dropped in some idioms in which the word after the possessive begins with *s*: *for conscience' sake; for appearance' sake; for goodness' sake*.

When a name ends with a sibilant letter that is silent, keep the possessive *s*: *Arkansas's; Duplessis's; Malraux's*. By custom, however, the possessive of an ancient classical name is formed with an apostrophe only: *Achilles' heel; Euripides' dramas*.

The apostrophe is used in expressions like *60 days' notice* and *20 years' imprisonment*. But: *60-day notice; a 20-year sentence; a sentence of 20 years*.

Also: *a year's worth; five days' worth; money's worth; a million dollars' worth; a penny's worth*. But, with the currency symbol: *$5 million worth*.

The expression *months pregnant* does not take an apostrophe; it is similar to *years old*.

Apostrophes are omitted in names of many organizations: *Citizens Union; Doctors Hospital; Teachers College*; etc. But if the word is plural before the addition of an *s*, keep the apostrophe: *Children's Court*. Also: *Ladies' Home Journal*.

Use no apostrophe in commonly accepted short forms like *cello, cellist, copter, chutist, phone, plane*. The apostrophe is used in abbreviations and contractions like *O.K.'d*.

Also see POSSESSIVES.

appall.

apparent. Do not confuse the adjective with the related adverb, which needs to be positioned precisely. People do not die of *apparent heart attacks* and they are not shot in *apparent robbery attempts*. Only real heart attacks and robbery attempts are dangerous. But someone can die *apparently of a heart attack*, and someone can be shot *apparently in a robbery attempt*.

apparent temperature. *See* HEAT INDEX.

Appellate Division.

Apple Computer Inc. (the manufacturer of the Macintosh and other computers).

application, in reference to computer software, is best confined to technical contexts. *Program* is one possible substitute.

apposition is a useful device in which one word or phrase is placed beside another, to define or explain it. In the sentence *Her husband, Chris, was late*; the first term (*her husband*) is explained by the second (*Chris*). The word or phrase in apposition ordinarily appears between commas (or, sparingly, between dashes); eliminating the commas around *Chris* would suggest that the wife has more than one husband. The two expressions in apposition should serve identical grammatical functions; they mean the same thing. Thus *He said he was Chris Lamb, the stage name of the soap opera star* is faulty because *he* could be *Chris Lamb*, but *he* could not be *the stage name*. In editing, test such a construction this way: Mentally delete the first expression of the pair, and see if the remaining sentence makes sense: *He said he was the stage name of the soap opera star*. A possible repair: *He called himself Chris Lamb, using the stage name of the soap opera star.*

appraise, apprise. *Appraise* means evaluate: *Have the house appraised for the insurance company. Apprise* means notify or inform.

April. Do not abbreviate except, when necessary, in tables or charts.

aquavit (not *akvavit*).

Arab Emirates. *See* UNITED ARAB EMIRATES.

Arabic numerals. Uppercase *A. Also see* ROMAN NUMERALS.

Arabic terms in place names include *Ain* (spring), *Bab* (gate), *Bahr* (sea, lake and sometimes river), *Bir* (well), *Birket* (pond), *Burj* (tower), *Dahr* (mountaintop), *Dar* (abode of), *Deir* (monastery), *Jebel* (mountain), *Jisr* (bridge), *Kafr* (hamlet), *Khan* (caravansary), *Marj* (meadow), *Nahr* (river), *Naqb* (pass), *Qasr* or *Kasr* (castle), *Ras* (promontory, cape), *Suq* (market), *Tell* (hill) and *Wadi* (dry riverbed, ravine).

In Egyptian usage, the standard Arabic *j* is pronounced as a hard *g*. Thus *Burg, Gebel, Gisr* and *Marg* appear in Egyptian place names instead of *Burj, Jebel, Jisr* and *Marj*.

French transliterations have become standard for North African names; thus *Djebel* and *Ouadi* instead of *Jebel* and *Wadi*. But see GEOGRAPHIC NAMES for the order in which references should be consulted on spelling.

Arabist.

Arab names and titles. Arab names are usually Arabic words governed by grammatical rules. Many names incorporate the definite article *al*. But the vowel may take the form of *a, e* or *u*, or disappear entirely as a result of elision. The *l* may appear as *d, dh, n, r, s, sh, t, th* or *z*. The article may be joined with the previous or the next word, or both. Except where other usage has become established (*Abdel Nasser; Abdullah*), use *al* hyphenated with the next word: *al-Sabah; al-Azhar*. Many Arabs drop the definite article from their names in English: *Ismail Fahmy*, not *al-Fahmy*. Omit the article in a personal name after the first reference: *Anwar el-Sadat; Mr. Sadat*. (But capitalize the article in a publication title and omit the hyphen: *Al Ahram*.)

Compound names should be left intact. The commonest are composed with the word *Abd* (Worshiper of): *Abdullah* (Worshiper of God); *Abdel Nasser* (Worshiper of the Victorious One); *Abdur Rahman* (Worshiper of the Merciful One).

Another compound is completed by *al-Din* (the Religion), which may appear in forms like *ed-Din, ed-dine, uddin*, etc.: *Kamal ed-Din* (the Perfection of the Religion); *Nureddin* (the Light of the Religion); *Allah-ud-Din* or *Aladdin* (the God of the Religion).

Allah or *ullah* (God) completes compound names like *Jad-Allah* (God giveth), *Nasrullah* (the Victory of God). *Abu* (Father of) and *ibn, bin* or *ben* (Son of) combine in names like *Abubakr, Abul Zalaf, Ibn Saud*. Do not capitalize *ibn* when it is preceded by a first or a middle name.

A Muslim Arab has at least three names—the given name, the father's given name and the grandfather's given name. The permanent family name, if there is one, follows. Use whichever family name the subject seems to prefer. Otherwise, in later references, use *Mr.* or the official title before the last name and treat it as a family name. When in doubt, repeat the full name in later references.

The Arab titles *Pasha* and *Bey*, both of Turkish origin, have been abolished. Royal titles, as in English, are used with the first name: *Prince Sultan ibn Abdel Aziz; Prince Sultan. Sheik* is the title of the rulers of the Persian Gulf principalities: *Sheik Abdullah al-Salem al-Sabah; Sheik Abdullah*. The title and the first name alone are enough in first references to rulers (kings, imams, emirs and sheiks) unless the full name is needed to distinguish between people with the same title and the same first name.

arboretums (not *arboreta*).

Arc de Triomphe, the (in Paris); *the arch*. In direct quotations, *the Arch of Triumph* is acceptable.

arch(-). Except before a proper name, the prefix forms solid compounds: archangel, archbishop, archdiocese, archduke, archenemy, archfiend, archrival.

Though the prefix usually means chief or principal, it sometimes connotes extremism, warranting caution with phrases like *archconservative, archradical, archliberal, arch-Protestant* and *arch-Republican. Also see* ULTRA(-).

archaeology. Also: *archaeological; archaeologist.*

Archbishop *Dale B. Lam of Hartford, Archbishop Lam, the archbishop.* Or: *the archbishop of Hartford, Dale B. Lam. The Most Rev.* is used before the name of the Anglican prelate who is the archbishop of Canterbury. *Also see* BISHOP; CANTERBURY, ARCHBISHOP OF; MOST REV., RT. REV.; REV.; VERY REV.

archetype.

architecture. Styles and schools are listed separately. *Also see* ARTS TERMINOLOGY.

arctic (n., adj.). Capitalize in geographic expressions: *Arctic Circle; Arctic Ocean; Arctic Current; Arctic zone; the Arctic;* etc. Lowercase in general references: *arctic cold; arctic fox;* etc. Also: *arctics* (overshoes).

area codes. *See* TELEPHONE NUMBERS.

Argentine(s) (n. and adj.) for the people of Argentina. Not *Argentinian.*

Arizona. Abbreviate as *Ariz.* after the names of cities, towns and counties.

Arizonan(s).

ark. Lowercase this term for the cabinet that houses the Torah scrolls in a synagogue. Also: *ark of the covenant,* for the biblical chest that held the stone tablets inscribed with the Ten Commandments.

Arkansas. Abbreviate as *Ark.* after the names of cities, towns and counties.

Arlington National Cemetery.

Armed Forces Day. The United States observes it on the third Saturday in May; dates differ in other countries.

Army. Capitalize in *United States Army, British Army, Soviet Army,* etc. It is *the Army* in later references to the United States Army, but lowercase for foreign armies. Also use *Army* for United States Military Academy sports teams.

Army corps. A United States Army corps (the parent unit of a division) is designated by Roman numerals: *II Corps.*

Army ranks, in descending order, and their abbreviations:

COMMISSIONED OFFICERS

Gen. *Stacy D. Milori; General Milori; the general.* (A general wears four stars.)

Lt. Gen. *Dana L. Cordeiro; General Cordeiro; the general.* (A lieutenant general wears three stars.)

Maj. Gen. *Lindsay M. Karitsa; General Karitsa; the general.* (A major general wears two stars.)

Brig. Gen. *Lee B. Cordeiro; General Cordeiro; the general.* (A brigadier general wears one star.)

Col. *Merrill C. Kuzu; Colonel Kuzu; the colonel.*
Lt. Col. *Lee L. Agneau; Colonel Agneau; the colonel.*
Maj. *Stacy M. Miel; Major Miel; the major.*
Capt. *Hilary C. Daan; Captain Daan; the captain.*
First Lt. *Hilary F. Kuzu; Lieutenant Kuzu; the lieutenant.*
Second Lt. *Alex S. Karitsa; Lieutenant Karitsa; the lieutenant.*

WARRANT OFFICERS
(They hold their posts on warrants, or certificates of appointment, rather than commissions. They rank below commissioned officers and above enlisted personnel.)
Chief Warrant Officer *Chris W. Arniotis; Mr.* (or *Ms., Miss* or *Mrs.*) *Arniotis; the chief warrant officer.*
Warrant Officer *Terry O. Daan; Mr.* (or *Ms., Miss* or *Mrs.*) *Daan; the warrant officer.*

NONCOMMISSIONED OFFICERS
(Enlisted supervisors.)
sergeant major of the Army. Do not use the five-word title before a name; do not capitalize it and do not abbreviate it. Make it *Lindsay M. Bildots, the sergeant major of the Army; Sergeant Major Bildots; the sergeant major.* (This title is held only by the Army's top enlisted member; it usually requires explanation.)
Command Sgt. Maj. *Tracy C. Arniotis; Sergeant Major Arniotis; the sergeant major.* (This title is held by the top enlisted member of a major headquarters within the Army.)
Sgt. Maj. *Stacy S. Kuzu; Sergeant Major Kuzu; the sergeant(s) major.*
First Sgt. *Lauren F. Daan; Sergeant Daan; the sergeant.*
Master Sgt. *Tracy M. Berenich; Sergeant Berenich; the sergeant.*
Sgt. First Class *Pat F. Karitsa; Sergeant Karitsa; the sergeant.*
Staff Sgt. *Ashley S. Lam; Sergeant Lam; the sergeant.*
Sgt. *Terry P. Agnello; Sergeant Agnello; the sergeant.*
Cpl. *Stacy L. Milori; Corporal Milori; the corporal.*

OTHER ENLISTED PERSONNEL
Specialist *Leslie M. Berenich; Specialist Berenich; the specialist.*
Pfc. *Chris F. Agneau; Private Agneau; the private.*
Pvt. *Alex V. Cordero; Private Cordero; the private.*
Also see RETIRED.
Army Sgt. Maj. Do not use this abbreviation for *sergeant major of the Army.* And because the five-word title is cumbersome, use it after the name, not before: *Lindsay*

M. Bildots, the sergeant major of the Army (with an explanation that the bearer is the sole holder of the Army's highest enlisted rank). In later references: *Sergeant Major Bildots*; *the sergeant major.*

aromatherapy.

arrondissements (French municipal districts). *See* ADDRESSES.

art. Styles and schools are listed separately. *Also see* ARTS TERMINOLOGY.

Art Deco (architecture, interior design and decorative arts). Capitalize in reference to the 1920's and 1930's style, sometimes called *style moderne* or *jazz modern. Also see* ARTS TERMINOLOGY.

article (news report). In writing about newspaper reports, ordinarily use *article* rather than the colloquial *story*. And *report* is the word for a broadcast news account. But sometimes informal references to journalism are just right: *How Nellie Bly got the story.* A fictional account is also a *story.* Avoid the old-fashioned *dispatch* in referring to a datelined article. Use quotation marks for the titles of magazine and newspaper articles, and capitalize the principal words.

articles (parts of speech). *See* A, AN, THE, and THE.

Art Nouveau (architecture, interior design and decorative arts). Capitalize when referring to the decorative style with its roots in the 1890's and the early 20th century. *Also see* ARTS TERMINOLOGY.

Arts and Crafts (architecture, interior design and decorative arts). Capitalize only in reference to the design movement that began in late-19th-century England. It encompasses the styles known as Prairie, Mission and Craftsman, among others. *Also see* ARTS TERMINOLOGY.

arts locations. In an arts review, the name of a well-known museum, gallery, theater or concert hall may be shortened to its conversational form in first and later references, provided the full name appears somewhere in the review, or in a fact box. Examples: *the Modern* (but not *MOMA*, for the Museum of Modern Art); *the Corcoran* (for the Corcoran Gallery of Art, in Washington); *the Met* or *the Metropolitan* (for the Metropolitan Museum of Art or the Metropolitan Opera, depending on context); *the Brooks Atkinson* (for the Brooks Atkinson Theater).

arts terminology. When dealing with art, architecture, music or literature, capitalize the name of a specific historical movement, group or style: *the Impressionism of Monet.* Lowercase such a term in a more generalized sense: *Chris Miel's paintings are impressionistic in manner.* The prefix *neo* or *post* is lowercased unless specifically adopted by a group or movement as part of its name: the *Post-Impressionism of Seurat,* but *Leslie Cordeiro works in a neo-Dada manner.* In architecture, scholars disagree significantly on the limits and definitions of many styles. In the 20th century, for example, a building designed in a loosely classical vein, like the old Pennsylvania Station in New York, is likely to be called *Classical, neo-Classical, classical revival* or *romantic classical.* In such cases, it is best to use a phrase like *a 20th-century building in the classical style*. Individual styles and movements are listed separately. *Also see* DANCE and MUSIC.

as. *See* AS IF and LIKE.

Ascap for the American Society of Composers, Authors and Publishers.

Ascension. Capitalize when the reference is to Jesus.

Ascii (pronounced ASK-ee) is the acronym for the American Standard Code for Information Interchange. The code is a basic pattern of electrical pulses used by computers to compose characters for text and communications. A document conveyed in this code is an *Ascii file.*

Asean for the Association of Southeast Asian Nations. Its members are Brunei, Cambodia, Indonesia, Laos, Malaysia, Myanmar, the Philippines, Singapore, Thailand and Vietnam.

Ashkenazi is the term for a Jew who settled in middle or northern Europe after the Diaspora, or that Jew's descendant. The plural is *Ashkenazim*, and the adjective is *Ashkenazic*. *Also see* JEW(S) and SEPHARDI.

Asian-American, applied to a citizen or resident of the United States, is preferred over *Asian*. But whenever possible, use a more specific description: *Korean-American; Vietnamese-American*. *Also see* -AMERICAN and ETHNICITY.

Asian, Asiatic. Use *Asian(s)* when referring to people. *Asiatic*, in this sense, is now generally considered disparaging.

as if. Use the phrase, instead of *like*, when what follows is a clause with its own verb: *He pedaled as if his life depended on it*. *See* LIKE.

    As if is shorter and more logical than its generally accepted synonym, *as though*. The logic is clear if you insert the words that are implied: *It looks as* [it would look] *if the Yankees won.*

as many. Avoid this mannerism: *twice in as many days; third in as many days*. The wording is untidy because the phrase *as many* requires a cardinal number for completion (*as many as two; as many as three*). Make it *twice in two days* and *third in three days*. With a cardinal number (*five times in as many days*), the phrase is more grammatical, but still journalese.

as much as. Write *as much as if not more than*; do not omit the second *as*. For greater readability, complete the first thought before beginning the second: *He travels as much as a correspondent, if not more.*

assassin, assassinate, assassination. Generally reserve these terms for a fatal surprise attack on a prominent person, or for the attacker in such a crime. The terms are not synonyms for *kill, killer, murder* or *murderer* (a usage that sometimes occurs in overliteral translation from other languages). *Also see* EXECUTE, EXECUTION.

assault weapons are semiautomatic pistols, rifles or shotguns with special features like large-capacity magazines, pistol grips or folding or telescoping stocks. They were originally designed as automatic weapons for military or police use. Those sold to civilians are modified to allow only semiautomatic fire. *Also see* CALIBER; CARTRIDGE; HANDGUNS; RIFLES; SHOTGUNS.

assembly. Capitalize in *United Nations General Assembly*; *the State Assembly*; etc. In later references: *the Assembly*. But it is *state assembly, state assemblies, an assembly*, etc., when the reference is not specific.

Assembly districts. Capitalize in specific references: *First Assembly District*; *11th Assembly District*.

assemblyman, assemblywoman. *Assemblyman Pat W. Agneau*; *Assemblywoman Pat Y. Agneau*; *Assemblyman* (or *Assemblywoman*) *Agneau*; *the assemblyman* (or *assemblywoman*); *Mr.* (or *Mrs., Miss* or *Ms. Agneau*). Also: *an assemblyman*; *an assemblywoman*; *assemblymen*; *assemblywomen*. *Also see* MEN AND WOMEN and TITLES.

assistant bishop. *See* BISHOP.

Assistant Chief *Tracy M. Anyell* (in police and fire departments); *Chief Anyell*; *the chief*. (In the New York City Police Department, the rank does not exist, though there are deputy chiefs.)

Assistant District Attorney *Robin T. Milori*; *Assistant District Attorney Milori*; *the assistant district attorney*.

Associated Press, The. It is *The Associated Press* in news articles. The abbreviation is A.P. or *The A.P.*, except in some credit lines and in datelines: *RECIFE, Brazil, June 10 (AP)* — etc. Use this credit on undatelined A.P. articles:

By The Associated Press

Associate Justice *Ashley R. Berenich* (of the United States Supreme Court); *the associate justice*; *Associate Justice Berenich* (or *Justice Berenich*); *the justice*.

association. Capitalize when part of the name of an organization, but not when standing alone. Also capitalize in *Association football* (British).

Association of the Bar of the City of New York. Use its informal name, *the City Bar Association*, in virtually all references.

as such. In this construction, *such* is a pronoun, requiring a noun for its antecedent. Thus: *She is an editor; as such, she assigns reporters*. But not *He works for The Times; as such, he covers medicine*.

astronaut. The Russian term is *cosmonaut*, but confine that to quotations and untranslated texts.

astronomical unit. This unit of length used in astronomy is the mean radius of the Earth's orbit around the Sun. It is approximately 93 million miles.

AstroTurf is a trademark for synthetic grass.

as well as. Unlike *and*, this phrase joins two items without creating a plural. The phrase introduces what is essentially a parenthetical aside, so the verb still agrees with the original subject: *Alex as well as Lee was late.* The verb is singular because *Alex* remains the sole subject.

as yet. When the phrase modifies a verb, it should usually be shortened to *yet*: *The tax rate has not been set yet.* When modifying an adjective, *as yet* can be useful (*as yet undecided*), but idiom prefers the whole cluster after a noun, not before: *The sheriff denounced the killer, as yet unidentified* (not *the as-yet-unidentified killer*, with or without hyphens).

AT&T Corporation was the American Telephone and Telegraph Company until 1994.

at-bat(s). As a noun, the baseball term is hyphenated, though *times at bat* will often be smoother in copy: *Cordero scored five runs in 12 at-bats.* Or: *in 12 times at bat.* See BASEBALL.

Athabasca (not *Athabaska*) for the town, lake, mountain and river in Canada.

Atlantic. The actual shoreline of the Atlantic Ocean is *the Atlantic coast*; the region of the United States lying along the shoreline is *the Atlantic Coast* or *the Atlantic Seaboard.* It is the *coast* in all subsequent references. Also: *North Atlantic*; *South Atlantic*; *Atlantic Coast States.*

Atlantic alliance. See NATO.

Atlantic Container Line (an ocean carrier).

Atlantic Monthly, The.

Atlantic Richfield Company announced an agreement in 1999 to be acquired by *BP Amoco.*

at large. Do not hyphenate *ambassador at large*, *delegate at large* or similar titles. But hyphenate the phrase when its rather awkward use as a preceding modifier is unavoidable: *The state will be filling three at-large seats.*

A.T.M. for *automated* (not *automatic*) *teller machine. A.T.M. machine* is redundant.

atmosphere (unit of pressure).

atomic age.

attaché. *Col. Lynn T. Agnello, the military attaché; the attaché.*

attempt (v.) is often stilted; *try* is more conversational.

attorney. Ordinarily use *lawyer* instead; it is less pretentious. And it is more precise: in many situations, an attorney (someone authorized to act for another) need not be a lawyer.

Attorney General *Chris T. Baranek; the attorney general.* The plural is *attorneys general.*

attribution. Readers judge The Times not only by its accuracy record but also by what they can gather about its reporting standards. How authoritative are the people it interviews? Are they in a position to know? How directly? If the information comes from people with vested interests, does The Times acknowledge that?

Ideally, any new disclosure in the paper would be attributed to someone by name and title. But solid newsworthy information is sometimes available only from people who are not free to let their names appear in print. That is most often the case in diplomacy and foreign intelligence, and nearly as often in the criminal justice system. The newspaper's choice is between incomplete attribution and omitting the facts, however authoritative the reporter knows them to be.

At such times, a reporter's duty is to bargain hard with the source for terms that conceal as little as possible of what the reader needs to gauge reliability. Blind attribution—*sources said*, for example—is more a tease than a signpost. Attribution should never amount to a truism: since *source* merely means a provider of information, *one source said* is equivalent to *somebody said*. And *informed* or *reliable source* is no improvement. (Would The Times quote an uninformed or unreliable one?) The objection is not to the word *source*, but to its emptiness without a meaningful modifier: *a Senate source*, for example, may be acceptable—unless, of course, it is possible to tell the reader still more.

Trail markers should be as detailed as possible. *United States diplomat* is better than *Western diplomat*, which is better than *diplomat*. Still better is *a United States diplomat who took part in the meeting*. And *a lawyer who has read the brief* or *an executive close to the XYZ Company* is far better than *a person familiar with the case*, a phrase so vague that it could even mean the reporter.

Readers value signs of candor: *The report was provided by a Senate staff member working to defeat the bill.*

Whatever device is adopted, it must be truthful and not misleading. Do not write *State Department officials* when quoting a single person. And do not write *another official* when citing someone who was named in the previous paragraph. Also avoid ludicrous evasions like *a senior official aboard Secretary Lamm's plane.* Something like *reporters traveling with Secretary Lamm were told* may actually take the reader closer to the source.

Also see ANONYMITY; FAIRNESS AND IMPARTIALITY; FICTIONAL DEVICES; LEAK; QUOTATIONS.

Aug. for *August* before numerals (*Aug. 16*), or in charts and tables.

auger, augur. An *auger* is a tool for boring holes. An *augur* is a fortuneteller or prophet. As a verb, *augur* means foretell. And an *augury* is a sign of things to come.

author, co-author. Use both words as nouns only, not as verbs.

authoress. Use *author* instead. *See* MEN AND WOMEN.

autobahn(s).

automatic weapons. *See* ASSAULT WEAPONS and HANDGUNS.

autumn (also *fall*).

auxiliary bishop. *See* BISHOP.

avant-garde (n. and adj.); *avant-gardism*; *avant-gardist*.

Ave. may be used after an avenue name, but only in headlines, charts and maps.

Avenue of the Americas (Manhattan). In headlines, *Ave. of Americas*. The older name, *Sixth Avenue*, remains idiomatic and may be used for special effect. In a difficult headline, *6th Ave.* is acceptable, provided the article subtly connects the two names. *The Sixth Avenue subway* is also acceptable, especially when juxtaposed with expressions like *the Eighth Avenue subway*.

avenues. *See* ADDRESSES.

average. *See* MEAN, MEDIAN, AVERAGE.

averse (unwilling or reluctant), **adverse** (opposed or unfavorable). Example: *Ms. Lamm was averse to going to court because she thought the ruling would be adverse.*

Avery Fisher Hall (at Lincoln Center).

avoid, evade. *Avoid* is the more neutral term, in a context like taxes or punishment. *Evade* carries a suggestion of deceit or irresponsibility. Tax *avoidance* is ordinarily legal; tax *evasion* is not.

Awacs (n. or adj., sing. or pl.) is an acronym for *airborne warning and control system*. There is no such word as *Awac*.

awe-struck.

a while, awhile. *They plan to stay for a while; They plan to stay awhile.*

AWOL for *absent without leave*.

ax.

Axis (the German-Italian-Japanese alliance of World War II).

ayes and nays.

B

B.A. or **A.B.** for Bachelor of Arts. Also: *a bachelor's degree*.

baby boom. As allusions to the population surge after World War II—between 1946 and 1964—*baby boom* and *baby boomer* are overused; ration them.

baby-sit, baby-sitting, baby sitter. The idiom is *he baby-sits for Leslie*, not *he baby-sits Leslie*.

baccalaureate.

bachelor's degree. But: *Bachelor of Arts*; *Bachelor of Science*; etc. Also: A.B. (where used) or B.A.; B.S.; etc.

back(-), (-)back. Most but not all compounds formed with *back* as a prefix are one word: backache, backboard, backbone, backbreaking, backdate, backdoor, backdrop, backfield, backfire, background, backhand, backhoe, backlog, backpack, backpedal, backrest, back room (n.), back-room (adj.), back seat (n.), back-seat (adj.), backslide, backstage, back stairs (n.), backstairs (adj.), backstop, backstretch, backstroke, backswing, back talk, backtrack, backup (n. and adj.), back up (v.), backwoods, backyard.

Compounds formed with *back* as a suffix are one word: comeback, fastback, flareback, halfback, hatchback, piggyback (adj. and v.), rollback, setback, throwback.

backlash. A *backlash* is a strong reaction to a previous protest or movement. Unless there is a *lash*, there is logically no *backlash*.

back of, in back of. *Behind* is more efficient: *the tree behind the barn*.

backward (not *backwards*).

bacteria is plural; the singular is *bacterium*. *Also see* GENUS AND SPECIES and E. COLI.

bad, badly. After a verb like *be, appear, look, feel, seem, smell* or *taste*, the word most often wanted is the adjective *bad*, not the adverb *badly*. (Example: *The soup tastes bad.*) That is because the verbs listed above are "linking" verbs—those that connect one part of a sentence to another. Linking verbs call for adjectives where other verbs would demand adverbs. Thus someone who smells *bad* should bathe; someone who smells *badly* should see a doctor.

bad-mouth (v.) is slang, and the vividness has been recycled out of it.

Baghdad.

Bahai. A *Bahai* is an adherent of *Bahaism*, a religion that stresses brotherhood and social equality.

Bahamas, the. Lowercase *the*, even in datelines.

Bahrain (not *Bahrein*). The nation is formed of a group of islands in the Persian Gulf.

Baikonur Cosmodrome (the space center in Kazakhstan).

bail. A defendant may be *freed on bail* or, for example, *freed on $10,000 bail*. But if the defendant fails to produce cash or a bond in the amount determined by a judge who has *set bail*, the defendant is *held in bail* or *in $100,000 bail*.

bait (torment or entice), **bate** (reduce or lower, as in *abate*). *Also see* BATED BREATH.

Baja California, the Mexican peninsula, is divided into two states: *Baja California* in the north (not *Baja California Norte*) and *Baja California Sur* in the south.

baked alaska.

balding for becoming bald. *Baldish*, once preferred, now sounds archaic.

ball(-). Some compounds formed with *ball* are hyphenated, some are solid and some are two words: ball bearing, ball boy, ball carrier (sports), ball club, ball field, ball-flower (architecture), ballgame, ball joint, ballpark, ballplayer, ballpoint, ballroom.

Ballet Russe, Ballets Russes. The spelling will depend on the troupe mentioned, its leader and the year cited: the *Ballets Russes* (1909 to 1929), the groundbreaking company founded by Serge Diaghilev; the *Ballets Russes de Monte Carlo*, founded in 1932 by René Blum and Wassily G. Voskresensky (also known as Col. W. de Basil), which changed its name to *Ballet Russe de Monte Carlo* in 1934; the *Ballet Russe de Monte Carlo*, a successor led by Léonide Massine starting in 1938 and later by Sergei Denham; and the *Original Ballet Russe*, led by Col. W. de Basil from 1939 to 1948.

Band-Aid is a trademark for an adhesive bandage.

bandanna(s).

bandoleer.

Bangladeshi(s). The citizens of Bangladesh. But use *Bengali(s)* for the ethnic group in Bangladesh or in the Indian state of West Bengal.

Banjul (in Gambia).

Bankers Trust New York Corporation (parent company of the Bankers Trust Company).

Bank of America Corporation was formed after a 1998 merger of the BankAmerica Corporation and the NationsBank Corporation.

bankruptcy, a legal state of insolvency, can be voluntary (requested by the insolvent person or business) or involuntary (requested by the creditors). If a company is fighting an involuntary request, do not describe it as bankrupt until a judge has approved the petition. A person or business in debt may seek help under different chapters of the bankruptcy law. Individuals usually file under *Chapter 7* or *Chapter 13*. Chapter 7 allows for a quicker settlement of the debt while Chapter 13 leads to the gradual payment of some or all of the debt. *Chapter 11* is used mostly by businesses seeking protection from creditors' lawsuits while they reorganize their finances; such businesses are not yet bankrupt. A business that files under Chapter 11 may be forced into Chapter 7, which normally leads to liquidation.

Bank Street College of Education (in New York City).

banned, barred. Ordinarily, people can be *barred*, but only actions and things are *banned*. (An exception, under the apartheid system in South Africa, was the *banning* of politically suspect people, a set of restrictions on their contacts with others.)

bar(-). Most but not all compounds formed with *bar* are solid: barbell, bar chart, bar code, bar graph, barkeep, barkeeper, barroom, bartender.

bar association. *See* City Bar Association.

Barbados. Its people are *Barbadians.* Informally, many on the island call themselves *Bajans.*

barbecue (n. and v.).

Barclays Bank.

Bard, in references to Shakespeare, is trite. Resist it.

Bard College (in Annandale-on-Hudson, N.Y.).

bar mitzvah (for a boy), **bat mitzvah** (for a girl). The noun applies both to the ceremony and to the young person honored by it.

Barnes & Noble (the bookstore chain).

Barneys New York is the retailer. *Barney's Inc.* is its parent company. Only the parent uses the apostrophe.

baron is the lowest rank of British nobility. *Lord* is the customary title for a British baron, in all references and never with a given name: *Lord Lamb.* In some other countries, *Baron* is used before a name. *Also see* PEERS.

baroness. This is the lowest rank for a woman in the British peerage. A woman who holds it in her own right is *Lady Lamb* in all references or may choose to be *Baroness Lamb* on first reference and *Lady Lamb* thereafter; the wife of a baron is always *Lady Lamb.* No given name is used in either case. In some other countries, *Baroness* is used more widely. *Also see* PEERS.

baronet (British rank). The holder is not a peer. *See* Sir.

baroque (art, architecture and music). Capitalize in references to the style of painting, sculpture and architecture developed in Europe in the 17th century. Also capitalize in references to music composed between 1600 and 1750, beginning with

Monteverdi and ending with Bach and Handel. Lowercased, *baroque* refers to any style with a tendency to dramatic, abundant and elaborate detail. *See* ARTS TERMINOLOGY.

barrio. It is a Hispanic neighborhood or district. Avoid any assumption that it is necessarily poor, rundown or crime-ridden.

BART, for Bay Area Rapid Transit, San Francisco's mass transit system.

Baruch College (part of the CITY UNIVERSITY OF NEW YORK).

baseball. Give scores in figures, but spell out all other numbers under 10: *Bildots pitched seven innings and scored two runs in the Mets' 3-2 victory.*

The best-known professional organization is *Major League Baseball.* But: *major leagues; minor leagues; major-league* (adj.). Major League Baseball organizes the *World Series* (*the Series*). The best-known youth organization is *Little League Baseball,* which organizes the *Little League World Series.*

The names of pitches are single words: *changeup; curveball; spitball.* The names of positions other than *shortstop, pitcher* and *catcher* are two words: *first baseman; left fielder.*

Hyphenate the noun *at-bat(s),* but often *three times at bat* will be smoother in copy. Also: *r.b.i.* (never *r.b.i.'s*). Avoid tired words and phrases like *all-time, autumn classic, frame, nightcap, Pale Hose, win* (as a noun), *winless,* etc.

Basel (in Switzerland).

bases. *See* MILITARY BASES.

basis is often a symptom of bureaucratese. *The revenues were counted on a day-to-day* (or *week-to-week*) *basis.* Make it *The revenues were counted day to day.*

basketball. Use figures for points and scores: *He scored 8 points in two minutes. They won, 99-98.* Do not use *trey* for 3-point goals or *deuce* for 2-point baskets. The best-known professional leagues are the *National Basketball Association* and the *Women's National Basketball Association.*

bas-relief.

basset (the dog).

Bastille, the.

bated breath (not *baited*) is held because of excitement, fear or other emotion. The word is related to *abated.*

bath(-), (-)bath. Most but not all compounds formed with *bath* as a prefix are one word: bathhouse, bathmat, bathrobe, bathroom, bath salts, bath towel, bathtub.

Compounds formed with *bath* as a suffix are two words: acid bath, blood bath, bubble bath, sponge bath.

bathyscaph (a deep-sea diving craft).

Batswana (sing. and pl.). The people of Botswana. The adjective is *Botswana.*

battalion. Capitalize in names: *Third Battalion; 10th Battalion.*

battle(-). Some compounds formed with *battle* are hyphenated, some are solid and some are two words: battle-ax, battle cry, battle fatigue, battlefield, battlefront, battleground, battle(s) royal, battle-scarred, battleship, battle station(s).

battles. Capitalize names that have become known in history: *the Battle of Lexington; the Battle of Waterloo; the Battle of Ypres; the Battle of Britain.* But: *the attack on Fort Sumter; the Normandy campaign; the battle for Split.*

baud. This unit, as a measure of the speed of data transmission, has largely been replaced by BITS PER SECOND.

Bavarian cream (the dessert).

Bay Area (the San Francisco region).

Bayreuth (in Germany).

BBC for the British Broadcasting Corporation. Spell out the name unless the context is clear.

B.C. As an abbreviation for *before Christ*, it follows the year or the century: *The town was founded in 73 B.C.; the town dates from the second century B.C.* But A.D., for *anno Domini*, or *in the year of the* [or *our*] *Lord*, is placed before the year (*in A.D. 73*) and after the century (*in the second century A.D.*).

B. Dalton Bookseller.

Beaux-Arts (art and architecture). Capitalize when referring to the École des Beaux-Arts in Paris, which had a significant effect on American architecture and art, and when referring to the style itself. *See* ARTS TERMINOLOGY.

bed(-). Most but not all compounds formed with *bed* are solid: bed-and-breakfast, bedchamber, bedclothes, bedfast, bedfellow, bed jacket, bed linen, bedpost, bed rest, bedridden, bedroll, bedroom, bedsheet, bedside, bedspread, bedspring, bedtime.

Bed Bath & Beyond (the store chain).

before is more conversational than *prior to*, and shorter.

beg the question does not mean pose the issue or avoid the issue. To *beg the question* is to assume the truth of the proposition one is trying to prove. The phrase is so often used loosely that it is likely to be misunderstood.

Beijing. But *Peking duck. See* CHINESE NAMES.

Beirut (in Lebanon).

Bekaa Valley (in Lebanon).

Belarus. The adjective is *Belarussian.*

Belize. Its capital is Belmopan.

Bell Atlantic Corporation became part of VERIZON COMMUNICATIONS in 2000.

Bellerose (in Queens and Long Island).

Bellmawr, Belmar. *Bellmawr*, N.J., is in Camden County. *Belmar*, N.J., is in Monmouth County.

Bellmore (in Nassau County, N.Y.).

BellSouth Corporation (the regional telephone company).

bellwether. Its original meaning was a sheep (that is, *wether*) that wore a bell and led the flock. By extension, the term means a trend indicator.

bemused is not a synonym for aloof, cocky or amused. It means stupefied or muddled.

benefited, benefiting.

Bengali(s). An ethnic group in Bangladesh and India. *Also see* BANGLADESHI(S).

Benghazi (in Libya).

Ben-Gurion International Airport in Israel serves Jerusalem and Tel Aviv.

Benzedrine (a trademark for an amphetamine).

Bergdorf Goodman.

Bering Sea.

Berlin is the capital of Germany. From the end of World War II until 1990 the city was divided into American, British, French and Soviet sectors. The Soviet sector, *East Berlin*, was the capital of East Germany. The three other sectors, together forming *West Berlin*, were part of West Germany.

Berlin Wall; *the wall* (the one that stood from 1961 to 1989).

Bermuda shorts.

Bermuda Triangle. It is an area in the Atlantic bounded by Bermuda, Puerto Rico and Florida in which many ships are said to have disappeared mysteriously.

Bern (in Switzerland).

beset (v.) is stilted and is best replaced by conversational synonyms like *harass* or *trouble*.

besiege.

best(-). Compounds formed with *best* are usually hyphenated when they precede the nouns they modify: *best-dressed*; *best-informed*; *best-liked*; *best man*; *best-paid*; *best-selling*. In general, the hyphens are omitted when the compound adjectives follow the nouns they modify: *A survey found newspaper readers best informed*. *Also see* BEST-SELLER LIST.

best-seller list. Make it *the New York Times best-seller list* when the newspaper's name serves as a modifier or *The New York Times's best-seller list* when the newspaper's name serves as a noun. But the books are *best sellers*.

bettor (one who wagers).

between. In a range of prices or quantities, this phrasing is wordy: *The project will cost between $1.2 million and $1.6 million*. Use the more graceful "to" construction: *The project will cost $1.2 million to $1.6 million*. See AMONG, BETWEEN.

Bhopal (in India).

Bhutan. Its residents are *Bhutanese*.

bi(-). Compounds formed with *bi* are not hyphenated: biannual, bicameral, bicentennial, bicultural, bidirectional, biennial, bifocal, bilateral, bilingual, bimonthly, bipartisan, biplane, bisexual, bistate, bivalve, biweekly. *Also see* BIANNUAL, BIENNIAL; BIMONTHLY; BIWEEKLY; SEMIANNUAL; SEMIYEARLY; SEMIMONTHLY; SEMIWEEKLY.

biannual, biennial. *Biannual* means twice a year, as do *semiannual* and *semiyearly*. *Biennial* means every two years. For comprehension, when possible write *twice a year* or *every two years*.

Bible, biblical. Capitalize *Bible* (but not *biblical*) if the reference is to the Old Testament or the New Testament. But: *The style manual is their bible. Also see* GOSPEL(S) and SCRIPTURE(S).

Bible Belt for regions, especially in the South, where evangelical fervor is strong. Take care to avoid a disparaging tone.

BID for business improvement district, but only when the context is clear.

bid (v.). Use the word freely in the context of auctions or business contracting. But resist it in headlines as a synonym for *urge* or *request*; that usage sounds archaic. In the sense of greeting or saying goodbye, the past tense is *bade*. In bridge games and in business uses, the past tense is *bid*.

big. Use it as an adjective. The colloquial use as an adverb (*they won big*) is hackneyed, as is the related slang *they failed big time*.

Big Bang theory.

Big Board. *See* NEW YORK STOCK EXCHANGE.

Big Three (or *Four, Five*, etc.). Construe as a plural. Numerals may be used in headlines: *Big 3*.

big time. When it is used as a noun, it is two words: *That novel put her in the big time*. When it is an adjective that precedes what it modifies, it is hyphenated: *He was a big-time gambler*. Used as an adverb, it is two words (*He regretted his decision big time*), but it is also slang and a cliché.

bikini (bathing suit).

billion. A billion is 1,000 million. *See* DOLLARS AND CENTS; NUMBERS; NUMBERS, ROUND.

Bill of Rights. The first 10 amendments to the Constitution. Do not shorten it to *the bill* in later references. Also capitalize for the Bill of Rights enacted in Britain in 1689.

bills, legislative. *See* ACTS, AMENDMENTS, BILLS AND LAWS.

bimonthly means every two months; *semimonthly* means twice a month. For comprehension, use *every two months* or *twice a month*.

biodiversity. The term refers to the interdependence and preservation of all forms of life on earth. Except in a proper name—*the Hall of Biodiversity*, for example, at the American Museum of Natural History—simpler phrases are preferred.

biological parents. Use this term, not *natural parents*, when it is necessary to distinguish between birth parents and adoptive ones. But adoptive status should not be mentioned unless it is relevant and its relevance is clear to the reader.

bird's-eye (adj.). But the brand of frozen food is *Birds Eye*.

birth(-). Some compounds formed with *birth* are solid and some are two words: birth canal, birth certificate, birth control, birthday, birth defect, birthmark, birthplace, birthrate, birthright, birthstone.

bisexual. Do not use the slang shorthand *bi*.

bishop. Lowercase the title except when it directly precedes a name. Here is a guide to the use of the title in various churches:

EPISCOPAL

The Episcopal Church is headed by the *presiding bishop*. In first references: *Presiding Bishop Ashley B. Lamb of the Episcopal Church*. In later references: *Presiding Bishop Lamb*; *the presiding bishop*; *Bishop Lamb*; *the bishop*.

Bishops head dioceses and hold other posts. *Suffragan bishops* assist bishops of dioceses. *Bishops coadjutor* are suffragans with the right of succession. *Assistant bishops* (usually retired bishops) perform duties for bishops of dioceses but are not formally installed.

Omit *the Rt. Rev.* before the names of bishops. In first references, use the titles given in the previous paragraph: *Bishop Ashley B. Lamb of New York*; *Suffragan Bishop Ashley B. Lamb of New York*. Also: *the bishop of New York*, *Ashley B. Lamb* (or *the suffragan bishop of*, etc.). In later references, use simply *Bishop Lamb* or *the bishop*.

LUTHERAN

Lutherans in the United States rarely use the term *bishop*. When they do, this is the style for a first reference: *the Rev. Ashley B. Lamb, bishop of Missouri*. In later references: *Bishop Lamb*; *the bishop*.

METHODIST

In the United Methodist Church, the style for a first reference is *Bishop Ashley B. Lamb of Massachusetts*. Later references: *Bishop Lamb*; *the bishop*.

MORMON

Mormon bishops head wards: *Bishop Ashley B. Lamb of the Manhattan Ward*; *Bishop Lamb*; *the bishop*.

ORTHODOX

The style of the Eastern Orthodox Church is similar to the first- and later-reference style for other churches. But often a high-ranking clergy member adopts an ecclesiastical name and uses that name alone after the title in a first reference: *Archbishop Makarios* (*Makarios* means *Blessed*). For other titles used by the church, see METROPOLITAN and PATRIARCH. *Also see* EASTERN ORTHODOXY.

ROMAN CATHOLIC

Roman Catholic *archbishops* normally head archdioceses. *Bishops* normally head dioceses. *Auxiliary bishops* assist archbishops or bishops. Omit *the Most Rev.* before the name in almost all cases: *Archbishop Ashley B. Lamb of Hartford*; *Bishop Ashley B. Lamb of Hartford*; *Auxiliary Bishop Ashley B. Lamb of Hartford*; etc. Also: *the bishop of Hartford, Ashley B. Lamb* (or *the archbishop of*, or *the auxiliary bishop of*, etc.). In later references: *Archbishop Lamb, the archbishop*; *Bishop Lamb, the bishop*; *Auxiliary Bishop* (or *Bishop*) *Lamb, the auxiliary bishop* or *the bishop*. Superiors general of certain Catholic orders use *the Most Rev.* before their names.

Often, as in New York, the archbishop of a large archdiocese also holds the higher rank of *cardinal*; that title supersedes *archbishop*.

Also see ARCHBISHOP; CANON; CARDINAL; DEACON; DEAN; MOST REV., RT. REV.; REV.; SUPERIOR GENERAL; VERY REV.

bit. In computing, a *bit* (short for *bi*nary dig*it*) is an electrical pulse representing a 0 or a 1, a single basic unit of information, the smallest unit a computer can handle. Clusters of bits form characters, or bytes. *Also see* BYTE; GIGABYTE; KILOBYTE; MEGABYTE.

bits per second, or *b.p.s.*, is a measure of the amount of information being sent over a communication line. An older measurement, the *baud* rate, equaled the number of voltage or frequency changes in a second. It is seldom used now because improvements in data communication permit a variable number of bits to be transmitted in one baud.

bitter, bitters. *Bitter* is an ale, often ordered by the pint. *Bitters* is used as a medicine and as a flavoring in cocktails.

bivouac, bivouacking.

biweekly means every two weeks. *Semiweekly* means twice a week, but a few authorities accept *biweekly* in that meaning, too. For clarity, use *every two weeks* or *twice a week* instead.

black. Lowercase *black* and all racial designations derived from skin color (*white, brown, yellow, red*). *Also see* AFRICAN-AMERICAN, BLACK; ETHNICITY; HISTORICALLY BLACK.

black(-). Compounds formed with *black* are sometimes hyphenated, sometimes solid and sometimes two words: blackball, black box, blackjack, blacklist, blackmail, blackout, black tie (n. and adv.), black-tie (adj.), blacktop.

Black Muslim. Do not use this term for a member of the Nation of Islam, the black nationalist group founded by Elijah Muhammad in the 1920's. Most black Americans who are Muslim follow traditional Islam or are members of theological splinter groups. They are *black Muslims* but not *Black Muslims*.

blackout. In the sense of a curb on news reporting, it ordinarily refers to a rule that binds labor negotiators, trial participants or legislators, not journalists. The distinction should be made clear so readers will not infer that reporters or editors are conspiring to withhold information. Usually a paraphrase is clearer (*an agreement not to speak with reporters*, for example).

blame (v.). Use this construction: *The rescuers blamed the weather for the wreck.* Do not use *blame on: The rescuers blamed the wreck on the weather.* Though dictionaries accept both usages, the more traditional has logic on its side: Blame the cause, never the effect.

blast off (v.), **blastoff** (n.). Use only in references to rocketry.

Bleecker Street (in Greenwich Village).

blind. Apply the word only to those who have no sight. Others may have *limited sight* or be *partly blind*. Do not use euphemisms like *visually challenged* or *visually impaired. Also see* DISABILITY, DISABLED.

blitz, blitzkrieg.

blizzard. A storm is not a blizzard unless it meets the specifications set by the National Weather Service: winds of at least 35 miles an hour and considerable falling or blowing snow that reduces visibility to less than a quarter-mile.

bloc, block. A *bloc* is a group of people (or nations) with a common interest who are working together. A *block* is any number of people or things treated as a unit.

blockfront.

blond, blonde, brunet, brunette. Use the nouns *blond* and *brunet* for boys and men, and the nouns *blonde* and *brunette* for girls and women. Use the adjectives *blond* and *brunet* for people of both sexes, and for inanimate things.

Bloomberg News is a subsidiary of Bloomberg L.P., which provides financial information in many forms to traders, investors, newspapers and other subscribers. In datelined articles, put the name in parentheses: *CHICAGO, June 10 (Bloomberg News)* — etc. Use this credit on undatelined articles:

By Bloomberg News

Bloomingdale's (a subsidiary of Federated Department Stores).

blowout (n.), **blow out** (v.).

BMT for Brooklyn-Manhattan Transit, once a separate subway company in New York that became part of the city system in 1940. While the abbreviation survives in local idiom, it is confusing to newcomers and visitors. Except in direct quotations or historical contexts, make it simply *the N train* (or *line*); *the R train.*

B'nai B'rith, Bnai Zion. Note that one of these Jewish organizations uses no apostrophes. Do not use *the* before either name. The Anti-Defamation League is a division of B'nai B'rith.

board. Capitalize only when part of a name. Do not abbreviate, even in headlines.

board chairman (chairwoman). Lowercase the terms, and do not use as a false title (*the board chairwoman, Toby S. Kuzu,* not *board chairwoman Toby S. Kuzu*). Usually *chairman* (or *chairwoman*) *of the XYZ Company* can stand without *board.* Do not use *chairlady* or *chairperson.* In a general reference, *head of the board* is suitable for both sexes. *Also see* MEN AND WOMEN.

board of directors can usually be shortened to *the board* or *the directors.*

Board of Regents; *the Regents; the board.*

Boardwalk (in Coney Island, Atlantic City, etc.).

boast. Unless there is a real notion of taking pride, the verb, as a substitute for *have,* is an example of overreaching: *The school boasts three new computer rooms.*

boat(-). Many but not all compounds formed with *boat* are one word: boathook, boathouse, boatload, boatman, boat race.

boccie (the bowling game).

Boeing Company.

bogey. It is a noun meaning one over par in golf and a verb for making that score: *He scored a bogey; He bogeyed the third hole.* The plural is *bogeys. Also see* BOGY.

Bogotá (in Colombia).

bogy. A bugbear or a goblin or an evil spirit. The plural is *bogies. Also see* BOGEY.

bona fide. Without a hyphen, even as a preceding modifier.

bondholder.

bond ratings. *See* DEBT RATINGS.

booby trap (n.), **booby-trap** (v.).

book(-), (-)book. Most but not all compounds formed with *book* as a prefix are one word: book bag, bookbinder, bookcase, book club, book dealer, bookend, book jacket, bookkeeper, book learning, bookmaker, bookmark, bookmobile, bookseller, bookshelf, bookshop, bookstore, bookworm.

Most but not all compounds formed with *book* as a suffix are one word: bankbook, checkbook, guidebook, notebook, pocket book (a small book), pocketbook (a billfold, purse or handbag), reference book, schoolbook, storybook (n. and adj.), stylebook, textbook.

Book of Common Prayer.

books. Use their titles in quotation marks in news copy and capitalize the principal words (as defined in the entry on CAPITALIZATION). But omit quotation marks for the titles of standard reference works like dictionaries, encyclopedias and gazetteers. When an article deals substantially with a book, name the publisher and give the publication date, but not necessarily in the first few paragraphs.

Books on Tape is a trademark.

boost, booster. Suitable uses include these: *boost* (n. or v.) *over a wall; civic booster; morale booster; booster rocket.* But avoid journalese like *boost wages, boost taxes, boost a bill's chances.*

Border collie.

Border terrier.

Borders Books and Music (the retail chain).

"Boris Godunov" (the opera).

born again. The phrase applies to an evangelical Christian who has experienced an adult or adolescent conversion. As a modifier before a noun: *born-again.*

born, borne. Except in references to birth, use *borne* as the past participle of *bear*: a load, a cost and a grudge are *borne*, but a child is *born. Born* is used only in the passive voice and only when the focus is on the offspring: *Ashley was born in Ashtabula.* When the focus is on the mother, add an *e* (*Theo has borne three daughters*), even in the passive voice (*Three children were borne by Stacy*).

Borough of Manhattan Community College (part of the City University of New York).

Borough President *Stacy T. Lam of Queens; the borough president.* Never *the president.*

borscht. Also: *borscht belt* and *borscht circuit*, for the Catskill resort hotels and their nightclub entertainment in their heyday.

Börse (the German exchange). In most contexts, the English phrase is more comfortable.

Bosnia and Herzegovina split from Yugoslavia in 1992. Use the country's full name in datelines and formal contexts; in later references, normally just *Bosnia, Bosnian* and *Bosnians.* The country has two parts—the *Serbian Republic* (not to be confused with the Yugoslav republic of *Serbia*) and the *Muslim-Croat Federation.* It is often necessary to append an ethnic identification to the adjective *Bosnian*: *Bosnian Croat; Bosnian Serb* (as in *a Bosnian Serb militia*). But in a clear context, *Muslim* can stand alone.

Bosporus, the (not *Bosporus Strait*).

Boston Stock Exchange.

both means the two taken together. Do not use it in constructions like this: *Both towns are the same size*; make it *The two*, etc. *Also see* EITHER (. . . OR).

Botswana. Its people are *Batswana* (sing. and pl.). The adjective is *Botswana.*

Boulevard. Spell out and capitalize after a name in a news article: *Bruckner Boulevard.* The abbreviation may be used with a name (*Bruckner Blvd.*) in headlines, tables, charts and maps.

(-)bound. This suffix forms solid compounds except when it follows a proper name or produces an unaccustomed coinage: Africa-bound, deskbound, eastbound, fame-bound, housebound, musclebound, northbound, snowbound, southbound, vacationbound.

Bourse (French exchange). But the English phrase is usually more comfortable for American readers.

boutonniere.

bowl games. Capitalize their names: *Rose Bowl, Cotton Bowl, Orange Bowl,* etc. The National Football League designates its championship, the *Super Bowl,* with Roman numerals; the 1999 game, for example, was *Super Bowl XXXIII. Also see* SPORTS SPONSORSHIP.

box(-). Some compounds formed with *box* are one word, some are two words. Many compound adjectives formed with *box* are hyphenated: boxcar, boxholder, box kite, boxlike, box lunch, box office (n.), box-office (adj.), box score, box seat, box spring (n.), box-spring (adj.), box supper, boxwood.

boxing. Classes are *heavyweight, middleweight* and *lightweight,* but *junior welterweight.* Spell out the number of rounds below 10 and use figures for the time within a round: *2:03 of the sixth round.* Also use figures for the knockdown count: *a count of 8.*

boy. Reserve it for references to the very young, in the same contexts where *girl* would be appropriate. *Also see* MEN AND WOMEN.

boyfriend, girlfriend. The terms are informal and best reserved for teenagers.

Boy Scouts; *the Scouts; a scout.* The national organization is the *Boy Scouts of America.*

BP Amoco. In 1998, the Amoco Corporation and the British Petroleum Company merged to form *BP Amoco.* In 1999, BP Amoco announced an agreement to acquire the Atlantic Richfield Company.

bra is preferred to *brassiere* in all references.

brackets. In general, brackets signal the reader that the origin of information has shifted. Brackets should enclose a writer's or editor's insertions in a direct quotation, or an editor's additions to an article if they consist of material that the writer could not have supplied. (By contrast, PARENTHESES, outside a direct quotation, enclose clarifying material that was available to the writer.)

Brackets may be used—sparingly—in verbatim TEXTS AND EXCERPTS to explain an obscure name, expression or measurement, since the editor is not free to provide clues by altering the surrounding passages: *The bomber crashed 40 kilometers [about 25 miles] from the Chinese border.* Or: *Then I went to see Barany [Attorney General Lauren A. Barany of New Hampshire].* Note that the clarifying information about Barany has been concentrated in a single place—tidier than separate intrusions before and after the surname.

In a news article, such interruptions of a quotation divert attention to the editing process and should be a last resort. In their place, it is usually possible to use a partial quotation and paraphrase the cryptic term, or to adjust the surrounding phrasing for clarity: *"Then I went to see Barany," he said, a reference to Attorney General Lauren A. Barany of New Hampshire.*

To preserve the truthfulness of a dateline, brackets are used in an article to insert reporting obtained by editors from a news agency or from a correspondent distant from the datelined place. The inserted passage should specify its source, to help the reader understand the purpose of bracketing: *In Washington, the White House confirmed . . . or . . . The Associated Press reported. See* DATELINE INTEGRITY.

Often the bracketed passage mentions the timing of a news development. In such a case, since the insert is isolated from the dateline, *today* would be incorrect, but *yesterday* might confuse readers. Instead, name the day: *announced on Thursday.*

When bracketed material is longer than one paragraph, begin each paragraph with an opening bracket; use a closing bracket after the last paragraph only. Since brackets serve to isolate an insert from the dateline, they have no purpose in an undatelined article. There, added reporting should simply be woven into the copy, with suitable attribution.

If inserted material is from the same city and news organization as the rest of the article, but serves as a cross-reference to a separate article, brackets enclose the page reference only: *On Capitol Hill, meanwhile, the decision aroused indignation. [Page A15.]*

The position of punctuation before or after brackets is the same as with PARENTHESES.

Brahmin(s) for the priestly Hindu caste and for general references to aristocracy: *a Boston Brahmin.*

branded. In the sense of labeled, the word is used without *as*: *He branded the charge false* (not *as false*).

brand names may be used when they convey useful information or add color. If used, they should be capitalized. *Also see* TRADEMARK, SERVICE MARK.

brand-new.

Brasília (the capital of Brazil).

Brazil nut.

breach, breech. A *breach* is a breaking or violation (*breach of promise; breach of the peace; a breach in a dike*). The overworked allusion to Shakespeare's "Henry V" is "Once more *unto* the breach" (not *into*). *Also see* MORE HONORED IN THE BREACH.

A *breech* is the lower or back part of something (*breechcloth, breeches buoy*). *Breeches* (colloquially, *britches*) are trousers that extend just below the knee. And a *breech birth* is a feet-first delivery.

bread(-). Compounds formed with *bread* can be one word, two words or, in the case of compound adjectives, hyphenated: bread and butter (n., in the sense of livelihood), bread-and-butter (adj.), breadbasket, breadboard, breadbox, bread crumbs, breadfruit, bread line, breadstick, breadwinner.

break(-). Compounds formed with *break* can be one word, two words or hyphenated: breakaway (adj.), break away (v.), breakdown (n.), break down (v.), break-even (adj.), break even (v.), break-in (adj. and n.), break in (v.), breakneck, breakoff (n.), break off (v.), breakout (n.), break out (v.), breakthrough (n.), break through (v.), breakup (n.), break up (v.), breakwater.

breaststroke.

bribe(-). Compounds formed with *bribe* are one word: bribegiver, bribegiving, bribetaker, bribetaking.

Brick Township (in New Jersey).

bridal, bridle. *Bridal* refers to brides and weddings. *Bridle* refers to a horse's harness and, figuratively, to various kinds of restraints and controls.

bride. Beware of expressions like *his bride*, which imply an unequal marriage partnership. And use *wife* after the wedding bells stop ringing. Better still, call both spouses by their names. *Also see* MEN AND WOMEN and WIFE.

bridge. Capitalize *North, East, South, West.* Lowercase *spades, hearts, diamonds, clubs* and *no-trump*, which is both singular and plural: *one no-trump; three no-trump.*

Also lowercase names of cards and spell them out when they appear singly: *ace, king, queen, jack, ten, nine, eight, seven, six, five, four, three* (never *trey*), *two* (or *deuce*). Use initials and numerals hyphenated, for two or more cards in combination: *He led into South's A-9 combination* (not *ace-nine*). Use lowercase *x* as a symbol substituted for a numeral: *His holding in diamonds might have been K-x-x.*

Use numerals for all points above *one* in counting the value of a hand: *His hand was worth only 3 points; He had a 3-point hand; He had only one point.* Also use numerals for all match points or international match points except *one*. In scoring, use numerals for all points except a fraction that is not combined with a whole number: *370 points; 379½ points; 2½ points; one-half point; half a point.* The acronym *imp(s)* is acceptable in first and later references to international match points: *The Bildots team won the match by 67 imps.*

In giving the distribution or division of a bridge hand or suit, always use numerals with hyphens: *He had a 5-3-3-2 hand; They hoped the suit would be divided 3-1.*

In the bridge column, courtesy titles are not used before surnames in later references. But use them in news articles when bridge players are mentioned, except in passages where actual play is being reported.

Bridgeport, University of (in Connecticut).

Brig. *Lauren W. Karitsa* (in British or other foreign armed forces); *Brigadier Karitsa; the brigadier.*

Brig. Gen. *Lee P. Cordeiro; General Cordeiro; the general.*

bring, take. Use *bring* to mean movement toward the speaker or writer; *take* means movement away from the speaker or writer (in fact, any movement that is not toward the speaker or writer). So the Canadian prime minister cannot be *bringing* a group of industrialists to a conference in Detroit, except in an article written from Detroit. Since datelines do not govern headlines, *bring* in a Times headline usually refers to movement toward New York, or toward the United States.

Bristol-Myers Squibb Company (the pharmaceutical maker).

Britain (not *Great Britain*). But when a locating word is required after the name of a city or a town (in a dateline or an article), use *England, Scotland, Wales* or *Northern Ireland. Also see* DATELINES.

British, Briton(s). The people of Britain; this group includes the English, the Scottish, the Welsh and in some general contexts the Northern Irish. Use the more specific terms when they apply. Do not use *Brit(s)* or *Britisher(s)*.

British Airways.

British Broadcasting Corporation. *See* BBC.

British Columbia (Canadian province). Do not abbreviate after the names of cities and towns, even in datelines.

British Commonwealth is the former term for what is now the COMMONWEALTH.

British Petroleum Company merged with the Amoco Corporation in 1998 to form *BP Amoco.*

British titles are listed separately.

broadband (n. and adj.), for high-capacity communication links, especially those on the Internet.

broadsheet (n. and adj.), for a standard-size newspaper, but only in a clear publishing context.

brokerage. Use the word to mean a broker's line of work—that is, serving as an intermediary. But use *brokerage firm*, in full, to mean an organization in that business.

Bronx Community College (part of the CITY UNIVERSITY OF NEW YORK).

Bronx, the. The article, always lowercase, is part of the name except in mailing addresses, headlines, charts and maps.

Bronx-Whitestone Bridge. In a casual reference, *Whitestone Bridge* can stand alone.

Bronx Zoo. Use the informal name in virtually all references. In a detailed article, it may be useful to mention the official name, *the Bronx Zoo Wildlife Conservation Park.* The zoo is operated on city property by the WILDLIFE CONSERVATION SOCIETY.

Bronze Age.

Brookings Institution.

Brooklyn-Battery Tunnel.

Brooklyn Botanic Garden. But: *the New York Botanical Garden* (in the Bronx).

Brooklyn College (part of the CITY UNIVERSITY OF NEW YORK).

Brooklyn Heights; *the Heights.* In first references, use no article before *Brooklyn.* In headlines: *Brooklyn Hts.*

Brooklyn Navy Yard. The former military installation is now a small-business development center.

Brooklyn Public Library. It is independent of the New York Public Library.

Brooklyn Union Gas Company (a subsidiary of the KeySpan Energy Corporation).

Brothers. Spell out *Brothers* (or *Brother*) in a company or similar name. Also: *Dana Karitsa & Brothers* (never *and*, in this construction). The abbreviation *Bros.* or *Bro.* may be used in a company name in a headline, table or chart. *See* COMPANY AND CORPORATION NAMES.

brownstone. It is a house with a facade of brown sandstone. Not all town houses or row houses are brownstones.

Bruges (in Belgium), rather than the Flemish name, *Brugge.*

brunet, brunette. *See* BLOND, BLONDE, BRUNET, BRUNETTE.

Brünnhilde.

brush fire.

brussels sprouts.

B.S. for Bachelor of Science. Also: *a bachelor's degree.*

B.T.U. for British thermal unit. A *B.T.U.* is the amount of heat needed to increase the temperature of a pound of water by one degree Fahrenheit.

Budget Message. The president's and, if it is formally so called, a governor's or a mayor's.

buffalo(es).

bug (electronic). A *bug* is a listening device concealed to pick up sounds in a room or other area. A *tap* is a device connected to a telephone to capture conversations from the line. Do not use quotation marks around either expression or its related verb forms.

building names. Capitalize the names of governmental buildings, churches, office buildings, hotels, specially designated rooms, etc.: *the Capitol* (state or national); *Criminal Courts Building; Empire State Building; First Presbyterian Church; Grand Central Terminal; Inter-Continental Hotel; Oak Room; Ohio State Penitentiary;* etc.

buildup (n. and adj.), **build up** (v.).

bulimia.

bullet. It is the projectile that leaves the barrel of a rifle, a handgun or a machine gun. The ammunition supplied for such a weapon, or loaded into it, is not a bullet but a *cartridge* (also known as a *round*). A cartridge consists of the bullet plus casing, an explosive charge (powder) and a primer, the small explosive that ignites the charge. The casing remains after the bullet has been fired. *Also see* SHELL.

bullpen.

bull's-eye (when the reference is not to the eye of a bull).

Bundestag (the German legislature). Except in unusually detailed references to the system or passages conveying local color, *Parliament* is a more accessible term for nonspecialized readers.

bungalow. A small one-story house, often with an attic.

Bunsen burner.

bureau. Capitalize in names of government or private agencies (*Bureau of Indian Affairs*), but not in references to news bureaus (*the Washington bureau of The New York Times*).

bureaucrat means a functionary, but usually also a faceless and rigid one. Use it with care, or use a neutral synonym.

burgeoning. The word's loose use, to mean booming or spreading, has gained acceptance (to the point of being a cliché). But careful writers and knowing readers still use it only to mean budding.

burglary. *See* LARCENY, BURGLARY, ROBBERY, THEFT and MUGGING.

Burkina Faso is the former Upper Volta. The capital is Ouagadougou.

Burlington Northern Santa Fe Corporation, the parent of the Burlington Northern and Santa Fe Railway Company.

Burmese (n. and adj., sing. and pl.). The people of Myanmar, formerly Burma. The country name may also be used as an adjective, but the more familiar *Burmese* aids comprehension. Refer to the language as *Burmese*.

Burmese names. When used in full on first reference, a Burmese name includes a courtesy title that is considered essential: *U* for a man, *Daw* for a married woman, *Mah* for an unmarried woman, *Maung* or *Ko* for a young man or a boy. Thus an article should normally refer to a Burmese man, on first reference, as *U*; for example, *U Soe Myint*. When possible, use a governmental or professional title instead (*President, Gen.* or *Dr.*, for example) and drop the *U*. In a later reference, a Burmese man without such a title should be called *Mr.*: *Mr. Soe Myint*. A woman without a title should be *Ms., Mrs.* or *Miss* in later references. Burmese can have either one name (*U Nu; U Lwin*) or two (*U Kyaw Soe; Dr. Hla Han*); if two, use both names in later references: *Mr. Kyaw Soe; Dr. Hla Han*.

bus, bused, buses, busing (all v.) for transporting by bus. The expression *forced busing* is polemical; use *court-ordered busing*.

bushel. It is equal to four pecks or eight gallons. The United States bushel is equal to 35.24 liters; the British imperial bushel, 36.37 liters.

business directories and guides. Use their titles without quotation marks; capitalize principal words.

businessman, businesswoman. But: *business owner; small-business man; small-business woman. Businesspeople* is acceptable, but not *businessperson;* in a general reference use a phrase like *business manager* or *business executive. Also see* COMPOUND WORDS and MEN AND WOMEN.

bust, for arrest, is slang, and usually out of place in news articles.

buyback (n. and adj.), **buy back** (v.).

buyout (n. and adj.), **buy out** (v.).

by(-). Except before a vowel, compounds formed with *by* are one word: by-election, bylaw, byline, bypass (n. and v.), bypath, byplay, byproduct, byroad, bystander, byway, byword.

bylines. In the news pages, bylines are centered, with the name in bold capitals:

By HILARY J. McMIEL

If two writers merit equal credit, use one of these styles:

By HILARY J. McMIEL
and LESLIE P. DANN Jr.

By HILARY J. McMIEL and LESLIE P. DANN Jr.

If the principal reporter has received major assistance, or if only one member of the pair has visited the location designated in the dateline:

By HILARY J. McMIEL
with LESLIE P. DANN Jr.

By HILARY J. McMIEL with LESLIE P. DANN Jr.

When more than two reporters share credit:

> *This article is by* **Lee Cordero, Hilary J.** **McMiel** *and* **Leslie P. Dann Jr.**

> *This article was reported by* **Lee Cordero,** **Hilary J. McMiel** *and* **Leslie P. Dann Jr.** *and written by Ms. Cordero.*

> *This article is based on reporting by* . . . etc.

Also see CREDIT LINES; DATELINES; SIGNATURES.

byte. The term for one character—a letter or number, for example—stored or processed by a computer. It is composed of a string of bits, or electrical pulses, usually eight per byte. *Also see* BIT; GIGABYTE; KILOBYTE; MEGABYTE.

byzantine. Capitalize in reference to the Byzantine Empire, the Eastern Orthodox Church or the architectural style of the Byzantine Empire. Lowercase in general references to deviousness or complexity.

C

cabdriver. Also: *cabby*; *cabbies*. But: *gypsy-cab driver*.

cabinet is lowercase, even for a national or state government: *the cabinet*; *President Miel's cabinet*; *a cabinet minister*.

cabinet titles, United States and foreign, are capitalized only when they precede names: *Secretary of Labor Terry J. Karitsa*; *Finance Minister Ashley C. Lamb*; *the secretary*; *the minister*; *a secretary*; *a minister*; *the secretaries*; *the ministers*. *Also see* TITLES.

CAD-CAM for computer-aided design and computer-aided manufacturing, but only in unmistakable technical contexts, and not in headlines.

caddie (golf), **caddy** (tea), **Caddy** (the car, colloquially).

Cadet *Dale P. Lamm*; *Cadet Lamm*; *the cadet* (for students at the Air Force and Coast Guard academies and West Point).

Caesarean section.

cafe. No accent except in a proper name or a foreign phrase.

Cairene(s) (the people of Cairo).

cairn terrier.

caliber measures the internal diameter of a firearm barrel. For rifles and pistols, the caliber is usually rendered in millimeters or hundredths of an inch. For naval guns and artillery, some calibers are stated in inches. Use figures in giving the calibers of weapons and ammunition: *.22 rifle* (or *.22-caliber rifle*); *7.2-inch gun*; *11-inch cannon*. Most sporting rifles are between .22 and .458 caliber. Some common ones are .222 Remington, .243 Winchester, 7x57-millimeter Mauser, .30 Carbine, .30-30, .30-'06 (note the apostrophe), .308 Winchester, .35 Remington and .375 H&H Magnum. The most common calibers for military rifles are 5.56 millimeter (the M-16) and 7.62 millimeter (the AK-47 and the M-14).

Some common handgun calibers are .22, .22 Magnum, .25, .32 Colt, .32 Special, 9 millimeter, .357 Magnum, .38 Special, .40 Smith & Wesson, .44 Magnum and .45 Colt. *Millimeter* may be abbreviated (as *mm.*) in headlines, tables and charts. *Also see* BULLET; CARTRIDGE; HANDGUNS; MAGNUM; RIFLES; SHELL; SHOTGUNS.

California. Abbreviate as *Calif.* after the names of cities, towns and counties.

Caltech in later references to the California Institute of Technology.

Cambodia, Cambodian(s). The language may also be called *Khmer*, and the predominant ethnic group is Khmer.

Cambodian names. Cambodians' names assume a variety of forms. If it is known without doubt that part of a name is a surname, or is used alone by Cambodians, that part may stand alone in later references: *Prince Norodom Ranariddh*; *Prince Ranariddh*. In a headline: *Ranariddh*. In most cases, though, for consistency and certainty, repeat full names: *Sam Rainsy*; *Mr. Sam Rainsy*. Or *Gen. Ke Kim Yan*, with the title abbreviated in all references because the name is unchanged. (But if his title were, say, *Maj. Gen.*, it could later be shortened to *General*, spelled out.)

Cameroon (not *Cameroons* or *Cameroun*).

camp(-). Most but not all compounds formed with *camp* are one word: camp chair, campfire, campground, campsite, campstool.

Camp David (the presidential retreat near Thurmont, Md.).

Canada. Use province or territory names (spelled out) instead of the country name after the names of cities and towns, but only if a locater is necessary. (Often it is unnecessary; see STATE ABBREVIATIONS.) When the names of provinces or territories stand alone in articles, *Canada* is often unneeded.

Canada goose (not *Canadian* goose).

Canadian Broadcasting Corporation (CBC).

Canadian National Railway.

Canadian Pacific Ltd. (the parent company of the Canadian Pacific Railway, formerly the CP Rail System).

Canadian provinces and territories are listed separately. Do not abbreviate their names after the names of cities and towns, even in datelines.

canal. Lowercase in later references to the *Panama Canal*, the *Suez Canal* and others.

Canal Zone, in historical references to the strip of land on both sides of the Panama Canal when it was controlled by the United States.

Canard Enchaîné, Le (the French weekly newspaper of satire and investigative reports).

cancel, canceled, canceling, cancellation.

Cancún (in Mexico).

candelabrum (sing.), **candelabra** (pl.).

candle(-). Compounds formed with *candle* are one word: candleholder, candlelight, candlepower, candlestick.

canine. Use the word as an adjective meaning *of dogs*. Used as a noun meaning *dog*, for the sake of variation, it is trite.

cannon, canon. A *cannon* is a piece of artillery, or a gun mounted on a plane; the plural is *cannons*. A *canon* is a body of literature or church laws, an Episcopal clergy member or a basic principle.

Canon *Hilary V. Lamm; Canon Lamm; the canon.* A canon is an Episcopal clergy member connected with a cathedral or assigned to a bishop.

Cantabrigian(s). The people of Cambridge, England, or students and graduates of Cambridge University. But phrases using *of Cambridge* are usually less stodgy.

cantaloupe.

Canterbury, archbishop of. *The Most Rev. Morgan C. Barany, archbishop of Canterbury; Archbishop Barany; the archbishop of Canterbury; the archbishop. Also see* MOST REV., RT. REV.

canto(s).

Canton (in China) is now known as *Guangzhou. See* CHINESE NAMES.

canvas (cloth), **canvass** (to survey, poll or solicit).

capability. *Ability* and *capacity* are shorter, less stilted and almost always preferred.

Cape Canaveral (in Florida) is the home of the *John F. Kennedy Space Center.* The related installation at Houston is the *Lyndon B. Johnson Space Center.*

Cape Town (in South Africa).

Cap Haitien.

capital (city), **capitol** (building). Always lowercase *capital* (meaning principal city). Capitalize *Capitol,* meaning a specific national or state building. Lowercase general and plural references to such buildings: *the country needed a capitol; three state capitols won architecture awards.* Also: *Capitol Hill.*

Capital Cities/ABC Inc. has changed its name to *ABC Inc. See* ABC.

capitalization. Styles for capitalization are given in separate listings. A word, phrase or abbreviation listed without discussion should normally be capitalized or lowercased as shown.

In cap-and-lowercase headlines, capitalize all nouns, pronouns and verbs, and all other words of four or more letters. Handle shorter words as follows:

CAPITALIZE		LOWERCASE		
No	*Off*	*a*	*en* (in *en Route*)	*or*
Nor	*Out*	*and*	*for*	*the*
Not	*So*	*as*	*if*	*to*
	Up	*at*	*in*	*v.* (in legal contexts)
		but	*of*	*vs.*
		by	*on*	*via*

Handle infinitives this way: *to Be; to Do; to Go.*

Uppercase the first word of any line in a main headline, or in a bank inside the paper. V-shaped banks (inverted pyramids) on Page A1 are different: treat them as if they were one continuous line, so the first word of the second or third line should be lowercased if it is in the lowercase list above. Uppercase any word directly after a dash in a bank. Uppercase any word directly after a colon in a headline. And always uppercase the last word of a headline or a bank.

Some of the "little" headline prepositions occasionally turn into adverbs, modifying the preceding word; in those situations, they are capitalized: *Mayor Drops In*; *Meeting Drones On*; *Governor Stands By Her Position*. Sometimes even as a preposition, such a word will attach to the preceding verb and should be uppercased: *Cared For by His Mother*; *Attended To in an Emergency Room*. But idioms like *Call on, Call for* and *Wait on*, when followed by objects, do not fall into that category, and the prepositions remain lowercase: *Mayor Calls on President to Yield*; *Senator Calls for Decision*. A few expressions can occur in both forms: *They Waited on Tables* but *Customers Were Waited On in Turn*.

When the preposition *for* takes the place of a verb meaning *supports* or *advocates*, capitalize it: *Mayor For Health Insurance Plan*.

In general, capitalize both parts of a hyphenated compound in a headline: *Cease-Fire*; *Able-Bodied*; *Sit-In*; *Make-Believe*; *One-Fifth*. When a hyphen is used with a prefix of two or three letters merely to separate doubled vowels or to clarify pronunciation, lowercase after the hyphen: *Co-op*; *Re-entry*; *Pre-empt*. But: *Re-Sign*; *Co-Author*. With a prefix of four letters or more, capitalize after the hyphen: *Anti-Intellectual*; *Post-Mortem*. In sums of money: *$7 Million*; *$34 Billion*.

For the treatment of large decorative letters that begin articles, see INITIAL LETTERS.

Capt. *Hilary P. Daan*; *Captain Daan*; *the captain*. This applies to military, maritime, fire and police captains.

captions. A caption should normally explain what readers cannot see for themselves in the picture (*President Karitsa appealing for the education bill at a teachers' conference in Washington yesterday*) and should omit the obvious (*licking an ice cream cone* or *shaking hands*). Captions about fresh news may be written in the present tense (*Firefighters carry an injured crew member from the wreckage of the cargo plane*). But if the caption includes a past time element like *yesterday*, the verb must change to a participle (*carrying*) or to the past tense (*carried an injured crew member yesterday*). A caption recalling history or old news can use only the participle form or the past tense.

If space requires the omission of "little words" like *a* or *the*, drop the leftmost ones first (*After third inning, the Yankees changed pitchers*). Once the reader's mental ear has heard *the* or *a*, it strains to hear all such words and senses awk-

wardness if they are missing. Similarly, a caption may begin with a sentence fragment (*Spectators at the Capitol yesterday*). But once a complete sentence has appeared, the ear demands full sentences until the end.

Because captions may be read hastily and punctuation overlooked, caption
writers should avoid parenthetical clauses that flash backward and forward in
time: *Secretary Yagyonak, who was killed in the crash, boarding the aircraft yesterday.* Instead follow the sequence, first to last: *Secretary Yagyonak boarding the aircraft yesterday before his death in the crash.*

Caraqueño(s) (the people of Caracas).

carat. The unit of weight used for gemstones. It equals about 200 milligrams. Not to
be confused with a *karat*, the measure of the fineness of gold. Pure gold is 24
karats. And a *caret* was a mark used by writers and editors in the days before
cursors.

cardinal (Roman Catholic). *Cardinal Dale T. Cordeiro*; *Cardinal Cordeiro*; *the cardinal.* Use a given name on first reference, even for the cardinal who is archbishop
of New York. Church authorities no longer place *Cardinal* between given name
and surname. Capitalize in the official name of a group: *the College of Cardinals.*

CARE may be used in all references to the Cooperative for Assistance and Relief
Everywhere. Reserve the full name for articles dealing with the agency in detail.

care(-). Most compounds formed with *care* are one word: carefree, caretaker,
careworn. *Caregiver* is so spelled, but is social science jargon.

careen, career. Precise writers reserve *careen* to mean tilt or heel over (as a ship might).
The verb for moving at high speed is *career*.

career. Through headline compression, the phrase *of his career* has mutated into *her
sixth career victory* and *his second career knockout.* Invest two short words in the
more graceful *sixth victory of her career*, etc.

cargo(es).

Caribbean can stand alone to mean the sea. It can also refer to the area and its people. *See* West Indian.

carmaker.

Carnegie Institute (in Pittsburgh), **Carnegie Institution** (in Washington).

Carnival Cruise Lines.

Carolina. *N. Carolina* and *S. Carolina* may be used in headlines when necessary (and
more readily in the sports pages) to avoid the ambiguity of *Carolina* alone.

carousel.

car pool (n. and adj.), **car-pool** (v.), **car-pooling** (n. and v.).

carriers are transportation companies that move cargo. *Shippers* are the owners of the
goods.

Cartier (not *Cartier's*) is the jeweler.

cartridge. It is the ammunition for a rifle, a handgun or a machine gun. The cartridge (also called a *round*) includes the bullet, the projectile that leaves the barrel when the weapon is fired. The other components are the explosive charge (powder), the primer (a small explosive that ignites the charge) and the casing, which remains after the bullet has been fired. *Magnum* is the term for a cartridge that has more striking power than others of the same size. *Also see* CALIBER and SHELL.

case(-). Most but not all compounds formed with *case* are one word: casebook, case history, case law, caseload, casework, caseworker.

casket. Use *coffin* instead.

cast(-). Some compounds formed with *cast* are one word, some are two and a few are hyphenated: castaway (n.), cast iron (n.), cast-iron (adj.), castoff (n. and adj.).

caster (a furniture wheel), **castor** (an oil-producing bean).

catalog.

catchment area is jargon for the district served by a social service or health agency. Except in direct quotations, use a conversational term like *district* or *service area*.

cater-corner, cater-cornered (not *catty-corner*).

Cathedral Church of St. John the Divine.

Catholic does not necessarily mean Roman Catholic. If there is room for doubt, use *Roman Catholic* in repeated references.

Catskill Mountains; *the Catskills*. But as an adjective: *Catskill* (without the *s*). And the town is *Catskill*, N.Y.

cause célèbre.

cave-in (n.).

CB for citizens' band radio.

CBC for the Canadian Broadcasting Corporation.

CBS. The *CBS Corporation* agreed in 1999 to merge with Viacom Inc. CBS's major divisions are *the CBS Station Group*, the radio and television stations owned by the company; *CBS Television*, which includes CBS Entertainment and various production and distribution operations; and *CBS Cable*. Other divisions are *CBS News*, *CBS Sports* and *CBS Affiliate Relations*. (Do not attribute a *CBS News* production to *CBS-TV*.) The major division names, as well as *CBS* alone, may be used in first references. *CBS*, standing alone, may be best when several networks are mentioned together: *ABC, CBS, CNN and NBC will televise the news conference*.

CD('s) for compact disc(s), the audio recording medium. Also: *C.D.* for certificate of deposit, provided the context is clear.

C.D.C. for the Centers for Disease Control and Prevention.

CD-ROM for compact disc read-only memory, the computer storage medium.

C.D.T., C.S.T. for Central Daylight Time and Central Standard Time. *See* TIME.

cease-fire (n. and adj.).

cedilla. *See* ACCENT MARKS.

celebrant, celebrator. In careful usage, a *celebrant* officiates at a religious rite, typically a Mass. A merrymaker is a *celebrator*.

cellist, cello. No apostrophes, and note the spelling of the longer forms: *violoncellist* and *violoncello*.

Celsius, centigrade. The temperature scale used in the metric system. In it, zero represents the freezing point of water, and 100 degrees is the boiling point at sea level. To convert to Fahrenheit, multiply by 9, divide by 5 and add 32. The preferred term is *Celsius*, for the name of the system's inventor, a Swede; *centigrade* (lowercased) is used less often. The abbreviation for either name is *C*, so a temperature in this scale is written 20°C (without a period). *Also see* FAHRENHEIT; KELVIN; TEMPERATURES.

cement. Use *concrete* instead to mean the material that forms blocks, walls and roads. One ingredient is *cement*, the binding agent that is mixed with water, sand and gravel.

Centenary College (in Hackettstown, N.J.).

center (v.). Do not write *center around* because the verb means gather at a point. Logic calls for *center on, center in* or *revolve around*.

center(-). Most but not all compounds formed with *center* are one word: centerboard, center field, centerfold, centerpiece.

Centereach (in Suffolk County, N.Y.).

Centerport (in Suffolk County, N.Y.).

Centers for Disease Control and Prevention. Though the former *Centers for Disease Control* (note the plural *Centers*) has changed its name, it still uses the abbreviation *C.D.C.*

centigrade. *See* CELSIUS, CENTIGRADE.

Central African Republic. Its capital is Bangui.

Central Conference of American Rabbis (a Reform group).

Central Daylight Time, Central Standard Time (C.D.T., C.S.T.). *See* TIME.

Central Intelligence Agency (C.I.A.); *the agency*. It is headed by the director of central intelligence, whose title does not include the word *agency. Also see* AGENT.

Central Park Zoo. Use the informal name in virtually all references. In a detailed article, it may be useful to mention the official name, *the Central Park Wildlife Center*. The zoo is operated on city property by the WILDLIFE CONSERVATION SOCIETY.

Centre Street (in Manhattan).

cents. *See* DOLLARS AND CENTS.

centuries. Lowercase and spell out through the ninth: *the eighth century, the 12th century*. Hyphenate the adjectival form: *18th-century poet*. Also, in almost all contexts, *the 1700's*, not *seventeen-hundreds*; and *mid-ninth century, mid-16th century*, *mid-1890's.* Understandings differ on when a century begins and ends; see YEARS, DECADES, CENTURIES.

chador. The traditional shawl or cloak of Muslim women. The plural is *chadors*.

chair. As a noun, it can mean an endowed professorship (*the Anyell Chair in Philosophy*) or a position in an orchestra (*first-chair players*). Do not use it to mean *chairman* or *chairwoman*. Avoid it as a verb meaning *lead a committee*; try *lead*, *head* or *preside over* instead. Similarly, avoid *co-chair* (n. and v.).

chairman, chairwoman. Also: *board chairwoman* and *chairman of the board*, although *board* is usually redundant with these titles; make it *chairwoman of the XYZ Company.* Do not use *chairlady* or *chairperson. Also see* CHAIR and MEN AND WOMEN.

chairman of the Joint Chiefs of Staff. Lowercase *chairman*, and use a comma to separate the expression from a name: *the chairman of the Joint Chiefs of Staff, Gen. (or Adm.) Alex L. Barany; Gen. (or Adm.) Alex L. Barany, chairman of the Joint Chiefs of Staff; General (or Admiral) Barany; the chairman.* In later references, *the Joint Chiefs* and *the chiefs.*

chaise longue (not *lounge*).

challenged. Do not use this euphemism for disabilities (*he is hearing-challenged*). Write instead that *he cannot hear* or that *she is partly blind. Also see* AFFLICTED; BLIND; CRIPPLE, CRIPPLED; DEFORMED; HANDICAPPED; IMPAIRED; VICTIM.

Chamber of Deputies; *the Chamber.*

Champagne, champagne. *See* WINES AND SPIRITS.

Champs-Élysées.

chancellor. For the head of a government, a governmental agency or a school system, make it *Chancellor Lee P. Milori; Chancellor Milori; the chancellor;* Mr. (or *Miss, Mrs., Ms.* or *Dr.*) *Milori.* In New York City the title is *schools chancellor*, also capitalized when it precedes the name. For nongovernmental chancellors (in universities, for example), lowercase, and separate the title from the name with a comma.

channels (television). Make it *Channel 2; Channel 13;* etc. Also: *WCBS-TV; WNET;* etc. For consistency in the news columns, avoid individual variations like *Thirteen/WNET.*

chaperon (not *chaperone*). Also: *chaperoned, chaperoning.*

chapter numbers. Capitalize them as proper names: *Chapter 16; Chapter 2.* In tables and charts, abbreviations may be used: *Ch. 16; Ch. 2. See* NUMBERED EXPRESSIONS.

characters (in books, plays, etc.). Use no quotation marks: *He played Hotspur.*

charge. Use the preposition *with.* (But after *accuse*, use *of.*) In an account of an arrest or a criminal proceeding, *charge* ideally means the formal allegation submitted to a court by a prosecutor or (in the case of an indictment for a serious crime) by a grand jury. At a minimum, *charge* may refer to the official allegation lodged by the police at the time of booking. But the informal, usually imprecise account given at the scene of a crime is not a charge. Thus: *The police accused Mr. Kuzu of having thrown a brick through the supermarket window and having threatened the manager with a pistol.*

chargé(s) d'affaires.

Charleston, Charles Town, Charlestown. *Charleston* is West Virginia's capital (in Kanawha County) and a South Carolina seaport. *Charles Town* is the seat of Jefferson County, W.Va. *Charlestown* is part of Boston.

charter. Capitalize when using the word with a specific city's name: *the Los Angeles City Charter; the city charter; the charter; a charter.* An exception: when the reference is to New York City's, uppercase *City Charter* standing alone. *Also see* UNITED NATIONS CHARTER.

Chase Manhattan Bank is a division of J. P. Morgan Chase & Company. *Chase* remains a brand name for many of the company's retail services. *J. P. Morgan* is the name for its wholesale businesses.

chassis (sing. and pl.).

chateau(s). But in a French name or phrase: *Château Lafite-Rothschild; the Rue des Châteaux.*

Château-Thierry (the World War I battle site in France).

cheat. Use this noun, not *cheater*, for a person who cheats.

Chechnya. Its people are *Chechens.*

cheese(-). Most but not all compounds formed with *cheese* are one word: cheeseburger, cheesecake, cheesecloth, cheese spread.

chef-owner is restaurant industry jargon. Make it *chef and owner.*

chemical elements and formulas. Do not capitalize the name of an element, even when using its mass number: *carbon 14; strontium 90; uranium 235.* Chemical formulas are set this way: H_2O; CO_2.

chess. Algebraic notation is used to report game scores and to describe moves in articles and columns. The abbreviations are *K* (king), *Q* (queen), *R* (rook), *B* (bishop) and *N* (knight). The pawn is not designated by name in algebraic notation: *14 Nb3, 29 Qd7;* but *1 e4, 29 gh.*

The names of the pieces are spelled out, lowercase, in general references: *The queen was trapped; Lamm freed his bishop on his 23rd move.*

Openings and major variations are capitalized: *King's Indian Defense; Dragon Variation; Exchange Variation of the Ruy Lopez.* Black and White are capitalized as nouns but not as adjectives: *With 8 e4, White seized the initiative.* But: *The white pieces were cramped.* The words *kingside* and *queenside* are lowercased as nouns or adjectives.

In articles and columns, black and white moves are not separated by punctuation: *5 c3 c5 6 Bc4 Nd7*. A black move standing alone or at the start of a sequence is preceded by an ellipsis: *3 . . . Bc7*.

Punctuation marks connoting criticism—like *!*, *?* or *!?*—are permissible in analyses but not in game scores. In game scores, *check* and *en passant* are omitted. *Mate* is lowercase and not separated from the move: *42 Qg8mate*.

The slash mark is used to denote pawn promotion: *44 e8/Q*. If more than one piece of the same type can move to a square, the rank number or file letter of the origination square is added: *41 R1d4, 27 . . . Nec6*.

In the chess column, courtesy titles are not used before surnames. In news articles, however, use *Mr.* (or *Mrs.*, *Miss* or *Ms.*) except when reporting actual play.

Chevron Corporation.

Chevy (colloquially), not *Chevie* or *Chevvy*.

Chicago Board of Trade (the commodity market).

Chicago Board Options Exchange (not Chicago Board *of* Options Exchange).

Chicago Mercantile Exchange.

Chicago Stock Exchange. Formerly the Midwest Stock Exchange.

Chicano (n. and adj.) refers to Mexican-Americans and their culture, but only some prefer the term, chiefly in the Southwest, while others object to it. Apply it with care, only to those who choose it. The feminine noun is *Chicana. Also see* ETH-NICITY; HISPANIC; LATINO; PUERTO RICO, PUERTO RICAN.

chickenpox.

Chief *Merrill H. Arniotis* (for police and fire ranks); *Chief Arniotis; the chief.*

chief delegate (diplomatic). Lowercase and use the preposition *to: Lynn B. Agneau, chief United States delegate to the Conference on the Law of the Sea; Ms. Agneau; the chief delegate.* Confine *delegate* and *chief delegate* to members of temporary or provisional delegations, like those at the annual General Assembly of the United Nations. For permanent bodies, use CHIEF REPRESENTATIVE, REPRESENTATIVE and, when appropriate, AMBASSADOR.

chief executive officer can usually be trimmed to *chief executive.* Informally the abbreviation is nonetheless *C.E.O.*

Chief Judge *Robin T. Anyell* (of the Court of Appeals in New York State, and of the state itself); *Judge Anyell; the chief judge.*

Chief Justice *Dana L. Milori; Chief Justice Milori; the chief justice.* It is *chief justice of the United States,* not *of the Supreme Court.*

chief master sergeant of the Air Force. Lowercase the full title and use a comma to separate it from the name, without abbreviation: *Lindsay E. Bildots, the chief master sergeant of the Air Force; Sergeant Bildots; the sergeant.* The title is held by only one person at a time, the highest-ranking enlisted member of the Air Force. It ordinarily requires explanation.

chief of staff. Lowercase, and use a comma to separate the title from the name: *Gen. Chris R. Lam, chief of staff; the chief of staff; the White House chief of staff, Pat L. Kuzu.*

Chief Petty Officer *Lindsay T. Milori; Chief Milori; the chief petty officer.*

Chief Rabbi *Hilary I. Bildots of Britain* (or any country where the title is used); *Hilary Bildots, chief rabbi of Britain; the chief rabbi; Rabbi Bildots; the rabbi.* In Israel, Sephardic and Ashkenazic Jews have separate chief rabbis. Follow the same styles for *grand rabbi* in countries where that title is used.

chief representative (diplomatic). Lowercase and use the preposition *at*: *Merrill T. Lamb, chief United States representative at the World Health Organization; Dr. Lamb, the chief representative.* Confine *representative* and *chief representative* to assignments to permanent bodies, like the United Nations. (But do not ordinarily use *permanent representative*, a diplomatic jargon term that overstates the tenure.) For temporary or periodic meetings, use CHIEF DELEGATE, DELEGATE and, when appropriate, AMBASSADOR.

Chief Warrant Officer *Chris A. Arniotis; Mr. Arniotis; the chief warrant officer.*

chili(es) for the pepper(s) and for the food term adopted into English as *chili con carne.* But spell it *chile* in a Spanish-language phrase: *chile serrano.*

China. Standing alone, it means the mainland nation. Use the formal name, *the People's Republic of China*, in texts and direct quotations only. *Also see* COMMUNIST CHINA and TAIWAN.

Chinese (n., sing. and pl.; also adj.). The people are always *Chinese*; never use the disparaging *Chinamen* or *Chinaman*, except in an inescapable direct quotation.

Chinese names. A personal name ordinarily consists of the family name followed by a given name (*Zhu Rongji*, for example; in later references, *Mr. Zhu* or *Prime Minister Zhu*).

English spellings of mainland Chinese words and names are governed by the official system known as Pinyin (the term means "transcription"). Many of the Roman letters approximate their accustomed English sounds. The exceptions most jarring to non-Chinese-speaking readers are *q* (which sounds like *ch*, as in cheek) and *x* (which sounds like *sy*, so that the province name *Xinjiang* is pronounced *syin-jyang*). When either letter occurs in a name newly prominent in the news, supply the pronunciation. (*See* PRONUNCIATION KEYS.)

Women do not ordinarily take their husbands' names. The usual title with a woman's surname is *Ms.*, unless she has a professional, military or specialized title.

When an English "conventional form" is recognized for a Chinese place name, use it: *Hong Kong, Inner Mongolia, Tibet* and *Yangtze River*, for example. (*See* GEOGRAPHIC NAMES.)

For names in Hong Kong and in areas outside Beijing's influence (notably in Taiwan), non-Pinyin preferences should be followed. A usual style is based on the older system known as *Wade-Giles* (with its apostrophes omitted): *Tung Chee-hwa*; *Chiang Pin-kung*.

Some Chinese, most often in Hong Kong, in Taiwan or overseas, westernize their names: *Martin Lee*; *Elsie Leung*.

Names of historic figures keep traditional spellings: *Confucius*; *Sun Yat-sen* (but this group does not include *Mao Zedong* or *Zhou Enlai*). Also use familiar spellings for menu items like *General Tso's chicken*. And when reporting on an art exhibition, follow the style used in the catalog. *Also see* DYNASTIES.

chip (not *microchip*).

chitchat.

chock-full.

choice is a partisan term in the context of abortions. *See* ABORTION.

chord (music, mathematics), **cord** (spinal, vocal).

chow chow (a dog), **chowchow** (pickled vegetables).

Christ. *See* JESUS.

Christian Church (Disciples of Christ). The parenthetical phrase is part of the official name that must be used in a first reference. In later references: *the Disciples*. The CHURCHES OF CHRIST and the UNITED CHURCH OF CHRIST are separate denominations.

Christian Era.

Christian Methodist Episcopal Church. In later references: *C.M.E.*

Christian Science. The denomination is formally *the Church of Christ, Scientist*. Members belong to branch churches (for example, *the Fourth Church of Christ, Scientist*) and may also hold membership in the *First Church of Christ, Scientist*, which is in Boston and is known as the Mother Church.

Do not use *the Rev.*; the church has no clergy. Members are elected for designated terms to fill the posts of *first reader* and *second reader* in local congregations and the Mother Church. There is also a president of the denomination. The church supports *lecturers*, who speak about Christian Science throughout the world.

Christmas. Also *Christmas Day*. Never abbreviate to *Xmas* or any other form.

Chrysler Corporation merged with Daimler-Benz in 1998 to form *DaimlerChrysler A.G.*

church. Capitalize the word in the name of an institution (*the Roman Catholic Church*; *the Episcopal Church*) or a building or congregation (*the First Presbyterian Church*; *the Church of SS. Peter and Paul*). But: *a Roman Catholic church*; *an Episcopal church*. In all later references, to building or organization: *the church*.

church and state. Do not capitalize when used in this sense: *conflict between church and state*; *church-state issue*.

churches and other religious organizations are listed separately.

Churches of Christ. This Protestant denomination broke away from the Christian Church (Disciples of Christ) early in the 20th century.

Church of Christ, Scientist. *See* CHRISTIAN SCIENCE.

Church of England. This episcopal church is the established church of England, automatically headed by the country's reigning monarch. Its primate is the archbishop of Canterbury. *The Anglican Church* may be used in first references. In later ones, *the church* is usually enough. *Also see* ANGLICAN COMMUNION; CANTERBURY, ARCHBISHOP OF; EPISCOPAL.

Church of Jesus Christ of Latter-day Saints. In first and later references it may be called by its less formal name, *the Mormon Church*, so long as the full title appears at least once in any major article about it. *See* MORMON CHURCH.

Church of the Brethren.

Church of the Holy Sepulcher (in Jerusalem).

chute, chutist. They may be used in headlines for *parachute* and *parachutist*.

C.I.A. for the Central Intelligence Agency. It is headed by the director of central intelligence. The director's title does not include *agency*. *Also see* AGENT.

cigarette.

Cigna Corporation.

Cincinnati.

cinéma vérité for realistic documentary techniques in film.

Cineplex is a trademark. The generic term for a multiscreen theater is *multiplex*.

circumflex. *See* ACCENT MARKS.

Citigroup Inc., formed in 1998 through the merger of Citicorp and the Travelers Group Inc., is the parent of Citibank and Salomon Smith Barney.

Citroën.

city. Capitalize when the word is an integral part of an official name or of a regularly used nickname: *New York City*; *the City of New York* (the corporate name in legal matters); *Kansas City*; *Mexico City* (not the official *Mexico, D.F.*); *Windy City*; *City of Light*. Also capitalize when *City* is appended to a place name to avoid ambiguity: *Panama City*, for example. (In an unambiguous context, use *Panama* alone as the city or country name.)

Lowercase *city* in all first and later references like these: *the city*; *city government*. In forms like *city of Boston*, lowercase except in the rare legal contexts calling for a corporate name: *The chief defendant was the City of Boston.* When the word stands alone, lowercase even in that situation: *The city sued the state.* If there is a possibility of confusion between city and state, use *New York City* or *New York State*. When necessary in context, capitalize *City* (or *State*) with the name of an agency or with an official title (*the City Planning Commission*; *City Comptroller Terry N. Cordero*).

In a headline, because the newspaper's readership is nationwide, do not use *City* standing alone to mean New York, except with an overline or similar label that makes the meaning clear, or in a locally distributed section.

City Bar Association should be used in virtually all references for the Association of the Bar of the City of New York.

City Charter (New York City's); *the charter. Also see* CHARTER.

City College (in New York). It is a four-year college of the CITY UNIVERSITY OF NEW YORK. Its nickname, *C.C.N.Y.*, though unofficial, may be used for special effect.

City Council; *the Columbia City Council; the Council.* In references to New York City, *the City Council* can stand alone.

city names. For guidance on appending state abbreviations, see DATELINES and STATE ABBREVIATIONS.

City of London for the financial district. In later references, when the context is clear, *the City.*

City University of New York. It consists of two-year and four-year colleges and graduate and professional programs. Individual institutions or campuses like City College are units of the City University. *CUNY* is acceptable in later references and in headlines. The system's Web site provides information about the City University and its campuses:

http://www.cuny.edu

Also see STATE UNIVERSITY OF NEW YORK and UNIVERSITY OF THE STATE OF NEW YORK.

citywide.

Civil Service. But: *civil servant.*

Civil War, for the one in the United States (1861-65). Use *the War Between the States* in direct quotations or texts only. Also: *the Spanish Civil War* (and others); *the civil war.*

(-)clad. Most but not all compounds formed with *clad* are hyphenated: copper-clad, half-clad, ironclad, snow-clad, steel-clad.

claim is not a neutral synonym for *say.* It means assert a right or contend something that may be open to question.

Clarkson College (in Omaha), **Clarkson University** (in Potsdam, N.Y.).

class(-). Some compounds formed with *class* are hyphenated, some are one word and some are two: class-action (adj.), class action (n.), class book, class day, classmate, classroom.

Also: *class of 1993* (or '93).

Class A, Class B. Capitalize such designations (of stocks, for example) as proper nouns. Also see NUMBERED EXPRESSIONS.

classical (architecture). Capitalize when referring generally to Greek and Roman architecture. For more recent buildings that are classical in spirit, it is best to use more specific descriptions: *a building with arches and pediments in the classical style. Also see* ARTS TERMINOLOGY and NEO-CLASSICAL.

classical, classicism (music). Capitalize *Classical* and *Classicism* when referring to the style of music centered in Vienna roughly from 1770 to 1840, notably the works of Haydn, Mozart and Beethoven. The lowercased terms refer less specifically to music of the European tradition. *See* ARTS TERMINOLOGY.

clean(-). Some compounds formed with *clean* are one word and some are hyphenated: clean-cut, cleanshaven, cleanup (n.).

clear(-). Some compounds formed with *clear* are one word and some are hyphenated: clear-cut, cleareyed, clearheaded, clear-minded, clearsighted.

clemency, amnesty, pardon. *Clemency* is leniency or mercy shown by someone in power. An *amnesty* is a general pardon, usually for political offenses, granted to a group. A *pardon* is a release from punishment or forgiveness of an offense, granted to an individual.

clergy. Like *army*, the noun is collective, referring not to individuals but to the group. For individuals, use *clergymen, clergywomen, clergy members* or *members of the clergy*. References to *three clergy* or *many clergy*, or to *training clergy*, are jargon.

clerical titles are listed separately.

cliché. Also (adj.): *clichéd.*

climactic (relating to a climax), **climatic** (relating to the climate).

climax. Use it as a noun. As a verb (*The program climaxed with fireworks*), it is journalese.

clock time. *See* TIME.

clockwise, counterclockwise.

close-up (n., adj.). But the adverb is two words: *Seen close up, the mountain is purple.*

closing, closure, cloture. In references to shutdowns (of airports, businesses, streets, etc.), use *closing(s)* rather than the stilted *closure(s)*. And use *cloture* (not *closure*) for the parliamentary procedure that cuts off debate in the United States Senate.

club(-). Some compounds formed with *club* are one word and some are two words: club car, club chair, clubhouse, clubman, club owner, clubroom, club sandwich, club soda, clubwoman.

club officers. Do not capitalize their titles.

clumber spaniel.

Cmdr. *Alex J. Miel; Commander Miel; the commander.*

CNN for Cable News Network.

co(-). Some compounds formed with *co* are one word and some are hyphenated: co-author (n. only), co-chairman, co-chairwoman, co-defendant, coed, coeducation, coequal, coexist, coexistence, cohabitation, commingle, co-op, cooperate, cooperation, cooperative (n. and adj.), coordinate, coordination, co-maker, co-owner, co-pilot, co-signer, co-star, co-worker.

Most verbs coined with *co-* (like *co-author* and *co-write*) sound contrived and should be avoided (with a phrase, for example, like *Ms. Karitsa wrote the book with Mr. Dann*). But *co-produce* and *co-sign* are acceptable.

Co. for Company, but only after a name in a headline, a table or a chart. *See* COMPANY AND CORPORATION NAMES.

coalition. A *coalition* is a group of groups, often joined together for a limited purpose despite differing interests. Use caution in accepting the claim of an advocacy group that it is a true coalition, with broad support. If that is not established, resist the term.

coast. Lowercase when referring to an actual shoreline: *Atlantic coast; Pacific coast; east coast; west coast;* etc. Capitalize when referring to specific regions of the United States: *Atlantic Coast; Pacific Coast; Gulf Coast; West Coast; East Coast.* Do not capitalize in references to more local areas: *the New Jersey coast* (but: *the Jersey Shore*). Do not use *the Coast* (or *on Coast*) to mean the West Coast.

Coast Guard Academy for the United States Coast Guard Academy in New London, Conn.

Coast Guard, coast guardsman. Lowercase *coast guardsman* and do not use it before a name. Also avoid incongruity by using substitute terms for women who are members: *Coast Guard members; Coast Guard women;* or *Coast Guard men and women.*

Coast Guard ranks, in descending order, and their abbreviations:

COMMISSIONED OFFICERS

Adm. *Lynn L. Karitsa; Admiral Karitsa; the admiral.* (An admiral wears four stars.)

Vice Adm. *Alex M. Barany; Admiral Barany; the admiral.* (A vice admiral wears three stars.)

Rear Adm. *Dale A. Agnello; Admiral Agnello; the admiral.* (A rear admiral may wear one or two stars.)

Capt. *Hilary C. Daan; Captain Daan; the captain.*

Cmdr. *Lauren P. Miel; Commander Miel; the commander.*

Lt. Cmdr. *Morgan A. Bildots; Commander Bildots; the commander.*

Lt. *Lee T. Kikondoo; Lieutenant Kikondoo; the lieutenant.*

Lt. j.g. *Stacy R. Milori; Lieutenant Milori; the lieutenant.*

Ensign *Chris L. Arniotis; Ensign Arniotis; the ensign.*

(They hold their posts on warrants, or certificates of appointment, rather than commissions. They rank below commissioned officers and above enlisted personnel.)

Chief Warrant Officer *Leslie C. Anyell*; Mr. (or Ms., Miss or Mrs.) *Anyell*; *the chief warrant officer.*

Warrant Officer *Terry M. Daan*; Mr. (or Ms., Miss or Mrs.) *Daan*; *the warrant officer.*

NONCOMMISSIONED OFFICERS

(Enlisted supervisors.)

master chief petty officer of the Coast Guard. Do not use this title before a name, and do not abbreviate or capitalize it. Make it *Theo H. Lam, the master chief petty officer of the Coast Guard.* Then explain that it is the highest enlisted rank in the service. In later references: *Mr. Lam, Master Chief Lam.*

Master Chief Petty Officer *Hilary R. Baranek*; *Chief Baranek*; *the chief.*

Senior Chief Petty Officer *Lauren S. Cordeiro*; *Chief Cordeiro*; *the chief.*

Chief Petty Officer *Lindsay T. Milori*; *Chief Milori*; *the chief.*

Petty Officer First Class *Merrill M. Yagyonak*; *Petty Officer Yagyonak*; *the petty officer.*

Petty Officer Second Class *Tracy A. Karitsa*; *Petty Officer Karitsa*; *the petty officer.*

Petty Officer Third Class *Dale H. Miel*; *Petty Officer Miel*; *the petty officer.*

OTHER ENLISTED PERSONNEL

Seaman *Lindsay D. Daan*; *Seaman Daan*; *the seaman* (male or female).

Seaman Apprentice *Alex H. Kuzu*; *Seaman Kuzu*; *the seaman* (male or female).

Seaman Recruit *Chris R. Lam*; *Seaman Lam*; *the seaman* (male or female). *Also see* RETIRED.

Cobleskill (with only one *b*) is in Schoharie County, N.Y.

coca, coco, cocoa, coconut. *Coca* is the tropical plant that yields cocaine. *Coco* is a palm tree, and its fruit is a *coconut*. The chocolate drink is *cocoa*, made from *cacao* beans.

Coca-Cola, Coke are trademarks.

co-chair. Use *co-chairman* or *co-chairwoman* instead. For a general reference, try *co-leader.*

c.o.d. for cash on delivery or collect on delivery.

code of conduct. The phrase has a specialized meaning in the United States military. It is the name of a document that governs the behavior of troops in the face of the enemy or in captivity. For other sets of rules (about dating, for example), use *code of behavior* or another paraphrase.

codes. Lowercase *penal code, building code,* etc. Capitalize titles like *Code of Civil Procedure, Code Napoléon.*

coed. As a noun meaning woman in a coeducational school, the term is dated and often considered belittling. But the adjective *coed,* standing for *coeducational* (as in *coed schools*), can be useful in headlines, if only as a last resort. *See* COLLEGE BOY, COLLEGE GIRL and MEN AND WOMEN.

Coeur d'Alene (in Idaho).

coffee(-). Compounds formed with *coffee* are sometimes one word and sometimes two words: coffee break, coffeecake, coffeehouse, coffee maker, coffee mill, coffeepot, coffee table.

But: *kaffeeklatsch,* not *coffee klatch.*

coffin. Use this word instead of the euphemistic *casket.*

Cognac, cognac. *See* WINES AND SPIRITS.

cognoscenti. It is plural, meaning experts. The singular, rarely seen, is *cognoscente.*

Cohoes (in Albany County, N.Y.).

cohort. In informed usage, a *cohort* is not an individual but a group with some common bond. A *cohort of elk breeders* meets the test. A *vandal and two of his cohorts* does not.

Col. *Merrill N. Kuzu; Colonel Kuzu; the colonel.*

cold war. But note the punctuation when the modifier is attached to a prefix: *post-cold-war economies; pre-cold-war relationships.*

collectible.

College Board, the. A national organization of schools and colleges, the board sponsors college admission tests and other programs. The best-known exams are the *reasoning test* and the *subject tests* (in more than 20 fields). Together those are known as the *Scholastic Assessment Tests* (always plural, never abbreviated). SAT, a trademark used by the board, is no longer considered an abbreviation and does not stand for any test name. For comprehension, therefore, the component tests are best called *the College Board reasoning test* and *the College Board subject tests* (or *College Board chemistry test,* etc.). Even more informally: *the College Boards.* In headlines: *College Tests* or the like. The *SAT* trademark may also be used, sparingly.

Similarly the board's preliminary tests, for high school students, may be cited informally as *the preliminary College Board exams.* The official name, too technical for the news columns, is *PSAT/NMSQT* (officially not an abbreviation, but derived from *Preliminary SAT* and *National Merit Scholarship Qualifying Test*).

The board's formal name, virtually never needed in articles, is *the College Entrance Examination Board.*

college boy, college girl. Use *college man, college woman* or, better, *college student.*

college names. Verify them carefully; Web sites are often the most current source. It is, for instance, *Iona College*, but the *College of New Rochelle*. For consistency in the news columns, lowercase *the* in a college name, regardless of individual styles. Omit *College* or *University* freely in a mention of a well-known institution: *She graduated from Purdue.* (It is rarely necessary to make a distinction when the undergraduate college bears the same name as its university: *He is a Harvard sophomore.*) Do not ordinarily use *school* to mean *university.*

College of Cardinals.

College of New Jersey. It was formerly Trenton State College. Before 1896, Princeton University was known as the College of New Jersey, but the two institutions are not related.

College of Staten Island (part of the CITY UNIVERSITY OF NEW YORK).

College of St. Elizabeth (in Convent Station, N.J.).

collide, collision. Only two objects in motion can collide. If the phrase *collided with* seems to fix blame, avoid it by using this construction: *a truck and a bus collided.*

colloquialisms. Words bearing the label *colloquial* (or its equivalent, *informal*), in the dictionary or in this manual, occur naturally in speech and in writing that emulates the casualness of speech. Expressions like *kids, hole up, trendy, pricey* and *for kicks* are examples. They should be confined to features and light contexts (often in style, sports and the arts), and used without quotation marks or other signs of self-consciousness. The fresh effect can curdle, though, if the phrases chosen are faddish (like *flap*, meaning a fuss). *Also see* SLANG.

colon. For the placement of a colon alongside other punctuation, see PARENTHESES and QUOTATION MARKS.

The colon can introduce a word, a phrase, a sentence, a passage, a list or a tabulation. For its use in introductions to verbatim material, see TEXTS AND EXCERPTS. The colon is also used for clock times (*10:30 a.m.*) and, in sports, for the times of races (*2:55; 4:10:23*).

As punctuation within a sentence, the colon can be effective: *Today is the dead center of the year, or as near dead center as you can get: 182 days gone by, 182 to come.*

Ordinarily lowercase the word after a colon. This is especially true if the colon is used between complete clauses, to underscore their relationship more emphatically than a semicolon would: *He had reason to be afraid: the war was only weeks away. To err is human, to forgive divine: that is a noble sermon.* As an exception, the word after a colon is capitalized if it begins a complete sentence formally introduced by what precedes it: *She promised this: The company will make good all the losses.* In news copy, though, resist the staccato mannerism that uses the colon as a kind of trumpet fanfare, in place of a verb (*The reason: they want the Midwestern farm vote*). And in headlines, uppercase any word directly after a colon.

While a comma introduces a direct quotation of one sentence that remains within the paragraph, use a colon to introduce longer quotations.

Colonial (architecture). Capitalize in reference to structures built when America was a colony; for more recent buildings, its preferred use is as a modifier: *colonial style*. *Also see* GEORGIAN.

Colonie (in Albany County, N.Y.).

color. *See* PEOPLE OF COLOR.

Colorado. Abbreviate as *Colo.* after the names of cities, towns and counties.

colorblind.

colored. In most United States racial contexts, the term is offensive, except in a proper name like *National Association for the Advancement of Colored People*. In South Africa, however, *colored* (n. and adj.) and *coloreds* are the accepted terms for people of racially mixed ancestry; in that sense, lowercase and use the American spelling, not *coloured*.

Columbia-Presbyterian Medical Center is now part of NEW YORK-PRESBYTERIAN HOSPITAL.

Columbia University. In many casual references, *Columbia* can stand alone, for the university or for its undergraduate college.

Columbus Day, the second Monday in October, is a federal holiday.

columns. Uppercase principal words in their titles, usually without quotation marks: *Metropolitan Diary*; *Sports of The Times*. As an exception, use quotation marks if a column title cannot be easily recognized as such or reads awkwardly with the surrounding words.

combat, combated, combating.

comedian is suitable for a man or a woman. Do not use *comedienne*. *See* MEN AND WOMEN.

Comédie-Française.

comma. For the placement of a comma alongside other punctuation, see PARENTHESES and QUOTATION MARKS.

In general, do not use a comma before *and* or *or* in a series: *The snow stalled cars, buses and trains*. But use a comma in sentences like this to avoid confusion: *A martini is made of gin and dry vermouth, and a chilled glass is essential*.

If commas appear within the items of a series, separate the items themselves with semicolons. In that case, keep even the final semicolon, before the *and*. *See* SEMICOLON.

Commas should be used in compound sentences before conjunctions like *and, but* and *for: They left early, and their mother said they would arrive before lunch*; *The track was slow, but the betting was fast*; *They were impatient, for their test scores were due any day*. When the clauses are exceptionally short, however, the comma may be omitted: *Nero fiddled and Rome burned*. Also: *The comma is small but mighty*.

Use commas to enclose a nonrestrictive clause (that is, a clause providing incidental extra information): *The house, which was 100 years old, was still in good condition*. A restrictive clause, providing necessary identification, does not go between commas: *The second book that she wrote was a best seller*. Do not use the comma after an identifying noun used in this way: *The painter van Gogh had a hard struggle*. The absence of commas in *His brother Alex was best man* means that the bridegroom has more than one brother. If there is only one brother, *Alex* should be surrounded by commas. Thus a monogamous society must be well supplied with commas: *Her husband, Leslie, was absent*.

Between adjectives in a series or a pair, use a comma if the adjectives convey equal significance—that is, if they could comfortably be connected by *and*: *a tired, disillusioned politician*; *quick, easy solutions*. But: *a gray iron cot*; *a wiry old carpenter* (no comma because the phrases *iron cot* and *old carpenter* are bound together more closely than the rest of each expression).

Use the comma to introduce a quotation of one sentence or less: *He said, "I shall return."* For quotations of more than one sentence use the COLON. A comma may also introduce a paraphrase similar in form to a quotation but without quotation marks: *The question is, How high will prices rise? He said, Yes, he would accept the job.* But: *He said yes. She said no.*

Do not use a comma after *that* in this construction: *He said that for more than a year and a half, the problem had been ignored*; *She pledged that whatever the cost, she would close the deal*. (The material directly after *that* is not parenthetical; it is introduced by *that*, just as the rest of the sentence is.)

In general, use the comma for figures in thousands (*1,250 miles*; *$12,416.22*). But do not use it in designations of years (in dates), street numbers, box numbers, room numbers or telephone numbers.

In financial copy, precise use of the comma is often needed to avoid confusion: *The stock advanced 3 points, to 21*. The comma makes it clear that the range of advance was not between 3 and 21, but upward from 18.

Do not use a comma before an *of* indicating place or position: *Morgan S. Lam of Brooklyn*; *President Dana J. Kikondoo of Tanzania*. (Exception, to avoid royal overtones when a given name stands alone: *Survivors include her son, Howard, of Lenox, Mass.*) In ages, heights, distances, time, etc., expressed in the following form, the comma is omitted: *4 years 9 months 21 days*; *6 feet 3 inches tall*; *2 hours 15 minutes 10 seconds*.

Commas are not used in names like these: *Lauren B. Cordero Jr.* (or *Sr.*); *Stacy R. Karitsa IV.*

Commas are used when constructions like this are unavoidable: *the Salem, Ore., public schools*; *a Columbus, Ohio, newspaper.* But it is smoother to write *the public schools of Salem, Ore.* For a clarifying insertion in a proper name, use parentheses: *The Columbus (Ohio) Citizen*; *Centerville (Ill.) General Hospital.* Here, too, a phrase after the name—*in Ohio*; *in Illinois*—is preferred.

In a date with the day omitted, use no comma: *He said he left Boston in April 1975 and never returned.* But when giving both day and year, use a comma between them. And in that case, a comma or other punctuation mark must always follow the year. Do not use this construction: *He said that May 5, 1999 was not a happy day.*

Commack (in Suffolk County, N.Y.).

commandant of the Marine Corps. Do not use as a title before a name. Make it *Gen. Hollis P. Cordero, the commandant of the Marine Corps.*

commander. Use the term instead of *commanding general* when it is otherwise made clear that the bearer is a general: *Maj. Gen. Hollis T. Cordeiro, commander of the First Infantry Division.* Also use it instead of *commanding officer*, since invariably a unit commander or police commander is an officer. *Also see* CMDR.

commander in chief. Lowercase, without hyphens, and use a comma to separate the title from a name.

commanding general, commanding officer. Though used officially, the phrases are redundant when referring to someone who is clearly identified as a general or an officer. Use *commander* by itself: *Maj. Gen. Hollis F. Cordeiro, commander of the First Infantry Division.* Also: *the division commander*; *the precinct commander.* *Also see* CMDR.

Command Sgt. Maj. *Tracy N. Arniotis*; *Sergeant Major Arniotis*; *the command sergeant major* or *the sergeant major.* The title designates the senior enlisted member of a major command.

commission. Capitalize only when part of a name. Do not abbreviate, even in headlines.

Commissioner *Stacy S. Lam*; *the commissioner.* Also use this form for titles like *police commissioner* and, in New York City, *parks commissioner* (note the plural).

commitment.

committee. Capitalize only when part of a name. Do not abbreviate, even in headlines. *See* CONGRESSIONAL COMMITTEES AND SUBCOMMITTEES.

common(-). Some compounds formed with *common* are one word and some are two. Most compound adjectives are hyphenated: common law (n.), common-law (adj.), commonplace, common sense (n.), common-sense (adj.), commonweal, commonwealth.

Common Market. A predecessor to the Eᴜʀᴏᴘᴇᴀɴ Uɴɪᴏɴ.

Commonwealth, formerly the British Commonwealth. It is an association of sovereign states joined in recognizing the British monarch as head of the Commonwealth, though not in all cases as the head of their states. The current membership is listed in the World Fact Book maintained by the Central Intelligence Agency on the World Wide Web for public use:

http://www.odci.gov/cia/publications/factbook/appc.html

Commonwealth of Independent States. It was established in 1991 to coordinate relations between former Soviet republics and to oversee the dissolution of the Soviet Union. The members were Armenia, Azerbaijan, Belarus, Georgia, Kazakhstan, Kyrgyzstan, Moldova, Russia, Tajikistan, Turkmenistan, Ukraine and Uzbekistan. In later references: *the organization,* to avoid confusion with the Cᴏᴍᴍᴏɴᴡᴇᴀʟᴛʜ.

communiqué.

communism. Capitalize only when referring to the Communist Party movement. Lowercase in references to the philosophy: *The residents of Brook Farm sought to achieve communism.*

Communist. Capitalize as a noun for a member of the Communist Party and as an adjective referring to the party. Lowercase in references to the philosophy.

Communist China. The name of the country is simply Cʜɪɴᴀ. *Communist China* is acceptable to make a special point—a contrast, for example—or in a quotation. The official name, *the People's Republic of China,* is used only in texts and quotations.

Communist Party.

community. Apply this word cautiously to ethnic, racial or interest groups (*the black community, the gay community*). It implies a unanimity that may or may not exist. (It is, however, a proper term for a neighborhood.)

compact disc. *Also see* ᴅɪsᴄ, ᴅɪsᴋ.

companion is a suitable term for an unmarried partner of the same or the opposite sex. In the case of a gay couple, resist *longtime companion,* originally a euphemism and now a parodied cliché; substitute, for example, *companion of 27 years. Also see* ʟᴏᴠᴇʀ and ᴘᴀʀᴛɴᴇʀ.

company (military). *Company A; Company H; Headquarters Company; the company.* (For clarity, avoid the reversed *A Company, H Company,* etc.) Company nicknames, using the words of the phonetic alphabet (*Charlie Company* or *Hotel Company,* for instance), should be confined to quotations or feature contexts. They will often require graceful explanation for readers unfamiliar with military usage.

company and corporation names. In articles, spell out *Company, Corporation, Industries, Brothers, Associates,* etc., when they are part of a name. Generally use the full name of a company on first reference. For major corporations with names that are household expressions (*Microsoft, General Motors, General Electric*), the terms *Company, Corporation,* etc., may be omitted even from first references. When *Company* or *Corporation* is part of a full name, conversational English calls for *the* in front of the name.

Omit *Inc.* or an equivalent foreign abbreviation (*Ltd., S.A., S.p.A., G.m.b.H., N.V.,* etc.) in the name of any company that incorporates another company term (*Company, Corporation, Industries,* etc.). When using *Inc.* or an equivalent foreign abbreviation, do not surround it with commas (*EarthLink Inc. is declaring a dividend*).

Headlines, charts and listings may freely use the abbreviations *Bros., Co.* and *Corp.* in the names of companies. Even in ordinary news copy, listings or enumerations of companies may omit *Company, Corporation,* etc.

Use the ampersand (&) in place of *and* when the company's name consists of personal names (*Procter & Gamble*) or when *and* directly precedes a company term (*J. P. Morgan Chase & Company*); other examples include *& Brothers, & Associates, & Sons,* etc. This rule means that most names of law firms, accounting firms, etc., require the &. For consistency within the news columns, apply Times style to all such names. Some railroad names and other business names use the ampersand without fitting these rules; they are listed separately.

When using abbreviations in later references, generally replace *and* with an ampersand, as in *A.&P.* In a headline, a thin space may follow the ampersand, to balance the space created by the preceding period.

Use periods in company abbreviations when the initials stand for words (*I.B.M.* for the International Business Machines Corporation). Use no spaces between initials, except for those derived from a personal name, which take thin spaces (*J. C. Penney*). If a company has adopted letters without periods as its formal, incorporated name, follow that style (*the RCA Corporation; AT&T; the USX Corporation,* formerly United States Steel). In detailed discussion of such a company, it is useful to recall the former name.

If an acronym (an abbreviation pronounced as a word) is used for later references, it should generally be upper-and-lowercase, not all caps (*Alcoa,* for the Aluminum Company of America). But *the RAND Corporation* because the name is an acronym shorter than five letters. For consistency in names that often appear close together, omit periods in all abbreviations for broadcast networks, stations and services: *ABC; CBS; NBC; CNN; PBS;* etc.

When a company name calls for unconventional capitalization, heed any preference that requires up to three capitals in a word. If the capitals exceed three, upper-and-lowercase the name except for proper nouns that appear within it. Thus: *PepsiCo Inc.* and *the SmithKline Beecham Corporation.*

Apply the term *firm* to partnerships, not normally to corporations. But make an exception for brokerage houses, which are *member firms* of an exchange regardless of whether they are incorporated, and for law, accounting and architecture groups comprising the equivalent of partners, even if actually incorporated.

When mentioning a subsidiary of a publicly traded company, identify the parent also, provided the news might attract investors' interest. This applies inside and outside the business pages, but an exception may be made if the subsidiary is very well known or bears a name similar to the parent's. Outside the business pages, the parent may also be omitted when the subsidiary is mentioned primarily for its artistic or cultural activities (a book publisher or record company, for example).

Many company and corporation names, including some exceptions to these rules, are listed separately.

company officers. Do not capitalize their titles: *She was elected president of the company; They complained to the treasurer, Dale T. Kikondoo.*

compare. Use *compare to* when the intent is to liken things: *The book compared the quarterback's role to the job of a company's vice president for operations.* When the intent is to compare and contrast, or just to contrast, use *compare with: They compared Terry's forecasting with Dana's and found Dana more accurate.*

comparisons. Avoid phrases like *times larger* or *times taller;* they rarely say what the writer means. Something *three times larger* is actually *four times as large*, since each of the "times" is added to the original dimension or amount. Make it *seven times as large* or *three times as tall.* As for quantities that are *five times smaller*, they cannot exist. *One time smaller* amounts to subtracting 100 percent, and winding up with zero. Make it *one-fifth as much*, or *one-fifth as large.*

complementary, complimentary. Use *complementary* and its forms to describe things that fit together to form a whole: *Her math skills complemented his writing; they were complementary.* Use *complimentary* to mean flattering. *Complimentary* is also used in sales literature to mean free, but journalism favors the unpretentious word: *free.*

compound words are generally listed in the entries for individual prefixes and suffixes. For those not shown in this manual, consult the dictionary. (*See* SPELLING.) In general, a compound that would be hard to decipher at a glance should be hyphenated rather than solid. To avoid incongruity, a compound noun that is ordinarily solid should be separated when the first part is modified by an adjective: *businessman*, for example, becomes *small-business man; sailmaker* becomes *racing-sail maker; schoolteacher* becomes *public-school teacher.*

When a compound modifier is formed by an adjective before a noun, it is usually hyphenated: *They wore well-tailored gray suits.* But omit the hyphen when the phrase follows what it modifies: *The suits were well tailored.* More examples appear in the entries for ILL(-) and WELL(-). *Also see* HYPHEN.

comprise means *consist of.* The whole comprises the parts: *The alliance comprises 35 organizations.* Not: *Thirty-five organizations comprise the alliance.* And do not write *comprised of. See* INCLUDING.

comptroller. Reserve this term for a government official who bears the title officially. The federal government has a *comptroller general* and a *comptroller of the currency.* New York State and New York City each have a *comptroller.* Capitalize the title before a name (*Comptroller Lindsay T. Daan*), but lowercase elsewhere. Use *controller* for the financial officer of a business.

CompuServe.

computer programs. *See* SOFTWARE.

Comsat Corporation.

concert halls. *See* ARTS LOCATIONS.

concerto. Capitalize in a title: *Mozart's Piano Concerto in E flat (K. 271); Mozart's "Coronation" Concerto.* But: *the concerto.* Also: *concertos* (pl.), but *concerti grossi. See* MUSIC.

Concorde (the British-French supersonic airliner).

concrete. *See* CEMENT.

Condé Nast.

conditional tenses. When a sentence expresses the dependence of one event on another, convey the two ideas in verb tenses that work together—always matched, never mixed:

- *If Governor Agnello runs, Mr. Karitsa will be on her ticket.* (An *if* clause in the present tense; a *then* clause in the future tense.)
- *If Mr. Karitsa refused the job, Dr. Arniotis would get it.* (An *if* clause in the past tense; a *then* clause in the conditional tense.)
- *If Dr. Arniotis had wanted the job, he would have said so.* (An *if* clause in the past perfect tense; a *then* clause in the conditional perfect.)

condo, condominium. *Condo* is useful in headlines and in articles as a later reference to a condominium.

Con Ed for the Consolidated Edison Company. Also: *Con Edison.*

Confederate States of America, the official name of the Confederacy. *Also see* CIVIL WAR.

Conference Board (a business-sponsored nonprofit research organization).

confidant (n., masc.), **confidante** (n., fem.).

confined. People with illnesses or disabilities do not necessarily consider themselves *confined* to their beds, homes or wheelchairs; the term may exaggerate their limitations. Write instead that they *use wheelchairs* or are *housebound* or *bedridden.* When possible, be specific about the causes: *He has used a wheelchair since losing* *his legs in Vietnam; She cannot leave home for fear of catching an infection. Also see* DISABILITY, DISABLED.

confrere.

Congo, Congo Republic. The two neighboring countries in central Africa use nearly identical names, and the distinction requires care. For the country farther east, formerly known as Zaire, with Kinshasa as its capital, use *Congo*, without a preceding *the* (and not the full name, *the Democratic Republic of Congo*). For clarity, it is helpful to mention the name of the capital.

For the country to the west, with Brazzaville as its capital, use *the Congo Republic* (not the full name, *People's Republic of the Congo*). Again, mention the name of the capital.

Congo River (not *the Zaire*).

congregationalism is a form of Protestant church structure that vests ultimate authority in local congregations or their representatives. Denominations so organized include the SOUTHERN BAPTIST CONVENTION and the UNITED CHURCH OF CHRIST. This form of organization contrasts with the episcopal system used by some other denominations, including the UNITED METHODIST CHURCH. Capitalize *Congregational* in the name of an individual church or in a reference to the denomination descended from the New England settlers, now part of the United Church of Christ.

Congressional. Capitalize in reference to the United States Congress only.

Congressional committees and subcommittees. Capitalize committee names: *Ways and Means Committee; Appropriations Committee*. But: *the committee*. Also capitalize the formal name of a subcommittee, if it is terse enough to use in an article: *Senate Permanent Subcommittee on Investigations*. And: *the subcommittee*. Many names, though, are long or complex and should be paraphrased, in lowercase: *the House ethics committee* (in place of the formal *House Committee on Standards of Official Conduct*). If the paraphrase includes the formal name of a parent committee, capitalize the parent's name: the *House Foreign Affairs subcommittee on aid to Ruritania*.

congressman, congresswoman. The titles traditionally apply to members of the House, not the Senate: *Congresswoman Lauren E. Cordero; Congresswoman Cordero; the congresswoman*. The preferred title, though, is *representative*.

Connecticut. Abbreviate as *Conn.* after the names of cities, towns and counties.

Connecticut College (in New London).

Conrail, the Consolidated Rail Corporation, was purchased in 1998 by the CSX Corporation and the Norfolk Southern Corporation. In 1999, they divided it between them.

conscience(-). Most but not all compounds formed with *conscience* are two words: conscienceless, conscience money, conscience-stricken.

Also: *for conscience' sake.*

(-)conscious. Most but not all compounds formed with *conscious* are hyphenated: air-conscious, class-conscious, clothes-conscious, music-conscious, self-conscious (and *un-self-conscious*), style-conscious, unconscious.

consensus. Not the redundant *consensus of opinion* and not *general consensus*.

conservative. Capitalize as noun or adjective in the name of a political party or movement, or in reference to members of that group: *Four Conservatives voted with the prime minister.*

Conservative Judaism. It is a branch of the religion that retains traditional ritual (Hebrew-language worship, for example) but with moderate adaptation to modern life. Its houses of worship are *synagogues,* not temples. *Also see* ORTHODOX and REFORM, REFORMED.

Conservative Party.

consist of usually introduces a full list: *His team consists of 11 Ph.D.'s; The meal consists of 10 courses.* Use *includes* to introduce a partial listing: *His team includes two shortstops. Also see* COMPRISE.

Consolidated Edison Company (Con Ed or Con Edison).

Consolidated Rail Corporation. *See* CONRAIL.

Constable *Hilary T. Lamm; Constable Lamm; the constable.*

constitution. Capitalize when referring to the specific constitution of a nation or a state, but lowercase *a constitution* in general references. Also: *constitutional; unconstitutional.*

constitutional amendments. Capitalize formal titles of amendments to the United States Constitution (which include the numbers): *Fifth Amendment; 15th Amendment.* But lowercase informal titles (*the income tax amendment*) except for words that are capitalized in their own right: *the Prohibition amendment. Also see* ACTS, AMENDMENTS, BILLS AND LAWS.

Consul *Robin E. Dann; Consul Dann; the consul.* Similarly capitalize *consul general* in front of a name only. (The plural is *consuls general.*)

consulate (or **consulate general**). Lowercase when standing alone. But: *the United States Consulate; the French Consulate General.* (The plural is *consulates general.*)

Consultation on Church Union. An organization working for the merger of several major denominations in the United States.

Consumer Price Index; *the price index; the index.* It is a measure of the retail prices of a specific list of goods and services. Do not describe it as a *cost-of-living index* because it does not take account of income taxes and some other factors in the cost of living.

Consumer Product Safety Commission.

contact (v.). A conservative minority of authors and teachers still object to the verb *contact* as business jargon. But it is valuable as a terse synonym for *get in touch,* when the method of communication is beside the point: *Contact a physician.*

Those who wish to please the traditionalists may seek substitutes: *write, call, fax, consult, meet, phone, visit.*

container port, container ship.

continent. Lowercase after a name: *African continent*; *North American continent*; *European continent.* Capitalize *the Continent* or *Continental* only when it means Europe.

Continental Airlines.

Continental Divide, the Rocky Mountain ridge that separates rivers flowing east from those flowing west. In later references: *the divide.*

continental shelf, continental slope. The *continental shelf* is the gradually sloping submerged surface between a continent's coast and the *continental slope*, which descends more steeply to the ocean bottom.

continual (over and over again), **continuous** (unbroken).

contractions. In straightforward news copy, spell out expressions like *is not, has not, have not, do not, are not, will not,* etc. Contractions are acceptable in quotations, in texts and transcripts, in light or humorous copy and in headlines and subheadings of all kinds.

contretemps. It is an embarrassing mishap, not the confusion that follows.

control, controlled, controlling.

controller. Use *controller* for the financial officer of a business. But use *comptroller* for a government official with that formal title. *Also see* COMPTROLLER.

controversial. This completely acceptable word becomes an unfair shortcut when attached to the name of a person, program or institution without elaboration: it places the subject under a sinister cloud without stating any case. At a minimum the issue should be specified soon after the word appears. Once that is done, the need for the adjective will often — though not always — evaporate.

conventions (political). *See* NATIONAL CONVENTIONS.

convince, persuade. *Convince* should be followed by an *of* phrase or a *that* clause: *She convinced the teacher of her ability*; *She convinced her sister that it was too late.* But *convince* cannot be followed by a *to* phrase; in such a case, *persuade* is required: *He persuaded his sister to take the day off.* (*Persuade* is more versatile than *convince* and can be followed by any of the three constructions.)

cookie (not *cooky*).

coolly.

co-op. The preferred first (and later) reference for a cooperative. In cap-and-lowercase headlines, it is *Co-op.*

Cooper-Hewitt National Design Museum. This name may be used in most first references. On later references: *the Cooper-Hewitt* or *the National Design Museum.* The formal name is *Cooper-Hewitt, National Design Museum, Smithsonian Institution* (with two commas).

Coopers & Lybrand, the accounting firm, was merged in 1998 into *PricewaterhouseCoopers L.L.P.*

Coordinated Universal Time. Use this term, which has replaced *Greenwich Mean Time*, for the world standard. It is the equivalent of the old system but corrected by atomic clocks to take account of the earth's rotation. The abbreviation, chosen as a compromise that would favor neither English nor French, is *U.T.C. See* TIME.

Copiague (in Suffolk County, N.Y.).

Copper Age.

copter, for helicopter.

Coptic Church. The principal Christian church in Egypt. It has its own patriarch. *See* EASTERN ORTHODOXY.

copy(-). Most but not all compounds formed with *copy* are one word: copybook, copycat, copy desk, copy-edit (v.), copy editor, copyright, copywriter.

copy (in art). *See* FAKE, FORGERY, COPY.

copyright, patent. A *copyright* is legal ownership vested in the author of an original work (fiction, nonfiction, music, drama, art or photography, for example), giving the owner the sole right to reproduce, distribute, display or publish it. Copyright protects the form of expression, but not the ideas and facts themselves. A *patent* is legal ownership vested in the inventor of a process or device, who is given the exclusive right to produce, sell or use it. Copyrights and patents are granted for limited periods. In news copy (but not necessarily in credit lines), omit the copyright symbol (©). *Also see* TRADEMARK, SERVICE MARK.

cord (vocal and spinal), **chord** (music and mathematics).

CORE for the Congress of Racial Equality.

co-respondent means the "third party" accused of adultery in a divorce case. Not, it is hoped, *correspondent.*

Corn Belt.

Corp. Spell out *Corporation* in company and similar names in news articles. It may be abbreviated to *Corp.* in headlines, charts and tables when used with the name of a company. *See* COMPANY AND CORPORATION NAMES.

corporal. *See* CPL.

Corporation for Public Broadcasting. It receives federal money for distribution to individual stations and to National Public Radio and the Public Broadcasting Service. *Also see* NPR and PBS.

corporations. *See* COMPANY AND CORPORATION NAMES.

corps (military). Capitalize only when part of a name: *Adjutant General's Corps; Army Corps of Engineers; Artillery Corps; Signal Corps; the corps. Also see* MARINE CORPS. For numbered corps (units larger than divisions), use Roman numerals: *X Corps.*

Corpus Christi (in Texas).

corralled.

corrections. Because its voice is loud and far-reaching, The Times recognizes an eth-
ical responsibility to correct all its factual errors, large and small (even mis-
spellings of names), promptly and in a prominent reserved space in the paper. A
correction serves all readers, not just those who were injured or who complained,
so it must be self-explanatory, tersely recalling the context and the background
while repairing the error.

A complaint from any source should be relayed to a responsible editor and in-
vestigated quickly. If a correction is warranted, it should follow immediately. In
the rare case of a delay longer than a month, the correction should include an explanation (saying, for example, how recently the error was discovered or why the
checking took so long). If the justification is lame or lacking, the correction
should acknowledge a reporting or editing lapse.

The correction should appear, of course, in any regional editions that carried
the error. If the error, or the entire faulty article, appeared in only some copies, the
correction should say so. When the correction refers to an error in a preprinted
section of the current day's paper, it gives a page number.

Seldom should a correction try to place blame or deflect it outside The
Times; the effort might appear defensive or insincere. But when an error has occurred under the byline or credit of a blameless staff member or news agency, the
correction may cite an editing error or a transmission error. And if The Times has
been misinformed by an institution or a reference work that should have been authoritative, the error may be attributed: . . . *included an erroneous profit figure from
the company's annual report.* Note, though, that the attribution is light-handed
and given in passing (not, for example, *Because of erroneous information from the
Karitsa Company . . .*).

For clarity, the first sentence of a correction should characterize the error
without repeating the faulty information (*misstated the 1998 profit of the Karitsa
Company's heavy equipment group*). At the end, after supplying the facts, the correction may usefully remind readers of the specific error (*It was $480 million, not
$480 billion*).

For the handling of more general lapses (those of fairness, balance and perspective), see EDITORS' NOTES.

correspondent. It is not the word for the "third party" accused of adultery in a divorce
suit; that is *co-respondent.*

Corsica. Use *Corsica* rather than *France* after the names of Corsican cities and towns.
See DATELINES.

cortege.

Cortes (the Spanish legislature). Except in unusually detailed references to the system
or passages conveying local color, *Parliament* is a more accessible term for nonspecialized readers.

Cortland, Cortlandt, Courtlandt. *Cortland* is the city and county in upstate New York; *Cortlandt* is the town in Westchester County, N.Y.; *Courtlandt Avenue* is in the Bronx.

cosmonaut. Use *astronaut* instead except in untranslated texts or direct quotations.

cost, when used as a verb, requires a direct object (*The error cost her $500*) or an adverb (*The mistake cost him dearly*). When used with only an indirect object (*The snub will cost her*), the word is slang or dialect.

cost of living. Hyphenate only when the term precedes what it modifies: *The union negotiated a cost-of-living adjustment.* Economists define the cost of living as the sum needed to pay taxes and buy needed goods and services. It differs from the CONSUMER PRICE INDEX.

Cotton Belt.

councilman, councilwoman. *Councilman* (or *Councilwoman*) *Lee E. Baranek*; *Councilman* (or *Councilwoman*) *Baranek*; *the councilman*; *the councilwoman*. Also: *the councilman* (or *councilwoman*) *at large*. For a group of both men and women, use *council members*. *Also see* MEN AND WOMEN and TITLES.

Council of Churches of the City of New York. It represents Protestant and Eastern Orthodox congregations.

Council of Economic Advisers. The council advises the president on economic matters and helps prepare the president's annual economic report to Congress.

councilor (council member), **counselor** (adviser or embassy official).

count. In non-British rankings of nobility, this title is the equivalent of EARL. Use it in first and later references (never *Lord*). When the title is territorial, capitalize the first reference as a full name: *the Count of Paris; the count*. Some Europeans have modified protocol and use the title with given name and surname; individual preferences should be honored. *Also see* PEERS.

counter(-). It forms solid compounds: counterargument, counterattack, counterbalance, countercharge, counterclaim, counterclockwise, counterculture, counterespionage, counterintelligence, counterintuitive, counterirritant, countermand, countermeasure, counteroffensive, counteroffer, counterpart, counterplot, counterpoint, counterproductive, counterproposal, counterpunch, counterrevolution, countersign, countersink, counterspy.

Countess *Lamb; Lady Lamb; the countess*. In Britain, the woman bearing this title is the counterpart of an earl, or she is the wife of an earl. In some other countries, she is the equivalent of a count, or the wife of a count. (A count is the non-British equivalent of an earl.) Use no given name. If the title is territorial, treat it as a capitalized full name on first reference: *the Countess of Dannford; Lady Dannford*. *Also see* PEERS.

countries. *See* GEOGRAPHIC NAMES.

country(-). Most but not all compounds formed with *country* are one word: country club, countryman, countryside, countrywide, countrywoman.

county. Capitalize when part of a name: *Kings County; Union County.* But: *the county; the county government.* For plurals: *Kings and Union Counties.*

County Clerk *Pat T. Agnello; the county clerk.*

County Executive *Morgan R. Cordeiro; the county executive.*

County Legislature; *the Legislature.*

coup de grâce.

coup d'état. *Coup* can usually stand alone when the context is clear.

couple may be either singular or plural. Used in reference to two distinct but associated people, *couple* should be construed as a plural: *The couple were married in 1952. The couple argued constantly; they* [not *it*] *even threw punches.* When the idea is one entity rather than two people, *couple* may be treated as a singular: *Each couple was asked to give $10; The couple was the richest on the block.* In general, *couple* causes fewer problems when treated as a plural.

Used colloquially, to mean a handful or a few, *couple* should always be followed by *of* (*a couple of pomegranates,* never *a couple pomegranates*).

court cases. Use their names in roman type without quotation marks, and abbreviate *versus* as *v.* Example: *Yagyonak v. the City of New York.* (In all other contexts, the abbreviation is *vs.*) In a quotation or a text, use quotation marks around a citation that would otherwise be hard to recognize: *"This is what 'Nixon' tells us," the judge said.* Give docket numbers when reporting appellate decisions in important cases (*Burlington Industries Inc. v. Ellerth,* No. 97-569) and identify all the judges if the decision is by a panel. In cap-and-lowercase headlines, lowercase *v.*

court decisions. In reporting the decision of a panel (in the federal appellate courts, for example), always name the judges and say how each voted. Lawyers and scholars cannot evaluate the opinion without this information.

courtesy titles. Use *Mr., Mrs., Miss* or *Ms.* with surnames in the news columns for second and later references to people who do not bear specialized titles, like DR., GEN. or GOV. Exceptions are few and are set out in this entry.

First name, middle initial (if any) and surname normally appear on first reference, without a courtesy title. For a woman, later references are to *Ms. Milori,* unless the woman asks to be known as *Miss* or *Mrs.;* the choice is hers, and reporters should seek her preference. In an exceptional case, typically on the society pages, a woman may wish to be known by her husband's name: *Mrs. Morgan H. Berenich,* and then *Mrs. Berenich.*

In general, government officials may be *Dr., Mr., Mrs., Miss* or *Ms.* after being introduced by their main titles: *Gov. Toby K. Lamm; Governor Lamm; Ms. Lamm.* But judges and uniformed personnel (military, police, fire) keep specialized titles in all references. Religious titles vary by denomination and are listed separately.

Some people younger than 18 should receive courtesy titles, and some should not: their role in the news is the guide. A teenager who achieves distinction in a normally adult field (scientific discovery, for example, or musical competition) might well merit *Ms.*, *Miss* or *Mr.* But in a schoolroom setting, *Robin* would seem more natural. If a title seems inappropriate, call the subject *Robin* or *Robin Agnello* in all references; do not use fusty phrases like *the Agnello boy* or *the Cordero girl* or *the Lamm youth*.

Use a courtesy title in a headline for special effect only, or if the surname would be misleading and a full name will not fit: *Mrs. Clinton*; *Mr. Thatcher*.

Omit courtesy titles with most names in sports articles (even on the front page), though titles are sometimes appropriate for names occurring in purely political, civic or business roles: *Ms. Barany threw out the first ball*. In other articles, omit a courtesy title for a sports figure mentioned in an athletic role, but use the title when the name appears in other connections. In an athlete's obituary, omit the title in passages covering the sport, but use the title in those passages recounting other phases of the subject's life—a later business career, for example. Copy about chess or bridge should follow the sports style.

Omit courtesy titles with surnames of historic or pre-eminent figures no longer living: *Curie*; *Hitler*; *Lenin*; *Napoleon*; *Newton*; *Woolf*. This style also applies, especially in the arts and sometimes in science, to eminent figures still living. Examples might have included *Bernhardt*, *Callas*, *Einstein*, *Picasso* and *Stravinsky* before their deaths. In an arts review, the judgment of eminence should ordinarily be left to the critic.

Omit a courtesy title with a coined or fanciful stage name to avoid appearing overliteral. *Meat Loaf* and *Little Richard*, for example, keep their full names, without title, in all references.

Foreign equivalents of the courtesy titles—*M.*, *Mme.*, *Mlle.*; *Herr*, *Frau*, *Fräulein*; *Señor*, *Señora*, *Señorita*; *Signor*, *Signora*, *Signorina*; etc.—should be used only for special effect (as they appear in this paragraph: some abbreviated, some spelled out). The foreign titles may also be used when they occur in an English-language passage that is being quoted. But if they occur in a translated quotation, translate them, too.

The Times Magazine and the Book Review, edited in the more literary style of a weekend periodical, omit all courtesy titles.

courthouse. Exception: *United States Court House* at Foley Square.

Courtlandt Avenue (in the Bronx). *Also see* CORTLAND, CORTLANDT, COURTLANDT.

court(s)-martial.

Court of St. James's, St. James's Palace. The United States ambassador to Britain may also be called the *United States ambassador to the Court of St. James's*, but only in contexts that warrant the ceremonial flavor.

courtroom.

courts. Capitalize the names of courts: *Appellate Division*; *County Court*; *Court of Appeals*; *Court of Claims*; *Court of Criminal Jurisdiction*; *International Court of Justice* (the *World Court*); *Supreme Court*; *Surrogate's Court*; etc.

Later references to a court or to its presiding officer are lowercased: *the court*. Also lowercase these and similar terms: *administrator, appellant, coroner's jury, master, receiver, referee in bankruptcy*.

In the federal system, the appellate courts below the Supreme Court are *the United States Courts of Appeals*. An individual one is the *United States Court of Appeals for the Fifth Circuit*, not *the Fifth Circuit Court of Appeals*. (New York and Connecticut are in the Second Circuit; New Jersey is in the Third Circuit.) At the next lower level are the United States District Courts. A single one may be referred to as the *United States District Court* or the *Federal District Court*. In New York, it is usually important to distinguish between the court for *the Southern District* (in Manhattan, also covering the Bronx and Westchester County) and *the Eastern District* (in Brooklyn, also covering Queens, Staten Island and Long Island).

Note that in the New York State system, the Supreme Court is not the highest court. The higher ones are the Appellate Division of the State Supreme Court and ultimately the Court of Appeals. Any article about the Appellate Division should name the affected judicial department: for example, *the First Judicial Department* (or *First Department*) covers Manhattan and the Bronx.

The use of JUDGE and JUSTICE varies among courts, even within federal and state systems. *See* those entries, as well as ASSOCIATE JUSTICE; CHIEF JUDGE; CHIEF JUSTICE; MAGISTRATE JUDGE.

Also see SUPREME COURT and WORLD COURT.

Court TV for the Courtroom Television Network.

cover-up (n. and adj.), **cover up** (v.).

C.P.A. for certified public accountant.

Cpl. *Stacy K. Milori*; *Corporal Milori*; *the corporal*.

CP Rail System is now the Canadian Pacific Railway, a subsidiary of Canadian Pacific Ltd.

C.P.U. for a computer's central processing unit.

crab(-). Most compounds formed with *crab* are two words: crab apple, crab grass, crab meat.

crack(-). Most but not all compounds formed with *crack* are one word: crackbrained, crackdown, crackpot, crackup (n.), crack up (v.).

crackerjack is slang for *excellent* or *outstanding*. *Cracker Jack* is the trademark for glazed popcorn.

craft (v.). As a verb meaning make with skill, *craft* is the grandiose language of sales literature. Consider substitutes like *make, devise, shape* and *fashion*.

crèche.

credit lines (for articles). The Times's credit style assumes that bylined articles are the newspaper's own, unless otherwise attributed in a credit line. Thus bylined articles written by The Times's staff, stringers or contributors require no credit line. Copy without a byline, if written locally, is also assumed to be The Times's own and requires no credit.

But if the copy carries a dateline without a byline, readers must be told what news organization provided the reporting from a remote site.

Thus credit lines for articles in the news columns are used or omitted as follows:

COPY BY TIMES WRITERS OR CONTRIBUTORS
Bylined copy, with or without a dateline: No credit line.
Unbylined, nondatelined copy: No credit line.
Unbylined copy, with dateline:

By The New York Times

COPY FROM NEWS AGENCIES
Datelined copy, on Page 1 and inside the paper (see DATELINES):

TUSCALOOSA, Ala., March 7 (AP) —
ABIDJAN, Ivory Coast, May 19 (Agence France-Presse) —

In an exceptional case, the copy may appear with a byline:

By THEO T. KARITSA

TUSCALOOSA, Ala., March 7 (Reuters) —

Nondatelined copy:

By Agence France-Presse
By The Associated Press
By Bloomberg News
By Dow Jones
By Reuters

COPY FROM OTHER NEWSPAPERS
Copy supplied by another newspaper or a newspaper group, with or without a dateline:

New York Times Regional Newspapers
The Press-Democrat, Santa Rosa, Calif.
Cox Newspapers

In an exceptional case, the credit may appear with a byline:

By S. P. AGNELLO
New York Times Regional Newspapers

credit lines (for photos and illustrations). Ordinarily The Times credits the creator or the supplier, or both, for every photo, map and illustration in the paper. (As an exception, credit may be omitted for thumbnail photos and illustrations, especially those used in indexes, billboards and tables of contents.) Above all, a credit should convey meaning: if the phrasing merely satisfies the supplier or the lawyers without clearly telling the reader who did what, rewrite it, improvising a style if necessary.

Generally department heads will determine who deserves credit. The wording and format follow:

The main style for a staff-produced map or chart:

The New York Times

The main style for any staff photo, or for a staff map or chart reflecting special effort:

Toby H. Dann/The New York Times

For a freelance on assignment:

Toby H. Dann for The New York Times

For an unassigned freelance:

Toby H. Dann

For a news agency, outside organization or press pool:

Associated Press
Reuters
CNN
Pool photo
Agence France-Presse
New York City Ballet

For multiple photos or illustrations:

Photographs by Toby H. Dann/The New York Times
Illustrations by D. R. Cordero/The New York Times

For a Times map or chart, embellished by an individual illustrator, whether staff or freelance:

The New York Times; illustration by L. T. Dann

In special cases, for a shared staff effort on a map or chart:

> Leslie S. Miel and Lindsay Baranek/The New York Times

For grouped photos:

> Top left, A. T. Agnello/The New York Times; top right, Associated Press;
> center, Amnesty International; bottom right, General Motors

For special merit:

> TOBY H. DANN/The New York Times
> Photographs by LEE T. LAMM/The New York Times
> M. L. Karitsa/Associated Press
> M. L. KARITSA/Associated Press

When more than one organization is cited in a credit, separate the names with a comma for clarity.

For a Times special assignment by an outside agency:

> Associated Press, for The New York Times

For a special assignment by an agency photographer:

> Leslie T. Karitsa/Magnum, for The New York Times
> L. D. Agnello/AP, for The New York Times

For a photo produced by one organization and transmitted by another:

> White House, via Associated Press
> CNN, via Associated Press
> Pool photo, via Associated Press

crematory, crematories. Preferable to *crematorium(s)*. Do not use *crematoria*.

crepe de Chine.

crepe(s), for the food. But: *crêpes suzette*.

crescendo. A crescendo is not a peak of intensity but a gradual increase in force, intensity or loudness. It is the trip to the peak.

crew, like *army* or *navy*, is a collective noun. It refers not to individuals but to all the members of a group. In references to individuals, use *crewmen, crew members* or *members of the crew*. References to *three crew* or to *selecting crew* are jargon.

Criminal Courts Building.

cripple, crippled. Do not use these words when mentioning disabilities (*she is a cripple; he was crippled by polio*). Instead: *She lost the use of her legs to polio; He has been unable to walk since an automobile accident in 1992. Also see* AFFLICTED; CHALLENGED; DEFORMED; DISABILITY, DISABLED; HANDICAPPED; IMPAIRED.

crisscross.

criterion (sing.), **criteria** (pl.).

criticize can be a partisan term when followed by a *for* phrase: *She criticized the president for breaking his promises.* That phrasing assumes that the president really broke them. Make it *accused the president of breaking his promises.*

critique has gained acceptance as a verb but precise writers still use it only as a noun. Suitable verbs include *analyze, assess, comment on, criticize* and *review.*

Croatia (the country), **Croat(s)** (n., the people), **Croatian** (adj.).

crocus(es).

cross(-). Most compounds formed with *cross* are one word, some are hyphenated and some are two words: crossbar (sports), crossbones, crossbow, crossbred, crosscheck, cross-country, crosscurrent, cross-examination, cross-examine, cross-examiner, cross-fire, cross hair(s), crosshatch, cross-index, cross-legged, crossover (n.), cross-purpose, cross-question (n. and v.), cross-reference (n. and v.), crossroad, cross section, crosstown, crosswalk, crossword puzzle.

Cross Bay-Veterans' Memorial Bridge (over Beach Channel, in Queens).

Croton-on-Hudson (in Westchester County, N.Y.).

crunch. As a noun meaning *showdown* or *crisis, crunch* is slang and faddish.

crystallize.

C-Span, for the Cable-Satellite Public Affairs Network and its primary television channel. Also: *C-Span 2,* its second channel.

CSX Transportation Inc.

Cubism (art). Capitalize in reference to the style of painting and sculpture created by Picasso and Braque from 1907 onward. *See* ARTS TERMINOLOGY.

cuff links.

cul-de-sac(s).

cult, in a religious context, suggests that a group holds bizarre views and manipulates its members. Unless that is established, consider a more neutral term, like *sect.*

Cultural Revolution. Capitalize references to the one in China that lasted from 1966 to 1976. But: *a new cultural revolution; a cultural revolution.*

(-)culture. Most but not all compounds formed with *culture* are one word: counterculture, subculture, tissue culture.

Cummings, E. E. (not *e. e. cummings*). Except in his poetry, he used conventional capitalization.

Cunard Line.

CUNY is acceptable on later references and in headlines for the CITY UNIVERSITY OF NEW YORK.

cup. A measuring cup holds 8 fluid ounces or 16 tablespoons.

cupful(s).

Curaçao.

currencies. *See* FOREIGN CURRENCIES.

curriculums (not *curricula*).

curriculum vitae is too lofty for news copy. Use *résumé* instead.

Custom House.

Cutchogue (in Suffolk County, N.Y.).

cutlines. *See* CAPTIONS.

Cuyahoga is the name of a county and a river in Ohio. *Cuyahoga Falls* is an Ohio city.

cyber(-). It is a prefix, not a word, forming solid compounds except with a proper name: *cyberrevolution, cybervoting, cyber-Shakespeare* (in jest, presumably). Ration these coinages.

cyberspace (the realm of computer networks).

cyclone. It is an area of low atmospheric pressure and spiraling winds, but the term is used in parts of the United States for a tornado and in the Indian Ocean region for a hurricane. Specify the meaning, or rephrase the passage. *See* HURRICANE and TORNADO.

Cypriot(s). The people of Cyprus.

czar, czarist. Use these spellings rather than the less familiar *tsar.* Also: *czarina.* Capitalize the title before a Russian royal name only: *Czar Nicholas; the czar.* Lowercase *czarist(s).* Also lowercase figurative references, like *baseball czar, drug czar, economic czar*, etc., but those terms are overworked.

Czechoslovakia divided in 1993 into the Czech Republic and Slovakia. The adjective was *Czechoslovak*, not *Czechoslovakian*.

Czech Republic. Formerly the western part of Czechoslovakia. The capital is Prague. *Also see* SLOVAKIA.

D

D.A. for district attorney, but only in a quotation or a text, or for special effect.

dachshund(s).

Dacron is a trademark.

dad. Reserve this colloquialism for folksy contexts, and lowercase except when it substitutes for a proper name: *I'll bet Dad was quite a hit in his senior class show; Tracy's dad was in it, too. Also see* FATHER.

Dada. Capitalize in reference to the art movement that emerged in Europe and New York during World War I. Members of this movement are *Dadaists. See* ARTS TERMINOLOGY.

DaimlerChrysler A.G. was formed in 1998 with the merger of Daimler-Benz and the Chrysler Corporation.

Dakota. *N. Dakota* and *S. Dakota* may be used in headlines when necessary (somewhat more readily in the sports pages) to avoid the ambiguity of *Dakota* alone.

Dalai Lama. Because the holder uses no other name, uppercase the title as if it were a full name.

Dalles, The (in Oregon). An exception to the usual preference for lowercasing *the*.

Dame *Ashley Anyell; Dame Ashley* (but never *the dame*). The honor is comparable to a knighthood, and the bearer is not a peer. A dame who marries retains her title unless her husband holds a higher rank: *Dr. Hilary J. Cordero and Dame Ashley Anyell de Cordero.*

damn it. The expression is two words, but like other profanity it should not be used without a compelling reason. *See* OBSCENITY, VULGARITY, PROFANITY.

dance. Capitalize in a title: *Schubert's German Dances*; *"Dance of the Hours"*; *"Danse Macabre."* But lowercase in a generic sense: *Balanchine's dances; a modern dance.* Similarly, lowercase individual dance styles, except when used in a title: *a Chopin waltz, Chopin's Waltz in A flat; a gavotte, the "Ascot Gavotte" from "My Fair Lady."* *See* ARTS TERMINOLOGY and MUSIC.

Danzig. Use *Gdansk*, the Polish spelling, rather than this German one, except in historical contexts.

D.A.R. for the Daughters of the American Revolution.

Dardanelles, the (not *Dardanelles Strait*).

Dar es Salaam (the capital of Tanzania).

dark(-). Some compounds formed with *dark* are one word, some are hyphenated and some are two words: dark-eyed, dark-haired, dark horse (n.), dark-horse (adj.), darkroom (photography), dark-skinned.

dash. The dash is often misused for the comma: *Pat—who was badly hurt last year—was pronounced fit today.* And it is often overused. A sentence with more than two dashes is confusing because a reader cannot distinguish between the asides and the main narrative.

Dashes properly surround a series punctuated by commas: *The governor will face many problems—unemployment, declining revenue and rising costs—in the election year.* Here, too, the dash is needed for clarity: *The costs—taxes and lawyers' fees—were higher than expected.*

Also use the dash to mark an abrupt change in continuity of expression: *"The balance of payments is—but you know all that."* A sudden cutoff of conversation or Q. and A. dialogue should be marked by a two-em dash (double length):

"Your Honor," she said, *"please let me finish my——"*

"Overruled!" the judge shot back.

(A quotation that trails off indecisively is treated differently. *See* QUOTATIONS.) In a dateline, a dash follows the date: SCRANTON, *Pa., March 11*—etc.

The dash may also precede *namely, viz., i.e.* and similar words or abbreviations. Do not use a dash alongside a comma, a semicolon or a colon.

Because newspaper columns are usually narrow, with few words to a line, the dash should be surrounded by spaces; they provide openings for the computer to distribute spacing evenly when justifying the type.

The dash used in news copy is one em wide. Do not use the shorter en dash (–), except as a minus sign. And in headlines (other than banks), avoid both dashes because they are ungainly in large type; usually the meaning can be conveyed with a colon, a semicolon or parentheses. *See* HEADLINES.

DAT for digital audiotape.

data is acceptable as a singular term for information: *The data was persuasive.* In its traditional sense, meaning a collection of facts and figures, the noun can still be plural: *They tabulate the data, which arrive from bookstores nationwide.* (In this sense, the singular is *datum*, a word both stilted and deservedly obscure.)

databank.

database.

date line for the place on the globe where a new day begins. But: *dateline*, at the top of a news article.

dateline integrity. Because believable firsthand news gathering is The Times's hallmark, datelines must scrupulously specify when and where the reporting took place. A dateline guarantees that a reporter (the bylined one, if there is a byline) was at the specified place on the date given, and provided the bulk of the information, in the form of copy or, when necessary, of notes used faithfully in a rewrite.

With instantaneous worldwide communication, writers are able to reflect events occurring anywhere. But the reader is owed an accounting of the source for any detailed reference to events remote from the dateline: credit to news agencies, for example, or to telephone interviews, or witnesses' reports on the Internet.

Editors may supply background or clarifying material within a datelined article, if the insertions are carefully checked and could reasonably have come from the writer, given adequate time or convenient references. But any substantive reporting added to an article must be isolated from the dateline — either enclosed in brackets or appended as a "shirttail," beneath a dash and a separate heading. Such material should be credited to its source, with a discrete dateline when that is appropriate. *See* BRACKETS.

If publication is delayed, the article should carry the most recent date on which the reporter or stringer was at the scene and able to update or reconfirm the facts. If the delay is more than a week, the date should be dropped from the dateline. For example, an article datelined *BRUSSELS, Feb. 1* is publishable in the papers of Feb. 2 through Feb. 8. In the paper of Feb. 9 or later, the dateline would be simply *BRUSSELS*, without a date. At that point, any phrasing that might *imply* a more recent visit by the reporter should be restated for accuracy. *Next Tuesday*, for example, would be misleading if the reporter departed more than a week before that day. But *on Feb. 23* is acceptable because it could have been written truthfully when the reporter was on the scene.

Events occurring after the reporter's departure from the datelined place cannot truthfully be reported under the dateline, with or without a date. If those events are secondary, they may be treated in a bracketed insert, a shirttail or an adjoining brief article, with the information source credited. If the events are central to the account, the dateline should be removed; the reporter's earlier presence on the scene may be demonstrated gracefully in the narrative.

The name of a military base or (most sparingly) an aircraft, ship or train may serve as a dateline, if that was the origin of the reporting. Note, however, that if an "en route" article describes the journey's end, and events afterward, it can no longer truthfully carry such a dateline.

Roundups should follow a rule of reason. If they are written in New York with information from a variety of sources, they should be undatelined and the sources should be specified. A roundup on a Midwestern or a national subject written by a reporter in Chicago would properly carry a Chicago dateline; one that had nothing to do with Chicago but was written by a reporter who just happened to be there should be undatelined.

Occasionally an article about an event in one city may be more effectively written from another, perhaps because it requires the expertise of a specialized reporter remote from the scene. If the writer's locale is visibly relevant—Rome, for example, for an article about a pope's travels elsewhere—the locale may serve as a dateline. Otherwise the article should omit a dateline. In either case, the writer must verify that the event occurred as planned and specify how the facts were learned.

datelines. Generally the news sections use datelines on articles originating outside New York City. This is the usual form of a news dateline:

> KIGALI, Rwanda, March 14—

In feature sections and on many columns, the "shoulder" style is used (flush right, without a date; capitals and small capitals for city name only):

> PORT OF SPAIN, Trinidad and Tobago

For a news agency article:

> EDMONTON, Alberta, March 14 (Reuters) —
> DIXVILLE NOTCH, N.H., Feb. 10 (AP) —

If an article reports developments so current that the dateline is identical with the publication date, alert the reader by naming the day:

> CINCINNATI, Friday, Sept. 18 —

A date is omitted from the dateline when an article is published more than a week after the reporter has left the scene. *See* DATELINE INTEGRITY.

In shipboard datelines, use a locating phrase (but not an imprecise one, like *at Sea*):

> ABOARD U.S.S. HARRY S. TRUMAN, off South Korea, July 16 —

With some exceptions (see below), a domestic dateline includes the state (abbreviated as shown in this manual's separate state listings), a Canadian dateline the province (spelled out) and any other foreign dateline the country. But some distinctive national regions abroad are customarily named in place of the country; examples include Sicily, Sardinia, Corsica, Scotland, Wales and Tasmania.

When the names of the city and the state or country are identical or nearly so (*Panama, San Salvador*), use only one, except in the cases noted on the lists that follow. *UNITED NATIONS* appears in datelines without further identification. Local zoned sections omit the state from datelines within their coverage areas.

Domestic and foreign place names that should stand alone in datelines are listed here. In an article, however, writers and editors should feel free to omit the state or country after *any* place name that is identifiable in context, especially in a series of names when others stand alone.

UNITED STATES

ALBANY
ALBUQUERQUE
ANCHORAGE
ATLANTA
ATLANTIC CITY
BALTIMORE
BOSTON
BUFFALO
CHICAGO
CINCINNATI
CLEVELAND
COLORADO SPRINGS
DALLAS
DENVER
DES MOINES
DETROIT
EL PASO
FORT WORTH
HARTFORD
HOLLYWOOD
HONOLULU
HOUSTON
INDIANAPOLIS
IOWA CITY
JERSEY CITY
LAS VEGAS
LOS ANGELES
MEMPHIS
MIAMI

MIAMI BEACH
MILWAUKEE
MINNEAPOLIS
NASHVILLE
NEWARK
NEW HAVEN
NEW ORLEANS
OKLAHOMA CITY
OMAHA
PHILADELPHIA
PHOENIX
PITTSBURGH
ROCHESTER
SACRAMENTO
SALT LAKE CITY
SAN ANTONIO
SAN DIEGO
SAN FRANCISCO
SEATTLE
ST. LOUIS
ST. PAUL
SYRACUSE
TRENTON
TUCSON
VIRGINIA BEACH
WASHINGTON
WHITE PLAINS
YONKERS

Note that KANSAS CITY datelines always specify a state (*Kan.* or *Mo.*).

FOREIGN

ALGIERS	LUXEMBOURG
AMSTERDAM	MACAO
ATHENS	MADRID
BANGKOK	MANILA
BEIJING	MEXICO CITY
BERLIN	MILAN
BOMBAY	MONACO
BONN	MONTREAL
BRASÍLIA	MOSCOW
BRUSSELS	MUNICH
BUDAPEST	NEW DELHI
BUENOS AIRES	OSLO
CAIRO	OTTAWA
CALCUTTA	PANAMA
CAPE TOWN	PARIS
COPENHAGEN	PRAGUE
DJIBOUTI	QUEBEC
DUBLIN	RIO DE JANEIRO
EDINBURGH	ROME
FRANKFURT	SAN MARINO
GENEVA	SAN SALVADOR
GIBRALTAR	SHANGHAI
GLASGOW	SINGAPORE
GUATEMALA CITY	STOCKHOLM
THE HAGUE	TEHRAN
HAVANA	TEL AVIV
HONG KONG	TOKYO
ISTANBUL	TORONTO
JERUSALEM	TUNIS
JOHANNESBURG	VENICE
KUWAIT	VIENNA
LISBON	WARSAW
LONDON	ZURICH

Also see BYLINES and CREDIT LINES.

datelines, unfamiliar. An obscure dateline should be explained high in the article. A deft phrase will usually do: *… in Indian towns like this one in northern Argentina.*

dates. Use a numeral for the day when it follows the name of the month: *April 1, 1996.* In the rare case of a day that precedes the month (usually in a quotation), use this form: *the 6th of January.* An exception: *the Fourth of July.*

When day, month and year are given together, use a comma after the day, and use a comma or some other punctuation after the year: *He said he left Ho Ho Kus on April 16, 1995, to return to Burkina Faso.* When month and year are given without a day, use no comma after the month, and punctuation can usually be omitted after the year: *He said he left Ho Ho Kus in April 1995 to sail the Gulf of Kutch.*

Also *see* MONTHS and YEARS, DECADES, CENTURIES.

day(-). Most compounds formed with *day* are one word, some are hyphenated and some are two words: daybed, daybreak, day care, daydream, daylight, daylong, day room, day school, day student, daytime, day-to-day (adj.), daywork.

Day 1. Capitalize, and use a figure.

day care is not hyphenated, even as a modifier: *day care center.*

Day-Glo is a trademark for fluorescent paints or for the agent that produces their brilliant colors.

daylight time. Lowercase the expression standing alone: 9 *a.m., daylight time.* But *Eastern Daylight Time* (and *Central, Mountain* or *Pacific*). Abbreviations: *E.D.T., C.D.T., M.D.T., P.D.T.* Also note the full expression: *daylight saving time,* not *savings.* By act of Congress, the legislatures in states that span time zones may choose to observe daylight time or not. For those that do, the law sets the changeover times as 2 a.m. on the first Sunday in April (when clocks are set forward one hour) and 2 a.m. on the last Sunday in October (when they are set back an hour). Also *see* TIME.

days. *See* DATES.

D.C. for District of Columbia. Omit *D.C.* after the city name except when there is a likelihood of confusion with Washington State. Also *see* DISTRICT.

D.D. for Doctor of Divinity, an honorary degree that does not justify the use of *the Rev. Dr.* or *Dr.* with names. Also *see* DR.

D-Day. The *D,* an unavoidable redundancy, stands for *Day.* The expression, popularly identified with the Normandy landing on June 6, 1944, is used by military planners to lay out the timetable for any operation before its exact date is chosen. Similarly: *H-Hour,* the *H* standing for *Hour.*

D.D.S. for Doctor of Dental Surgery.

DDT for the insecticide. The full name, ludicrously long, need almost never be used.

de (the particle). *See* PERSONAL NAMES AND NICKNAMES.

de(-). Ordinarily close up compounds formed with *de* unless the prefix is directly followed by an *e* or an uppercase letter: deactivate, debrief, decaffeinated, declassified, de-emphasize, de-escalate, dehumanize, deinstitutionalize, demilitarize, de-Stalinization, detoxify, devaluation.

But hyphenate *de* compounds that would otherwise be hard to read: *de-ice.*

deacon. Deacons are members of one of the three orders of Christian ministry. (Priests or ministers constitute another order and bishops the third.) In the

Roman Catholic and Episcopal churches, the diaconate is one stage through which a candidate for the priesthood passes on the way to ordination, and it requires the completion of a course of study. There are also "permanent" and "perpetual" deacons for whom the diaconate is a final position, usually part-time and unpaid. These deacons are able to perform most functions of priests, including the distribution of holy communion, but may not consecrate the elements of bread and wine. In other churches, deacons usually oversee the charitable activities of a congregation, and the post does not require special theological training.

The Episcopal form of address is *the Rev. Ashley B. Daan, deacon of,* etc. In later references, it is *Mr., Mrs., Miss, Ms., Dr.* or *the deacon,* but not *Deacon Daan.* For deacons of the Roman Catholic and other churches, use this form: *Ashley B. Daan, a deacon of,* etc., with later references as in the Episcopal style.

dead(-). Some compounds formed with *dead* are one word, some are hyphenated and some are two words: deadbeat, deadbolt, dead center, dead end (n.), dead-end (adj.), dead heat, deadline, deadlock, deadpan, dead weight, deadwood.

deaf. Apply the term to someone who cannot hear at all. Others may be *hard of hearing* or *have partial hearing.* If possible, cite the extent of the hearing loss. *See* DISABILITY, DISABLED; DUMB; IMPAIRED; MUTE.

dean. In the Episcopal Church, it is the title for the dean of a cathedral and sometimes for the head of a seminary: *the Very Rev. Lauren M. Barany, dean of the Cathedral Church of St. John the Divine; Dean Barany; the dean.* Also: *Lauren M. Barany, dean of Harvard College* (or *dean of students*); *Professor Barany* (or *Mr., Dr., Miss, Mrs.* or *Ms. Barany*); *the dean.* Also see ARCHBISHOP; BISHOP; CANON; DEACON; MOST REV., RT. REV.

death(-). Most but not all compounds formed with *death* are two words: deathbed, death camp, death chamber, death house, death knell, death penalty, death rate, death row, death squad, deathtrap, deathwatch.

debark. Dictionaries accept this word and *disembark* equally. An economical writer may prefer the shorter one: why put people aboard (with the *em-* prefix) only to walk them back down the gangway (*dis-*)?

debt ratings. The two most widely followed companies that judge the investment risk of long-term debt securities are Moody's Investors Service Inc. and Standard & Poor's Rating Service.

Moody's uses nine broad ratings: *Aaa, Aa, A, Baa, Ba, B, Caa, Ca* and *C.* Bonds rated *Aaa* are judged to be of the best quality and those rated *C* are regarded as extremely poor. Moody's adds numerical modifiers (1, 2 and 3) to indicate whether a bond is in the upper, middle or lower part of the range: *Aa2; Baa3.*

S.&P. has 10 main grades: *AAA, AA, A, BBB, BB, B, CCC, CC, C* and *D.* It often uses a plus or minus sign on grades from AA through CCC: *AA–; B+.* For a minus symbol, use the en dash (–).

debut. Use it as a noun (*made a debut*) or a modifier (*debut recital*), never as a verb (*debuted*).

debutante.

Dec. for *December* before numerals (*Dec. 17*), or in charts and tables.

decades should usually be given in numerals: *the 1990's; the mid-1970's; the 90's.* But when a decade begins a sentence, it must be spelled out (*Nineteen-eighties solutions are no longer adequate*); often that is reason enough to recast the sentence. Decade nicknames are spelled out and capitalized: *Gay Nineties; Roaring Twenties. Also see* PLURALS *and* YEARS, DECADES, CENTURIES.

decimals. Use figures for all numbers that contain decimals: *3.4 inches of rain; 22.25 inches of snow.* If the figure is entirely a decimal, use a zero before the point: *0.3 inch.* An exception: *.22-caliber rifle. Also see* FRACTIONS *and* NUMBERS.

Be wary of false precision in using decimals. Taking a statistic beyond the decimal point is misleading if one or more numbers in the calculation are estimates or rounded with many zeros. For example, when a company reports that its net income rose to $685 million from $545 million, describing the increase as 25.7 percent implies a precision that cannot be genuine because both original numbers are approximations.

decimate originally meant kill every 10th member of a group. But dictionaries agree that it has come to mean destroy or kill a large part of something. Because the notion of one-tenth remains, do not couple *decimate* with other fractions or percentages: *The bomb decimated a quarter of the division.*

decisions. In the United States (in contrast with Britain), they are *made*, not *taken*.

décor.

decry is stilted and archaic-sounding. Substitute verbs include *deplore* and *denounce*.

deductible.

deejay. Use *D.J.* instead for disc jockey.

deep(-), (-)deep. Most but not all compounds formed with *deep* as a prefix are hyphenated: deep-rooted, deep-sea (adj.), deep-seated, deepwater (adj.).

Compounds formed with *deep* as a suffix are hyphenated: ankle-deep, waist-deep.

Deep South.

de facto.

defense. Do not use as a verb, even in sports contexts.

defensible (not *defendable*).

defining moment is a journalistic cliché.

definitions. To avoid seeming to patronize the reader who already knows, place a definition or explanation ahead of the term being defined when possible: *the 20th-century composers Ashley Lamb and Lauren Milori* or *the buildings, land and machinery that make up a company's fixed assets* (rather than *Ashley Lamb and*

Lauren Milori, 20th-century composers, or *a company's fixed assets—its buildings, land and machinery*). The explanations slip by unnoticed because they occur before the reader realizes what term is being defined.

deformed. Use more specific, less disparaging terms in referring to disabilities. *Also see* CRIPPLE, CRIPPLED; DISABILITY, DISABLED; HANDICAPPED; IMPAIRED.

defuse, diffuse. Similar pronunciation may lead to spelling confusion: The verb for removing danger is *defuse*—that is, *remove a fuse. Diffuse* can be an adjective meaning *spread out* or, in the case of a speech, *wordy;* it can also be a verb meaning *spread.*

degrees. Many academic degrees are listed separately. *Also see* TEMPERATURE.

deity. Capitalize terms like *God, Holy Ghost* (or *Holy Spirit*), *Son of Man, the Supreme Being* (but: *a god; gods; a supreme being*). In references to God, Jesus or Allah, in keeping with current practice even in most church publications, lowercase personal pronouns (*he, him, his, thee, thou, thine*) as well as the relative pronouns (*who, whom, whose,* etc.).

déjà vu. In precise writing, the term refers to the *illusion* of reliving an event that has in fact not occurred before. The looser use, to mean re-experiencing a real event, is trite.

Delancey Street (in New York City).

Delaware. Abbreviate as *Del.* after the names of cities, towns and counties.

delegate (diplomatic). Lowercase and use the preposition *to: Lynn B. Agneau, United States delegate to the Conference on the Law of the Sea; Ms. Agneau; the delegate.* Confine *delegate* and *chief delegate* to members of temporary or provisional delegations, like those at the annual General Assembly of the United Nations. For permanent bodies, use CHIEF REPRESENTATIVE, REPRESENTATIVE and, when appropriate, AMBASSADOR.

delegate at large. No hyphens.

Delta Air Lines.

Delta Queen Steamboat Company.

demagogy.

démarche. It means a diplomatic maneuver, but consider a more conversational synonym.

demi(-). Compounds formed with *demi* are one word: demigod, demimonde, demitasse.

Democrat (n.), **Democratic** (adj.), for the party and its members. Do not use *Democrat* as a modifier (*the Democrat party*); that construction is used by opponents to disparage the party.

Democratic national chairman (or *state* or *county chairman* or *chairwoman*). *Lindsay E. Kuzu, Democratic national* (or *state* or *county*) *chairman; the national* (or *state* or *county*) *chairwoman.*

Democratic National Committee (or *State* or *County Committee*); *the national* (or *state* or *county*) *committee*; *the committee*.

Democratic National Convention (or *State Convention*); *the national* (or *state*) *convention*; *the convention*.

Democratic Party.

denouement.

department. Capitalize it in the name of a government agency, national, state or municipal: *State Department*; *Conservation Department*; *Police Department*. For most federal departments, the briefer form *State Department* is preferred to *Department of State*. Do not capitalize the names of academic or commercial departments: *physics department*; *English department*; *customer service department*. The abbreviation (*Dept.*) may be used in charts and tables, but not in news articles. It may also be used in headlines, but only in a governmental proper name: *Justice Dept.*; *State Dept.*; *Conservation Dept.*; *Police Dept.*; *Fire Dept.*; etc.

depose. The legal term means testify under oath or question under oath. Usually those phrases are more comfortable for readers. But *deposition*, for a sworn statement, is clear enough.

depression. A *depression* is a period of decreased business activity, falling prices and widespread unemployment. It is longer and more severe than a recession. Capitalize the word when it refers to the Depression of the 1930's, which is also called *the Great Depression*.

Dept. *See* DEPARTMENT.

Deputy Chief *Leslie M. Agnello*; *Chief Agnello*; *the chief*.

deputy. Capitalize only when it is part of a title preceding a name: *Deputy Prime Minister Merrill D. Lamb*; *the deputy prime minister*. Because most Americans think of *deputy* as a synonym for *assistant*, it is usually best to avoid the term in the foreign sense of *member of Parliament*. Also see TITLES.

Deputy Inspector *Pat T. Daan*; *Inspector Daan*; *the inspector*.

de rigueur. Both *u*'s are de rigueur.

desegregation, integration. The words are not synonymous. *Desegregation* means ending the separation of racial or ethnic groups. *Integration* means bringing them into full, equal association.

desiccate (dry out).

design, as a verb, suggests the shaping of physical things. For intangibles like laws and policies, more precise substitutes include *intend*, *devise* and *plan*: *The law is intended to reduce trade deficits*.

-designate. *Ambassador-designate Ashley T. Lamb*; *Secretary-designate Dana U. Agnello*. But other phrasing is less awkward: *Ashley T. Lamb, the ambassador-designate*; *Dana*

U. Agnello, who was nominated as secretary of defense last month. In cap-and-lower-case headlines, capitalize *Designate.*

Detective *Hilary P. Kuzu; Detective Kuzu; the detective.* (In the New York City Police Department, detectives are usually assigned to detective squads or bureaus, not to individual precincts.)

détente, a diplomatic term, is serviceable in both articles and headlines, but also stuffy. *Easing of tension* or an equivalent phrase may be more conversational. *Also see* RAPPROCHEMENT.

determine usually implies the truth of what is being reported: *The police determined that the wounds were self-inflicted.* Neutral terms include *said* and *concluded.*

Deutsche mark is acceptable in direct quotations, in texts or for special effect, but ordinarily use just *mark* or *German mark.*

"Deutschlandlied" ("Song of Germany"), the German national anthem. The title "Deutschland Über Alles" was dropped after World War II.

devil. Capitalize it in references to Satan, but lowercase *devils* and *a devil.*

devout. An overused word, in clichés like *devout Catholic.* Without knowing the writer's criteria, the reader cannot tell whether this means simply churchgoing or something less, or more.

Dexedrine is a trademark.

Dhahran (in Saudi Arabia).

Dhaka (formerly *Dacca*) is the capital of Bangladesh.

diabetes. When possible, differentiate between *Type 1* diabetes (also known as *insulin-dependent diabetes*) and *Type 2* (also known as *non-insulin-dependent diabetes*). Type 1 diabetes is also called juvenile diabetes, but because it is found in many adults, that name is misleading. A major research and fund-raising organization is, however, the *Juvenile Diabetes Foundation.*

diagnose. The disease, not the patient, is diagnosed. Do not write: *She was diagnosed with cancer.*

dial (v.) still means enter a telephone number, even on a push-button keypad.

dialect. The writer should consult an editor, and both should hesitate, before trying to render dialect in direct quotations. The results are likely to be subjective (since they depend on the home region of speaker and listener) and will strike at least some readers as patronizing. After all, national leaders and corporate executives have been known to say "gonna" and "hadda" and perhaps "y'all." Even writers with the keenest ears and most thorough notes must satisfy themselves that readers will understand why a class or group is being tarred selectively with quirks. Usually the decision should be that word order and turns of phrase paint a clearer picture than eccentric spelling. A classic Times article captured the Lower East Side of Manhattan when it quoted an onlooker, spelling intact, about the inevitable hot dog vendor at a political campaign appearance: *"Sure. For Rockefeller he gives discounts."*

diarrhea.

diaspora. Capitalize in references to the epoch in which the Jews were dispersed after the Babylonian exile, or to the body of people who were dispersed then. Lower-case in other references to scattering of national or ethnic groups.

Dictaphone is a trademark for a dictation machine.

dictionaries. Set their names in roman type, without quotation marks; capitalize the principal words. *See* SPELLING.

die-hard (n. and adj.).

dieresis. *See* ACCENT MARKS.

diesel.

Diet. It is the Japanese legislature. But except in unusually detailed references to the system or passages conveying local color, *Parliament* is a more accessible term for nonspecialized readers.

dietitian (not *dietician*).

different. To satisfy the most exacting readers, use *different* with *from*, in front of a noun: *Newspaper writing is different from poetry.* When *different* unavoidably figures in a comparison with a full clause (including its own verb), *different than* is accepted by many authorities: *Newspaper writing is different than it was 25 years ago.* But if a graceful change can convert the phrasing to allow *different from*, it should be made: *Newspaper writing is different from what it was 25 years ago.*

The adjective is unneeded in a construction like this: *She acted for three different reasons.*

diffuse, defuse. Similar pronunciation may lead to spelling confusion: *Diffuse* can be an adjective meaning *spread out* or, in the case of a speech, *wordy*; it can also be a verb meaning *spread*. The verb for removing danger is *defuse*—literally, remove a fuse.

dilemma does not mean simply a problem; it means a choice between disagreeable alternatives.

dilettante(s).

DiMaggio Highway. At least in formal references, what was once the *West Side Highway* is now *Joe DiMaggio Highway.*

dimensions, measurements, weights and proportion. When they consist of two or more elements, or when a decimal is used, state them in figures, even those below 10: *2 by 4; 7 feet 3 inches by 10 feet 5 inches* (no commas); *5 feet 10 inches tall; 6-foot-5; 6 years 5 months 13 days old; 8 pounds 3 ounces; 5 parts gin 1 part vermouth; 2 to 1; odds of 4 to 3; 8-to-1 shot; 50-50.* Also: *2½ by 4; 15½-foot tree.* But: *a two-by-four* (for the piece of lumber).

When giving a single dimension or measurement below 10, spell it out, even when it includes an ordinary fraction: *three and a quarter miles long*; *six feet tall*; *eight-pound baby*; etc. In most contexts, a spelled fraction should be expressed in the conversational form *three and a half*, not *three and one-half*.

But with a decimal: *6.5-inch snowfall*.

Diners Club, a trademark, has no apostrophe.

diphtheria.

director. Do not capitalize: *Tracy J. Bildots, director of the Federal Bureau of Investigation*; *Dale F. Lam, the director of central intelligence*; *Stacy W. Daan, a director of General Motors*. *Also see* TITLES.

Director General *Ashley B. Karitsa*; *Director General Karitsa*; *the director general*. No hyphens in this or similar titles, like *secretary general*.

disability, disabled. Mention disabilities only when their pertinence will be clear to the reader. It is acceptable to speak of someone's physical or mental *disability*, but more specific descriptions are preferred: *She cannot walk because of multiple sclerosis*. When possible, treat *disabled* as an adjective or a verb. As a noun (*the disabled*) it may seem to equate widely diverse people and undervalue the productive parts of their lives. *Also see* CRIPPLE, CRIPPLED; HANDICAPPED; IMPAIRED.

disburse (lay out money), **disperse** (scatter or spread out).

disc, disk. Use *disc* in references to phonograph records (*disc jockey, discography*), optical and laser-based devices (*compact disc, laser disc, videodisc*), farm implements (*disc harrow*) and brakes (*disc brake*). Use *disk* in references to the magnetic storage devices used with computers (*floppy disk, hard disk*) and to the fiber and cartilage between the vertebrae (*slipped disk*).

discharge. *See* FIRE, FIRING.

disco. An acceptable substitute for *discothèque* in all references. The plural is *discos*.

discomfort index. The term has been replaced by HEAT INDEX.

discreet, discrete. *Discreet* means prudent, or trustworthy with secrets. *Discrete* means separate or standing alone.

disembark. Dictionaries accept this word and *debark* equally. An economical writer may prefer the shorter one: why put people aboard (with the *em-* prefix) only to walk them down the gangway (*dis-*) again?

disinterested, uninterested. *Disinterested* means unbiased or impartial; *uninterested* means bored or indifferent.

disk. *See* DISC, DISK.

diskette, for a floppy disk. *See* DISC, DISK.

dismiss. *See* FIRE, FIRING.

dispatch. *See* ARTICLE.

distances. Many common units of distance used in the English-speaking countries, as well as many metric units, are listed separately. *Also see* METRIC SYSTEM.

district. Capitalize in a name: *Second Election District*; *10th Assembly District*; *17th Congressional District*; *District of Columbia*. The abbreviation (*Dist.*) may be used in charts and tables, but not in articles or headlines. *The District*, standing alone as a synonym for the District of Columbia, conveys an undesired insider flavor for readers outside Washington. Reserve it for special contexts warranting that tone. *See* D.C.

Also lowercase in expressions like *garment district, flower district* and *Flatiron district.*

District Attorney *Lynn R. Berenich*; *District Attorney Berenich*; *the district attorney*; *Ms. Berenich*. The plural is *district attorneys*. *Also see* D.A. and TITLES.

District of Columbia. *See* D.C.

dived (not *dove*) is the past tense of *dive.*

Divine Liturgy.

division (corporate or governmental). Lowercase: *Chevrolet division of General Motors*; *antitrust division of the Justice Department.*

division (military). Spell out numerical designations through the ninth and then use figures: *Fifth Division*; *34th Division*; *the division*. In later references, the name of an infantry division may be informally shortened by dropping the word *infantry*: *First Division* instead of *First Infantry Division*. But never, for a division, simply *the First Infantry*; that wording signifies a regiment, now ordinarily defunct but commemorated in the naming of separate battalions (*Fifth Battalion, First Infantry*). *See* REGIMENT.

divorcé(e). The term conveys a whiff of censure. Write instead—and only when pertinent—that a man or woman has been divorced or that a previous marriage ended in divorce. *Also see* MEN AND WOMEN.

D.J. (not *deejay*), for disc jockey.

D.M.D. for Doctor of Dental Medicine. *Also see* DR.

DNA may stand alone in most references for *deoxyribonucleic acid*, the material in a cell nucleus that contains the genetic code.

Dobbs Ferry (in Westchester County, N.Y.).

dock(-). Most but not all compounds formed with *dock* are one word: dock hand, dockmaster, dockside, dockyard.

doctor. *See* DR.

doctorates (earned and honorary). *See* DR.

dollars and cents. Sums of dollars and cents are usually given in figures: *5 cents*; *25 cents*; *$10*; *$12.25*; *$10,629*. But: *$1 million*; *$3.6 million*; *$895 million*; *$1.53 billion*; etc. Also: *$3 million to $6 million* (not *$3 to $6 million*); *$300,000 to $1 million*. In the simple adjective form, do not use a hyphen: *$2.5 million investment*. But hyphens must be used in longer modifiers, like these: *a $10-to-11-billion increase*; *a $2-million-a-year job.*

When it is desirable to leave sums in the millions or billions unrounded, they are expressed in the ordinary way: *$1,913,658* or *$5,937,600,823*.

Although those forms should be followed in general, it is sometimes appropriate to spell out indefinite and round sums: *a million-dollar budget*; *a million and a half dollars*; *half a million*; *a hundred dollars, more or less*; etc.

With money, in any currency, the rule of spelling below 10 does not apply: *4 cents*; *$4*. The cent symbol (*3¢*; *26¢*) may be used in headlines, financial quotations and tables or charts, but *cent* or *cents* should be spelled out in news articles: *9 cents apiece*; *26 cents a dozen*; *1-cent tax*. (But: *He said he would not give them one cent.*)

Use apostrophes in expressions like *a million dollars' worth* and *a penny's worth* (they are possessive because they mean, in effect, the worth *of a penny*). But drop the apostrophe when using the currency symbol: *$5 million worth*.

All these guides apply to sums of money both in articles and in headlines. But in headlines it is usually better to round an uneven sum that appears in the article (*$1.9 Million*, rather than *$1,913,658*) unless the exactness is important. The dollar sign may be omitted as a last resort to save a good headline that would not fit otherwise: *4.9-Billion Budget*. (Note the hyphen, which is used in the modifier form when the dollar sign is omitted.)

Also see MONEY; NUMBERS; POUNDS AND PENCE.

Dolley Madison was the wife of James. *Dolly Madison* is an ice cream and a bakery.

Dom Pérignon.

door(-). Most but not all compounds formed with *door* are one word: doorbell, doorjamb, doorkeeper, door key, doorknob, doorman, doormat, door prize, doorsill, doorstep, door-to-door (adj.), door to door (adv.), doorway.

DOS for disk operating system, the software that manages basic functions in most personal computers. The almost ubiquitous Microsoft version is MS-DOS.

dos and don'ts. Use no apostrophes to form the plurals of "words as words"—that is, words being discussed as objects, apart from what they ordinarily symbolize. Also: *ifs, ands or buts*; *yeses and noes*; *ayes and nays*.

Dostoyevsky, Fyodor. But in most references, *Dostoyevsky* will do.

dot-com is a business colloquialism for an Internet company.

double(-). Some compounds formed with *double* are one word, some are hyphenated and some are two words: double agent, double-barreled, double-blind, double boiler, double-breasted, double-check, double cross (n.), double-cross (v.), double-dealing, double dipping, double-dyed, double-edged, double entendre, double-faced, double fault (n.), double-fault (v.), doubleheader, double jeopardy, double-jointed, double-park, double-quick, double standard, double talk.

doughnut (not *donut*).

Dowager *Marchioness of Bute*; *the Lady Bute*; *the marchioness*. Capitalize the first reference as if it were a full name. A dowager peeress in Britain is the earliest surviving widow of a holder of the title. A more recent widow uses her given name before the title: *Alice Marchioness of Bute*; *Lady Bute*; *the marchioness*. Also see PEERS.

Dow Jones & Company. It publishes The Wall Street Journal and other publications, mostly business-related. It also operates Dow Jones Newswires, Dow Jones Interactive Publishing (including a publications archive) and other business news ventures. It compiles the *Dow Jones industrial average*, the *Dow Jones transportation average*, the *Dow Jones utility average* and the *Dow Jones composite average*, among other indexes. In later references and in headlines, the industrial average may be referred to as *the Dow*. In datelines: RECIFE, *Brazil, June 10 (Dow Jones)* — etc. Use this credit line on undatelined articles:

By Dow Jones

down(-). Most but not all compounds formed with *down* are one word: downbeat, downcast, downdraft, downfall, downgrade, downhearted, downhill, download, down payment, downpour, downright, downspout, downstage, downstairs, downstream, downswing, down-to-earth, downtown, downtrodden, downturn, downwind. But resist DOWNPLAY.

Down East (n., adj. and adv.). In, to or into New England, especially coastal Maine. The term alludes to *downwind* sailing, since the prevailing coastal wind is from the southwest.

downplay. An ungainly leftover from the age of penny-a-word telegram economies. Make it *play down*.

Down syndrome (not *Down's*). The older terms *mongolism* and *mongoloid* are now considered disparaging. Also see DISABILITY, DISABLED.

Dr. should be reserved for those with earned doctorates. Physicians' or dentists' titles should be used in all references: *Dr. Alex E. Baranek*; *Dr. Baranek*; *the doctor*. Others with earned doctorates, like Ph.D. degrees, may choose to use the title or not; follow their preference. Do not use the title for someone whose doctorate is honorary.

draconian. Lowercase, except in references to ancient Greece.

draft (not *draught*), for a current of air. Also: *draft beer*; *draft horse*; *draftsman*.

dramatic means *like a drama, theatrical, filled with conflict and emotion*. So there cannot be, for example, *a dramatic change in wheat yields*.

draperies is preferred to *drapes*.

Drew University (in Madison, N.J.).

drop-kick (n., v., adj.), **drop-kicking**.

drought (not *drouth*).

drunk. *He was drunk* (when the adjective follows the noun). But: *a drunken driver*; *drunken driving*.

dry dock (n.), **dry-dock** (v.).

dub. In the sense of naming or labeling (*They dubbed it the Curriculum Outreach Plan, or COP*), the overfancy word is best left for knighthood ceremonies.

duchess. Capitalize the first reference as a full name: *the Duchess of Lambsford; the duchess.* No given name, and never *Lady. Also see* PEERS.

dueling, duelist, with a single *l.*

due to. Careful writers avoid this phrase unless *due* functions as an adjective, with a specific noun to modify: *The shutdown was due to snow* (with *shutdown* as the modified noun). But not *The schools were closed due to snow*; make it *because of* snow instead. As a test, mentally ask each time: "*What* was due to an illness [or an emergency, etc.]?" If the sentence offers no single noun to answer the *what* question, use *because of.* At the start of a sentence (notably the infamous *Because of an editing error*), the needed phrase is nearly always *because of.*

duke. Capitalize the first reference as a full name: *the Duke of Lambsford; the duke.* No given name, and never *Lord. Also see* PEERS.

Duma (the lower house of the Russian legislature). Except in unusually detailed references to the system or in passages conveying local color, *Parliament* is a more accessible term for nonspecialized readers.

dumb has become a term of disparagement. Do not use it for someone who cannot speak. Instead use *mute* or say the person *cannot speak*, preferably specifying why. *Also see* DEAF and DISABILITY, DISABLED.

dumbfound, dumbfounded.

Dumpster is a trademark for a trash hauling bin.

Dun & Bradstreet. In a later reference, sparingly, and in a headline if the context is clear: *D.&B.*

du Pont, duPont, DuPont. The full, formal name of the company is *E. I. du Pont de Nemours & Company.* In later references, *the DuPont Company*, or just *DuPont.* In any article that deals with the company only peripherally, the shorter forms may be used even on first reference. The trademark for its products is *DuPont.* The company was founded by Eleuthère Irénée du Pont. Many of his descendants spell their name *duPont.* In either form, the particle *du* in the personal name should be lowercased except when it begins a sentence or a headline. *Also see* PERSONAL NAMES AND NICKNAMES.

Dupont Circle (in Washington).

Düsseldorf.

Dutch, Dutchman(men) and **Dutchwoman(women)** for the people of the Netherlands. Also *Netherlander(s)*, but never *Hollander(s)*. The adjectives are *Dutch* and *Netherlands.*

Dutchess County (in New York), with a *t.*

DVD for a digital versatile disc, a digital videodisc or the technology.

dynasties. *The Ming dynasty; the dynasty.* In China, the dynasties are *Shang, Zhou, Han, Wei, Song, Yuan, Ming and Qing. Also see* CHINESE NAMES.

Reserve *dynasty* to mean a significant period (a few generations, surely more than two) in which control of a government or region remained in the same family. Looser uses, to mean any family-run company, are trite.

E

each other, one another. Two people look at *each other*; more than two look at *one another*. In the possessive: *each other's books*, never *each others'*.

Earl *Lamb*; *Lord Lamb*; *the earl*. Never use a given name. When the title is territorial, capitalize the first reference as if it were a full name: *the Earl of Lambsford*; *Lord Lambsford*; *the earl*. In non-British systems, the equivalent title is *count*, used in first and later references. *Also see* PEERS.

earned-income tax credit.

earth, moon, sun. Lowercase, except in the specialized context of astronomy, usually in juxtaposition with other bodies and without a preceding *the*: *How do Mars and Earth fit into that pattern?* (The absence of *the* is not the test for capitalization, as *down to earth* and *move heaven and earth* demonstrate.)

earthquakes. Seismologists now usually express the intensity of an earthquake in *moment magnitude*, a measure of how much of the earth moved at the moment of the shock, and how far. (Older magnitude scales, including the Richter and the Mercalli, now mostly disused, reflected local effect but not necessarily the overall severity of a quake.) Early reports of an earthquake should refer to a *preliminary magnitude*, based on the best available estimates: *The quake had a preliminary magnitude of 6.5.* For most large earthquakes, seismologists revise the early estimate and produce a more precise figure, which can be described simply as the *magnitude*. Do not use the term *Richter scale*.

The moment magnitude scale is logarithmic: an earthquake with a magnitude of 6 releases 32 times as much energy as a magnitude 5 quake and about 1,000 times as much as a magnitude 4 quake.

It is imprecise to compare quakes measured on different scales. The San Francisco earthquake of 1906, for example, was 8.3 on the Richter scale, but is calculated at 7.9 on the moment magnitude scale.

The word for a shock is *temblor*, not *tremblor*.

earth satellites. Designate them with Arabic numerals and without quotation marks: *GOES 7*; *DFH 3*; *Sputnik 5*; etc. *Also see* ROCKETS.

east. Capitalize when referring to the region of the United States, to Asia, to the Communist bloc during the cold war or to a more local region so known: *East Texas.* Lowercase as a point of the compass.

East Bank, West Bank (of the Jordan River). Capitalize so long as the terms have political significance. Do not hyphenate the words as modifiers when they are capitalized.

East Berlin, West Berlin. *See* BERLIN.

Eastchester, East Chester. *Eastchester,* N.Y., is in Westchester County. *Eastchester* and *Eastchester Bay* are neighborhoods in the Bronx. *East Chester,* N.Y., is in Orange County.

east coast. Capitalize when referring to the region of the United States lying along the shoreline of the Atlantic Ocean; lowercase when referring to the actual shoreline.

East End (of London or Long Island).

eastern. Capitalize when referring to the eastern region of the United States, to Asia or to the countries that supported Communism in the ideological division of the world: *Eastern Europe.* But: *eastern New York; eastern France; eastern half;* etc.

Eastern Daylight Time, Eastern Standard Time (E.D.T., E.S.T.). *See* TIME.

Easterner. Capitalize when referring to a native or resident of the Eastern United States.

Eastern Hemisphere; *the hemisphere.*

Eastern Orthodoxy. A branch of Christianity that came into being after the Great Schism of 1054, it consists of 11 national churches and 4 patriarchates, which cover broader regions. The Ecumenical Patriarchate of Constantinople has jurisdiction over the Greek Orthodox Archdiocese of America. In the United States there is no single Orthodox church; rather there are several dozen separate ethnic churches, including the Orthodox Church in America and the Greek Orthodox Archdiocese. The nine largest cooperate through the Standing Conference of Canonical Bishops. *Also see* EASTERN RITE.

Eastern Rite (Roman Catholicism). It is a group of ethnic churches that accept the ecclesiastical authority of the Roman pope but follow an Eastern liturgy. Some have patriarchs. They operate with considerable independence, but any major decision, like a change in canon law, requires papal approval. Examples include the Ukrainian Catholic Church, the Syrian Catholic Church, the Greek Catholic Church and the Melkite Church. *Also see* EASTERN ORTHODOXY.

Eastern Seaboard, the region of the United States lying along the Atlantic coast. Also: *the Atlantic Seaboard.*

Eastern Shore. The area in Maryland and Virginia that is east of Chesapeake Bay.

East Germany. *See* GERMANY.

East Hampton, Easthampton. It is *East Hampton* in Suffolk County, N.Y., and in Connecticut. (Spellings for nearby Suffolk towns differ: *Bridgehampton, Southampton, Westhampton.*) But: *Easthampton,* in Massachusetts.

East Meadow (in Nassau County, N.Y.).

Eastport (in Suffolk County, N.Y.).

East Side. Capitalize it as a regularly used designation for a section of a city. In London: *East End.*

East Texas.

easygoing.

éclat.

E. coli is the abbreviation commonly used in place of *Escherichia coli,* the species name for bacteria that contaminate food and water. In the biologists' designation *E. coli O157:H7,* the character preceding the numerals is a letter *O,* not a zero. *Also see* GENUS AND SPECIES.

ecology, ecological. These words refer to the interdependence between living organisms and the environment. They are not synonymous with *environment* and *environmental,* which refer to conditions and influences that affect an organism.

e-commerce, for electronic marketing and ordering on the Internet. In a headline: *E-Commerce;* at the start of a sentence: *E-commerce.*

Economic Message. The president's and, if it is formally so called, a governor's or mayor's.

Ecstasy. Uppercase the nickname of the hallucinogenic drug known scientifically as MDMA.

Ecuadorean(s).

ecumenical council. *See* FIRST VATICAN COUNCIL and SECOND VATICAN COUNCIL.

ecumenical patriarch. *See* EASTERN ORTHODOXY.

edgy. Use the adjective to mean tense or nervous, but avoid the faddish meaning of *far out* or *on the edge;* that sense gained cliché status almost overnight.

edition(s), issue. *Issue* and *edition,* for newspapers, are not interchangeable. An *issue* means all the copies printed on a given day. There may be several *editions* of one *issue.* When referring to the full run of one day's paper use *the Nov. 5 issue* or simply *The New York Times of Nov. 5.* In citing only part of a day's run, use terms like *first edition, last edition, early editions, late editions* or if necessary *some copies of the first edition of Nov. 5.* Often *issue* and *edition* are both superfluous: *The change was first reported yesterday in The Boston Globe.*

editorial, news. In references to a newspaper, reserve *news* for the news columns and staff; reserve *editorial* for the opinion pages and their staff. The distinction cannot be applied, though, in the magazine business, which uses *editorial staff* and *editorial content* to mean everything outside the advertising columns.

editor in chief. No hyphens.

editors' notes acknowledge (and rectify, when possible) lapses of fairness, balance or perspective—faults more subtle or less concrete than factual errors, though often as grave and sometimes graver. Examples might include The Times's failure to seek a comment from someone denounced or accused in its columns, or the omission of one party's argument in a controversy, resulting from haste in fitting the article into too small a space. Or the editors may have discovered that a free-lancer, assigned to review a book, failed to divulge a conflict of interest.

The possessive is always plural: *editors' note.* A note is published only after consultation with senior masthead editors to ensure that it is as fair to the staff as to readers and to the people mentioned. The purpose is to restore perspective while assuring readers that The Times's slip did not typify its standards or policy.

The note begins by recalling the date, placement and content of the faulty article, in a sentence or two. In another few phrases, it then summarizes the passage that created the problem. It goes on to state the fault, preferably in a terse way that sheds light on The Times's journalistic practice without preaching: *In fairness, the company should have been asked for its response to the accusation.* If possible, the note then supplies what was lacking earlier: *Yesterday the company denied that its prices were out of line, citing the unusual cost of its raw materials.*

Another example: *Ms. Agnello's own book was reviewed unfavorably last year by the author she was reviewing. The Times has a policy against assigning a review in those circumstances. Ms. Agnello says she was unaware of it.*

E.D.T., E.S.T. for Eastern Daylight Time and Eastern Standard Time. *See* TIME.

E. E. Cummings (not *e. e. cummings*). Except in his poetry, he used conventional capitalization.

E.E.O.C. for the Equal Employment Opportunity Commission.

effect. *See* AFFECT, EFFECT.

e.g., representing two Latin words, *exempli gratia,* means *for example.* Not to be confused with I.E.

egg roll (the food), **egg rolling** (the frolic).

Eglin Air Force Base (not *Elgin*), in Florida.

Egypt in all references to the Arab Republic of Egypt.

EgyptAir (the Egyptian airline).

E. I. du Pont de Nemours & Company. *See* DU PONT, DUPONT, DU PONT.

1800's, 19th century. In almost all contexts, use numerals for centuries after the ninth. Also: *mid-1800's; mid-19th century.* When unavoidable, at the start of a sentence or for special effect: *eighteen-hundreds. Also see* YEARS, DECADES, CENTURIES.

either, either . . . or. When *either* is the subject, the verb is singular: *Either of the cars is available.* When *either* and *or* link singular terms, the verb is singular: *Either the* *car or the truck is available*. When *either* and *or* link a singular term and a plural one, put the plural term second and use a plural verb: *Either the car or the trucks are available*. If the mixture of terms and verbs gets awkward, recast the sentence: *The car is available, and so are the trucks*.

In an *either/or* construction, the terms that follow the two words should be parallel in form and purpose: *The chef bakes either pies or cakes daily* (not *either bakes pies or cakes*). The same principle applies to *neither/nor* and *both/and*.

El Al Israel Airlines. *El Al* will do for most references.

élan.

elderly. Use the term with care. Some readers of any age may object to the label. Phrases like *people in their 70's and older* are preferable. In writing about medicine or social policy, try to specify whose definition is being used.

-elect. *President-elect Lauren F. Cordero*; *Vice President-elect Dale C. Agneau*; *Morgan D. Baranek, the governor-elect*; *the senator-elect*. In cap-and-lowercase headlines, *Elect* is also capitalized.

Election Day. But: *election night*.

election district. *See* DISTRICT.

Electoral College. But: *electoral vote(s)*.

electrical, electronic. A light bulb and a motor are *electrical*. A television set and a computer are *electronic*; the term denotes a controlled flow of electrons through a vacuum, a gas or a semiconductor.

11th hour. But: *11th-hour* (modifier preceding a noun).

elite, elitism, elitist. No accents.

Elizabeth Marine Terminal. The shipping depot in New Jersey is *the Elizabeth Marine Terminal*, not *Port Elizabeth*. Its formal name, *the Elizabeth Port Authority Marine Terminal*, should be reserved for articles that deal centrally with its structure.

ellipsis. The symbol for an omission should appear rarely in the news columns because it diverts attention to the editing process. (*See* QUOTATIONS.) But ellipses are used freely in verbatim TEXTS AND EXCERPTS.

The ellipsis consists of three periods. Separate them with thin spaces (. . .), which prevent a line break from occurring between them. Use an ordinary space before and after the three dots. If an omission falls at the end of a sentence, place the regular period right after the last word, followed by a space, then the ellipsis: *All the news that's fit. . . .*

To mark the omission of one or more whole paragraphs, use the symbol the same way, at the end of the last paragraph before the deleted material; do not follow the more academic style of centering the ellipsis on a separate line.

Ellis Island.

"El Malei Rahamim" ("Lord Full of Mercy"), a Jewish memorial prayer.

Elmsford (in Westchester County, N.Y.).

El Niño, La Niña. *El Niño* is the periodic climate phenomenon in which tropical Pacific Ocean waters become unusually warm. It causes changes in global weather patterns, including increased rainfall in some areas and drought in others. South Americans applied the name (the Child, an allusion to the Christ Child) because the change occurs around Christmas.

La Niña is the periodic phenomenon in which tropical Pacific Ocean waters become unusually cold. This causes changes in global weather patterns, including temperatures colder than normal in some regions and warmer than normal in others. The nickname, Little Girl, was coined to contrast with *El Niño* (as was another, less used nickname, *El Viejo* — the Old Man).

For euphony, omit *El* or *La* when any such term directly follows *a* or *the*.

El Salvador. The capital is *San Salvador* and the people are *Salvadorans*.

Élysée Palace. Without *the*.

e-mail, for electronic mail. The short form is preferred in nearly all references and ordinarily needs no explanation. Also: *an e-mail message*, but not *an e-mail*. In a cap-and-lowercase headline it is *E-Mail*, and at the beginning of a sentence *E-mail*. For comprehension, an e-mail address (like *miel@nytimes.com*) should ideally be contained in a single line of type. *Also see* INTERNET ADDRESSES.

Emancipation. Uppercase in references to the freeing of the slaves in the United States.

embarrassment.

embassy. Lowercase when standing alone. But: *the United States Embassy; the French Embassy; the Argentine and Chilean Embassies; the United States Embassies in Argentina and Chile.*

emcee. Use *M.C.* instead for *master of ceremonies*.

emeritus. It should be *Dr. Dana T. Arniotis, professor emeritus of physics.* Or *emeritus professor of physics*, a smoother phrase because it keeps *professor of* intact. But never *professor of physics emeritus.* Dictionaries accept *emeritus* for both men and women, but *emerita* may be used for a woman who prefers it.

emigrate, immigrate. *Emigrate* refers to departure from a homeland; *immigrate* refers to arrival in a new country. Either word can be followed by *from* or *to*, depending on the context: When focusing on life or conditions in the old country, write, *She emigrated from Sweden* or *She emigrated to Canada.* When focusing on life or conditions in the new country, write, *She immigrated from Sweden* or *She immigrated to Canada.*

The related words *emigrant* and *immigrant* are both acceptable, though *emigrant* is rare. An *emigrant* leaves a homeland; an *immigrant* arrives in a new country. Again, the use in a phrase depends on the context. If the focus is on the old country, write, *She is an emigrant from Sweden* or *She is an emigrant to Canada.* But if the focus is on the new country, write, *She is an immigrant from Sweden* or *She is an immigrant to Canada.*

> *Also see* ILLEGAL IMMIGRANT.

émigré (masc. and fem.). The word connotes departure from a homeland for political reasons.

eminent, imminent. *Eminent* means prominent. *Imminent* means impending. (*Immanent*, a theological term rarely seen in news copy, refers to the presence of God in the universe.)

emir. *See* ARAB NAMES AND TITLES.

emirates. *See* UNITED ARAB EMIRATES.

Emmy Award(s); *the award(s); the Emmy(s).* Articles dealing centrally with the awards should mention that they are presented by the Academy of Television Arts and Sciences.

empanel. Spell it *impanel* instead.

Emperor *Akihito; the emperor.*

Empire State (New York State's nickname).

employee(s).

emporiums (not *emporia*).

Empress *Michiko; the empress.*

empty-handed.

enamored. Use preposition *of* or *with*.

encyclical. In the Roman Catholic Church, an encyclical is a formal communication from the pope to the bishops. Encyclicals usually deal with doctrine.

encyclopedia. Exception: *Encyclopaedia Britannica*, but only when its full title is used. Use encyclopedia titles without quotation marks; capitalize the principal words.

ended, ending. Use *ended* for the past, *ending* for the future: *the weather for the period ended last Tuesday; the weather for the period ending next Friday.*

enforce. But: *reinforce.*

England. Use this name, not BRITAIN, after the names of cities and towns when a locating term is needed. *Also see* UNITED KINGDOM.

English, Englishman(men) and **Englishwoman(women)** for the people of England, but not for the people of the rest of the United Kingdom. *See* BRITISH, BRITON(S).

enlisted military ranks are listed separately. *Also see* MILITARY RANKS.

enormity, enormousness. *Enormity* refers to horror or great wickedness; *enormousness* refers to size: *the enormity of the crime; the enormousness of the national debt.*

enroll, enrollment.

Ensign *Chris J. Kikondoo; Ensign Kikondoo; the ensign.*

ensure, insure. *Ensure* means guarantee or make safe: *The hit ensured a Yankee victory.* *Insure* means buy or issue insurance: *She insured her camera against theft.*

entr'acte.

entree.

entrepôt.

enumeration. When spelling out ordinal numbers before the items in a list or series, write *first, second, third,* etc., not *firstly, secondly,* etc.

When introducing a series of items that begin with paragraph marks (¶) or bullets (•), use a complete sentence, sparing readers the need to glance backward repeatedly to complete the thought (*The bill also includes these provisions: . . .*).

envelop (v.), **envelope** (n.).

environment, environmental. These words refer to the conditions and influences that affect an organism. They are not synonymous with *ecology* and *ecological,* which refer to the interdependence between the organism and the environment.

Environmental Defense is the organization formerly known as the Environmental Defense Fund. The name was changed in 2000.

E.P.A. for the Environmental Protection Agency (federal).

épée.

epic (adj.) means heroic and majestic, or legendary in importance. Bestow such hyperbole sparingly.

epilepsy, epileptic. A person with epilepsy should preferably be described that way. Use *epileptic* as an adjective (*an epileptic seizure*). Some people with the condition object to being called *epileptics,* believing that the label submerges their identity in a single aspect of their lives. *Also see* DISABILITY, DISABLED.

episcopal. Capitalize the adjective in references to the Episcopal Church and its members and clergy: *an Episcopal minister.* Use *Episcopalian(s)* for its members, as a noun only. The lowercase term *episcopal* refers in general to bishops, of any faith: *episcopal rank,* etc. For that meaning, it is often clearer to rephrase: *A meeting of bishops,* etc. *Also see* ANGLICAN COMMUNION.

Episcopal Church, rather than Protestant Episcopal Church, is acceptable in virtually all references. (The longer version remains technically correct and is sometimes used.) Use this style for a local church: *Trinity Episcopal Church.* Also: *an Episcopal church; Episcopal churches.* Never *Episcopalian church.* Also see ANGLICAN COMMUNION.

Episcopalian(s) is a noun only, for members of the Episcopal Church.

epithet, expletive. An *epithet* is a word or phrase of description, often but not always disparaging (*bean counter,* for example, for an accountant). An *expletive* is a swearword or obscenity. In rare cases, when it is necessary to show that such a word has been excised from a quotation, a text or a transcript, insert *[expletive]* in brackets;

it is redundant to add *deleted*. For a discussion of ethnic, racial, religious and sexual epithets, see SLURS. *Also see* OBSCENITY, VULGARITY, PROFANITY.

equaled, equaling.

Equal Employment Opportunity Commission (E.E.O.C.).

equally as. Do not use the words together; one will do.

Equator. But: *equatorial.*

Ericson, Leif (the explorer). But verify the spellings used for places bearing his name; they vary.

Erisa for the Employee Retirement Income Security Act, the federal law that regulates employee benefit plans. It is not a headline term and nearly always needs explanation.

Eskimo(s) is the most recognizable term for the native people in Alaska and Canada. Many of those people, though, especially in Canada, now prefer *Inuit*, which may be used in articles about specific groups who choose it, so long as the connection of the two terms is made clear.

ESP for extrasensory perception.

ESPN for the cable television service.

(-)esque. Familiar compounds with *esque* as a suffix are not hyphenated: Chaplinesque; humoresque; Kafkaesque; picturesque; Romanesque; statuesque.

Do not ordinarily hyphenate unfamiliar terms or those coined for effect (*Armaniesque; divaesque; Hiltonesque*), but ration such uses to avoid triteness.

estates. Use the names of houses and estates without quotation marks: *Blair House; the Elms.*

Estée Lauder (the cosmetics company).

esthetic. Use *aesthetic* instead.

etc. for et cetera. It rarely serves much purpose in news writing, except for special effect.

ethics can be singular or plural. Use a singular verb when the word refers to an art or science: *Ethics is a branch of philosophy.* But use a plural verb in reference to practices: *Her ethics are beyond reproach.*

ethnic. Use the word freely as an adjective (*ethnic group*), but not as a noun except in direct quotations. The political coinage (*white ethnics*) is condescending.

ethnicity should be mentioned only when it is pertinent and its pertinence is clear to the reader. The ethnicity of a candidate is pertinent if she uses it to appeal for votes. The ethnicity of a person sought by the police may be an essential part of a physical description. But the ethnicity of a person convicted of a crime is not pertinent unless the case has ethnic overtones that are worth describing in the coverage.

ethnic slurs. *See* SLURS.

étude.

Eucharist. In the Roman Catholic and Anglican (Episcopal) traditions, *eucharist* is a synonym for HOLY COMMUNION. The adjective is *eucharistic*. Uppercase either term when it is used as the name of a religious service; lowercase when designating the sacrament that is part of the service.

euphemisms are devices to conceal harsh or unattractive truths. They rarely belong in the newspaper. In news copy (other than direct quotations and texts), people *die*; they do not *expire* or *pass on*.

Euratom for the European Atomic Energy Community. *See* EUROPEAN UNION.

euro(s) for the unified currency used by many European countries. After it was introduced, on Jan. 1, 1999, national currencies like the German mark were to remain in existence for three more years, but with specified values relative to the euro. National currencies were to be withdrawn early in 2002. See EUROPEAN UNION.

Eurocurrency, Eurodollar. *Eurocurrency* is money held in banks outside its country of origin. *Eurodollars* are United States dollars held in banks outside the United States, especially in Europe. These and similar coinages should be used only when their meaning is clear. Not to be confused with EURO(S).

European Community. *See* EUROPEAN UNION.

European Economic Community (former organization). *See* EUROPEAN UNION.

European Free Trade Association; *the association.* Do not use the unfamiliar acronym *EFTA* except in a direct quotation or a text.

European Monetary Union. *See* EUROPEAN UNION.

European Union. Established in 1991, it is the umbrella organization intended to integrate the trade practices, fiscal and monetary policies and military programs of its member countries. In 1999, they were Belgium, France, Germany, Italy, Luxembourg and the Netherlands (the founders of what was the European Economic Community) plus Austria, Britain, Denmark, Finland, Greece, Ireland, Portugal, Spain and Sweden.

Three older bodies exist within the union: the *European Community* (previously called the European Economic Community, or informally the Common Market), the *European Atomic Energy Community* (or Euratom) and the *European Coal and Steel Community*. An arm of the European Union is the *European Monetary Union*.

Resist *E.U.* in headlines; *Europe* or *Europeans* will usually do.

evade, avoid. *Evade* carries a suggestion of deceit or irresponsibility. *Avoid* is the more neutral term, in a context like taxes or punishment. Tax *avoidance* is ordinarily legal; tax *evasion* is not.

evangelical. The preferred term for conservative Protestants of many denominations who describe themselves as born again. Only a small minority of evangelicals would describe themselves as FUNDAMENTALIST, so the terms are not synonymous.

And to some readers, *fundamentalist* can carry a pejorative suggestion of rigidity or primitivism.

Evangelical Lutheran Church in America.

evangelist. In lowercase, it is a term for a preacher of the Christian Gospel, a revivalist. When capitalized, singular or plural, it is used only in references to Matthew, Mark, Luke and John, the Evangelists who wrote the Gospels.

even(-). Some compounds formed with *even* are one word, some are two words and some are hyphenated: even break, evenhanded, even money (n.), even-money (adj.), even-steven.

ever(-). Most but not all compounds formed with *ever* are one word: ever-faithful, evergreen, everlasting, evermore, ever-present, ever-ready.

every(-). Most but not all compounds formed with *every* are one word: everybody, everyday (adj.), everyone (pron.), everything (pron.), everywhere.

But in some instances: *every one*. See EVERYONE, EVERY ONE.

everybody, everyone. Always singular. *See* ANYBODY, ANYONE, EVERYBODY, EVERYONE, NO ONE, SOMEONE and EVERYONE, EVERY ONE.

everyone, every one. The one-word form is a pronoun meaning all the people, or everybody: *Everyone came to the seance*. The two words (a modifier and a noun) mean each one of a group: *Every one of her predictions came true*; *Every one of the defendants was heard*. Note that *everyone* (like *everybody*) is singular: *He wanted everyone to become a veterinarian*. Not: *to become veterinarians*. *Also see* ANYBODY, ANYONE, EVERYBODY, EVERYONE, NO ONE, SOMEONE.

ex(-). Use the hyphen when *ex-* means former: *ex-champion*; *ex-president*; *ex-tennis player*. In articles, *former* is generally preferred, but *Ex-* is almost always used in headlines (and the word after the hyphen is capitalized). Do not hyphenate Latin phrases like *ex officio*, even in modifier form (*ex officio chairman*), or expressions like *ex cathedra, ex dividend, ex parte, ex post facto*.

excerpts are *from* documents, speeches, etc., not *of* them. Principles of editing verbatim documents appear in TEXTS AND EXCERPTS.

exchanges. Many major stock and commodity exchanges are listed separately.

exclamation point. For the placement of an exclamation point alongside other punctuation, see PARENTHESES and QUOTATION MARKS.

In news writing, the exclamation point is rarely needed except in quotations of shouted or deeply emotional phrases: *"Watch out!" the pedestrians called. "Hang him!" the crowd shouted. "That is a monstrous lie!" he roared*. When overused, the exclamation point loses impact, as advertising demonstrates continually.

execute, execution. *Execute* means put to death under a criminal sentence. It is not a synonym for *kill, murder* or *assassinate*. *Also see* ASSASSIN, ASSASSINATE, ASSASSINATION.

executive branch (of the United States government). Also: *legislative branch*; *judicial branch*.

Executive Mansion.

executive order (by a president of the United States). But capitalize when citing one by number: *Executive Order 39*.

exhilarate.

exit numbers. Capitalize them as proper names: *Exit 127*; *Exit 16*. *See* NUMBERED EXPRESSIONS.

exorbitant.

Export-Import Bank; *the bank. Ex-Im Bank* may also be used in quotations, and in headlines when the context is clear.

exposé (n.).

Expressionism (art, literature, music). Capitalize only in reference to the painting, sculpture and literary movements that emerged in Germany and Austria in the early 1900's. *See* ABSTRACT EXPRESSIONISM and ARTS TERMINOLOGY.

Express Mail is a service mark of the United States Postal Service.

expressway. Capitalize in names: *Long Island Expressway*. But: *the expressway*.

extra(-). Most but not all compounds formed with *extra* are one word: extra-base hit, extracurricular, extra-fine, extrajudicial, extra-large, extramarital, extramural, extraordinary, extrasensory, extraterrestrial, extraterritorial.

Exxon Mobil Corporation was formed in 1999 through the merger of the Exxon Corporation and the Mobil Oil Corporation. While the Exxon trademark long ago replaced Esso in the United States, the old brand name is still used overseas.

eyewitness. In general *witness* is preferred.

E-ZPass is a trademark for the cashless toll collection system.

F

F.A.A. for the Federal Aviation Administration.

facade. No cedilla beneath the *c*.

facilities. It is an acceptable general term for buildings, plants, recreational equipment and the like. The singular *facility*, applied to an individual place, is bureaucratic and should be replaced by specifics when possible: *base, building, factory, laboratory, office, pier, plant, warehouse*, etc.

facsimile. When the reference is to the conventional *fax* process, use that word instead, in all references.

fact-finding (adj.).

faculty, like *army* and *clergy*, is collective, referring not to individuals but to the group. For individuals, use *faculty members* or *members of the faculty*. References to *three faculty* or to *hiring faculty* are jargon.

fade(-). Most but not all compounds formed with *fade* are hyphenated: fade away (v.), fadeaway (n.), fade-in (n.), fade in (v.), fade-out (n.), fade out (v.).

Fahrenheit. The temperature scale commonly used in the United States. In it, the freezing point of water is 32 degrees and the boiling point is 212 degrees. In general, ordinary references to temperature do not specify the scale. (*See* TEMPERATURE.) In the special cases that require mention of the scale, use the style *86 degrees Fahrenheit* or (usually in tables) *48°F*, without a space before or after the degree symbol and without a period after the *F*. To convert a Celsius or centigrade temperature to Fahrenheit, multiply by 9, divide by 5 and add 32. *Also see* CELSIUS, CENTIGRADE and KELVIN.

Fairfield University (in Fairfield, Conn.).

Fair Lawn (in New Jersey).

Fairleigh Dickinson University (in Madison and Teaneck, N.J.).

fairness and impartiality. The news columns take no sides and play no favorites, in what they cover or what they omit. When reporting on conflict, they give all parties a chance to be heard. If a person or institution is criticized in an article, the subject must have an opportunity to reply. If the attack is detailed or occurs in a deeply researched article, time and space must be allowed for the subject's thoughtful comment. A reporter must make every effort to reach those criticized. If they cannot be found, the article should say what effort was made, over how long a time, and tell why it did not succeed. (*Could not be reached for comment* is too perfunctory an explanation.)

Conflict does not automatically dominate the news. An article about an initiative (by government, business or any institution) should normally report the development before setting out critics' objections or focusing on its vulnerability, and the headline should reflect that priority.

The Times forgoes innuendo: an accusation that would not be acceptable if made outright cannot be implied through sly juxtaposition, the print equivalent of a cocked eyebrow.

Writers and editors should guard against word choices that undermine neutrality. If one politician is *firm* or *resolute*, an opponent should not be *rigid* or *dogmatic*. If one country in a conflict has a *leadership* while the other has a *regime*, impartiality suffers. Negative overtones, in coverage of a figure in the news, are easily detected and repaired. But worshipful overtones can be a more insidious form of partiality, giving their subject an advantage over rivals.

Divisive issues like religion, politics, abortion and race relations call for extra sensitivity to neutrality in language. For an example, see ABORTION.

Special care must be taken when partisan information comes from news sources who are identified incompletely or not at all. They should not be permitted the appearance or the reality of hiding behind the newspaper when attacking others. *See* ANONYMITY.

And when, despite all efforts, The Times slips from neutrality, it is prompt and thorough in rectifying errors or lapses of fairness. *See* CORRECTIONS and EDITORS' NOTES.

fake, forgery, copy (art). A *fake* or *forgery* is made with the intent to deceive. A *copy* can be a study or a work in homage to another artist. *Also see* REPLICA.

fall (autumn).

false titles. Do not make titles out of mere descriptions, as in *harpsichordist Dale S. Yagyonak*. If in doubt, try the "good morning" test. If it is not possible to imagine saying, for example, "Good morning, Harpsichordist Yagyonak," the title is false.

A limited exception applies to sports articles: team names and positions (*third baseman, Yankee catcher*) may be used in front of names. *Also see* TITLES.

Fannie Mae, in later references, for the Federal National Mortgage Association. Its bonds are known as *Fannie Maes*.

fantasy (music). In titles that include the word without quotation marks, use the English spelling: *Schubert's Fantasy* [not *Fantasia*] *in C for Violin and Piano* (*Op. 159*). *See* MUSIC.

F.A.O., sparingly, for the Food and Agriculture Organization (not *Agricultural*).

F. A. O. Schwarz (the toy store), with thin spaces between the personal initials.

far(-). Most but not all compounds formed with *far* are hyphenated: far-fetched, far-flung, far-off, far-ranging, far-reaching, farseeing, farsighted (all adj.). Also: *faraway* (adj.), but *far away* (adv.).

Far East. It comprises Australia, Cambodia, China, Indonesia, Japan, Laos, Malaysia, Myanmar, New Zealand, North Korea, the Philippines, Singapore, South Korea, Taiwan, Thailand and Vietnam.

farm(-). Most but not all compounds formed with *farm* are one word: farm club (sports), farmhand, farmhouse, farmland, farm out, farm team, farmyard.

Far North.

Farrar, Straus & Giroux (the publisher).

Farrell Lines (the ocean carrier).

farther, further. Use *farther* for distance, *further* to mean additional or continued.

Far West, for the region of the United States.

FASB may be used sparingly, in financial contexts, for the Financial Accounting Standards Board. No periods because it is an acronym, pronounced FASS-bee.

Fascism, fascist. Capitalize in historical references to the Italian Fascist movement and party or to their members. But: *The Senator said his rival was a fascist* (or *had fascist tendencies*).

fast breeder reactor. Sometimes called a *fast reactor* or a *breeder reactor*, it produces more nuclear fuel than it consumes.

Fatah. *See* AL FATAH.

father. Lowercase except when it substitutes for a proper name: *Ask Father to lend you the spatula. Also see* DAD.

Father (clerical title) is used in later references to Roman Catholic and Orthodox priests, and to Episcopal priests who choose that style: *The Rev. Morgan J. Lamm*; *Father Lamm.*

Father's Day.

fatwa (a decree by an Islamic religious leader).

fauvism (art). Capitalize when referring to the exuberant, bright-colored paintings of Matisse and other French artists in the early 20th century. Lowercase when referring generically to a style employing splashy, bright color. *See* ARTS TERMINOLOGY.

faux, meaning artificial or imitation, has a place in art and design writing. Elsewhere it is pretentious.

faux pas.

fax (adj., n. and v.). It is short for *facsimile*, but the short form is preferred in references to the office equipment and its technology.

F.B.I. for the Federal Bureau of Investigation.

F.C.C. for the Federal Communications Commission.

F.D.A. for the Food and Drug Administration, sparingly and in headlines.

F.D.I.C. for the Federal Deposit Insurance Corporation.

featherbedding is the labor practice of requiring more workers than necessary to do a job. Applied to a specific workplace or dispute, the term is partisan: what the management calls featherbedding the union may call a necessity for productivity or safety. (For bedclothes, the spelling is *feather bedding*.)

Feb. for February before numerals (*Feb. 12*), or in charts and tables.

Fed, the, in later references to the Federal Reserve Board and in headlines.

federal (architecture and decorative arts). Capitalize when referring to the buildings and furniture built in the United States after the establishment of the federal government and through the early 19th century, and characterized by adaptations of classical forms. Modern buildings of a similar design should be labeled *federal style*. *See* ARTS TERMINOLOGY.

federal (governmental). Capitalize when part of a proper name (*Federal Reserve Board*; *Federal Bureau of Investigation*) but lowercase in other uses: *federal courts*; *federal troops*; *federal agents*.

Federal Building, capitalized, may be used alone when it is part of the name of a specific building and the identity is clear. Otherwise, on first reference, use a name like *the Jacob K. Javits Federal Building*.

federal courts. *See* COURTS.

Federal Election Commission; *the commission.* The abbreviation, *F.E.C.*, is not recognizable enough for headlines and should generally occur only in direct quotations.

Federal Emergency Management Agency. In later references, *the agency* or, rarely, *FEMA* (which is too obscure for headlines).

Federal Energy Regulatory Commission. In later references, *the commission* or *the agency.* The acronym *FERC* may occur in direct quotations.

Federal Hall National Memorial. This building, at Wall and Nassau Streets in New York City, is the former Subtreasury Building.

Federal Highway Administration. Do not abbreviate. Use *the administration* or *the agency* instead.

Federal Home Loan Mortgage Corporation has officially been renamed FREDDIE MAC.

Federal Housing Administration. In later references, sparingly, the *F.H.A.*

Federal Reserve Board. In later references, *the Federal Reserve*; *the Reserve*; *the board*; *the Fed.* Also, *the Federal Reserve System*; *the Federal Reserve Bank of New York* (or *Boston*, etc.); *the system*; *the bank*.

Federal Trade Commission. In later references, sparingly, *the F.T.C.*

Federation of Jewish Philanthropies. The New York regional organization is now part of the merged UJA-FEDERATION OF NEW YORK.

fellow (adj.). Do not hyphenate: *fellow American, fellow citizen, fellow traveler, fellow worker*, etc.

fellowships and scholarships. *Nieman fellow; White House fellow; a fellow of the university; the Nieman fellowship.* Also: *Fulbright scholar; Rhodes scholar; Rhodes scholarship.*

FEMA, but rarely, in later references to the Federal Emergency Management Agency.

female, male. In references to people, the nouns *woman, man, girl* and *boy* are most natural. If a construction unavoidably warrants *male* and *female*, use them as adjectives, not nouns. Avoid affixing *male* and *female* to occupational titles (*male nurse, female judge*) in ways that imply that they "normally" belong to only one sex. Preferably write, for example, *women on the faculty* or *men on the faculty. Also see* MEN AND WOMEN.

feminism, feminist. *See* MEN AND WOMEN.

feng shui is the traditional Chinese practice of finding auspicious locations for buildings, cities and graves.

Ferris wheel.

fete. No accent except in a proper name or a foreign phrase (*Salle des Fêtes*). As an English noun or verb, though, *fete* usually sounds contrived and old-fashioned.

fewer, less. Use *fewer* for people or things that can be counted one by one: *Fewer than 100 taxidermists attended.* If the number is one, write *one vote fewer*, not *one fewer votes* or *one fewer vote.* Use *less* for things that cannot be counted: *Most shoppers are buying less sugar.* Also use *less* with a number that describes a quantity considered as a single bulk amount: *The police recovered less than $1,500; It happened less than five years ago; The recipe calls for less than two cups of sugar.*

few who. The construction *one of the few who* requires a plural verb: *She is one of the few editors who parse perfectly.* (It is equivalent to *Of the few editors who parse perfectly, she is one.*)

F.H.A. for the Federal Housing Administration, sparingly.

fiancé (masc.), **fiancée** (fem.).

Fiberglas is a trademark. But *glass fiber* and (usually better) *fiberglass* are generic terms.

fictional devices. The Times's reporting sets out to be truthful in every detail. No reader should find cause to suspect that the paper would knowingly alter facts. For that reason, The Times refrains outright from assigning fictional names, ages, places or dates, and it strictly limits the use of other concealment devices.

　　If compassion or the unavoidable conditions of reporting require shielding an identity, the preferred method is to omit the name and explain the omission. (That situation might arise, for example, in an interview conducted inside a hospital or a school governed by privacy rules.) If a complex narrative must distinguish among several shielded identities, it may be necessary to use given names with last initials or, less desirable, given names alone (*Hilary K.*; *Ashley M.*; *Terry*). Descriptions may serve instead (*the lawyer*; *the Morristown psychotherapist*). As a rare last resort, if genuine given names would be too revealing, real or coined single initials (*Dr. D*; *Ms. L*) may be used after consultation with senior editors. The article must gracefully indicate the device and the reason. *Also see* ANONYMITY.

fief means land or domain. So *fiefdom* is redundant.

Field Marshal *Viscount Montgomery of Alamein*; *Viscount Montgomery*; *Lord Montgomery*; *Field Marshal Montgomery*. It is never *Marshal Montgomery*.

Fifth Amendment. Avoid expressions, like *took the Fifth Amendment*, that imply a scheme to escape justice. Neutral phrases include *invoked her Fifth Amendment right* or *cited his Fifth Amendment right against self-incrimination*.

figuratively. Do not use *literally* when *figuratively* is meant: *The Democratic leaders are literally walking a tightrope.*

figures. *See* NUMBERS and NUMBERS, ROUND.

file name (not *filename*).

filet, fillet. Use *filet* if the term is French: *filet mignon*. But make it *fillet* if the term is English: *fillet of sole*.

Filipino(s). The people of the Philippines, male and female. The adjective is *Filipino* or *Philippine*.

Filipino names. Do not use accent marks, even in the names that are Spanish in origin.

filmmaker.

films. Put their titles in quotation marks, with principal words capitalized.

filmstrip.

final (sports). A one-game or one-match championship is a *final*. A championship series can be called *finals*.

finalize. Though the dictionary blesses it, *finalize* has a bureaucratic sound.

"Finnegans Wake." No apostrophe; James Joyce omitted it from the title of his novel for the sake of a wordplay.

fire(-). Most but not all compounds formed with *fire* are one word: fire alarm, firearm, fireball, firebase, fireboat, firebomb (n. and v.), firebomber, firebombing, firebrand, firebreak, firebug, fire chief, fire company, firecracker, fire door, fire drill, fire engine, fire escape, fire extinguisher, firefight, firefighter, firefly, firehouse, fire hydrant, firelight, fire marshal, fireplace, fireplug, firepower, fireproof, fire sale, firestorm, firetrap, fire truck, fire wall, fire warden, firewood, fireworks.

Fire Department; *the department*. In headlines, *Fire Dept.* is acceptable. *Also see* NEW YORK FIRE DEPARTMENT.

Firefighter *Merrill E. Anyell*; *Firefighter Anyell*; *the firefighter*. This is the rank in the NEW YORK FIRE DEPARTMENT. *Also see* FIREMAN, FIREWOMAN.

fire (v.), **firing** (n.). These terms, once colloquial for the removal of an employee, are now standard English. But use them only for a dismissal resulting from employer dissatisfaction or from a dispute over job performance. *Discharge, dismiss* and *dismissal*, while less abrupt-sounding, should also be confined to that sense. None of the terms apply to a resignation under criticism or departure by mutual consent. Nor do they apply to employees' removal as a cost-cutting measure, or to reduction of a work force; the terms in that case are *lay off* (v.) and *layoff* (n.).

fireman, firewoman. *Firefighter* is preferred in virtually all references.

fire wall. Two words, for the physical kind or the computer security system.

firm (n.). Technically, a firm is an unincorporated partnership or business. But idiom permits the term for *member firms* of securities exchanges, even if incorporated, and for professional groupings of lawyers, architects, accountants, etc. *Also see* COMPANY AND CORPORATION NAMES.

first, firstly. Use *first*, not *firstly*, in enumerations.

first(-). Some compounds formed with *first* are one word, some are hyphenated and some are two words: first aid (n.), first-aid (adj.), first base, first baseman, firstborn, first-class (adj.), first floor (n.), first-floor (adj.), first grader, firsthand (adj., adv.), at first hand, first-rate (adj.), first strike (n.), first-strike (adj.).

first come first served. Hyphenate when the phrase is used as a modifier before a noun: *the first-come-first-served tradition.* Otherwise, omit all punctuation: *the principle of first come first served.*

first in first out. Hyphenate when the phrase is used as a modifier before a noun: *the first-in-first-out system.* Otherwise, omit all punctuation: *the principle of first in first out.* Also, in later references, but only in unmistakable business contexts, *FIFO.*

first lady. Lowercase, and always standing alone or separated from the name by a comma: *the first lady, Leigh C. Lamm.* The term applies to the wife of a president, a prime minister, a governor or a mayor in her public role as a spouse, but use her name instead when her independent activities make news.

First Lt. *Hilary N. Kuzu; Lieutenant Kuzu; the lieutenant.*

First Sgt. *Lauren U. Daan; Sergeant Daan; the sergeant.*

First Vatican Council. An assembly of the bishops of the Roman Catholic Church that was held in 1869-70. In later references, use *Vatican I.* Follow the same style for the Second Vatican Council, held 1962-65. It is *Vatican II.*

fiscal year. The term means the 12-month period used by a company or a government for its bookkeeping. Write *the 1998 fiscal year*, not *fiscal 1998*. The federal government's fiscal year begins on Oct. 1, so the period between Oct. 1, 1998, and Sept. 30, 1999, was *the 1999 fiscal year*. If a company's fiscal year does not correspond to the calendar year, say when it begins or ends: *The division was profitable* *in the 1998 fiscal year, which ended June 30. If the fiscal and calendar years co-incide, make it simply The division was profitable in 1997.*

Fishers Island (in New York). But it is *Fisher Island* in Florida.

fit. *Fitted* is the preferred past tense and past participle.

fit to a T.

fjord (not *fiord*).

flack, flak. Both words are slang. *Flack* is a noun for a press agent and a verb for drumming up publicity. *Flak,* a cliché derived from the German for antiaircraft fire, means criticism.

flag(-). Most but not all compounds formed with *flag* are one word: flagman, flagpole, flagship, flagstaff, flagstone, flag stop, flag-waving, flagwoman. But: *American-flag ship* in reference to a ship of American registry.

flag-draped coffin. A journalese cliché. (Even *the coffin was draped with a flag* is an improvement.) In a picture caption the phrase also commits the sin of telling readers something they can see for themselves.

flap. As a noun to mean fuss or controversy, *flap* is colloquial and trite.

flaunt, flout. *Flaunt* means show off; *flout* means defy or show contempt.

fleet. Capitalize only when part of a title: *Atlantic Fleet; British Grand Fleet.* Also: *Sixth Fleet.*

fleur(s)-de-lis.

flier can mean a pilot, a fast train or a leaflet. Not *flyer.*

Flight Lt. *Stacy H. Barany* (British and other air forces); *Flight Lieutenant Barany; the flight lieutenant.*

flight numbers. Capitalize them as proper names: *Flight 9; Flight 111.*

floor leader should be lowercased and separated from the name by a comma: *Representative Lee H. Milori, the Democratic floor leader;* or *the floor leader, Lee H. Milori.*

floppy disk. The portable storage medium used in a computer. Also: *diskette.* But see DISC, DISK.

Florida. Abbreviate as *Fla.* after the names of cities, towns and counties.

Florida East Coast Railway.

Floridian(s).

flounder, founder. *Flounder* means stumble or flail; *founder* means sink or collapse.

flout, flaunt. *Flout* means defy or show contempt; *flaunt* means show off.

Floyd Bennett Field (in Brooklyn) was New York City's first airport. Now a Coast Guard air station and part of a national park.

Flushing Meadows-Corona Park (in Queens).

flyer. See FLIER.

focused.

foe means enemy. Despite its usefulness in headlines, it is an exaggeration for most political campaigns. Use *rival* or *opponent* instead.

(-)fold. With this suffix, spell out any numeral that can be written as a solid word: *twofold; threefold; twentyfold; hundredfold; thousandfold; millionfold.* When the numeral cannot be written solid, use figures followed by a hyphen: *22-fold; 106-fold; 200-fold; 3,000-fold.* Any numeral above nine may be used in a headline: *10-fold; 100-fold;* etc. *Twofold* means multiplied by two. *Also see* MANIFOLD, MANYFOLD.

Folies-Bergère.

folk(-). Most but not all compounds formed with *folk* are two words: folk dance (n.), folk-dance (adj.), folklore, folk medicine, folk music, folk-rock, folk singer, folk song.

folks will have a place in the occasional feature article about homespun America. Otherwise it strikes a false note in the news columns and often sounds condescending.

follow(-). Compounds formed with *follow* are hyphenated: follow-through (n.), follow-up (n. and adj.).

following is almost always more cumbersome than *after* in this construction: *He went home after the game.*

Fond du Lac (in Wisconsin).

fondle. It means caress or stroke in a tender way. The word is not suitable for descriptions of rape, assault or unwelcome advances. *Grab, grope* or *touch* may be more appropriate.

Food and Agriculture Organization (F.A.O.), not *Agricultural.*

Food and Drug Administration. In later references, sparingly, and in headlines, *F.D.A.*

fool(-). Compounds formed with *fool* are one word: foolhardy, foolproof, foolscap.

foot(-). Most but not all compounds formed with *foot* are one word: foot brake, footbridge, foot-candle, footgear, foothill, foothold, footlights, footlocker, footloose, footman, footnote, footpad, footpath, foot-pound, footprint, footrace, footrest, foot soldier, footsore, footstep, footstool, footwear, footwork.

footage. As a synonym for film or videotape, *footage* is jargon.

foot-and-mouth disease (not *hoof-and-mouth disease*).

football. Give points, scores and yards in figures: *Milori ran for only 3 yards; Lam scored 9 points in the second quarter; Columbia won, 13-6.* Spell out the numbers of downs.

The best-known professional organization is the *National Football League;* its annual championship, the *Super Bowl,* is designated by Roman numerals. The 1999 game was *Super Bowl XXXIII.*

Avoid *grid, gridder, win* (as a noun), *pigskin* and similarly tired terms.

forbear, forebear. *Forbear* means refrain. *Forebear* means an ancestor. (*Forebearer* is not a word.)

Ford Motor Company.

fore(-). Most but not all compounds formed with *fore* are one word: forebode, forecourt, forefather, forefront, forehand, foreknowledge, foremast, foreordain, forepaw, foreplay, forerun, foresee, foreshadow, foreshorten, foreshow, foresight, forestall, foretaste, foretell, fore-topmast, fore-topsail, forewarn. *Also see* FORBEAR, FOREBEAR; FOREMAN, FOREWOMAN; FOREWORD; FORGO, FOREGO.

forego. *See* FORGO, FOREGO.

foreign currencies. When amounts of foreign money are mentioned in news articles, they should be converted into dollars at the latest available exchange rates: *The price was 100 French francs, or $17.* (The translation may appear in parentheses when that is smoother.) Use the symbol (£) for the British pound, but spell out other currency names, including foreign dollars: *100 Canadian dollars, or $74.* When a foreign sum is given in round numbers, round the translation as well, especially if the details are immaterial. *See* DOLLARS AND CENTS; EURO(S); FRANCS AND CENTIMES; MONEY; POUNDS AND PENCE.

Foreign Legion. Capitalize only in reference to the French force. On later references: *the legion.*

Foreign Minister (or *Secretary*) *Morgan I. Yagyonak*; *the foreign minister* (or *foreign secretary*); *the minister* (or *secretary*). *Also see* TITLES.

Foreign Ministry (for a specific one). In later references, *the ministry.*

foreign names. Within The Times, all departments should consult the foreign copy desk about individual spellings and usage adopted on the advice of correspondents or at the request of foreign personalities. If a Russian or other foreign cultural figure performs or records often in the West and is the subject of extensive advertising or promotion, use the artist's preferred spelling. The goal is to avoid inconsistency between highly visible publicity materials and the news columns. More general guides to personal and place names may be found on these Web sites operated by the Central Intelligence Agency for public use:

> http://www.odci.gov/cia/publications/factbook/index.html
> http://www.odci.gov/cia/publications/chiefs/index.html

This stylebook is the authority, however, for the use or omission of accent marks and for the handling of names covered by these specific entries: ACCENT MARKS; ARAB NAMES AND TITLES; BURMESE NAMES; CAMBODIAN NAMES; CHINESE NAMES; FILIPINO NAMES; GEOGRAPHIC NAMES; JAPANESE NAMES; KOREAN NAMES; LAOTIAN NAMES; MALAYSIAN NAMES; RUSSIAN NAMES; SPANISH NAMES; THAI NAMES; VIETNAMESE NAMES.

Foreign Service. Capitalize when referring to the career diplomatic service of the United States; otherwise lowercase: *She was formerly general director of the Foreign Service*; *He was in the British foreign service.*

foreign words. Follow English capitalization style in the foreign title of a literary or artistic work, or the proper name of an organization. (For the single exception, see SONGS.) German nouns are always uppercased in German phrases, but lowercase them when they occur in English phrases: *The professor sighed, her weltschmerz showing.* (Usually, though, English synonyms are less pretentious and thus preferred.) *Also see* ACCENT MARKS; CAPITALIZATION; ITALICS; TITLES.

foreman, forewoman. Do not use *forelady* or *foreperson. Also see* MEN AND WOMEN.

foreword. It is the introduction to a book (the *word* be*fore* Chapter 1). Do not confuse with FORWARD.

forgery (in art). *See* FAKE, FORGERY, COPY.

forgo, forego. *Forgo* means refrain. *Forego*, which is relatively rare, means precede. Thus: *foregone conclusion*, an outcome determined be*fore*hand.

formal wear.

former. It is the preferred modifier before a title (*former commissioner*), though *Ex-* is useful in headlines (with an uppercase letter after the hyphen).

Avoid uses of *former* that force the reader to glance back (*Ms. Agnello and Mr. Dann waged hard campaigns, and the former prevailed*). Rephrase and name names.

Formica is a trademark.

formulas (not *formulae*).

for-profit, as a modifier, has an artificial sound. Use *profit-making* or *commercial* instead. Also: *nonprofit* rather than the contrived *not-for-profit.*

forswear.

fort. Spell out in news copy and capitalize as part of a name: *Fort Hamilton.* The abbreviation (*Ft.*) may be used with the name in a headline, a chart, a list or a map.

fortnight. Use *two weeks* instead.

fortuitous means happening by chance. It does not mean fortunate.

49er(s). There is no apostrophe in the name of the football team. And a person who went to California in search of gold in 1849 was a *forty-niner.*

forward (not *forwards*) means up front or toward the front. Do not confuse with FOREWORD.

founder, flounder. *Founder* means sink or collapse; *flounder* means stumble or flail awkwardly.

founding fathers. Lowercase the expression. And unless referring narrowly to the authors of the Constitution, seek a phrase (like *founders* or *colonists*) that un-self-consciously encompasses both sexes.

401(k) for a retirement savings plan financed by employee contributions, often with employer matching funds. It takes its name from the section of the Internal Revenue Code that authorized it. Plural: *401(k)'s.*

Fourth Estate. Capitalize when the reference is to the public press.

Fourth of July. Also *Independence Day.*

fowl (sing. and pl.).

fractions. When fractions appear by themselves in ordinary copy, follow these spelling styles: *one-half inch* (not ½ *inch*); *one-half an inch; half an inch* (preferred); *two-tenths; one-twentieth; one twenty-first; one-thirtieth; one thirty-second; 21 thirty-seconds; one-hundredth; two-hundredths; two one-hundredths; 20 one-hundredths; twenty-hundredths; 21-hundredths; one-103rd; twenty-five 103rds; nine-thousandths; nine one-thousandths; nine-1,009ths; 63 one-thousandths.*

In these examples the numerator and the denominator are connected by a hyphen when neither includes a hyphen: *one-twentieth.* But it is *one twenty-third* when an element does include a hyphen. Also note that numerals are used to render fractions like *103rd,* which would be cumbersome if spelled out. Finally, spell out the first element in *twenty-five 103rds* to avoid a confusing pileup of numerals.

Use numerals wherever the fraction appears with a full number in ages, pairs of dimensions, etc.: *3½-year-old; 3½ by 2½* (or *3.5 by 2.5*). In other cases, follow the rule for spelling out below 10: *He reigned for six and a half years* (smoother in this case than *one-half*). *His reign lasted 31½ years. See* DECIMALS and NUMBERS.

framers (of the Constitution). Lowercase.

frame-up (n.).

Franco-. In references to France, use the more conversational *French-American, French-German,* etc.

François.

francophone. In general, use *French-speaking* instead.

francs and centimes. Spell out when the figures are given: *5 francs; 5.40 francs; 15 million francs; 15 centimes. See* FOREIGN CURRENCIES and NUMBERS, ROUND.

Frankfurt (in Germany).

Franklin D. Roosevelt Drive. In headlines and in later references: *F.D.R. Drive; the drive.*

fraternal societies. Capitalize their names: *Knights of Columbus; Masons; Odd Fellows;* etc. Lowercase the titles of officers, and separate them from the name with a comma: *the grand ruler, Tracy B. Miel; Merrill C. Yagyonak, the exalted ruler; the sachem.*

Frau, Fräulein. *See* COURTESY TITLES.

Fraunces Tavern.

freakish (adj.). It is a *freakish storm*, not a *freak storm*.

Freddie Mac is the official name of the federally chartered, publicly held company formerly known as the Federal Home Loan Mortgage Corporation. Its securities are *Freddie Macs*.

free(-). Some compounds formed with *free* are one word, some are hyphenated and some are two words: free agent, freebooter, free fall, free-for-all (n. and adj.), free-form (adj.), free hand (n.), freehand (adj.), freehanded (adj.), freelance (n., v. and adj.), freelancer, freeload (v.), freeloader, freeloading (n. and adj.), free port, free-spoken, free-standing, freestyle (swimming; n. and adj.), freethinker, freethinking (n. and adj.), free throw (basketball), free trade, freeway, freewheel (v.), freewheeler, freewheeling (n. and adj.), free will (n.), freewill (adj.).

free means without cost. *For free* is colloquial; avoid it.

freedom fighter is a polemical term. Confine it to direct quotations.

free state, slave state. Lowercase, in references to the situation before the Civil War.

free world is the language of opinion, even in a historical reference to the cold war. Confine it to the editorial pages and direct quotations.

French(-). Do not hyphenate a compound with *French* except when forming an adjective: French bread, French cuff, French door, French dressing, French-fried potatoes, French fries, French pastry, French roll, French toast, French window.

French, Frenchman(men), Frenchwoman(women).

frère.

freshman. For the class and a member of that class, man or woman. If an exceptional context warrants avoiding *-man*, use *first-year student(s)*. But not *freshwoman(women)* or *freshperson(s)*.

friend of the court (legal term). *See* AMICUS CURIAE.

Friends. *See* QUAKERS.

Frigidaire is a trademark.

Frisbee is a trademark.

front-runner, front-running. Hyphenate both expressions. And use them with caution because they can influence an election by creating a bandwagon effect. They can also return to embarrass the writer and the newspaper if used so early in the process that a candidate's popularity is little tested. If the label is warranted, the ranking should generally be attributed.

F.T.C. for the Federal Trade Commission, sparingly and in headlines.

Führer.

Fujiyama, Mount Fuji. But not *Mount Fujiyama*.

fulfill, fulfilled.

full time (n. and adv.), **full-time** (adj.).

fulsome means not just abundant but offensively excessive.

fun. Though the commercials may someday win respectability for *fun* as an adjective (*a fun vacation*), the gushing sound argues for keeping the word a noun.

fundamentalist. As a religious term, the word should be used with care because of its connotations of rigidity. In Christian contexts, it is best applied only to those who so define themselves. Many conservative Protestants prefer to be called EVANGELICAL. In references to Islam and other non-Christian religions, equate *fundamentalism* to doctrinal conservatism only; do not assume or imply a link to militancy or terrorism.

fund, funded, funding. As a verb, *fund* is needed in some financial contexts; it means, for example, set aside capital to earn interest. But in general contexts (*The state funded the research*), it is jargon; use *financed* or *paid for*.

fund-raiser, fund-raising.

funeral director may be used interchangeably with *undertaker*. Do not use *mortician*.

further. *See* FARTHER, FURTHER.

fused participles. *See* PARTICIPLES AS NOUNS.

futurism (art). Capitalize in reference to the movement begun in 1909 in Italy. Lowercase in general references to forward-looking art. *See* ARTS TERMINOLOGY.

G

gag order, gag rule. Though lawyers consider the terms merely factual, their effect in the news columns is pejorative. Except in direct quotations or texts, paraphrase them. And remind readers that a rule of silence ordinarily binds the negotiators, trial participants or legislators, not the journalists who cover them. *Also see* BLACKOUT.

gaiety, gaily.

Galápagos Islands.

gale. Use this term if the wind meets the National Weather Service's specifications for a gale—39 to 54 miles an hour. *Also see* HURRICANE and STORMS.

galleries. *See* ARTS LOCATIONS.

gallon. A gallon equals four quarts. A United States standard gallon is roughly 3.8 liters. A British imperial gallon is roughly 4.5 liters.

Gambia (not *the Gambia*). Its capital is Banjul and its people are *Gambians*.

gambit. In careful usage, a gambit is an *opening maneuver* (in chess, for example, a sacrifice) to gain a strategic advantage. Do not use the word merely to mean tactic.

gaming is a euphemism. Ordinarily use *gambling* instead, except in official names and direct quotations.

gamut, gantlet, gauntlet. A *gamut* is a scale of notes, or any complete range; someone can *run the gamut* literally or figuratively. A *gantlet* is a flogging ordeal in which an offender runs between lines of tormentors bearing sticks. A *gauntlet* is a long glove, the kind duelists wore; it can be *thrown down* to issue a challenge or *taken up* to accept one. (Some authorities, but not this one, accept *gauntlet* to mean the ordeal also.)

gamy, gamier, gamiest.

gantlet. *See* GAMUT, GANTLET, GAUNTLET.

G.A.O. in headlines, sparingly, for the General Accounting Office (not *Government Accounting Office*), an investigative arm of Congress.

garçon.

Garden State (New Jersey's nickname).

Gardiners Island (in Suffolk County, N.Y.).

garnish, garnishee. Both are properly used as verbs in the sense of putting a lien on property or wages to satisfy a debt. But *garnishee* is more common (despite objections by lawyers), perhaps because the more usual meaning of *garnish* is adorn or decorate. As a noun, *garnishee* means the person served with a legal *garnishment*.

gasification, gasify. But: *liquefaction; liquefy.*

Gaspé Peninsula.

(-)gate. The use of *gate* as a suffix in the news columns (*Irangate, Travelgate*), equating current controversies with the 1973-74 Watergate scandal, carries polemical overtones. Watergate culminated in President Nixon's resignation in the face of a House committee vote to seek impeachment on charges that included obstruction of justice and abuse of authority. If a writer considers a more recent episode comparable, the case should be made straightforwardly.

Gateway National Recreation Area (bordering lower New York Bay).

GATT for the General Agreement on Tariffs and Trade.

Gatwick Airport (near London).

gauge.

gauntlet. *See* GAMUT, GANTLET, GAUNTLET.

gay (adj. and n.) is preferred to *homosexual* in references to social or cultural identity and political or legal issues: *gay literature*. Use *homosexual* in specific references to sexual activity and to psychological or clinical orientation. *Gay(s)* may refer to homosexual men or more generally to homosexual men and women. In specific references to women, *lesbian* is preferred. When the distinction is useful, write *gay men and lesbians. Also see* SEXUAL ORIENTATION.

gay rights. Advocates for gay issues are concerned that the term may invite resentment by implying "special rights" that are denied other citizens; the advocates prefer phrases like *equal rights* or *civil rights for gay people*. But the shorter phrase is in wide use and often indispensable for confined headlines. When it occurs, define the issues precisely.

gazetteers. Use their titles without quotation marks, and capitalize the principal words. *See* GEOGRAPHIC NAMES.

Gdansk. Use this Polish name, not the German *Danzig*, except in historical references.

G.E. for the General Electric Company.

gefilte fish.

gelatin (not *gelatine*).

Gen. *Stacy J. Milori; General Milori; the general.*

gender, sex. In general, *gender* is the grammatical classification of words as masculine, feminine or neuter and *sex* is a characteristic of living things. Use *sex* in unambiguous phrases like *sex discrimination* and *single-sex schools*. But *gender* has taken on new meaning in social and political contexts. Use *gender,* for example, in idioms like *gender gap* and in references arising from its use in legislation or other legal documents. Use it, too, when necessary to avoid confusion with physical sex or to avert double meanings. In other words, *gender* is not to be, well, confused with *sex.*

General Accounting Office (not *Government Accounting Office*), an investigative arm of Congress. In headlines, sparingly: G.A.O.

General Assembly for the United Nations and for the lower house in some state legislatures; *the Assembly.*

Generalissimo *Hilary T. Cordero*; *General Cordero*; *the generalissimo* or *the general.* (The title now occurs mostly in historical references.)

general staff. *The French General Staff*; *the general staff*; *a general staff.* Capitalize in formal references to the headquarters organization at the top of the country's armed forces or army. Lowercase for the general staff of a subordinate command, like a brigade, a division, a corps or a field army.

Generation X. The term for people born in the 1960's and 1970's. Also: *Gen X*; *Gen Xer(s).* All of the terms are faddish, and the short forms are slang as well.

Genet, Jean, for the 20th-century French playwright. But *Genêt* for the 18th-century French diplomat known as Citizen Genêt.

gentleman. Except in jesting or teasing contexts, *gentleman* is obsolete for *man,* just as *lady* is obsolete for *woman.*

genus and species. A biological species is a group of individuals capable of interbreeding and producing fertile offspring. The name of a species is always preceded by the name of the genus, the larger category of which it is a division. Use roman type, and capitalize only the genus name: *Homo sapiens.*

In later references, names may be abbreviated in some contexts: *E. coli* for *Escherichia coli.* If a subspecies name is used, it must be accompanied by genus and species names: *Homo sapiens neanderthalensis.*

The more comprehensive taxonomic classifications of plants and animals are, in ascending order, family, order, class, phylum and kingdom. Capitalize the names of all such classifications except kingdom: *the phylum Protozoa.* But nouns and adjectives derived from such classifications are not capitalized: *protozoan* (n. and adj.).

geographic names. For quick reference, some place names are listed separately in this manual. In general, the first authority for the spelling of domestic place names not listed here is the United States Postal Service's National Five-Digit ZIP Code and Post Office Directory. But do not use the Postal Service's two-letter abbreviations for state names; the preferred abbreviation is shown in this manual under each state's full name. For names not given here or in the Post Office Directory, consult the Geographic Names Information System maintained by the United States Geological Survey and the Board on Geographic Names on the World Wide Web:

http://mapping.usgs.gov/www/gnis

The first authority for the spelling of foreign place names not listed here is the latest edition of Webster's New World College Dictionary. For names that do not appear here or in the dictionary, consult the current edition of the National Geographic Atlas of the World. For names found in none of those three places, consult the Geonet Names Server maintained by the National Imagery and Mapping Agency on the World Wide Web:

http://164.214.2.59/gns/html/index.html

When alternative spellings exist for foreign place names, use what geographers call the "conventional form" for English. Thus, for example, use *Munich*, not *München*, and *Moscow*, not *Moskva*. Retain accent marks in French, Italian, Spanish, Portuguese and German names only. If an umlaut (ö) is omitted as a result of this rule, do not follow the practice of some languages in adding an *e* after the affected vowel.

Abbreviate *Saint* and *Sainte* as *St.* and *Ste.* when they occur in place names, domestic or foreign. But spell out *Fort* and *Mount* as part of a name. The abbreviations *Ft.* and *Mt.* may be used in headlines, charts, tables or maps.

Also see Arabic terms in place names.

Georgia. Abbreviate the name of the state as *Ga.* after the names of cities, towns and counties. Do not abbreviate the name of the former Soviet republic.

Georgian (architecture). Capitalize when referring to the simple, straightforward style of buildings, usually of brick, built in the era that began with the reign of King George I; Georgian is a more precise term for what is generally called Colonial. In reference to a recent building, a modifier like *Georgian style* or *Georgian design* is preferred. *See* arts terminology.

Germany. The capital is Berlin. The plural is *Germanys*, not *Germanies*. From 1945 to 1990, the country was divided into West Germany (officially the Federal Republic of Germany) and East Germany (officially the German Democratic Republic).

gerunds. *See* participles as nouns.

get, got, gotten. In American English, *gotten* is the usual participle, rather than *got*, as in *She had gotten the mail each morning.* But: *I've got a headache* and *I've got to get going*, etc. Except in a handful of idioms, like *get going*, *get lost* and *get sick*, do not substitute *get* for *is* or *are*. Write *the class is tested weekly*, not *the class gets tested weekly*.

ghetto(s). In its current sense, *ghetto* means a poor neighborhood inhabited by members of a minority, usually black. Do not assume that all sections of a predominantly black area—Harlem, for instance, or the South Side of Chicago—are slums or places where only poor people live. *Also see* INNER CITY.

G.I. The colloquial term, derived from *government issue*, for American soldiers. The plural is *G.I.'s*; avoid a plural possessive. No longer official, if it ever was, *G.I.* remains useful in headlines. It can stand for American troops in general, but not for members of the Air Force, the Marines or the Navy.

gibe means jeer or taunt. *Jibe*, colloquially, means conform; in sailing, it means shift.

G.I. Bill of Rights for the post-World War II laws that once financed both college education and home mortgages for veterans and now provide them with educational assistance. In later references, *the G.I. Bill* or a paraphrase, but not *the bill* because there have been many bills over the years.

giga(-). Compounds formed with *giga*, which means one billion, are not hyphenated, except in rare use before a vowel: gigabyte; gigacycle; giga-electron; gigaton; gigawatt.

   Hyphenate terms coined for effect (*giga-ego*; *giga-mansion*), but ration that use to avoid triteness.

gigabyte. About a billion bytes of information, or enough computer memory to store about a billion characters. In technical contexts, it is abbreviated *GB: a 2GB hard disk. See* BIT; BYTE; KILOBYTE; MEGABYTE.

gild the lily is an accepted phrase for overembellishment, but writers who wish to delight the exacting reader will use Shakespeare's actual words, from "King John": "To gild refined gold, *to paint the lily.*"

gilt-edged.

Ginnie Mae for the Government National Mortgage Association, the government agency that buys pools of mortgages from lenders and sells securities to the public. The securities are *Ginnie Maes*.

girl. Reserve *girl* for references to the very young; use it only in contexts where *boy* would be appropriate. It is a *saleswoman*, not a *salesgirl*, and a *college student*, not a *college girl*. *Also see* COED and MEN AND WOMEN.

girlfriend, boyfriend. The terms are informal and best reserved for teenagers.

Girl Scouts; *the Scouts; a girl scout.* The national organization is *Girl Scouts of the U.S.A.*

giveaway (n.).

gladiolus (sing.), **gladioli** (pl.).

glamour, glamorize, glamorous.

Glens Falls (in New York).

glitzy is trite, except in passages making light of the term or its tone. Possible substitutes include *dazzling, pretentious, sparkling, ornate* and *gaudy*. *Glitz*, more trite still, is a back-formation from a cliché.

G.M. for the General Motors Corporation.

G.M.A.T. for the Graduate Management Admissions Test, administered by the Educational Testing Service.

G.N.M.A. or *Ginnie Mae* for the Government National Mortgage Association.

G.N.P. for the gross national product, the value of a nation's goods and services, including those produced by its citizens working abroad.

goal(-). Some but not all sports compounds formed with *goal* are one word: goalkeeper, goal line, goal mouth, goal post, goaltending.

gobbledygook.

God (Supreme Being). Lowercase *he, him, his, thee, thou, who* and *whom* when the reference is to God, Jesus, the Holy Ghost (or the Holy Spirit) or Allah.

goddamn, goddamned, goddamn it. The expressions are lowercased. Like other profanity they should not be used without a compelling reason. *See* OBSCENITY, VULGARITY, PROFANITY.

god(-). Compounds formed with *god* are one word; those formed with *God* are hyphenated: godchild, goddaughter, goddess, godfather, God-fearing, God-forsaken, God-given, godless, godlike, godmother, godsend, godson, godspeed.

(-)goer. Compounds formed with *goer* are one word: churchgoer, moviegoer, operagoer, playgoer, theatergoer.

Golan Heights; *the heights.*

golf. Spell out the number of holes, tees and strokes below 10: *He took six strokes on the ninth hole; She fell behind on the 10th hole.* But use numerals for scores: *He shot a 6.* Also: *72-hole tournament; 2-foot putt; 95 yards; par 4; par-4 hole; two-over-par 6; on the green in 2.* The totals of out and in play are given this way: *36; 36-72.* Handicap totals: *83-10-73.* Clubs are described as an *8-iron*, a *2-wood*, etc.

Competition is held at *medal play* (lowest score wins) and *match play* (direct elimination). Some tournaments combine the two, with qualifying medal play preceding match play. The Grand Slam of golf consists of the Masters, the United States Open, the British Open and the P.G.A. Championship.

Birdie, bogey and *par* may be used as nouns or verbs. *Hole in one* takes no hyphens.

gonzo, slang for *madcap*, is faddish and, for many readers, obscure.

goodbye(s).

Good Friday.

good night (farewell).

good will. But hyphenate when it directly precedes a noun: *a good-will offering.*

G.O.P. may be used as a synonym for the Republican Party in headlines and direct quotations, but in articles it should be used only to achieve a special (*Grand Old Party*) effect.

Gore-Tex is a trademark for laminated weatherproof fabrics.

gospel(s). Capitalize when referring to any of the four books of the Bible so named or when using the word in the sense of the Christian message: *He preached the Gospel.* Lowercase in other references: *She is a famous gospel singer; He swore he was telling the gospel truth.*

gothic (art, architecture and literature). Capitalize in references to the Goths, the medieval period (*Late Gothic* art), the style of architecture and the genre of literature, but not in references to printing: *gothic type.* Also lowercase in general references to gothic images like dark and stormy nights and castles. *See* ARTS TERMINOLOGY.

Gothic novel.

Götterdämmerung (twilight of the gods). Use quotation marks when the reference is to Wagner's opera so named.

gourmet has been drained of meaning by commercial overuse, especially as an adjective (*gourmet cat food*). Words like *epicure, food lover* and *judge of fine cooking* now serve better.

governance is a stuffy way to say things like *management* or *control* or *governing.*

government. Lowercase, as noun or adjective, except in proper names: *United States government; Pakistani government; Colorado government; government bonds; government agents.* But: *Government Printing Office.*

governmental. Lowercase unless it is a part of a name.

Gov. *Lauren J. Daan; Governor Daan; the governor. Also see* GOV. THOMAS E. DEWEY THRUWAY and TITLES.

Governor-elect *Tracy J. Lam; Governor-elect Lam; the governor-elect.* But in cap-and-lowercase headlines: *Gov.-Elect Lam.*

Governor General *Chris L. Agneau; Governor General Agneau; the governor general.* No abbreviation and no hyphen, in references to the British crown's symbolic representative in a Commonwealth country. Plural: *governors general.*

Governors Island (in New York).

Gov. Thomas E. Dewey Thruway. Normally use *New York State Thruway* or *New York Thruway,* reserving the full name for articles that deal centrally with its operation or history. In later references: *the Thruway.* It is operated by the New York State Thruway Authority.

goy (sing.), **goyim** (pl.). These Yiddish words meaning non-Jew(s), while often used lightly, amount to ethnic slurs.

grader. Do not hyphenate in reference to school classes: *first grader, sixth grader, 10th grader,* etc. But: *third-grade pupil.*

graduate (v.). A person may *graduate from* a school or *be graduated from* it. But never *They graduated high school.*

Graduate Management Admissions Test (G.M.A.T.).

graffiti. Usage now accepts the word as a singular when it means the practice or phenomenon of drawing on walls: *Graffiti has cost the city $2.5 million this year.* In references to the scrawls themselves, *graffiti* may be used as a plural: *The graffiti were not there yesterday.* Strictly speaking, a single wall marking is a *graffito*, but the expression is pedantic; use *scrawl* or *marking* or *drawing* instead.

Seen in a museum or gallery, graffiti can be art. But in writing about streets and public places, avoid *graffiti artist(s)*, a phrase that strikes some readers as condoning vandalism.

gram. Convert grams to ounces by multiplying the number of grams by 0.035: *The gold-bearing rock weighed 56 grams, about 2 ounces.* But when *gram* is used in nutritional measurements, do not convert: *Each cookie has 10 grams of fat.* See MET-RIC SYSTEM.

Grammy Award(s); *the award(s)*; the *Grammy(s)*. Articles dealing centrally with the awards should mention that they are presented by the National Academy of Recording Arts and Sciences.

Grand Central Terminal.

grande dame (sing.), **grandes dames** (pl.).

grandmother. Describe a woman as a *grandmother* (or *mother*) only when her family status is pertinent and its pertinence is clear to the reader. The best test is whether, if the subject were a man, *grandfather* would be used. *Also see* MEN AND WOMEN.

Grand Rabbi. *See* CHIEF RABBI.

Grand Slam. Uppercase in references to the four major tournaments in golf (the Masters, the United States Open, the British Open and the P.G.A. Championship) and the four in tennis (the Australian Open, the French Open, Wimbledon and the United States Open).

Grand Teton National Park.

Grand Trunk Western Railroad.

Grants Pass (in Oregon).

graphic. In general contexts and in articles about publishing, use the term as a modifier only: *graphic design*; *graphic designer* (and *graphics editor*, but not *graphics designer*). As a singular noun (*a graphic tracing wheat prices*), the word is publishing jargon and should usually be replaced by *graph*, *chart*, *diagram*, etc. The singular noun is accepted in technology contexts: *the program inserts a graphic into a document.* The plural, though, is standard English in all contexts, in the sense of design: *a magazine distinguished by innovative graphics.*

grave accent. *See* ACCENT MARKS.

gray. But: *greyhound.*

great(-). Hyphenate all relationship words beginning with *great*: great-aunt, great-grandchild, great-granddaughter, great-grandfather, great-great-grandfather, great-grandmother, great-grandparent, great-grandson, great-nephew, great-niece, great-uncle.

Great Atlantic and Pacific Tea Company (A.&P.).

Great Britain. Shorten it to Britain in ordinary news copy.

Great Lakes; *the lakes.* They are Lakes Superior, Michigan, Huron, Erie and Ontario.

Great Salt Lake (in Utah).

Great South Bay (in New York).

Greek Catholic Church. A Roman Catholic church of the Eastern Rite.

Greek Orthodox Archdiocese of America.

Greek Orthodox Church. It is the established church of Greece and, like the Russian Orthodox Church, is one of the autonomous Eastern Orthodox churches. *See* Eastern Orthodoxy; metropolitan; patriarch.

Greek Revival (architecture). Capitalize when referring to the simple and austere building style. *See* arts terminology.

Green Berets. It is the informal name of the Special Forces, the Army's antiguerrilla troops. Mention both names when the units figure more than casually in an article. *Also see* Special Operations.

greenmail is the purchase of a large block of a company's stock in the hope that the management, fearing a takeover, will pay a premium to buy it back. When the word is used, explain it.

Greenwich Mean Time has been replaced as the world standard by Coordinated Universal Time. Use that term instead. *Also see* time.

Greenwich Village. In later references, *the Village.* Do not use quotation marks, even when *Village* stands alone in a headline. If the context is not clear, use a more specific place name, like *Washington Square.*

Green-Wood Cemetery (in Brooklyn).

gross domestic product. It is the total value of the goods and services produced in a country in a specified period. It has replaced the gross national product as the United States government's principal measure of the country's output.

gross national product. It is the total value of the goods and services produced by a country in a given period, including those produced by its citizens who are working abroad. In later references (sparingly) and in headlines: G.N.P.

groundbreaking.

Group Capt. *Ashley B. Kikondoo* (in British and British-influenced foreign air forces); *Group Captain Kikondoo; the group captain.*

Group of 7 for the conference of industrialized nations. In direct quotations, but not ordinarily in headlines: G-7. In some contexts, when Russia is included: *Group of 8.*

grow (v.) can be used without a direct object in many contexts: *flowers grow; unemployment grows; businesses and governments grow.* With a direct object, *grow* sounds natural in references to living things: *grow flowers*; *grow wheat*; *grow a beard*; *grow antlers*. The newer usage of *grow* to mean expand (*grow the business*; *grow revenue*) is business jargon, best resisted.

grown-up (n. and adj.).

grueling.

G-7. *See* GROUP OF 7.

GTE Corporation became part of VERIZON COMMUNICATIONS in 2000.

Guadalupe, Guadeloupe. *Guadalupe* is a common place name in Central and South America. But in the West Indies, the name is *Guadeloupe*.

Guangzhou (in China) was formerly known as Canton. *See* CHINESE NAMES.

Guantánamo, Guantánamo Bay (in Cuba). In direct quotations or in feature contexts involving the United States naval base there, the nickname *Gitmo* may be used.

guarantee, not *guaranty*, except in proper names.

Guatemala City, the capital of Guatemala. Omit the country name after the city name. *Also see* DATELINES.

gubernatorial. Though favored by political insiders, the adjective is stilted. When possible, choose more conversational phrasing: *the campaign for governor*; *the election of a governor*.

guest. Do not use as a verb except in direct quotations.

guide(-). Some compounds formed with *guide* are one word and some are two words: guidebook, guide dog, guideline, guidepost, guide rail.

Guinea, Guinea-Bissau. *Guinea* is a former French colony on the west coast of Africa. Its capital is Conakry and its people are *Guineans*. *Guinea-Bissau*, much smaller and to Guinea's northwest, is a former Portuguese colony. Its capital is Bissau. Its people can be called Guineans only when the context distinguishes them from the people of Guinea.

gulf coast. Capitalize when referring to the region of the United States lying along the Gulf of Mexico; lowercase when referring to the actual shoreline.

Gulf Stream for the ocean current. But: *the Gulfstream Aerospace Corporation* makes *Gulfstream* aircraft.

gulf war. Lowercase, and reserve the term for use after first references to the Persian Gulf war of 1991, in which the United States and allied countries supported Kuwait after an invasion by Iraq.

gun may be used loosely in reference to any firearm. *See* HANDGUNS; RIFLES; SHOTGUNS.

gun(-). Most but not all compounds formed with *gun* are one word: gunboat, gun dog, gunfight, gunfire, gunman, gunner, gunplay, gunpoint, gunpowder, gunrunner, gunship, gunshot, gun-shy, gunsmith.

Gunnery Sgt. *Lindsay K. Kuzu; Sergeant Kuzu; the sergeant.*

Gutenberg, Johann.

Guyana. Its capital is Georgetown and its people are Guyanese.

Gypsy, Gypsies, in references to the ethnic group also known as *Romany*. Many Gypsies, especially in Europe, refer to themselves by the plural noun *Roma*. Also, lowercased: *gypsy cab*; *gypsy-cab driver*; *gypsy moth*.

H

habitué (masc. and fem.).

hacker originally referred to any skilled manipulator of software. It now connotes mischievous, malicious or illegal manipulation.

Hades. But lowercase *hell*.

haftara, a reading from the Prophets during a Jewish Sabbath or festival service, supplementing the reading from the Torah. Despite a frequent assumption, the term is derived not from *Torah* (hence the spelling difference) but from the Hebrew for *dismissal*. Plural: *haftarot*.

Hagatna, formerly Agana, is the capital of Guam.

Haggadah. The Passover text recited at a Seder. Plural: *Haggadot*.

Hague, The. An exception to the usual preference for lowercasing *the*.

hair(-), (-)haired. Most but not all compounds formed with *hair* as a prefix are one word: hairball, hairbreadth, hairbrush, haircut, hairdo, hairdresser, hairdressing, hairless, hairline, hairpiece, hair shirt, hairsplitting, hairstyle, hair trigger (n.), hair-trigger (adj.).

As a suffix, *haired* is usually hyphenated: brown-haired, fair-haired, longhaired, red-haired, etc.

Also: *harebrained*, not *hairbrained*.

hajj, hajji. *Hajj* is the pilgrimage to Mecca that every Muslim is obliged to make. A *hajji* is a Muslim who has made that pilgrimage.

Halakha. The part of the Talmud devoted to unwritten laws that are based on an oral interpretation of Jewish Scriptures.

half(-). Most compound adjectives that use *half* as a prefix are hyphenated, but some are solid: half-afraid, half-baked, half-cocked, half-done, half-dozen, half-full (adj. only), halfhearted, half-hourly (adj., adv.), halfway.

Compound nouns that use *half* as a prefix can be solid, hyphenated or open: half-and-half (the drink), halfback, half brother, half dollar, half dozen (n.), half gainer (diving), half-holiday, half-hour (n. and adj.), half-life, half-moon, half nelson (wrestling), half note (music), half pay, halfpenny, half shell, half sister, half size, half sole, half time (n., except sports), halftime (n., sports), halftone, halftrack, half-truth. When in doubt, consult the dictionary.

Also: *cut in two*; *break in two* (not *in half*, unless the measurement is exact).

half-mast, half-staff. As a sign of mourning, flags on ships and at naval installations ashore are flown at *half-mast*; flags elsewhere ashore are flown at *half-staff*.

hall(-). Compounds formed with *hall* are one word: hallmark, hallway.

Halloween.

halo(s).

Hamas (the militant Islamic movement in the Middle East).

Hamtramck (in Michigan).

hand(-), (-)hand. Most but not all compounds formed with *hand* as a prefix are one word: handbag, handball, handbill, handbook, handcuff, handful(s), hand grenade, handgun, hand-held, handmade, hand-me-down, handoff, handout (n.), handrail, handsaw, handshake, hands-off, hands-on, handspring, handstand, hand-to-hand, hand-to-mouth, handwriting.

As a suffix, *hand* is sometimes hyphenated and sometimes solid: beforehand, left-hand (adj.), longhand (writing), right-hand (adj.), shorthand.

handguns. A *handgun* or *pistol* is a weapon that can be held and fired with one hand. It may be a *semiautomatic*, with the ammunition stored in a magazine or clip, usually in the handle; a *revolver*, with the ammunition stored in a cylinder that turns with each shot to align a fresh cartridge; a *derringer*, with a round in each of two barrels; or a *single-shot pistol*. The discharge of a handgun is called a shot. *Also see* BULLET; CALIBER; CARTRIDGE; RIFLES; SHOTGUNS.

handicapped. Use more specific terms for disabilities when possible. Many people with disabilities believe that the broad term exaggerates their limitations—because, for example, a person in a wheelchair is not *handicapped* if the workplace provides ramps. *Also see* CHALLENGED; CRIPPLE, CRIPPLED; DISABILITY, DISABLED; IMPAIRED.

hangar (an airplane shed); **hanger** (a clothes hook or the like).

hanged, hung. A person is *hanged*; a picture is *hung*.

hansom cab. A *hansom cab* is a covered, two-wheeled carriage with a driver's seat above and behind the cab. The carriages commonly seen in New York City are *victorias*, which have four wheels and a driver's seat in front.

Hanukkah (Festival of Lights).

Hapag-Lloyd A.G. (the German ocean carrier).

Hapsburg (not *Habsburg*).

hara-kiri.

harass.

Harcourt Inc. (formerly Harcourt Brace & Company).

hard(-). Some compounds formed with *hard* are solid, some hyphenated and some two words: hardball, hard-bitten, hard-boiled, hard core (n.), hard-core (adj.), hardcover, hard-earned, hard hat (the noun for the headgear and, in slang, its wearer), hard-hat (adj.), hardhearted, hard landing, hard-line (adj.), hard-liner, hard pressed, hard rock, hard-wired, hardwood, hard-working.

harebrained.

hark, hark back, harken, hearken. Both *hark* and *hearken* mean listen attentively. *Harken* is a variant spelling of *hearken. Hark back* means return to an earlier point.

Harper's Magazine.

Harrods (the London department store). Without an apostrophe.

Harry S. Truman. Use a period after the initial, though he had no legal middle name.

Hart Island (in Long Island Sound, part of the Bronx).

Hartsdale (in Westchester County, N.Y.).

Harvard Business School may be used in most references rather than the full name, *the Harvard Graduate School of Business Administration.* Use *B school* in direct quotations only, or for feature effect.

Harvard University. In most casual references, *Harvard* can stand alone, for the university or for its undergraduate college.

Hasbrouck Heights (in Bergen County, N.J.).

Hasid (n., sing.), **Hasidim** (n., pl.), **Hasidic** (adj.). Use *Hasidism* for the beliefs of the Jewish sect.

hassle. In the sense of struggle or bother, *hassle* is slang.

Hastings-on-Hudson (in Westchester County, N.Y.).

hatrack.

haves, have-nots (n.).

Havre de Grace (in Maryland).

Hawaii. Do not abbreviate after the names of cities, towns and counties, even in datelines.

hay(-). Nearly all compounds formed with *hay* are one word: hay fever, hayfield, hayloft, haymaker, hayrick, hayride, haystack, haywire.

H-bomb may be used for hydrogen bomb in later references and in conversational contexts. In cap-and-lowercase headlines: *H-Bomb.*

HDTV for high-definition television in later references, sparingly, and in headlines.

he, him, his, thee, thou, who, whom. Lowercase, even in references to God, Jesus, the Holy Ghost (or the Holy Spirit) or Allah.

he or she may be used as a last resort to avoid an unwanted assumption of maleness or femaleness in a general reference. (Also *him or her* and *his or hers.*) But preferred solutions are those that spare the reader all traces of a writer's struggle. Try the plural construction: *A doctor always bills his patients,* for example, may be changed to *Doctors always bill their patients*. Or rewrite the sentence so that no pronoun is required: *The doctor always bills the patient. Also see* ANYBODY, ANY- ONE, EVERYBODY, EVERYONE, NO ONE, SOMEONE; MAN, MANKIND; and MEN AND WOMEN.

head (n.). A specific organizational title is preferred (*president, chairman, chair- woman, director*), because the vagueness suggests superficial reporting.

head(-). Most but not all compounds formed with *head* are one word: headache, headband, headboard, head cold, headdress, headfirst, headgear, headhunter, headlight, headlong, head-on, headphone, headrest, headroom, headset, head start, headstone, headstrong, head-to-head, headwaiter, headwaters, headway, headwear, headwind. *Also see* HEADMASTER, HEADMISTRESS.

headlines should ideally be written in the standard English of a simple sentence. As a test of the reader's comfort, it should be possible to convert a headline into a straightforward sentence merely by restoring the "little words" that have been omitted for copy fitting. On Page 1 and in most news sections, each line of a head should express a self-contained idea, grammatically independent of the other lines. But even in feature sections, line breaks should occur at natural breathing points.

When reporting an accident, a crime or a disaster with a range of estimates of dead and injured, the headline should use the conservative figure. (As an excep- tion, if experience suggests that an earthquake or a typhoon, for example, is likely to do vast damage because of its location, a general prediction like "hundreds" may be appropriate for the headline.) This rule should not affect the rounding of other kinds of numbers and decimals (*see* NUMBERS).

Headlines on fresh news almost always use the present tense: *Men Walk on Moon*. If the headline relates a current action to an earlier one, drop back only one level in time, to the past tense: *Governor Signs Bill She Opposed* (not the past perfect *Had Opposed*). When recalling history or newly disclosing a past develop- ment, also use the past tense: *Miel Left Millions to College*.

To save space, the verb *to be* (in forms like *is, are, was*, etc.) can be omitted, but only from the first phrase of a headline or a bank, as shown here by the brack- ets: *State [   ] Facing Deficit, Governor Asserts*. But never *Governor Asserts State [   ] Facing Deficit*, because the omission from a later phrase creates distorted English. And if any "little words" (verbs or articles) must be omitted for space, drop the left- most ones first. Once the mind's ear has "heard" an *a* or a *the*, it finds later omis- sions dissonant.

A bank may begin with a verb, omitting a subject, but only if the implied sub- ject is identical with the actual one in the headline above.

Thus:	But not:
Cordeiro Plans China Trip	*Cordeiro Plans China Trip*
Will Argue for Human Rights	*Will Ask Him for Trade Deal*

Short, active verbs work best. Avoid archaic-sounding ones like *beset, decry* and *score* (in the sense of denounce). Even the graying ones, like *bid* (meaning request), should be a last resort.

In headings of all kinds (including those for charts and lists), use single quotation marks instead of doubles. In general, use a semicolon between headline clauses, even if the second shares a subject with the first: *Governor to Run Again; Pledges a 'Clean, Tough Fight.'* In a multiple-line head, the semicolon should normally fall at the end of a line.

Except in desperation, do not use a comma to mean *and* in a phrase like *Taxes, Wages Expected to Rise.* Do not use a question mark to mean *maybe* or to suggest tentativeness (*Governor to Run Again?*). In a special case, usually for humor, the first part of a headline may end with a period. In that case, for balance, another period should appear at the end:

U.S. Embassy Passes Into History. Coming Soon: Real Estate Deals.

(The rule does not apply to exclamation points and question marks; if they appear in midheadline, they do not create a need for punctuation at the end.)

Resist using dashes because they are ungainly in headline type; usually the meaning can be conveyed with a colon, a semicolon or parentheses. The objection applies equally to the half-width en dash (–) except when it is used, properly, as a minus sign. But make an exception for the cone-shaped banks on Page 1; they customarily use full-length dashes rather than semicolons between clauses or ideas.

Additional headline conventions apply to OBITUARIES. *Also see* CAPITALIZATION.

headmaster, headmistress. Lowercase and separate the title from the name with a comma: *Merrill V. Barany, the headmaster; the headmistress.* In a general reference: *the head of the school.*

headquarters. Treat it as a plural noun in ordinary uses: *Procter & Gamble's headquarters are in Cincinnati.* But use a singular verb in this kind of military construction: *Headquarters wants the battalion to move out.* Capitalize this way: *First Army Headquarters; the headquarters.* Do not use *headquarter* as a verb: *The company is headquartered in Philadelphia.*

health care is not hyphenated, even when it serves as a modifier: *health care plan.*

hearing examiner. *See* ADMINISTRATIVE LAW JUDGE.

heart(-), (-)hearted. Most but not all compounds formed with *heart* as a prefix or a suffix are one word: heartache, heartbeat, heartbreak, heartbroken, heartburn, heartfelt, heartland, heartless, heart-rending, heartsick, heart-to-heart, heartwarming, halfhearted, hardhearted, lionhearted, softhearted.

heart condition. Every heart has some kind of condition. Write *heart ailment, disease,* etc., instead.

heat(-). Most but not all compounds formed with *heat* are two words: heat exhaustion, heat lightning, heat pipe, heatproof, heat pump, heat sink, heatstroke, heat wave.

Heathrow Airport (near London).

heat index. It is a measurement devised by the National Weather Service to express the combined effect of high temperature and high humidity on human comfort, health and safety. The index, sometimes called the *apparent temperature,* is expressed in degrees Fahrenheit, representing the sensation caused when a given air temperature interacts with a given level of relative humidity. For example, if the air temperature is 95 and the relative humidity is 55 percent, the heat index, as read from the Weather Service chart, is 110. The system replaced the *discomfort index* and the *temperature-humidity index.* In articles about heat waves, the index is a useful indicator of how harmful the weather may be. The Weather Service considers heat indexes of less than 80 comfortable. It regards those greater than 100 as hazardous and those greater than 110 as dangerous. The chart is on the World Wide Web:

http://www.nws.noaa.gov/er/mhx/hit.htm

heaven. Lowercase except in this sense: *I thank Heaven.*

hectare. An area equal to 10,000 square meters or 2.47 acres. Unless there is a special reason to use hectare figures, convert them to acres. And round figures should be rendered as round translations. *See* METRIC SYSTEM.

Heights, the. Capitalize in later references to Brooklyn Heights or Washington Heights. In headlines: *Brooklyn Hts.; Washington Hts.*

hell. Lowercase, but *Hades* is uppercase. As profanity and slang, *hell* should be resisted. *See* OBSCENITY, VULGARITY, PROFANITY.

Hell Gate (the narrow channel in the East River).

helmeted. *Helmeted police* and *helmeted troops* are journalese clichés. If it needs to be said, say *soldiers in helmets,* etc.

help (v.). Use the construction *help wondering,* as in *He cannot help wondering.* Not *He cannot help but wonder.*

helter-skelter.

hemisphere. Capitalize in references to the divisions of the earth: *Northern Hemisphere,* etc. But: *the hemisphere.*

Henry, O. The pen name of the short-story writer William Sydney Porter was *O. Henry* (not *O'Henry*).

her. In reference to countries or ships, use *it* or *its* instead.

Herakleion. Use *Iraklion* instead for the city in Crete.

herculean.

here(-). Compounds formed with *here* are one word: hereabout(s), hereafter, hereby. The following, all too pompous for most newspaper writing, are also solid: herein, hereinafter, hereto, heretofore, hereunder, herewith.

heretofore, hitherto. Both words mean *until now*. Do not confuse them with *theretofore*, meaning *until then*. All three words have their place, but it is in an old-fashioned legal brief. News writing calls for the simple phrases.

Her Majesty and similar designations should be used only in texts and quotations or for special effect.

Herr. *See* COURTESY TITLES.

herself, himself, myself. Reflexive pronouns serve to add emphasis (*She fixed it herself*) or to turn the action back to the subject (*He makes himself hard to find*). Do not substitute them for ordinary objects: *The meeting was between myself and the plumbers.* Make it *me and the plumbers*.

Hewlett-Packard Company.

Hezbollah is a Shiite Muslim militant group based in Lebanon and fighting with Iranian backing against the Israeli military presence in southern Lebanon. The name means Party of God.

HIAS may be used, without *the*, in later references to the *Hebrew Immigrant Aid Society*.

hide(-). Most but not all compounds formed with *hide* are one word: hide-and-seek (n.), hideaway (n.), hidebound, hide-out (n.).

high(-). Some compounds formed with *high* are one word, some are hyphenated and some are two words: highball (drink), high beam, highchair, high fidelity, highflier, high frequency (n.), high-frequency (adj.), high-grade (adj.), highhanded, high jinks, high jump, high-level (adj.), highlight (n. and v.), high-minded, high-powered (adj.), high-rise (adj.), highroad, high-tech, high-tension, hightop (shoe), highway, highwayman.

highbrow (n. and adj.) is colloquial and sometimes disparaging. Use it with care.

high commission. In diplomatic relations within the Commonwealth, high commissions take the place of embassies. Lowercase *high commission* when it stands alone. But: *the Nigerian High Commission*.

High Commissioner *Leslie T. Anyell; Leslie T. Anyell, high commissioner to Nigeria; High Commissioner Anyell; the high commissioner; Mr. (or Ms., Mrs. or Miss) Anyell*. In diplomatic relations within the Commonwealth, high commissioners take the place of ambassadors.

High Court. It is the name of a British court, among others. Do not use it as a variation for Supreme Court. Even in a narrow headline, *Justices* will do.

High Holy Days (Jewish; preferred to *High Holidays*): Rosh Hashana and Yom Kippur.

high jinks. Not *hijinks*.

high Mass. It is *sung* or *celebrated*, not *said*. *Also see* MASS.

high tea is often misused to suggest something elegant; that is *afternoon tea*. In Britain *high tea* is a hearty working-class supper.

highway. Capitalize in names: *Sunrise Highway*. But: *the highway*. See INTERSTATE SYSTEM and ROUTE.

hijack (v. only). Use *hijacking* for the noun and the modifier, even in headlines.

hike. Do not use *hike* as a synonym for *increase*, whether noun or verb.

Hill. In references to Capitol Hill, *the Hill* is Washington jargon. Use it only to convey an insider flavor.

himself. *See* HERSELF, HIMSELF, MYSELF.

Hindi (language), **Hindu** (religion).

hip-hop. The style of popular music, and the culture surrounding it, associated with RAP and break-dancing.

hippie(s).

hippopotamus(es).

His Holiness should not be used for the pope except in direct quotations and texts or for special effect.

His Majesty and similar designations should be used only in direct quotations and texts or for special effect.

Hispanic (n. and adj.) means descended from a Spanish-speaking land or culture. It may apply to many groups of Americans—to Puerto Ricans, for example, or Texans of Mexican origin—as well as to immigrants from Latin America or Spain. It does not denote a race; Hispanics can be of any race.

Perhaps because of the *ic* ending, some writers prefer to avoid *Hispanic* as a noun (*Hispanics* or *a Hispanic*). But avoidance of the noun should not take conspicuous forms—wooden phrases, for example, like *Hispanic people* or *Hispanic residents*. If *Hispanic* occurs in a series of ethnic designations, all should be modifiers (*black, Hispanic and Asian-American neighborhoods*) or none should.

LATINO, a synonym originally favored in the Southwest and the West, is gaining in use elsewhere, but for now *Hispanic* remains more widely preferred. When writing about specific people or groups, choose the term they prefer. And when a more specific identification is available—*Cuban, Puerto Rican, Mexican-American*—use it. Take care with *Spanish-speaking* and *Spanish-surnamed* because Hispanics do not necessarily speak the language and some have other kinds of names. *Also see* CHICANO; ETHNICITY; PUERTO RICO, PUERTO RICAN.

historically black. It is a specialized term, referring to colleges and universities that were founded for blacks. Do not use it to mean merely that a college is predominantly black.

historic, historical. *Historic* means important in history. Use it with caution for a current event, because history's verdict is rarely predictable by journalists, and the word suggests hyperbole. *Historical* means *about* history or *concerned with* history: *a historical novel, a historical exhibition.* Because the *h* is pronounced, precede either word with *a*, not *an*.

hit(-). Standing alone: *hit or miss; hit and run.* But when preceding the words they modify: *hit-or-miss; hit-and-run.* And in headlines, when necessary: *hit-run.*

hitherto. *See* HERETOFORE, HITHERTO.

Hitler. Ordinarily omit his first name. But if it is used, spell it *Adolf,* not *Adolph.*

H.I.V. for the human immunodeficiency virus. It is not *the AIDS virus,* but rather *the virus that causes AIDS*; the medical condition is defined not by infection but by a variety of physical effects that may ensue. A person who has the virus is *H.I.V. positive* or *infected with H.I.V.* Note that *H.I.V. virus* is redundant. *Also see* AIDS.

H.M.O. for health maintenance organization in later references and in headlines. The plural is *H.M.O.'s.*

hoard (a reserve, or to reserve), **horde** (a throng).

Hobson's choice means a "take it or leave it" offer: no choice at all.

Ho Chi Minh City (in Vietnam) is the former Saigon, renamed after the Communist takeover in 1975. It is often helpful to note that the old name remains in popular use.

hockey. Scores are given in figures: *The Rangers won, 3-0.* Numbers of goals below 10 and of periods are spelled out: *He scored three goals in the second period.* But: *The score at the end of the second period was 3-1.* The best-known professional organization is the *National Hockey League,* and its annual championship is the *Stanley Cup finals.*

hocus-pocus.

hodgepodge.

Ho Ho Kus (in New Jersey). No hyphens.

hoi polloi is Greek for *the many,* meaning the masses (and not, as sometimes supposed, for *the elite*). Do not precede the phrase with a redundant *the.* And unless the intent is unmistakably ironic, avoid the expression as patronizing.

(-)holder. Most but not all compounds formed with holder are one word: boxholder, householder, jobholder, leaseholder, officeholder, potholder, shareholder, stockholder. But: *preferred-stock holder.*

holdup (n. and adj.). A *holdup* man or woman *holds up* a victim during a *holdup.*

hole in one.

holiday references. Resist the journalese mannerism that draws holidays irrelevantly into articles about events that occur on or near them. Do not characterize a Dec. 24 assault as a *Christmas Eve shooting* or a Feb. 14 accident as a *Valentine's Day crash*. Forgo chestnuts (so to speak) like *'tis the season, deck the halls, all the trimmin's* and *ring in the new.*

holidays are listed separately.

Holland. Use only in historical references (in art, for example) to the western region of what is now the NETHERLANDS, or in references to North Holland and South Holland, provinces created from that region in 1840.

Holland America Line (the cruise ship operator).

holocaust. Uppercase in references to the Nazis' mass destruction of Jews during World War II. Lowercase *holocaust* in a more general reference to a firestorm. Resist applying the word casually to other massacres; there is a danger of hyperbole and of offending readers by trivializing the place of genocide in history.

holy communion. The Christian sacrament, celebrated by a minister, a priest or a bishop. The elements of bread and wine (or grape juice) are consecrated by the celebrant and then distributed or administered to the congregation. Uppercase the term when it refers to a religious service that incorporates the sacrament. Lowercase for the sacrament itself.

Holy Father should not be used in reference to the pope except in quotations and texts, or for special effect.

holy grail. Capitalize only in a reference to the cup or plate that was lost, according to medieval legend, after Jesus used it at the Last Supper. Lowercase the phrase in general references to a long and arduous search or to the object of such a search, but ration them; they are overused.

Holy See (the Roman see of the Roman Catholic Church).

Holy Week (the week before Easter).

home(-). Most but not all compounds formed with *home* are solid: homebound, homecoming, homeless, homemade, homeowner, home plate, homeroom, home rule, home run, homesick, homespun, homestretch, hometown, homework. *Also see* HOMEMAKER.

home, hone. A detection device (radar, for example) *homes in* on a signal source, behaving like a *homing* pigeon. *Hone*, an unrelated word, means *sharpen*; it is not used with *in*.

homemaker. Unlike *housewife*, the term does not define a person by marital status; it is therefore preferred. But resist the term unless occupation is the most pertinent way of identifying the woman, or a man in a similar situation. And do not use it in general references that presume this is women's usual situation. *See* MEN AND WOMEN.

home page, the introductory screen of a site on the WORLD WIDE WEB.

home port (n. and adj.). Do not use as a verb.

hometown. Do not write *his hometown of Peoria.* Make it *his hometown, Peoria.*

Homo sapiens. *See* GENUS AND SPECIES.

homosexuality. *See* ADMITTED HOMOSEXUAL; BISEXUAL; GAY; LESBIAN; SEXUAL ORIEN-
TATION.

Hon., for the Honorable. Use it in direct quotations or texts only, followed by a full
name: *the Hon. Lauren P. Lamb.*

hone. *See* HOME, HONE.

Honeywell Inc. merged with AlliedSignal Inc. in 1999 under the Honeywell name.

Hong Kong.

honorarium(s).

honored in the breach. *See* MORE HONORED IN THE BREACH.

honorifics. *See* COURTESY TITLES.

hoof-and-mouth disease. Make it *foot-and-mouth disease.*

hoof, hooves.

hoopla.

Hoosick Falls (in Rensselaer County, N.Y.).

hopefully. In the sense of *let us hope,* this adverb inflames passions. Widely heard in
speech, it is also approved by most dictionaries and usage manuals, in sentences
like *Hopefully, Congress will pass the law.* Grammarians equate that usage to uni-
versally accepted constructions with *frankly* and *mercifully.* But traditionalists insist that *hopefully* can be used only to mean *in a hopeful manner,* as in *The
ambassador sought hopefully for an agreement.* In surveys of skillful writers and
teachers, large majorities cling to the restriction. So writers and editors unwilling
to irritate readers would be wise to write *they hope* or *with luck.* With luck, writers
and editors will avoid wooden alternatives like *it is hoped* or *one hopes.*

horror-struck.

hors d'oeuvre(s).

horse(-). Some compounds formed with *horse* are one word, some are hyphenated and
some are two words: horse-and-buggy (adj.), horseback, horsecar, horse chestnut,
horseflesh, horsefly, horsehair, horsehide, horselaugh, horseman, horse opera,
horseplay, horseplayer, horsepower, horse race, horse racing, horseradish, horse
sense, horseshoe, horse trade (n.), horse-trade (v.), horse trader, horse trading,
horsewoman.

horse racing. Use figures for times of races: 2:39. Use fractions rather than decimals:
1:12⅘.

The first time prices are mentioned in an article, the type of bet should be
specified. *He paid $4.60 for $2 to win. He returned $18.40, $9.60, $5.40 for $2*

across the board. Exact odds should be used. If the odds are 35 cents to the dollar, the horse is 7 to 20 (or 7-20) rather than 1 to 3. If the payoff is $4.10 for $2, the odds are 21 to 20, not even money. Exception: If the price is comparatively high, the odds may be rounded. Thus a horse paying $38.20 for $2 may be listed as 18 to 1 rather than 181-10.

Thoroughbred horses run in *stakes* (sing. and pl.), harness horses in a *stake* (sing.) or *stakes* (pl.).

Harness races are *trotted* or *paced*, not *run*. The words *break* and *broke* should be used with care in harness articles. *He broke from the No. 4 post* could mean either that the horse started from that post or that he broke his stride.

For a horse mentioned in an article by name, use the pronoun *he* or *she*, not *it*. Gelded horses are *he*.

horsy, horsier, horsiest.

host. Do not use *host* as a verb except in direct quotations. In news articles, people should not *host* parties or broadcasts, just as no one *guests* them.

As a noun, *host* can refer to a man or a woman, but the widely used *hostess* seems free of the usual objections to grafted feminine endings.

Hostos Community College (part of the CITY UNIVERSITY OF NEW YORK).

hot-blooded.

hot dog (n.), hot-dog stand. But the slang verb meaning *show off* is spelled *hotdog* (and thus *hotdogger; hotdogging*).

hotels. Capitalize their names: *Plaza Hotel*. Generally *Hotel* follows the name.

hot line for a direct communications system for emergencies.

hour(-). Most but not all compounds formed with *hour* are one word: hourglass, hour hand, hourlong.

hours. *See* TIME.

house(-). Most but not all compounds formed with *house* are one word: house arrest, houseboat, housebound, housebroken, housecleaning, housecoat, housedress, housefly, household, househusband, housekeeper, housemaid, houseman, housemate, housemother, house organ, house party, houseplant, housetop, housewares, housewarming, housework. *Also see* HOUSEWIFE.

House of Commons; *the Commons.*

House of Lords; *the Lords.*

House of Representatives (United States); *the House.*

houses and estates. Capitalize but do not use quotation marks around their names: *Blair House.*

house-sit, house-sitting, house sitter.

housewife. The preferred term, when such a description is pertinent, is HOMEMAKER. *Also see* MEN AND WOMEN.

HTML for Hypertext Markup Language, the formatting system that allows a document to be displayed on the WORLD WIDE WEB.

HUD for the Department of Housing and Urban Development.

Humvee (derived from H.M.M.W.V., or high mobility multipurpose wheeled vehicle) is the nickname of the military vehicle that succeeded the jeep. The civilian version is called a *Hummer.*

(-)hundreds (of years). In almost all contexts, use the numerals (*1900's*, for example) rather than the words (*nineteen-hundreds*). *See* YEARS, DECADES, CENTURIES.

Hunter College (part of the CITY UNIVERSITY OF NEW YORK).

Hunters Point (in Queens).

Hunts Point (in the Bronx).

huppah (the Jewish wedding canopy).

hurly-burly.

hurricane. Do not call a storm a hurricane unless it meets the National Weather Service's hurricane specifications. The major requirement is winds near the center of the storm that reach or exceed 74 miles an hour.

The National Hurricane Center classifies hurricanes according to their intensity. Category descriptions are on the World Wide Web:

http://www.nhc.noaa.gov/aboutsshs.html

Use the hurricanes' assigned names sparingly, for necessary identification. But do not personalize the weather with pronouns like *his* or *her*, and do not attribute human traits to it (never, for example, *Bonnie behaved capriciously* or *Charlie showed his temper*). *Also see* GALE; STORMS; TROPICAL STORM.

Hyde Park (in Dutchess County, N.Y., and in London).

hymns. Use quotation marks around their titles, with principal words capitalized.

hypertext, a document transmission format used on the WORLD WIDE WEB. Hypertext pages include embedded "links," usually displayed as colored or underlined words, allowing rapid cross-reference to other Web pages. *Also see* HTML.

hyphen. Compounds formed with and without hyphens are listed separately or in entries for individual prefixes and suffixes.

Use the hyphen in constructions like *three-mile hike* and *30-car train* and to avoid confusion in words like *re-form* (meaning form again). *See* RE(-).

Do not use hyphens in compound modifiers when the meaning is clear without them: *sales tax bill; foreign aid plan; C minor concerto*. But: *pay-as-you-go plan* and *earned-income tax credit*. Hyphens inserted hastily or automatically can be misleading, since the first word may relate at least as much to the third word as to the second. For example: *airport departure lounge; fast breeder reactor; national health insurance*. Also use no hyphen in these forms: *navy blue skirt; dark green paint*.

In some compounds, the hyphen should be used to avoid ambiguity or absurdity: *unfair-practices charge*, not *unfair practices charge*. Note the separation of an otherwise solid compound in *small-business man* (not *small businessman*) and *parochial-school teacher* (not *parochial schoolteacher*). *See* COMPOUND WORDS.

Never use a hyphen after an adverb ending in *ly*: *a newly married couple*; *an elegantly furnished house*; *a perfectly explicit instruction*. But an adjective ending in *ly* may take the hyphen if it is useful: *gravelly-voiced*; *grizzly-maned*.

The special case of compound modifiers that precede nouns is demonstrated in the entries on ILL(-) and WELL(-). An example: *He wore a well-tailored gray suit.* But omit the hyphen when the words follow the noun they modify: *The suit was well tailored.*

Some other compound modifiers, typically those beginning with nouns, keep their hyphens regardless of position in a sentence: *They are health-conscious; The purchase was tax-free; The party describes itself as family-oriented; Stylebook editors are awe-inspiring.*

Use no hyphens in a title consisting of a principal noun with modifiers: *commander in chief; lieutenant general; attorney general; director general; editor in chief; delegate at large; secretary general.* (See separate listings.) But use the hyphen in a title that joins two equal nouns: *secretary-treasurer.*

When a modifier consisting of two or more words is bound together by quotation marks, the hyphen is redundant; thus *poison-pill defense* and *"poison pill" defense* are both acceptable, but *"poison-pill" defense* is not. A long phrase serving as a contrived modifier is best set off by quotation marks rather than hyphens: *her "fed up with business as usual" theme.*

Use the suspensive hyphen, rather than repeat the second part of a modifier, in cases like this: *On successive days there were three-, five- and nine-inch snowfalls.*

Some house numbers in Queens take the hyphen: *107-71 111th Street.*

Use the hyphen in a compound denoting national origin: *Italian-American; Japanese-American.* But *French Canadian* and *Jewish American*, for example, take no hyphen because both words denote current group membership rather than origin.

For a minus sign, use the en dash (–) rather than a hyphen.

Also see WORD DIVISION.

I

I- for *Interstate* in highway numbers: *I-95. See* INTERSTATE SYSTEM.

I. for *Island* in names. The abbreviation may be used in headlines and maps (*Easter I.*), but not in articles. Do not use it in references to Coney Island, which is a neighborhood though it was once an island, and do not use *Long I.* or *Staten I.* Plural: *Is.* (*Canary Is.*).

Iberia Airlines of Spain. In most references, *Iberia* will do.

I.B.M. for the International Business Machines Corporation. As a brand name, the abbreviation stands alone (*an I.B.M. computer*).

ICBM('s) for intercontinental ballistic missile(s).

ice(-). Some compounds formed with *ice* are one word, some are two and a few are hyphenated: ice bag, iceberg, iceboat, icebound, icebreaker, icecap, ice-cold, ice cream, ice field, ice floe, icehouse, iceman, ice milk, ice pack, ice pick, ice skate (n.), ice-skate (v.), ice storm, ice water.

ice age.

iced tea (not *ice tea*).

Icelandair (the Icelandic airline).

IC4A, in first or later references to the Intercollegiate Association of Amateur Athletes of America, but the full name should appear in major articles.

ID for identification, without periods because the letters do not stand for separate words.

Idaho. Do not abbreviate, even after the names of cities, towns and counties.

Id al-Adha, the Islamic Feast of Sacrifice, is celebrated 70 days after Ramadan, the holy month of daytime fasting.

Id al-Fitr is the Islamic festival marking the end of Ramadan, the holy month of daytime fasting.

idée fixe (an obsession).

i.e., for the Latin *id est*, means *that is*. It rarely has a place in news writing, but when it does, do not confuse it with E.G.

if. For the verbs and tenses to use in *if* clauses, see CONDITIONAL TENSES and SUBJUNCTIVE. *Also see* WHETHER.

ifs, ands or buts. No apostrophes.

I.L.A. for the International Longshoremen's Association.

I.L.G.W.U. *See* UNITE.

ill(-). Hyphenate a compound formed with *ill* only when it serves as an adjective before a noun: ill-advised, ill-conceived, ill-considered, ill-defined, ill-equipped, ill-fated, ill-gotten, ill-humored, ill-looking, ill-mannered, ill-natured, ill-prepared, ill-spent, ill-starred, ill-suited, ill-tempered, ill-timed, ill-treated, ill-used.

   The hyphen is not used when the words follow the nouns they modify: *The plan was ill timed.*

illegal immigrant is the preferred term, rather than the sinister-sounding *illegal alien.* Do not use the euphemism *undocumented.*

illegitimate. Do not refer to a child of unmarried parents as *illegitimate,* and avoid the stodgy *born out of wedlock.* If the parents' marital status is pertinent and the pertinence is clear to the reader, simply report that the parents are not married or that the child is the son or daughter of a single mother or father.

Illinois. Abbreviate as *Ill.* after the names of cities, towns and counties.

Illinois Central Railroad (a subsidiary of the Illinois Central Corporation).

ill will, good will. But hyphenate them when they directly precede nouns: *a good-will offering.*

imam. *See* ARAB NAMES AND TITLES.

I.M.F. for the International Monetary Fund. Also: *the monetary fund; the fund.*

immigrate, emigrate. *See* EMIGRATE, IMMIGRATE.

imminent, eminent. *Imminent* means impending. *Eminent* means prominent or outstanding. (*Immanent,* a theological term rarely seen in news copy, refers to the presence of God in the universe.)

impact. As a verb, it means *strike with force* (the way a meteorite strikes Earth, for example). Do not use it to mean *affect* or *have an effect*; in that sense, it is technical jargon.

impaired. In references to people with disabilities, it usually means a correctable or less than total loss of a function or ability. Someone with less than 100 percent hearing may be described as *hearing-impaired. Also see* BLIND; CHALLENGED; DEAF; DISABILITY, DISABLED; HANDICAPPED.

impala (sing. and pl.).

impanel.

imperial gallon. An imperial gallon, the standard British gallon, is equal to about 4.5 liters or 1.2 United States gallons.

implement. Used as a verb, *implement* is pompously bureaucratic (as is *implementation*). Use conversational phrases like *carry out, put in effect, fulfill, accomplish* or *do.*

imply, infer. A speaker or writer or a set of facts *implies* things (that is, gives hints). A hearer or reader *infers* things (that is, draws conclusions). Preserve the distinction.

important(ly). Avoid this construction: *He is tall. More importantly, he is young.* Make it *more important.* The phrase includes an implied *what is* (*What is more important, he is young*). Thus *important* is an adjective modifying *what.*

impostor.

impressionism (art). Capitalize when referring to the movement in painting, initiated by Monet and others in the 1860's. Lowercase in more general references to art of a generalized and unfocused manner. *See* ARTS TERMINOLOGY.

Impressionism (music). Capitalize in reference to the movement, mainly French, that developed in the late 19th and early 20th centuries in opposition to Romanticism. Debussy was its main exponent. *See* ARTS TERMINOLOGY.

in. When it precedes a noun and means fashionable or faddish, *in* should carry quotation marks: *Bell-bottom pants were the "in" thing to wear in the early 1920's.* But: *Bell-bottoms are in again.* The same would be true of *out,* meaning outmoded, but it almost never precedes the noun: *Tail fins are definitely out.*

in(-), (-)in. Generally the prefix *in-* forms solid compounds: inboard, inbound, incoming, indoor, infield, infighting, inpatient (n. and adj.). But: in-group (n.), in-house (adj., though jargon), in house (adv., and more jargon), in-law, daughter-in-law, father-in-law.

    The suffix *-in* forms hyphenated compounds: break-in, cave-in, sit-in (all n. only).

    Latin terms that have entered English in fields like law and medicine are never solid or hyphenated: *in absentia, in camera, in extremis, in loco parentis, in toto, in utero, in vitro.* (Often it is possible, though, to improve readability by using English instead.)

in as many. Avoid this journalese mannerism: *This was the second case in as many weeks.* As many as *second*? No. Make it *the second case in two weeks.*

inasmuch as.

Inauguration Day. Also: *Inaugural Address.* Uppercase only when the terms apply to the president of the United States.

Inc. or an equivalent foreign abbreviation (*Ltd., S.A., S.p.A., G.m.b.H., N.V.,* etc.) should be omitted when a name includes some other company term (*Company, Corporation, Industries,* etc.). Similarly omit the terms in casual references: *She admires I.B.M. for its marketing strategy.* When *Inc.* is used, omit surrounding commas (*AOL Time Warner Inc.*).

incident. An *incident* is a minor happening or disturbance. When used in reference to accidents or events that have serious consequences, the word seems to trivialize them.

including. A phrase introduced by *including* can be logical only when a positive expression or quantity is doing the "including": *Tenured professors, including Dr. Agneau, may lose their jobs.* If the subject is negative, use *not even* instead: *No one, not even Dr. Agneau, will lose a job.* If the emphasis is on smallness of numbers, *not even* will again be closer to the desired meaning: *Few public officials, not even the Democratic leaders, support the legislation.* Or: *Few public officials, even among the Democratic leaders, support the legislation.* Also see COMPRISE.

income. In discussing a company's earnings, do not use *income* alone. Make it *income before taxes* or *net income.*

incommunicado.

incredible, incredulous. *Incredible* means unbelievable. *Incredulous* means unbelieving.

IND for the Independent Subway System, once a separate New York City operation. While the abbreviation survives in local idiom, it is confusing to newcomers and visitors. Except in quotations or historical contexts, make it simply *the A train* (or *line*); *the D train.*

Independence Day is the holiday celebrated on July 4. Informally, *the Fourth of July.*

in depth. The smoother way to use the phrase is after a noun: *a survey in depth.* As a preceding modifier (*in-depth study*), it is both cumbersome and devalued by overuse in publicity releases.

indexes (not *indices*).

Indian. *See* AMERICAN INDIAN(S).

Indiana. Abbreviate as *Ind.* after the names of cities, towns and counties.

indirection is what Harold Ross of The New Yorker called the quirk of sidling into facts as if the reader already knew them. An example is this sentence, in a profile of a college athlete: *The 19-year-old also plays the piccolo.* The reader pauses to wonder whether the 19-year-old is the athlete or someone else. Journalese indirection probably appears most often in situations like this: After a lead reporting a Democratic senator's re-election, the second paragraph begins *Lynn N. Karitsa thanked his supporters at a rowdy celebration.* The reader must guess that Mr. Karitsa is the senator. Better to write *The senator, Lynn N. Karitsa. . . .*

indispensable.

individual is stilted as a synonym for *person.* Reserve it for contexts in which a person is being distinguished from a group: *Companies will be taxed, but not individuals.*

Indochina consists of Cambodia, Laos and Vietnam.

Indonesian names. Often an Indonesian, like Suharto, has only one name. On first reference, if the subject has a title, it should be used: *President Suharto,* or before he was president, *General Suharto.* But if he had no title, the style would be *Mr. Suharto* in all references.

Generally, the consonant combination *dj* should be changed to *j* (as in the place name *Jakarta*, not *Djakarta*) and the vowel combination *oe* should be changed to *u* (*Suharto*, not *Soeharto*).

industrial age.

Industrial Revolution. The one that began in England in the 18th century.

inequity (unfairness), **iniquity** (evil or wickedness).

infer, imply. A hearer or reader *infers* things—that is, draws conclusions. A speaker or writer or a set of facts *implies* things—that is, gives hints. Preserve the distinction.

information age.

infrared.

ingénue.

initial letters. When a decorative initial letter is used at the beginning of a line (ascending or descending), uppercase the rest of the word. If the initial occurs in a personal name, the title of an artistic or literary work, or a publication name, set the entire name in capitals. If the first word is a title (*Sir, Dr., Gen.,* etc.), uppercase the entire name. And if the line begins with a one-letter word, follow the initial with an en space, and set the next word in capitals:

I REMEMBER the night the storm broke.   A NIGHT like few others.

initials in names. Although full first names with middle initials (if any) are preferred in most copy, two or more initials may be used if that is the preference of the person mentioned: *L. P. Arniotis,* with a thin space between initials. In American usage, a single initial (*L. Arniotis*) is not usually proper, but that style may be used in lists and charts. Also, in a pen name or a well-established stage name: *B. Traven.*

Except for unusual effect, do not use famous initials (*J.F.K., L.B.J., F.D.R.,* etc.) as a substitute for a name, even in a headline.

Also see PERSONAL NAMES AND NICKNAMES.

initiate is usually a stilted way of saying *open, start* or *begin.*

in line, on line. Few besides New Yorkers speak of standing *on line.* Follow the usage of the rest of the English-speaking world: *in line.*

inner city. Used in references to poor or blighted urban areas and their residents, the phrase is euphemistic and often inaccurate. (Some "inner" areas of cities are privileged, even wealthy, and some "outer" ones are poor.) Whether the desired meaning is *poor* or *minority* or *black,* specific and direct language is better.

innocent, not guilty. In the American system, a defendant is presumed innocent and therefore never needs to prove innocence; it is guilt that must be proven, by the state. So a defendant's plea (or a successful one's verdict) is *not guilty* rather than *innocent.* The journalistic practice of writing *innocent* arose from a fear of omitting *not* in typesetting. But the distinction is worth preserving, even at the cost of an extra moment to check the copy.

innuendo.

inoculate.

input. To avoid jargon, confine the word (n. and v.) to its technical sense: data or programs entered into a computer, or the process of entering them.

inquire.

insane asylum. Except in direct quotations, replace this outmoded term with *mental hospital.*

insignia is both singular and plural. An alternative singular, *insigne,* is stilted; an alternative plural is *insignias.*

insist. It means declare firmly or persistently, often in the face of disbelief. The word should be used with care because it can suggest that the writer does not believe the speaker.

insofar as.

Inspector *Alex J. Cordero; Inspector Cordero; the inspector.*

install, installment.

instill, instilling.

Institute for Advanced Study (in Princeton, N.J.). *Study* is singular, and the institute is not part of Princeton University.

insure, ensure. *Insure* means buy or issue insurance: *She insured her camera against theft. Ensure* means guarantee or make safe: *The hit ensured a Yankee victory.*

integration. *See* DESEGREGATION, INTEGRATION.

intelligence. *See* AGENT.

Intelsat for the International Telecommunications Satellite Organization.

inter(-). Do not hyphenate compounds formed with *inter* except when it precedes a proper noun: interaction, inter-American, intercity, intercollegiate, intercontinental, interdenominational, interdisciplinary, interfaith, interlocking, intermarriage, international, interoffice, interracial, interstate.

Interboro Parkway (connecting Brooklyn and Queens) is now *Jackie Robinson Parkway.*

Intercollegiate Association of Amateur Athletes of America. The abbreviation *IC4A* may be used in first references, but the full name should appear in major articles.

interface. To avoid jargon, confine the term (n. and v.) to its technical meaning: a bridge of equipment or software, or both, allowing dissimilar devices or programs to communicate. By extension, *interface* (or *user interface*) also refers to the symbols and movements on a computer screen that translate abstract program structures into understandable human terms (folders, push buttons, recycling bins, hourglasses and the like).

Intermediate School. In first references (except anecdotal or colloquial ones), use *Intermediate School 201* (without *No.* before the numeral). In most later references: *I.S. 201*.

intern (n. and v.).

International Brotherhood of Teamsters. *See* TEAMSTER.

International Court of Justice (at The Hague); *the World Court*; *the court*.

international date line. Not *dateline*, for the place on the globe where the day begins.

International Labor Organization (I.L.O.). The membership of this United Nations body consists of labor delegates, management delegates and governmental delegates.

International Ladies Garment Workers Union. It was absorbed in a 1995 merger. *See* UNITE.

International Monetary Fund; *the monetary fund*; *the fund*. In headlines: *I.M.F.*

International style (architecture). Capitalize when referring to the austere 20th-century style of steel and glass. *See* ARTS TERMINOLOGY.

International Telecommunications Satellite Organization (Intelsat).

Internet, the. The global network of computer networks. Also: *the Net.*

Internet addresses include e-mail addresses (*hlamm@nytimes.com*) and Web site designations (*http://www.nytimes.com*). The Web address is known technically as a U.R.L. (for *uniform resource locator*). Provide it whenever an article refers to a Web site that readers might want to consult. Follow the owner's capitalization, no matter how eccentric; parts of some addresses are "case sensitive" (valid only when properly capitalized). If a site owner uses a final slash (/), include it. If the address ends a sentence, use the normal period. But rephrase if necessary to avoid following the address with a comma or other punctuation mark. Because *http://* is the most common start of an address, it may be omitted; Web software will supply it. But some addresses begin with other expressions (for example, *ftp://*), which must be specified.

For comprehension, confine an Internet address within a single line of type when possible, or treat it as a separate paragraph. If an address must break between lines, the split should occur directly *before* a slash or a dot that is part of the address (without an inserted hyphen, which could be misleading). To accomplish this, first see where the typesetting computer tries to break the line; then, if necessary, override it with a "justify" command at the preferred spot.

Interstate System (of highways). When the name of the system is required, use this shortened version instead of the full name, the *National System of Interstate and Defense Highways*. In later references: *the Interstate*; *the Interstate proposal*. A highway may be referred to as *Interstate 95*, *Route 95* or *Route I-95*. In headlines: *Rte. 95; I-95; Rte. I-95.*

into the breach. The cliché, drawn from Shakespeare's "Henry V," is "Once more *unto* the breach."

intra(-). Do not hyphenate compounds formed with *intra*: intramural, intrastate, intrauterine, intravenous.

Intracoastal Waterway.

intranet, an organization's internal network of computers. An intranet may be linked to the global INTERNET or may merely emulate the Net's formats and commands.

Inuit (sing. and pl.) is the ethnic designation now preferred, especially in Canada, by many of the native people known to outsiders as *Eskimo(s)*. Because *Eskimo* is more widely recognizable, it should remain the primary reference, but *Inuit* may be applied to specific groups who choose it, so long as the connection of the terms is made clear.

invalid (n.). Describing a person as an *invalid* is vague and undervalues the person's remaining abilities. Be as specific as possible: *He finds it painful to walk more than a few steps* or *She is unable to get out of bed. See* DISABILITY, DISABLED.

i.o.u.

Iowa. Do not abbreviate, even after the names of cities, towns and counties.

I.Q. for intelligence quotient.

Iraklion, not *Herakleion*, for the city in Crete.

iris(es).

Ironbound, the. A neighborhood in the eastern corner of Newark that took its name in the late 1800's from the railroad tracks that then surrounded it.

ironclad.

Iron Curtain. Uppercase in references to the Soviet bloc's isolation during the cold war, but use the expression only when polemical phrasing is appropriate, or in quotations. Lowercase in general references to *an iron curtain*.

irony, in precise usage, is a restrained form of sarcasm in which the intent of a phrase differs from its literal meaning, often for rhetorical effect (*His brilliant plan nearly bankrupted the company*). The looser use of *irony* and *ironically*, to mean an incongruous turn of events, is trite. Not every coincidence, curiosity, oddity and paradox is an irony, even loosely. And where irony does exist, sophisticated writing counts on the reader to recognize it. *Also see* PARADOX.

I.R.S. for the Internal Revenue Service.

IRT for Interborough Rapid Transit, an independent subway line in New York acquired by the city in 1940. While the abbreviation survives in local idiom, it is confusing to newcomers. Except in direct quotations or historical contexts, make it simply *the No. 9 train* (or *line*); *the 4 train.*

I.S. for Intermediate School in most later references: *I.S. 109*. In first references (except anecdotal or colloquial ones), spell out *Intermediate School 109* (without *No.* before the numeral).

Is. for Islands in proper names. The abbreviation may be used in maps and headlines (*Canary Is.*). The singular is *I.* (*Easter I.*).

I.S.D.N. for Integrated Services Digital Network, a technology that uses telephone lines to transmit digital data, images and voices.

(-)ish. Compounds formed with *ish* as a suffix are not hyphenated unless they include a number: amateurish; bluish; boyish; bullish; 40-ish; kittenish; prudish; sweetish.

Do not ordinarily hyphenate unfamiliar *ish* words or those coined for effect (*Clintonish*; *downtownish*), but ration their use to avoid cuteness.

Islam can mean not only the Muslim religion but also Muslims generally and the areas of the world where their religion is predominant. Islam's deity is Allah, and Muhammad is the religion's prophet. The adjective is *Islamic*.

Island, the, for Long Island, in later references.

issue, edition(s). Do not interchange. *See* EDITION(S), ISSUE.

it. In references to countries and ships, use the pronouns *it* and *its*, not *she* and *her*.

Italianate. Capitalize the architectural term, which has several meanings, most of them vaguely related to the idea of Italian villas. In the United States the style is characterized mostly by rounded window tops, often with elaborate cornices above them and atop the building itself. Many 19th-century brownstones in New York are considered Italianate. *See* ARTS TERMINOLOGY.

italic. Both *italic* and *roman* are lowercase in references to typefaces.

italics. News copy uses italics most sparingly, a convention rooted in the era of metal type, when they were usually inaccessible. Now, however, italics are available—for a quotation, for example, to convey the speaker's emphasis—but The Times's own writing should preferably express emphasis through word order and word choice. Do not use italics for GENUS AND SPECIES names or for publication names or cultural titles; see the separate style entries for those.

Also do not use italics for citations of court cases, but in a quotation or a verbatim text, substitute quotation marks around any occurrence that would otherwise be ambiguous (" 'Nixon' offers us a valuable example," the judge said).

While the news sections do not italicize foreign words, an exception is made for The Times Magazine and the Book Review, reflecting the more literary flavor of a weekly periodical. In those sections, use italics for words that are indisputably foreign—either absent from the English dictionary or included but labeled foreign. Commonly borrowed expressions like *haute cuisine* and *haute couture*, *gulag*, *glasnost* and *perestroika* remain in roman type, as do foreign proper names.

If in doubt, assume that a word is too familiar in English to be treated as foreign. And a lengthy foreign sentence (a quotation, ordinarily) is not italicized.

Italo-. Avoid, in adjectival references to Italy. Use *Italian-American, Italian-French,* etc.

Itar-Tass is the official name of the Russian government's press agency, but *Tass* is an acceptable first reference. *Itar* stands for Information Telegraph Agency of Russia. Tass was formed from the initials of the Russian words meaning Telegraph Agency of the Soviet Union.

its, it's. Beware of the confusion that may result from haste: *its* is the possessive form of *it* (meaning *of it*). The contraction *it's* means *it is* (or, less often, *it has*).

ITT is no longer the name of a single company; the ITT Corporation was split in 1995. Successor companies are *ITT Educational Services, ITT Hartford Mutual Funds* and *ITT Industries.* All trace their ancestry to the International Telephone and Telegraph Corporation.

IUD for intrauterine device (contraceptive).

Ivory Coast (not *Côte d'Ivoire*). The people are *Ivoirian(s)*.

Ivy League. Its members are Brown, Columbia, Cornell, Dartmouth, Harvard, the University of Pennsylvania (not Pennsylvania State), Princeton and Yale.

J

Jackie Robinson Parkway (the former *Interboro Parkway*, connecting Brooklyn and Queens).

jack-in-the-box(es); *jack-in-the-pulpit(s); jack(s)-of-all-trades; jack-o'-lantern(s).*

Jacob K. Javits Convention Center. In later references, and even in first references when terseness counts, *the Javits Convention Center* is acceptable.

jailer.

Jan. for January before numerals (*Jan. 10*) or in charts and tables.

J&R Computer World, J&R Music World (the Manhattan stores and their branches).

Jane's. The reference books are *Jane's All the World's Aircraft, Jane's Fighting Ships, Jane's Intermodal Transportation, Jane's Space Directory, Jane's Weapon Systems.* All without quotation marks.

Jap. As a term for *Japanese*, it is pejorative. Resist its use even in references to World War II attitudes.

Japan Airlines (JAL).

Japanese names. Use them in the customary Western fashion, with the surname after the given name: *Finance Minister Kiichi Miyazawa; Mr. Miyazawa.*

Java man (anthropological), not *Java Man.*

J. C. Penney Company. Use a thin space between initials.

jeep. Lowercase when referring to the military vehicle of World War II and later vintage; capitalize when referring to the civilian vehicle so trademarked.

Jehovah's Witnesses are members of a Christian denomination that holds the Bible to be literally true in every detail. They are notable for their door-to-door missionary work.

Jell-O is a trademark.

jerry-built means cheaply or shoddily made. Do not confuse with *jury-rigged*, which means intended for temporary or emergency use.

Jersey, as a short form for *New Jersey*, should be a last resort, in copy and in headlines; some New Jerseyans find it disparaging. The same is true of *Jerseyan(s).* A few idioms are exceptions: *Jersey Shore; North Jersey; South Jersey.*

Jersey City State College changed its name in 1998 to *New Jersey City University.*

Jersey Shore; *the shore.* But: *the New Jersey coast.*

Jesus. As a historical name, it is undisputed and therefore preferred. But in direct or in-direct quotations and explicit references to Christianity, *Christ* is also appropriate. Lowercase *he, him, his, who, whom,* etc., in references to Jesus, God or the Holy Ghost (or Holy Spirit).

Jet Ski is a trademark for a motorized water scooter.

Jet Train Airlines (the discount airline).

Jew(s). Use the word, unvarnished, in references to people of Jewish heritage or religion. Phrases like *member of the Jewish faith* strike some Jews as unwarranted euphemisms. Do not use *Jewess.*

In citing Eastern European Jewish ancestry, do not assign nationalities unless families claim them. For centuries, many Jews felt themselves excluded from the nations in which they lived, and built a society apart. So it is often more appropriate to write (when it is relevant) that a Jew is *the daughter of immigrants from Ukraine,* for example, than to call her *the daughter of Ukrainian immigrants.*

Also see CONSERVATIVE JUDAISM; ORTHODOX JUDAISM; REFORM, REFORMED; RECONSTRUCTIONIST JUDAISM.

J.F.K. or simply *Kennedy* in headlines and in later references to John F. Kennedy International Airport. Use *Kennedy International Airport* or *Kennedy Airport* in most first references. (But do not use *J.F.K.* to mean the former president, even in a headline, except for special effect.)

j.g. for junior grade: *Lt. j.g. Chris T. Yagyonak; Lieutenant Yagyonak; the lieutenant.*

J.H.S. for Junior High School in most later references: *J.H.S. 131.* In first references, (except anecdotal or colloquial ones), spell out *Junior High School 131* (without *No.* before the numeral).

jibe. Colloquially, it means conform. In sailing, it means shift. *Gibe* means jeer or taunt.

jihad. It is a holy war carried out by Muslims against the enemies of Islam.

Joe DiMaggio Highway. At least in formal references, the new name of the *West Side Highway.*

John F. Kennedy International Airport is the official name, but *Kennedy International Airport* or *Kennedy Airport* should be used in most first references. The single word *Kennedy* or the initials *J.F.K.* will do for most later references and for headlines when the aviation context is clear.

John Jay College of Criminal Justice (part of the CITY UNIVERSITY OF NEW YORK).

Johns Hopkins University (in Baltimore).

Johnson Space Center is an acceptable first reference to the Lyndon B. Johnson Space Center at Houston. In later references: *the space center. Also see* CAPE CANAVERAL.

Joint Chiefs of Staff; *the Joint Chiefs*; *the chiefs*. *Also see* CHAIRMAN OF THE JOINT CHIEFS OF STAFF.

joint meeting, joint session. When the two houses of Congress convene together to conduct official business—to hear the State of the Union address, say, or to count electoral votes—they are holding a *joint session*. But when they gather to hear a distinguished speaker, it is a *joint meeting* held while Congress is in recess.

journal names. *See* PERIODICAL NAMES.

J. P. Morgan Chase & Company was formed in 2000 by a merger of the Chase Manhattan Corporation with J. P. Morgan & Company. *J. P. Morgan* remains a brand name for the company's wholesale banking businesses. *Chase* remains the name for many of its retail services.

Jr., Sr. *See* JUNIOR, SENIOR.

Juárez (in Mexico).

Judaism. *See* CONSERVATIVE JUDAISM; ORTHODOX JUDAISM; REFORM, REFORMED; RECONSTRUCTIONIST JUDAISM.

Judge *Tracy T. Anyell*; *Judge Anyell*; *the judge*. Do not use *Mr., Mrs., Miss, Ms.*, etc., in later references. These courts use *judge*:
- All federal courts except the Supreme Court.
- The Criminal, Civil and Family Courts in New York City.
- State courts in Connecticut, New Jersey and most other states. But in New York, only the Courts of Appeals and Claims. (In the New York State Supreme Court and its Appellate Division, the title is JUSTICE.)

   Also see COURTS.

judgment.

judicial branch (of the United States government). Also: *executive branch*; *legislative branch*.

Juilliard School. Also: *the Juilliard Theater*.

jukebox.

July. Do not abbreviate except, when necessary, in tables or charts.

jumbo jet. An extra-large airliner like the 747.

June. Do not abbreviate except, when necessary, in tables or charts.

junior for the class and a member of that class. *See* JUNIOR, SENIOR.

Junior High School. In first references (except anecdotal or colloquial ones), use *Junior High School 131* (without *No.* before the numeral). In most later references: *J.H.S. 131*.

Junior, Senior. Use *Jr.* and *Sr.* (without commas) in names: *Lee Berenich Jr.* (or *Sr.*). In bylines: **By LEE E. BERENICH Jr.** Also: *Lee E. Berenich IV* or *Lee E. Berenich 4th*, depending on individual preference. If the preference is not known, use Roman numerals.

In a listing with surnames printed before given names, *Jr.* (or *Sr.*, or *IV*, etc.) comes last: *BERENICH, Lee E. Jr.*, not *BERENICH Jr., Lee E.*

junkie(s). In its original meaning, for an addict, the word is brutal slang. In other uses (notably *political junkie*), it remains slang, besides being a cliché that slights the enormity of addiction.

jury-rigged means intended for temporary or emergency use. Do not confuse with *jerry-built*, which means cheaply or shoddily made.

Justice *Lindsay M. Karitsa; Justice Karitsa; the justice* (or *the judge*). For a member of the United States Supreme Court, it is *the justice* or *the associate justice*. Do not use *Mr.*, *Mrs.*, *Miss*, *Ms.*, etc., in later references. Do not use *Mr. Justice* (or *Ms. Justice*, etc.) except in quotations, in texts or for special effect. *Justice* is also the title for the New York State Supreme Court and for its Appellate Division. *Also see* JUDGE.

juvenile diabetes. *See* DIABETES.

juvenile offenders and suspects. Often though not always, The Times shields the identity of a juvenile offender or suspect. Factors in the decision include the severity of the crime, the likelihood that the case will be tried in a juvenile court and the subject's prospects for eventual rehabilitation. *Every* decision to divulge such an identity or to withhold it should be discussed with a masthead editor or with the head of the news desk.

K

Kaaba is the sacred shrine at Mecca toward which Muslims turn when they pray.

Kaddish, the Jewish prayer for the dead, is recited in Aramaic, not Hebrew.

kaffeeklatsch (not *coffee klatch*).

Kansas. Abbreviate as *Kan.* after the names of cities, towns and counties.

Kansas City Southern Railway (a subsidiary of Kansas City Southern Industries).

karat. A *karat* is a measure of the fineness of gold. Pure gold is 24 karats, and one karat is equal to one twenty-fourth part of pure gold. Thus an object made of 18-karat gold contains 18 parts pure gold and 6 parts alloy. Not to be confused with *carat*, a unit of weight used for gemstones, which equals 200 milligrams. An *18-karat* gold ring might have a *1-carat* diamond. And of course a *caret* was a mark used by writers and editors before they had cursors.

Kashmir, Vale of.

Katmandu (in Nepal).

Katonah (in Westchester County, N.Y.).

Kazakhstan (the former Kazakh Soviet Socialist Republic).

Kean University (in Union, N.J.).

Kearny (in New Jersey). But: *Kearney, Neb.*

keen(-). Compounds formed with *keen* are hyphenated: keen-edged, keen-eyed, keen-sighted, keen-witted.

(-)keeper. Compounds formed with *keeper* as a suffix are generally one word: barkeeper, beekeeper, bookkeeper, gatekeeper, goalkeeper, groundskeeper, hotelkeeper, housekeeper, innkeeper, peacekeeper, scorekeeper, shopkeeper, storekeeper, timekeeper, tollgate keeper.

keeshond (the dog). The plural is *keeshonden*.

Kelvin. An international standard scale for temperature. Uppercase the system name, but lowercase the term for the unit, a *kelvin*. Do not use the redundant *degree(s) kelvin*. Like Celsius, the Kelvin scale reckons the difference between the freezing and boiling points of water as 100 units. But while Celsius places 0 at the freezing point, Kelvin begins its scale at absolute zero—the total absence of heat. The freezing point of water (0 degrees Celsius) is 273.15 kelvin and the boiling point is 373.15 kelvin. The abbreviation, ordinarily confined to tables, is uppercased, without a degree symbol: *373.15 K.* Also see CELSIUS, CENTIGRADE; FAHRENHEIT; TEMPERATURE.

Kennedy International Airport or *Kennedy Airport* should generally be used in first references rather than the official name, *John F. Kennedy International Airport.* Use *Kennedy* alone or *J.F.K.* in most later references and in headlines when the aviation context is clear.

Kentucky. Abbreviate it as *Ky.* after the names of cities, towns and counties.

ketchup (not *catchup* or *catsup*).

key (adj. and n.). In a phrase like *key provisions* or *key role*, the modifier is tolerable, though clichéd because of its usefulness in narrow headlines. And the provisions may be *a key* or *the key* to the passage of a bill. But resist this faddish use of *key* as an adjective (without a *the*) after the noun: *the lobbyists were key.* More established synonyms include *crucial* and *central.*

key(-). Many compounds formed with *key* are one word, but some are two: keyboard, key club, keyhole, Key lime pie, key money, keynote, keypad, key punch, key ring, keystone, keystroke, Key West.

KeySpan Energy Corporation (the parent of the Brooklyn Union Gas Company).

K.G.B., in historical references, for the Soviet secret police and intelligence apparatus. Its Russian initials stood for Committee for State Security. The name was used only from 1954 to 1991; for other periods, verify which of many successive names applied.

Khmer Rouge (usually plural).

kibbutz for the Israeli collective settlement. The plural is *kibbutzim.* Also: *kibbutznik* for a member.

kickoff (n.).

kidnap, kidnapped, kidnapping, kidnapper. Use *kidnapping* (never *kidnap*, even in headlines) for the noun and the modifier, to avoid a headlinese flavor.

kid(s). As a synonym for *child* or *children*, it is colloquial and usually too folksy.

kill (n.). One meaning of this noun is stream. Thus it is redundant, for example, to write *the Schuylkill River.* It is *the Schuylkill.*

Kill Van Kull (the strait between Staten Island and Bayonne, N.J.).

kilobyte. A *kilobyte* is about a thousand bytes (1,024, to be exact), or enough computer memory to store that number of characters. In technical contexts, abbreviate it as *K: an 800K data file. Also see* BIT; BYTE; GIGABYTE; MEGABYTE.

kilogram. One thousand grams, or roughly 2.2 pounds. *See* METRIC SYSTEM.

kilometer. A unit of length equal to 1,000 meters or approximately 3,281 feet. It is roughly equal to 0.6 of a mile or five-eighths of a mile. *See* METRIC SYSTEM.

kiloton. A *kiloton* is a unit used to measure the power of nuclear explosions. It is equal to the explosive force of one thousand tons of TNT. *Also see* MEGATON.

kilowatt-hours.

kimono(s).

kin is a collective plural meaning *relatives*; one person is a *kinsman* or a *kinswoman*.

kind, kinds. It is *that kind* and *those kinds*.

kindergartner.

kind of. Avoid this construction: *She bought that kind of a kumquat*. Omit the *a*.

King *Henry VIII*; *the king*; *Henry VIII*; and sometimes *Henry*. Capitalize *His Majesty*, but use it only in direct quotations or for special effect.

King James Version (of the Bible).

King, Martin Luther Jr. (the Rev. Dr.). See MARTIN LUTHER KING'S BIRTHDAY.

Kingsborough Community College (part of the CITY UNIVERSITY OF NEW YORK).

Kings Point (in Nassau County, N.Y.).

Kitty Litter is a trademark; the generic term is *cat litter* or *cat box filler*.

Klansman(men), Klanswoman(women) for members of the KU KLUX KLAN.

Kleenex is a trademark for facial tissues.

KLM Royal Dutch Airlines. In most references, *KLM* will do.

Kmart.

knee(-). Some but not all compounds formed with *knee* are hyphenated: knee breeches, kneecap, knee-deep, knee-high, kneehole, knee-jerk (adj.), kneejerk (n.), kneepad.

Knesset. It is the Israeli legislature. But except in unusually detailed references to the system or passages conveying local color, *Parliament* is a more accessible term for nonspecialized readers.

knight (British rank). The holder is not a peer. *See* SIR.

Knight Ridder, the newspaper company, no longer uses a hyphen or *Inc.* in its name.

knockdown (n.), **knock down** (v.).

knockout (n.), **knock out** (v).

knot. A knot is a unit of speed equal to one nautical mile (1.15 statute miles or 6,076 feet or 1,852 meters) per hour. So it is redundant to use *per hour* after knots, as in *10 knots per hour*.

know-how. It is colloquial, and a trite way to say *skill*.

knowledgeable.

known as. The phrase makes quotation marks redundant in a construction like *The practice is known as "greenmail."*

Kodak is a trademark for cameras, film and related products.

kopeck(s).

Koran. The sacred book of Islam. Muslims believe that its text comprises the words of Allah dictated to the Prophet Muhammad through the Angel Gabriel.

Korean names. Most Koreans follow the Chinese practice of putting family name first: *Prime Minister Kang Song San, Prime Minister Kang; President Kim Tae Chung, President Kim*. But the given names (*Song San; Tae Chung*), unlike those in

China, take the form of two separate words. In the past, some Koreans westernized their names (*Syngman Rhee*, for example; *Rhee* was the family name). This practice is now rarely seen.

Korean War (1950-53). In texts or quotations, *Korean conflict* is acceptable.

Kosciuszko Bridge (between Brooklyn and Queens, over the Newtown Creek).

kosher. Lowercase the term in its literal sense (meaning permissible under Jewish dietary law) or its slang one (meaning legitimate, in any field). Also: *glatt kosher* (stringently kosher by Hasidic standards) and *kashrut* (n., the system of dietary law).

Krazy Glue is a trademark.

Ku Klux Klan; *the Klan;* *the K.K.K.* A local unit is called a *Klan* or a *klavern,* and a member is a *Klansman* or *Klanswoman.*

Kuomintang (Chinese Nationalist), not *the Kuomintang Party. Tang* means party.

Kurile Islands.

Kwanzaa is a seven-day cultural festival celebrated by some black Americans. It begins on Dec. 26 and is based on African harvest customs.

L

labeled. Avoid the "as" construction: *She labeled the charge as false.* Make it simply *She labeled the charge false.*

"La Bohème."

Labor Day, the first Monday in September, is a federal holiday.

Labor Party (not *Labour*, even for the British party).

lack. Use the word to mean a shortage of something that is needed or desirable, not merely *absence.* Thus: *The skiers were frustrated by a lack of snow.* But: *The absence* [not *lack*] *of rain makes the island a perfect vacation spot.*

Ladies' Home Journal.

Ladies Professional Golf Association. No apostrophe. The abbreviation *L.P.G.A.* can be used in a first reference.

Lady. This title applies to the wives of British knights and baronets (who are not peers) and of barons, viscounts, earls and marquesses (who are). It also applies to women below the rank of duchess who are peeresses in their own right: *the Countess of Lambsford; Lady Lambsford.* For any of those ranks, the title is never followed by a given name: *Lady Dann,* not *Lady Hilary Dann.*

But the title is also applied to the daughters of earls, marquesses and dukes, and in those cases it precedes a given name: *Lady Mary Lamb; Lady Mary.* (Never, in such a case, *Lady Lamb.*)

When applied to the wife of the younger son of a marquess or a duke, the title is followed by the husband's given name: *Lady Douglas Anyell-Dann.* In later references, it is *Lady Douglas,* never *Lady Anyell-Dann.*

If a peeress in her own right or a peer's daughter marries, her title does not attach to her husband. If she outranks him, she keeps her title: *the Countess of Lambsford* (a peeress) *and her husband, Lt. Col. Edward Walter Cordero.* And *Lady Pamela Dann* (a peer's daughter) *and her husband, Michael Dann.*

For widows and divorced women, use this form: *Nancy Viscountess Anyell* or *Anne Lady Dann Cordero.* In later references it is *Lady Anyell* and *Lady Dann Cordero* (never *Lady Nancy Anyell* or *Lady Anne Dann Cordero*).

To distinguish between women of the same name, use any of these forms: *Lady (Elizabeth) Anyell* or *Lady Anyell, the former Elizabeth Dann* or *Lady Anyell, wife of Sir John Anyell* (never *Lady Elizabeth Anyell*, except for the daughter of an earl, a marquess or a duke).

lady. Except in wry contexts, *lady* is obsolete for *woman*, just as *gentleman* is obsolete for *man*. See FIRST LADY and MEN AND WOMEN.

La Guardia Airport.

La Guardia Community College (part of the CITY UNIVERSITY OF NEW YORK).

laissez-faire.

Laker Airways.

lambaste. When used to mean criticize or denounce, this colloquial verb is overworked and usually hyperbole.

lamb's-wool (adj.).

Lamont-Doherty Earth Observatory (at Columbia University).

Lance Cpl. *Dana F. Kuzu; Corporal Kuzu; the corporal.*

Lancet, The. Though it is published in Britain, do not call it *the British medical journal* because there is a publication called The British Medical Journal. Use a phrase like *the London-based medical publication.*

Lan Chile (the Chilean airline).

land(-), (-)land. Most compounds formed with *land* as a prefix are one word, but there are numerous exceptions: land bank, land contract, landfall, landfill, land grant (n.), land-grant (adj.), landholder, landlocked, landlord, landmark, land mine, landowner, land-poor, landscape, landslide, landward.

Compounds formed with *land* as a suffix are solid: cropland, dreamland, farmland, grassland, highland, inland, lowland, parkland, tideland, wonderland, woodland.

landmark. Use it as a noun; as a verb, it is jargon. Thus: *the theater was declared a landmark*, not *landmarked.*

Land Rover is no longer hyphenated.

Laotian names. Because of differences in ethnic backgrounds, Laotians' names assume a variety of forms. When possible, verify individual preferences. Most often a Laotian uses the first element of the name in later references: *Prince Souvanna Phouma; Prince Souvanna.* In a headline: *Souvanna.* In case of doubt, however, use the full name for all references: *President Khamtai Siphandon; Gen. Khamtai Siphandon*, with the title abbreviated in all references because the name is unchanged. (But if his title were, say, *Maj. Gen.*, it could later be shortened to *General*, spelled out.)

laptop (adj. and n.).

larceny, burglary, robbery, theft. *Larceny* is the wrongful taking of property (the equivalent, in nonlegal terms, of *theft* or *stealing*). Legal definitions of *burglary* vary among localities, but it must involve entering a building (not necessarily breaking and entering) and remaining unlawfully with the intent to commit a crime. *Robbery*, in its legal sense, is a larceny carried out through the use or threat of violence; it must be committed in the presence of the victim. In a broader sense, *rob* means plunder or rifle or loot. Thus, a safe may be *robbed*, as a person is *robbed*. The contents of the safe, or the wallet and watch of the victim, are *stolen. Also see* MUGGING.

largess (not largesse).

laser disc. *Also see* DISC, DISK.

lasso(s).

last in first out. Hyphenate when the phrase serves as a modifier before a noun: *the last-in-first-out system of accounting.* Otherwise, omit all the punctuation: *the principle of last in first out.* In later references, but only in clear business contexts: *LIFO.*

late (meaning dead). In general, use *the late* only with the name of a person who has recently died (*recent* being a synonym for *late*). For example, it is not needed in *the late Lyndon B. Johnson.* Avoid this redundancy: *She is the widow of the late Toby B. Karitsa.* And do not fall into this error: *Only the late Senator Miel opposed the bill.* He was almost certainly alive at the time.

Latino (n. and adj.) has the same meaning as HISPANIC: descended from a Spanish-speaking land or culture. (The feminine noun is *Latina.*) The use of *Latino*, long preferred in the West and the Southwest, is spreading in the United States; for now, though, *Hispanic* remains in wider use. When writing about specific people or groups, choose the term they prefer. Neither word denotes a race; *Latino* or *Hispanic* Americans can be of any race. When a more specific description is available—*Cuban, Puerto Rican, Mexican-American*—use it. Take care with descriptions like *Spanish-speaking* and *Spanish-surnamed* because Hispanic Americans do not necessarily speak the language, and some have other kinds of names. *See* CHICANO; ETHNICITY; PUERTO RICO, PUERTO RICAN.

latitude and longitude. Use these forms: *49 degrees north latitude; 24 degrees west longitude; 10 degrees 30 minutes south latitude.* Also: *prime meridian; Greenwich meridian; 17th parallel.*

latter. Avoid uses of *latter* that force the reader to glance back: *Both Mr. Miel and Ms. Agneau fought hard, but the latter prevailed.* Rephrase and name names.

Latter-day Saints. *See* MORMON CHURCH.

laughingstock.

launch, launching. In the naval and aerospace sense, use *launch* as a verb only: *They will launch the missile Tuesday. The ship was launched at Newport News.* For the noun and the adjective, use *launching,* even in tightly confined headlines: *The launching is scheduled for Tuesday; the launching pad.* In references to programs, candidacies, careers and other undertakings (but not military campaigns), use *open* and *begin* rather than the overworked *launch.*

Laundromat is a trademark.

laureate. Also: *Nobel laureate; poet laureate; J. J. Anyell, the poet laureate.*

law(-). Most but not all compounds formed with *law* are one word: law-abiding, lawbook, lawbreaker, lawmaker, lawman, lawsuit.

lawman is fine for western movies and other contexts that might also call for *passel* and *victuals.* Elsewhere use *law officer* or, better yet, an actual title.

laws. *See* ACTS, AMENDMENTS, BILLS AND LAWS.

lawsuits. The filing of a suit does not mean the plaintiff has a case, and the amount of the damage claim often bears no relationship to what a judge or a jury will eventually decide. Often a large dollar figure is used as a means of seizing headlines. Treat the content of the suit as merely one side in an argument, and seek a comment from the defendant. Ordinarily omit the amount of the claim from the headline and the lead; deal with it lower in the article, where the basis can be promptly put in perspective. An exception may be made if the plaintiff demonstrates that damages have been reasonably computed or if the article deals with the hyperbole surrounding such figures.

lay(-). Most but not all compounds formed with *lay* are one word: layaway (n.), layman, lay off (v.), layoff (n.), lay out (v.), layout (n.), layover (n.), layup (sports), laywoman.

lay, lie. Use *lay* to mean put down, or place. And it requires a direct object, the thing that is put or placed. Hens *lay* eggs. Bricklayers *lay* bricks. Healers *lay* hands upon the infirm. In every case, *lay* has an object—eggs, bricks, hands. In other tenses, *lay* takes these forms: *Hens laid eggs last week; Hens are laying eggs faster than ever; Hens had laid eggs before the sun rose.*

Lie means recline, or occupy a location. It does not take an object because the subject can accomplish those things alone. The idle rich *lie* on beaches. The restless *lie* awake. The faithful *lie* down in green pastures. Governors Island *lies* off Manhattan. Sleeping dogs just *lie.* The rich, the restless, the faithful, the island and the dogs need no help—no object to complete their actions. They simply lie there. And in other tenses, *lie* takes these forms: *The rich are lying on the beach despite the shaky economy; The rich had lain on the beach before moving to the slopes.*

Confusion arises because the past tense of *lie* also happens to be *lay,* playing a different role: *The idle rich lay on the beach yesterday.*

lay off (v.), **layoff** (n. and adj.). Use these terms for removals of employees to reduce a work force or cut costs, not for dismissals over job performance. *See* FIRE, FIRING.

lazy susan.

Lazard Frères & Company (investment bankers). Its French affiliate is *Lazard Frères et Compagnie.*

leach, leech. *Leach* is a verb for what liquids do when they percolate through a material. *Leech* is a noun for a bloodsucker, or a verb for the act of clinging like one.

leader. Resist phrases that anoint people to speak for others who have not had a chance to choose. Phrases like *black leader* and *spokesman for the Hispanic community* imply wide or universal agreement among people who may hold varied views. Except in unavoidable quotations, use more specific terms: *black ministers*; *pastor of the XYZ Baptist Church*; *Hispanic politicians*; *officers of Asian-American community groups.*

leak. In news reporting, a *leak* is an intentional disclosure by someone who chooses to remain anonymous. Some leaks are unsolicited; others are induced by diligent reporters. Some may serve a worthy purpose, others a selfish or underhanded one. When the source's motives can be gathered, they should be indicated in the article as fully as possible. Do not attribute a disclosure to a leak without knowing the exact circumstances; that can be unfair to a reporter in another organization whose enterprise tracked down the information. *Also see* ATTRIBUTION.

leatherneck. A synonym for a marine, but only in a direct quotation or in a feature context calling for a colorful effect.

leave alone, let alone. *Leave alone* means leave in solitude. *Let alone* means refrain from disturbing.

lectern, podium. A speaker stands *at* or *behind* a lectern and *on* a podium.

lectures. *See* SPEECHES AND LECTURES.

L.E.D. for light-emitting diode.

leech, leach. *Leech* is a noun for a bloodsucker, or a verb for the act of clinging like one. *Leach* is a verb for what liquids do when they percolate through a material.

left, leftist, left wing. Lowercase *left* unless the political divisions in a country are formally designated as *the Left, the Left Wing*, etc., or the word appears in a party name. Lowercase *leftist* unless the reference is to such a division or party, or to a member of it. Lowercase *left wing* or *left-wing* (adj.) unless the reference is to such a division or party.

left(-). Most compounds formed with *left* are either hyphenated or two words: left brain, left field, left fielder, left guard, left hand (n.), left-hand (adj.), left-handed, left-hander, leftover (n.), left wing (n.), left-wing (adj.).

Left Bank (the district in Paris).

legation. Lowercase when standing alone. But: *the Israeli Legation; the United States Legation.*

legendary is usually hyperbole. Use it with restraint.

legislation. When bills or regulations figure significantly in the news, the process should always be explained, and the copy should answer the question that naturally arises: What happens next? What steps remain? And what is the best estimate of the political outlook?

legislative bodies. Capitalize *Congress, Senate, House of Representatives* (or *House*), *Parliament, Legislature, Assembly,* etc., in any specific reference to a legislative body so named. *Parliament* should ordinarily be used in place of equivalent foreign terms like *Knesset* (Israel), *Diet* (Japan) and *Cortes* (Spain). Also: *parliaments; a parliament.*

legislative branch (of the United States government). *Also: executive branch; judicial branch.*

Legislature. Capitalize it when the reference is to one body officially so designated, or to a small number of bodies specifically identified: *the State Legislature; the Legislature; the California Legislature; the Wisconsin and Rhode Island Legislatures; the two Legislatures.* But: *many legislatures; several state legislatures;* etc. Also: *legislator(s); state legislator(s); California legislator(s).*

Lehman College (part of the CITY UNIVERSITY OF NEW YORK).

Leif Ericson (the explorer). But verify the spellings used for place names that commemorate him; they vary.

lend. *See* LOAN.

Lent, Lenten.

lesbian (adj. and n.). Lowercase except in the names of organizations. *Lesbian women* is redundant. *See* SEXUAL ORIENTATION.

lèse-majesté.

(-)less. Ordinarily close up compounds formed with *less* (even coined or jesting ones) unless the suffix directly follows an *l*: carless, computerless, dial-less, pitiless, rail-less, shell-less, tail-less, valueless, worthless.

lessen is a stilted word rarely found outside journalism. *Decrease* and *reduce* are more conversational.

less, fewer. *See* FEWER, LESS.

less than. The phrase is useful in many contexts but is sometimes partisan. It tends to play down an amount: *less than $10,000.* And *nearly $10,000* tends to play it up. A more neutral approach is *about $10,000.*

letup (n.).

letter(-). Compounds formed with *letter* can be one word, two words or hyphenated: letter bomb, letter carrier, letterhead, letterman (sports), letter opener, letter-perfect, letterpress, letter-quality.

level is stilted and rarely necessary in a passage like *on an informal level*. Make it *informally*.

levelheaded.

Levi's is a trademark.

levy, as a noun for *tax,* is archaic and at first glance, in a headline, looks distractingly like a surname.

L.I. may be used as a headline abbreviation for Long Island in editions and sections that circulate only in the New York metropolitan area. Do not use *Long I.* In datelines, the names of Long Island cities and towns should be followed by *N.Y.,* which should also be used in articles unless the context is otherwise clear. If necessary, mention deftly that the community is on Long Island.

liable suggests not just a probability but an unpleasant one. Write *Jaywalkers are liable to be arrested.* But: *The weather is likely to improve.*

liaison.

liberal. Do not capitalize as a noun or an adjective except in referring to a political party or movement so named, or to its members.

liberal-minded.

Liberal Party.

Liberty Island. Until 1956 it was Bedloes Island.

Library for the Performing Arts (a branch of the New York Public Library, at Lincoln Center).

libretto(s).

Liège (in Belgium). But the adjectives are *Liégeois* (masc.) and *Liégeoise* (fem.).

lie, lay. *See* LAY, LIE.

lieutenant governor. *Lt. Gov. Merrill S. Anyell; Lieutenant Governor Anyell; the lieutenant governor.*

life(-). Most but not all compounds formed with *life* are one word: lifeblood, lifeboat, life buoy, life cycle, life expectancy, life force, lifeguard, life insurance, life jacket, lifeless, lifelike, lifeline, lifelong, life net, life preserver, life raft, lifesaver, lifesaving, life science, life sentence, life-size, life span, lifestyle, lifetime, life vest, lifework.

lifestyle is shopworn in references to the values and consumption patterns of the well-to-do. And avoid phrases like *gay lifestyle,* which imply that all gay men and lesbians live the same way.

lighted, not *lit,* for the past tense of *light.* But in a variety of idioms: a *moonlit night, a bosky, sunlit dell* and *Her face lit up at the sight of me.*

light(-), (-)light. Most but not all compounds formed with *light* as a prefix are one word: light-footed, lightheaded, lighthearted, lighthouse, light opera, light pen, lightproof, lightship, lightweight (n., chiefly sports), light-year.

Compounds formed with *light* as a suffix are solid: firelight, flashlight, gaslight, highlight, lamplight, limelight, searchlight, sidelight, sunlight.

light-year. A unit of length (not of time) equal to the distance traveled by light in one year at the rate of 186,000 miles per second. That distance is approximately 5,878 billion miles.

likable.

like. The word plays many grammatical roles. The one that raises a usage issue is its sense as a preposition meaning *similar to*. In that guise it can introduce only a noun or a pronoun: *He deals cards like a riverboat gambler*. If in doubt about the fitness of a construction with *like*, mentally test a substitute preposition (*with*, for example): *He deals cards with a riverboat gambler*. If the resulting sentence is coherent, *like* is properly used.

But when *like* is used to introduce a full clause—consisting of subject and verb—it stops being a preposition and becomes a conjunction. Traditional usage, preferred by The Times, does not accept that construction: *He is competitive, like his father was*. Make it *as his father was*, or simply *like his father*. If the *as* construction (although correct) sounds stiff or awkward, try *the way* instead: *He is competitive, the way his father was*.

In other cases, if *like* fails the preposition test, *as if* may be needed: *She pedaled as if* [not *like*] *her life depended on it*.

When *like* is used correctly as a preposition, it faces another test. The items linked by *like* must be parallel and therefore comparable. Do not write *Like Houston, August in New York is humid*. That sentence compares August to Houston, not what its author meant. Make it *Like Houston, New York is humid in August*.

Like is the preferred expression (rather than SUCH AS) in this kind of phrase: *painters like Rubens*.

like(-), (-)like. Compounds with *like* as a prefix are hyphenated: like-minded, like-natured. But words with *like* as a mere first syllable are solid: likeness, likewise.

Compounds with *like* as a suffix are solid unless the main element ends in *l* or is a proper noun: businesslike, childlike, jewel-like, Reagan-like, shell-like. *Christlike* is an exception.

likely can be an adjective (*a likely story*) or an adverb. But when it is an adverb, idiom requires coupling it with *most, quite, rather* or *very*. This construction is dialect: *She will likely go*. This construction is proper, if a bit stilted: *She will most likely go*. This one is preferable: *She is likely to go*. Also see LIABLE.

Lilco was dismantled in 1998. *See* LONG ISLAND LIGHTING COMPANY.

lily of the valley.

Limburger (cheese).

linage (number of lines), **lineage** (descent).

Lincoln Center for the Performing Arts is the full name, but *Lincoln Center* will do in virtually all first references. Thereafter: *the center*.

Lincoln's Birthday, Feb. 12, is observed as a legal holiday in some states, including New York, New Jersey and Connecticut. Other states have designated the third Monday of February as *Presidents' Day*, to honor both Washington and Lincoln. The federal holiday on that day is officially *Washington's Birthday*.

line(-), (-)line. Compounds formed with *line* as a prefix are generally, but not always, solid: linebacker and lineman (football players), line judge and linesman (sports officials), line drawing, line drive, lineup (n.).

    Compounds formed with *line* as a suffix are usually solid: airline (though in some proper names it may be *air line*), bread line, coastline, deadline, shoreline, sideline, skyline, streamline, waistline.

lion's share is a cliché. It means not simply the largest share but the whole thing or almost all of it.

LIPA for the Long Island Power Authority, but sparingly, and only when the context is clear.

lip-sync, lip-synched, lip-synching (colloquial).

liquefaction, liquefy. The letter before the *f* is an *e*. But: *gasification, gasify.*

liquor. See ALCOHOLIC BEVERAGES and WHISKEY(S).

L.I.R.R. See LONG ISLAND RAIL ROAD.

Listserv is a trademark for an Internet mailing list or the software that manages one.

litchi. It is a Chinese evergreen tree or its fruit. The common term *litchi nut* is technically inaccurate.

liter. This metric unit is equal to the volume occupied by one kilogram of water under standard conditions; it is equal to one cubic decimeter or roughly 1.06 United States liquid quarts or 0.91 dry quart. See METRIC SYSTEM.

literally. Do not use it when *figuratively* is meant: *The Democratic leaders are literally walking a tightrope.* And when *literally* is used correctly, it is often unneeded.

Litt.D. or **D.Litt.** for Doctor of Literature.

littérateur.

Little League. The official youth baseball organization. Its championship is the Little League World Series.

living room (n.), **living-room** (adj.).

L.L.B. for Bachelor of Laws.

L.L.D. for Doctor of Laws.

Lloyd's (insurance exchange), **Lloyds** (bankers).

Lloyd's Register of Shipping.

L.N.G. for liquid (or *liquefied*) natural gas.

(-)load. Compounds formed with *load* are solid: busload, carload, shipload, truckload.

loan. Do not use *loan* as a verb. Use *lend* and, in the past tense, *lent* rather than *loaned.*

loath (adj.), **loathe** (v.). *Loath* means unwilling or reluctant. *Loathe* means hate.

localities and regions. Capitalize the names of specific localities and regions: *City of London* (financial district); *Left Bank*; *East Side*; *Midwest*; *Corn Belt*. Many such designations are listed separately.

located is often an excess word: *The feed store is located on Bortnicker Road.*

lock(-). Most compounds formed with *lock* are one word, but not all. Some examples: lockbox, lockjaw, locknut, lockout (n.), lock out (v.), locksmith, lock step, lockup (n.), lock up (v.).

Lockheed Martin Corporation.

logrolling.

Londonderry (in Northern Ireland).

Long Island. *See* L.I.

Long Island Lighting Company (Lilco) was dismantled in 1998. Its electricity operations were taken over by the LONG ISLAND POWER AUTHORITY and its gas operations by the Brooklyn Union Gas Company, a subsidiary of the KeySpan Energy Corporation.

Long Island Power Authority. In later references and in headlines, LIPA, but sparingly, and only when the context is clear.

Long Island Rail Road; *the Long Island*; *the railroad. L.I.R.R.* is acceptable in headlines.

longitude. *See* LATITUDE AND LONGITUDE.

long(-), (-)long. Most compounds formed with *long* as a prefix are one word, but some are hyphenated and a few are two words: longboat, long division, long-drawn-out (adj.), longhair (colloq.), longhaired, longhand, longhorn (cattle), long house, long jump (n., sports), long-jump (v., sports), long-lived, long-playing, long-range (adj.), long-run (adj.), longshoreman, long shot, longstanding, long-suffering, longtime (adj.), long wave (n.), long-wave (adj.), long-winded.

As a suffix, *long* forms a solid compound when it attaches to a one-syllable word ending in a consonant. The compound is hyphenated if the suffix directly follows a vowel or a word of more than one syllable: daylong, decade-long, hourlong, minute-long, mile-long, monthlong, second-long, weeklong, yearlong. Do not attach *-long* to a plural: instead of *weekslong delay*, write *a delay of weeks*.

Shorten expressions like *two-hour-long meeting. Two-hour meeting* says it all.

longshoreman. A *longshoreman* is a waterfront laborer. A *stevedore* can be either the laborer or the cargo loading company.

long ton. *See* TON.

Loop, the (the area in downtown Chicago).

Lord. This British title applies to barons, viscounts, earls and marquesses. Use it in all references to a baron (*Lord Lamb*) and in second and later references to the others. In those cases, the title is never followed by a given name. But the title also designates the younger sons of marquesses and dukes, for whom it is used this way: *Lord Charles Dann*; *Lord Charles*; but never *Lord Dann*. *Also see* PEERS.

Lord & Taylor.

Los Angeles, never *L.A.* except in direct quotations, not even in headlines. The people are *Angelenos,* not *Los Angelenos.*

Lotos Club.

Louisiana. Abbreviate as *La.* after the names of cities, towns and parishes (the equivalent of counties).

Louisianian(s).

lover is a suitable term for a partner in a literary or historic liaison or a highly visible romance between public personalities—in show business, for example. In writing about more private people, use the less flamboyant COMPANION or PARTNER.

low(-). Some compounds formed with *low* are one word, some are hyphenated and a few are two words. Some examples: lowball, low beam, low blow, lowbrow, low-cost, low frequency (n.), low-frequency (adj.), low-grade, low-key, lowland, low-level, low-pitched, low-pressure, low-priced, low-rise (adj.), low-tech, low-tension, low tide, low-water mark.

Low Countries, the. Belgium, the Netherlands and Luxembourg. But: *the Lowcountry* for the coastal area of South Carolina.

Lower California. *See* BAJA CALIFORNIA.

lowercase. It is one word, noun, verb and adjective.

Lower East Side (of Manhattan).

Lower Manhattan.

low Mass. It is said or celebrated, not sung. *See* MASS.

LP('s) for long-playing records.

L.P.G. for liquid (or *liquefied*) petroleum gas.

L.P.G.A. for the Ladies Professional Golf Association. No apostrophe.

Lt. *Dale A. Kikondoo* (military, fire or police); *Lieutenant Kikondoo; the lieutenant.* Also, for a lieutenant, junior grade, in the Coast Guard and the Navy: *Lt. j.g. Dale A. Kikondoo.*

Lt. Cmdr. *Morgan F. Bildots; Commander Bildots; the commander.*

Lt. Col. *Lee J. Agneau; Colonel Agneau; the colonel.*

Lt. Gen. *Dana B. Cordeiro; General Cordeiro; the general.*

Lt. Gov. *Ashley T. Lamb; Lieutenant Governor Lamb* (or *Mr., Ms., Miss* or *Mrs. Lamb*); *the lieutenant governor.*

Lucite is a trademark for a clear plastic.

Lufthansa German Airlines. For first references *Lufthansa* will do.

Lunar New Year (the Asian festival).

lunchroom.

Lutheran Church-Missouri Synod.

Luxembourg for the country, its capital, the Paris gardens and the museum.

Luxembourger(s). The people of Luxembourg.

Lycra is a trademark for spandex, the elastic fabric.

Lykes Brothers Steamship Company. For first references, *Lykes Brothers* will do.

Lyndon B. Johnson Space Center is the full name of the complex at Houston. But *Johnson Space Center* will do in virtually every first reference. Thereafter: *the space center. Also see* CAPE CANAVERAL.

Lyon (in France).

M

M. (for Monsieur). *See* COURTESY TITLES.

M.A. for Master of Arts. Also: *a master's degree.*

M.A.C., in later references, for the Municipal Assistance Corporation (in New York).

Macdougal Street (Greenwich Village), **MacDougal Street** (Brooklyn). Also, in Greenwich Village: *Macdougal Alley.*

Mace is a brand name for a stinging spray used to stun an attacker. Do not use *Mace* as a verb.

Macedonia. The name should stand alone to mean the country, formerly a republic in Yugoslavia. (International organizations use a longer variation in deference to Greece, which calls its northern district by the short name.) Macedonia is also a district in Bulgaria; when either district is in the news, use a phrase of explanation. Also: *Macedonian(s),* as a noun for the people and as an adjective.

machine gun (n.), **machine-gun** (adj. and v.). Also: *submachine gun.*

Mach 1, Mach 2, etc., for the speed of sound, twice the speed of sound, etc.

Macintosh (the family of personal computers manufactured by Apple Computer Inc.).

Mac, Mc. When a name with either prefix occurs in an all-uppercase context of any kind, including a headline, lowercase the *c* or *ac*; if lowercase type is unavailable, use small capitals: MACARTHUR, MCCLELLAN. Alphabetize such names as if all the letters were lowercase: *Mabley, MacAdam, Maynard, McNeil.*

macro(-). Compounds formed with *macro* are solid: macrobiology, macroclimate, macrocosm, macroeconomics, macroscopic.

Macy's (part of Federated Department Stores).

mad(-). Compounds formed with *mad* are one word: madcap, madman, madwoman.

Madagascar. Its capital is Antananarivo and its people are *Malagasy.*

madam (not *madame*), for the keeper of a bordello.

"Madama Butterfly" (the Puccini opera).

Madison, Dolley, was the wife of James. *Dolly Madison* is an ice cream and a bakery.

madras (fabric).

Maersk Sealand is the ocean carrier formed in 1999 when the Maersk Line bought Sea-Land Service.

magazine names. *See* PERIODICAL NAMES.

Magistrate Judge *Lynn H. Agnello; Judge Agnello; the judge.* If there is a risk of confusion with a district judge, in later references make it *Magistrate Judge Agnello* or
the magistrate judge.

Magna Carta (not *the Magna Carta*).

magnitude. *See* EARTHQUAKES.

Magnum designates a firearm that uses cartridges with an enhanced explosive charge,
or the cartridges themselves.

      Lowercase *magnum* to mean a double-size wine bottle, which holds 1.5 liters.

mah-jongg.

Maine. Abbreviate as *Me.* after the names of cities, towns and counties.

maintain means, among other things, *defend by argument.* It is not always a neutral
form of attribution. *He maintains that he is 45* hints that there is reason to think
he is, say, 50.

maître d'hôtel. The plural is *maîtres d'hôtel.* But *headwaiter(s)* is often less pretentious. Confine the truncated *maître d'* to direct quotations and light contexts.

Maj. *Stacy P. Miel; Major Miel; the major.*

Maj. Gen. *Lindsay R. Karitsa; General Karitsa; the general.*

major-domo(s).

Majorca. Use it (not *Mallorca* and not *Spain*) in datelines: PALMA, *Majorca.*

majority. A majority is more than half. Write about *a majority,* not *the majority,* unless
the reference is to an organized faction.

majority leader. Lowercased, and separated from the name by a comma: *Senator Lauren H. Baranek, the majority leader;* or *the majority leader, Lauren H. Baranek.*

make(-). Most but not all compounds formed with *make* are one word: make-believe,
makeover (n.), make over (v.), makeshift, makeup (n. and adj.), make-work.

(-)maker. Most compounds formed with *maker* as a suffix are solid: automaker,
bookmaker, carmaker, dressmaker, filmmaker, HOMEMAKER, moviemaker,
peacemaker, sailmaker, shoemaker, troublemaker, winemaker.

      But some other combinations, not so well established, should remain sepa-
rate words: carpet maker, decision maker, policy maker, steel maker.

Malagasy (sing. and pl., n. and adj.). The people of Madagascar.

Malay, Malayan, Malaysian. *Malay* (n. or adj.) refers to a member of an ethnic group,
Polynesian in background, found on the Malay Peninsula, or to the language of
that group. *Malayan* (n. or adj.) refers to any inhabitant of that peninsula or of
Malaya, the territory centering on the peninsula, which became part of Malaysia
in 1962. *Malaysian* (n. or adj.) refers to any inhabitant of Malaysia.

Malaysian names. Because of differences in ethnic backgrounds, Malaysian names
take a variety of forms. Always check to see which part of the name is used with a
courtesy title in later references. *Prime Minister Mahathir bin Mohamad,* for ex-

ample, is *Mr. Mahathir*. But *Foreign Minister Abdullah Ahmad Badawi* is *Mr. Badawi*.

male, female. In references to people, the nouns *woman*, *man*, *girl* and *boy* are most conversational. If a construction unavoidably warrants *male* and *female*, use them as adjectives, not nouns. Avoid affixing *male* and *female* to occupational titles (*male nurse*, *female judge*) in ways that imply they "normally" belong to only one sex. Preferably say, for example, *women on the faculty* or *men on the faculty*. See MEN AND WOMEN.

Mallorca (in Spain). *See* MAJORCA.

maneuver.

manhattan (the cocktail).

man-hour. It is an established business term, but phrases like *an hour of work* or *a payroll hour* better reflect the shared roles of the sexes.

manic, manically.

manifold, manyfold. *Manifold* means many-featured; *manyfold* means multiplied many times.

Manitoba (Canadian province). Do not abbreviate after the names of cities and towns, even in datelines.

man-made. The synonyms *artificial*, *manufactured* and *synthetic* better reflect the shared roles of the sexes.

man, mankind. Expressions built on *man* or *mankind* strike many readers as a slight to the role of women through history. In a few cases, those expressions may result unavoidably from idiom or a literary allusion. But the writer and editor should weigh the graceful alternatives: *humanity*, perhaps, or *human race* or *people*. And phrases like *common man* and *man in the street* can often be replaced by *ordinary people* or *the average person*. The dual goal should be to reflect the equality of the sexes and to avoid any awkwardness that would alert a reader to the effort involved. *See* HE OR SHE.

man (v.), **manned, manning.** To reflect the equal roles of the sexes, generally speak of *staffing* a project or department instead.

mannequin can mean either a clothes maker's dummy or a person who models clothes. In the second case, *model* is shorter and nowadays clearer.

manner born. The quotation, from "Hamlet," is *to the manner born*, not *the manor*.

mano a mano. Literally (in Spanish), *hand to hand*, in the sense of one-on-one confrontation.

man-of-war, men-of-war (warships).

manpower. To reflect the equal roles of the sexes, generally use terms like *labor*, *personnel* and *staffing* instead.

mansion is a subjective and sometimes disputed designation for a large house. The reader is better served by specifics: *30-room house*; *45-acre estate*. But the term is acceptable in phrases like *Executive Mansion*, for the White House, and *Governor's Mansion*.

mantel (shelf), **mantle** (cloak).

many(-). Most compounds formed with *many* are hyphenated: many-hued, many-sided. *Also see* MANIFOLD, MANYFOLD.

Mao Zedong. No longer spelled *Mao Tse-tung.* Also: *Chairman Mao*, and in many historical references just *Mao*, without a courtesy title. *Also see* CHINESE NAMES.

Marble Collegiate Reformed Church (in Manhattan).

March. Do not abbreviate except, when necessary, in tables or charts.

marchioness. Capitalize the first reference as a full name: *the Marchioness of Lambsford; Lady Lambsford; the marchioness.* Use the non-English equivalents *marquise* and *marchesa* where appropriate. *Also see* PEERS.

Mardi Gras.

margin means, among other things, the difference between two values. So a candidate who wins an election with 8,000 votes when the loser got 5,000 has a *margin* of 3,000. That candidate did not win *by an 8-5 margin* or *with a margin of 8,000 to 5,000.*

Mariana Islands. But: *the Marianas.*

marijuana.

marine(s). Capitalize *Marine(s)* as a synonym for the United States Marine Corps: *He enlisted in the Marines; a Marine landing.* But: *three marines; a company of marines; the corps.* If the word *soldier* or *soldiers* would fit logically in place of *marine* or *marines*, lowercase the *m.* If *Army* or *Air Force* can be substituted logically for *Marine* or *Marines*, uppercase the *M.*

Marine Corps ranks, in descending order, and their abbreviations:

COMMISSIONED OFFICERS

Gen. *Stacy T. Milori; General Milori; the general.* (A general wears four stars.)

Lt. Gen. *Dana A. Cordeiro; General Cordeiro; the general.* (A lieutenant general wears three stars.)

Maj. Gen. *Lindsay L. Karitsa; General Karitsa; the general.* (A major general wears two stars.)

Brig. Gen. *Lee C. Cordeiro; General Cordeiro; the general.* (A brigadier general wears one star.)

Col. *Merrill T. Kuzu; Colonel Kuzu; the colonel.*

Lt. Col. *Lee M. Agneau; Colonel Agneau; the colonel.*

Maj. *Stacy H. Miel; Major Miel; the major.*

Capt. *Hilary D. Daan; Captain Daan; the captain.*

First Lt. *Theo R. Kuzu; Lieutenant Kuzu; the lieutenant.*

Second Lt. *Alex T. Karitsa; Lieutenant Karitsa; the lieutenant.*

WARRANT OFFICERS

(They hold their posts on warrants, or certificates of appointment, rather than commissions. They rank below commissioned officers and above enlisted personnel.)

Chief Warrant Officer *Chris L. Arniotis*; *Mr.* (or *Ms.*, *Miss* or *Mrs.*) *Arniotis*; *the chief warrant officer.*

Warrant Officer *Terry M. Daan*; *Mr.* (or *Ms.*, *Miss* or *Mrs.*) *Daan*; *the warrant officer.*

NONCOMMISSIONED OFFICERS

(Enlisted supervisors.)

Sgt. Maj. *Stacy D. Kuzu*; *Sergeant Major* (or *Sergeant*) *Kuzu*; *the sergeant(s) major* or *sergeant.*

Master Gunnery Sgt. *Pat R. Agneau*; *Sergeant Agneau*; *the sergeant.*

Master Sgt. *Tracy D. Berenich*; *Sergeant Berenich*; *the sergeant.*

First Sgt. *Lauren S. Daan*; *Sergeant Daan*; *the sergeant.*

Gunnery Sgt. *Lindsay P. Kuzu*; *Sergeant Kuzu*; *the sergeant.*

Staff Sgt. *Ashley R. Lam*; *Sergeant Lam*; *the sergeant.*

Sgt. *Terry D. Agnello*; *Sergeant Agnello*; *the sergeant.*

Cpl. *Stacy H. Milori*; *Corporal Milori*; *the corporal.*

OTHER ENLISTED PERSONNEL

Lance Cpl. *Dana A. Lamb*; *Corporal Lamb*; *the corporal.*

Pfc. *Chris D. Agneau*; *Private Agneau*; *the private.*

Pvt. *Alex A. Cordero*; *Private Cordero*; *the private.*

Also see RETIRED.

marital status should be mentioned only when it is pertinent and its pertinence is clear to the reader. *Also see* MARRIED.

mark (currency). Except in quotations or for special effect, use just *mark* or, when clarification is needed, *German mark*, rather than *Deutsche mark*.

mark (v.). Resist the journalese use of *mark* to mean signify and, even more, to mean *is* or *are.* Write *The election is the third in seven years for Ruritania*, not *The election marks the third time Ruritania has voted in seven years.*

Maronite Church. A Roman Catholic church of the EASTERN RITE.

marquess. Capitalize the first reference as a full name: *the Marquess of Lambsford*; *Lord Lambsford*; *the marquess.* (Use the non-English equivalents *marquis* and *marchese* where appropriate.) And: *Marquess of Queensberry rules. Also see* PEERS.

Marrakesh for the city in Morocco.

married. *Got* is superfluous: *he married*; *she married.* Beware of phrases like *has a wife* that imply inequality in the relationship. *Also see* MEN AND WOMEN.

Marseille (in France).

marshal (n. and v.). Also: *marshaled*; *marshaling*.

Marshall Plan. The program to help European nations recover economically after World War II was officially known as the *European Recovery Program*. It was proposed in 1947 by George C. Marshall, the secretary of state.

Marshal of the Royal Air Force. This rank, the highest in the British air force, cannot properly be shortened, and *R.A.F. Marshal* is incorrect. But holders of the rank usually have other usable titles: *Marshal of the Royal Air Force Viscount Kuzu of Gerolstein*; *Viscount Kuzu*; *Lord Kuzu*.

martini (the cocktail).

Martin Luther King's Birthday is the preferred reference to the federal holiday observed on the third Monday in January. In a detailed article, save the full name of *the Rev. Dr. Martin Luther King Jr.* for a later mention.

Maryland. Abbreviate as *Md.* after the names of cities, towns and counties.

Mason-Dixon line. This short form is preferred to *Mason and Dixon's line*.

Mass (religious). Capitalize this and other formally named prayer services: *Divine Liturgy*; *the Eucharist*; *the Divine Eucharist*; *Friday Prayer* (Islam). But: *funeral Mass*; *high Mass*; *low Mass*; *nuptial Mass*; *requiem Mass*. High Mass is *sung*; low Mass is *said*. Masses are not held and do not take place; they may be *offered*, *celebrated*, *said* or *sung*.

Massachusetts. Abbreviate as *Mass.* after the names of cities, towns and counties.

massive. This overworked adjective is best reserved for references to physical bulk. A building or a mountain may be *massive*, but use a fresher description for a budget or a fire.

MasterCard.

Master Chief Petty Officer *Hilary Y. Baranek*; *Chief Baranek*; *the chief*.

masterful, masterly. *Masterful* means domineering or overpowering. *Masterly* means skillful.

Master Gunnery Sgt. *Pat S. Agneau*; *Sergeant Agneau*; *the sergeant*.

master's degree. But: *Master of Arts*; *Master of Science*; etc. Also: *M.A.*; *M.S.*; etc.

Master Sgt. *Tracy N. Berenich*; *Sergeant Berenich*; *the sergeant*.

Matamoras (Pa.), **Matamoros** (Mexico).

Matawan (N.J.), **Matewan** (W.Va.), **Mattawan** (Mich.), **Matteawan** (N.Y.).

matériel for military arms and equipment.

Matson Navigation Company.

matter-of-fact (adj.), **matter-of-course** (adj.). But: *as a matter of fact*; *as a matter of course*.

matzo(s).

Mawlid, the birthday of Muhammad.

May. Do not abbreviate, even before numerals or in charts and tables.

Mayagüez for the city in Puerto Rico.

Mayor *Lauren V. Barany*; *Mayor Barany*; *the mayor*; *Mr.* (or *Ms.* or *Mrs.* or *Miss*) *Barany*. Also: *Mayor Lauren V. Barany of Detroit*; *the mayors of Chicago and St. Louis*; *three former mayors*. But not *Detroit Mayor Lauren Barany*; the city name is not part of the title.

mayoral (adj.), **mayoralty** (n.).

Mays Landing (in Atlantic County, N.J.).

Mazatlán (in Mexico).

M.C., not *emcee*, for *master of ceremonies*.

McDonald's is operated by the McDonald's Corporation.

McDonnell Douglas Corporation. It is now a part of the Boeing Company.

M.D. for *Doctor of Medicine*. See Dr.

M.D.T., M.S.T. for *Mountain Daylight Time* and *Mountain Standard Time*. See TIME.

meager.

mean(-). With the exception of *mean time*, the astronomical term, compounds formed with *mean* are one word: meanspirited, meantime, meanwhile.

mean, median, average. In statistics, a *mean* is an average; a *median* is the figure that ranks midway in a list in ascending or descending order. For example, in a discussion of wages for 51 workers, the *mean* or *average* is the total of their pay divided by 51. The *median* is a wage that is higher than 25 of the wages and lower than the remaining 25. In a list with an even number of items—50, say, instead of 51—the median is the average of the two middle numbers. So if the 25th number in a listing is 200 and the 26th is 220, the median is 210.

meanwhile is too abrupt a transitional phrase when an article moves to reporting another event. The actual relationship of events should be expressed in a few words. And *In another development* is similarly skimpy.

measures. Many weights and measures are listed separately. See METRIC SYSTEM.

Medal of Honor; *the medal*. Not the *Congressional* Medal of Honor, though it is presented by the president "in the name of the Congress."

medals. Capitalize *Medal of Honor, Bronze Star, Purple Heart, Victoria Cross*, etc. But: *Olympic medal*; *gold medal*.

meddle, mettle. *Meddle*, the verb, means interfere. *Mettle*, the noun, means courage or excellence of character.

medevac, for medical evacuation (n. and adj.). As a verb: *medevac*; *medevacked*; *medevacking*.

Medgar Evers College (part of the CITY UNIVERSITY OF NEW YORK).

media. The term is often seen doing duty as a singular. But The Times, with a grammatically exacting readership, will keep it plural for now; the singular is *medium*.

Ordinarily expand the term, at least to *news media*. In discussion of news and information outlets, the word is meaningless when standing alone; politicians and publicity people have stretched it to embrace soap operas, talk shows, encyclopedias, technical journals and everything in between. And since the things in between include The Times, the discomfort of the embrace should be evident.

median. *See* MEAN, MEDIAN, AVERAGE.

Medicaid is a federal and state program that helps pay for health care for poor, elderly, blind and disabled patients and for poor families with children.

medical examiner. Lowercase the term, and separate it from the name with a comma: *The medical examiner, Toby Y. Anyell*; *Dr. Anyell* (or *Mr., Ms., Mrs.* or *Miss,* if the medical examiner is not a physician); *the medical examiner.* In many jurisdictions, the equivalent position is *coroner.*

Medicare is a federal health insurance program for people 65 or older and for disabled people.

medieval.

mega(-). Compounds formed with *mega*, which means one million, are not hyphenated, except in rare use before a vowel: megabucks (slang), megabyte, megacycle, mega-electron, megaton, megawatt.

Hyphenate terms coined for effect (*mega-merger, mega-series*), but ration that use to avoid triteness.

megabyte. A *megabyte* is about a thousand kilobytes, or a million bytes (actually 1,024 kilobytes, or 1,048,576 bytes). It is enough computer memory to store about a million characters. In technical contexts, it may be abbreviated *MB: a 1.44MB floppy disk. Also see* BIT; BYTE; GIGABYTE; KILOBYTE.

megahertz is a unit of frequency equal to a million hertz, or cycles per second. It is often used as a measure of radio frequency or of a computer's speed. The abbreviation (for technical contexts only) is *MHz: a 500 MHz computer.*

megaton. A megaton is the unit used to measure the power of a nuclear explosion. It is equal to the explosive force of a million tons of TNT. *Also see* KILOTON.

melee. It means a noisy, confused fight involving a number of people. A RIOT is not a melee.

Melkite Church. A Roman Catholic church of the EASTERN RITE.

member of Parliament. Always a lowercase *m*. The *P* is uppercased for a legislative body so named, or when *Parliament* substitutes for an equivalent foreign proper name. The abbreviation, seen occasionally in a quotation or a headline, is *M.P.*

memento(s).

memorabilia. It is plural; the Latin singular, never absorbed into English, is *memorabile.*

memorandums (not *memoranda*).

Memorial Day is observed in the United States on the last Monday in May.

ménage. Also: *ménage à trois.*

men and women. Times writing treats the sexes equally. It reflects a society that no longer assigns roles or occupations to men only or women only. Thus the copy shuns stereotypes and assumptions. Thoughtful writing is also un-self-conscious: it sidesteps offense without calling attention to the pitfalls. It may, for example, cite *spokesmen* and *spokeswomen,* but will refer to a mixed group as *press officers* rather than use the ostentatiously desexed *spokespersons. Councilwomen* and *councilmen* are, collectively, *council members,* not *councilpersons.* A company installs a *four-member management team,* not *four-man* but also not *four-person.* When referring impersonally to *anyone* or *someone,* the writer will find a construction that does not rely on *his* or *her* but also resists the conspicuously plural *they.* Example: *The conductor asked whether anyone had lost a ticket* — not *his ticket* or *her ticket,* and not *their ticket.* (*See* ANYBODY, ANYONE, EVERYBODY, EVERYONE, NO ONE, SOMEONE.)

 Seemingly innocent words can sound belittling. Do not, for example, label a woman a *housewife,* a *homemaker* or a *grandmother* unless the pertinence is obvious and an equivalent phrase would be used for a man in the identical context. Avoid old-fashioned descriptions like *attractive, blond, pert, glamorous* or *dapper;* supply meaningful specifics instead, for women and men equally.

 Test the relevance of marital or parental status in a sentence by mentally substituting a person of the opposite sex. And use *divorced man* or *divorced woman* in place of the lifted-eyebrow *divorcé(e).* When a woman's activities make news, omit mention of her husband unless his identity is pertinent or its omission would raise a genuine question. If a woman's name is Rockefeller, for example, readers should not have to guess whether she was born into the family or married into it, or which Rockefeller is her husband. The same is true for men married to women in the news.

 A phrase like *Hollis M. Cordero and his wife, Lynn,* assigns the woman unthinkingly to second rank. Instead write *Hollis and Lynn Cordero* and, equally often, *Lynn and Hollis Cordero.* In place of *he has a wife and two children,* write that *Mr. Cordero is married and has two children.* In a profile, *Secretary Anyell was born in Bethlehem, Pa., where her father was a steelworker* calls for some acknowledgment of her mother.

 Beware the automatic. The woman quoted in a supermarket, commenting on prices, may be a lawyer or a technician, just as a man might be; unless it is known and important that she is a *homemaker,* call her a *customer.* Call a new Congress member *a 44-year-old Staten Islander* rather than *a 44-year-old housewife* or *a blond mother of three.*

 For occupational terms, resist modifiers that imply a "norm" of maleness or femaleness: use *nurse*, not *male nurse*; also *judges*, not *women judges* and not *female judges*. When making a point of sex distinctions in a line of work, employ *man* and *woman* as nouns rather than modifiers: instead of *the rise of female managers in corporate ranks*, write *the rise of women in the ranks of corporate managers*. Resort to *male* or *female* to modify a job title only when unavoidable, and when the equivalent would be used for someone of the opposite sex in the same context.

In general references, use a neutral job title like *letter carrier* rather than *mailman*, and *police officer* rather than *policeman* or *policewoman*. Avoid most terms with grafted feminine endings; many suggest a secondary status: *comedienne, executrix, sculptress*. While *actress, hostess* and *waitress* remain widely accepted, *actor, host* and *waiter* suit both sexes, as does *server*. (Do not use *waitron, waitperson* or *waitstaff*.) *Headmaster* or *headmistress* is acceptable for an educator who uses the title, but write *head of the school* for the general term.

Sexual equality is no longer exotic, and its advocacy does not necessarily warrant the label *feminist* or *feminism*; apply the term only to those who choose it, and deftly indicate what they mean it to signify. When referring to the *women's movement*, be specific about the goals and actions involved. Avoid the outdated *women's liberation*, except in a historical reference. *Lib* and *libber* are condescending.

Use parallel courtesy titles for women and for men in all contexts, though women have a choice of title.

Also see ACTOR, ACTRESS; ASSEMBLYMAN, ASSEMBLYWOMAN; BOY; BUSINESSMAN, BUSINESSWOMAN; CHAIRMAN, CHAIRWOMAN; COED; COMEDIAN; CONGRESSMAN, CONGRESSWOMAN; COUNCILMAN, COUNCILWOMAN; COURTESY TITLES; DIVORCÉ(E); FEMALE, MALE; FOREMAN, FOREWOMAN; GENDER, SEX; GIRL; GRANDMOTHER; HEADMASTER, HEADMISTRESS; HE OR SHE; HOMEMAKER; HOUSEWIFE; LADY; (-)PERSON; POSTMASTER; WAITER, WAITRESS; WIDOW, WIDOWER.

Mennonites are members of an evangelical Christian sect opposed to military service and in favor of plain dress. *Also see* AMISH.

men's wear.

mental hospital is the preferred replacement for the outmoded *insane asylum*.

Mercedes-Benz. In later references, *Mercedes*. The plural, barely pronounceable but logical enough, is *Mercedeses* or, a bit more pronounceably, *Mercedes-Benzes*. The possessive is *Mercedes's* or *Mercedes-Benz's*—and yes, for the plural, *Mercedeses' and Mercedes-Benzes'*. The car is manufactured by DaimlerChrysler A.G., formed in 1998 through the merger of the Chrysler Corporation and Daimler-Benz of Germany.

merchant marine. Lowercase *United States merchant marine*, for the fleet of ships, though not for the people who staff them. A member of the merchant marine is *a merchant seaman* or *a merchant mariner*, not a merchant marine.

Merrill Lynch is acceptable in most references for *Merrill Lynch, Pierce, Fenner & Smith Inc.*, the brokerage firm. Merrill Lynch & Company is its parent.

Merrimack (the Confederate warship that fought the Monitor in the first battle between ironclads).

Met may be used to mean the *Metropolitan Opera* or the *Metropolitan Museum of Art* in later references and in headlines, provided that the music or art context is clear. Also: *the Metropolitan.* In a review, either short form may also serve as a first reference if the full name appears somewhere in the copy or in a fact box.

metaphor is not a synonym for *symbol* or *example.* A metaphor is a figure of speech in which a word or phrase usually applied to one thing is used for another. *A sea of troubles* is a metaphor, and so are the ever-popular *level playing field, sacrificial lamb* and *can of worms.* In software design, a metaphor is the expression of an abstract set of commands in borrowed physical terms: the *desktop*, for example, as a means of organizing files in personal computers.

meter. The basic unit of length in the metric system, equal to 39.37 inches, or roughly 1.1 yards. *See* METRIC SYSTEM.

Methodist Church. The Methodist Church merged with the Evangelical United Brethren Church in 1968 to form *the United Methodist Church.*

metric system. Many measurements are listed separately. Ordinarily convert measurements from the metric system to the American one. Delete the original measure unless it is truly useful, in which case use commas or another graceful device to set off the conversion: *The race was 100 kilometers, about 62 miles.* Conversions of rounded or even numbers should also be rounded: *125 grams, about 4 ounces* (not *125 grams, or 4.4125 ounces*).

metric ton. A *metric ton* is equal to 1,000 kilograms, or 2,204.62 pounds. (Outside the United States, it is often spelled *tonne.*) The *short ton*, the unit most commonly used in the United States (and called simply a *ton*), equals 2,000 pounds avoirdupois, or 907.20 kilograms. The *long ton*, used in Britain, equals 2,240 pounds, or 1,016.06 kilograms. *See* METRIC SYSTEM.

MetroCard, for the electronic fare collection system in New York City.

Metro-North Railroad; *Metro-North*; *the railroad.*

metropolitan (church title). This is a title given in the Eastern Orthodox churches to bishops of the rank just below patriarch. It is capitalized only when it directly precedes a name. *Also see* EASTERN ORTHODOXY and PATRIARCH.

Metropolitan Transportation Authority. In later references: *the authority.* In headlines: *M.T.A.* Its units are New York City Transit, which operates subways and buses; the LONG ISLAND RAIL ROAD; the Metropolitan Suburban Bus Authority, known as Long Island Bus; the METRO-NORTH RAILROAD; and the TRIBOROUGH BRIDGE AND TUNNEL AUTHORITY.

M-14, M-16. These are the designations of the 7.62-millimeter and 5.56-millimeter rifles used by the United States military. They are capable of automatic and semiautomatic fire. Also, from earlier eras: *M-1 rifle*; *M-1 carbine*. *Also see* BULLET; CARTRIDGE; HANDGUNS; RIFLES; SHELL; SHOTGUNS.

MGM for Metro-Goldwyn-Mayer Inc. An exception to the usual rule of using periods when the initials stand for words; the intent is consistency with the names of well-known subsidiaries like MGM/UA Distribution and MGM Grand Inc.

Michigan. Abbreviate as *Mich.* after the names of cities, towns and counties.

micro(-). The prefix forms solid compounds unless the second element begins with an *o* or, presumably in jest, a capital: microbar, microbrewery, micro-Cadillac, microcomputer, microclimate, microdot, microeconomics, micromanage, micro-organism.

microchip. Use *chip* instead.

Microsoft Corporation. In casual references, *Microsoft* can stand alone.

mid(-). Except before a proper noun or a number, compounds formed with *mid* are one word: midafternoon, midair, mid-America, mid-Atlantic, midchannel, midcontinent, midday, Mideast, midfield, midland, midlife, midmorning, midnight, midpoint, midocean, midsection, midship, midsize, midstream, midsummer, Midtown (Manhattan's), midtown, midway, midweek, Midwest, midwife.

　　　Also: mid-1960, mid-1960's, mid-'60, mid-60's, mid-ninth century, mid-16th century. *Also see* MIDDLE EAST and MIDDLE WEST.

middle(-). Some compounds formed with *middle* are one word, some are hyphenated and some are two words: middle age (n.), middle-aged (adj.), Middle Ages, middlebrow, middle class (n.), middle-class (adj.), middleman, middle-of-the-road (adj.), middle school, middle-sized, middleweight. *Also see* MIDDLE AMERICA; MIDDLE ATLANTIC STATES; MIDDLE EAST, MIDEAST; MIDDLE WEST, MIDDLE WESTERN, MIDWEST, MIDWESTERN.

middle age is generally considered to mean roughly 40 to 65. But when citing a finding or study, specify its definition.

Middle Ages.

Middle America for the middle class of the United States, especially in references to its values, but not for the central part of the country, which is *the Midwest* (preferred) or *the Middle West*.

Middle Atlantic States.

Middle East, Mideast. Use *Middle East* in news articles. Either term may be used in headlines. Do not use *Near East*. The Middle East comprises Cyprus, Egypt, Iran, Iraq, Israel, Jordan, Lebanon, Libya, Saudi Arabia, the Sudan, Syria, Yemen and the Persian Gulf emirates.

Middle West, Middle Western, Midwest, Midwestern. All forms may be used, though *Midwest* is preferred. Also: *Middle Western states; Midwestern states.*

midnight technically ends a day; the new one starts at 12:01 a.m. A reference to a strike deadline, a cease-fire, etc., should be clear and explicit about the day in question. *Also see* TIME.

Midshipman *Stacy K. Lamm; Midshipman Lamm; the midshipman* (for a man or woman enrolled at the United States Naval Academy).

Midtown Manhattan. Also, when the context is clear: *Midtown.*

Midway Airlines.

Midwest Express Airlines.

Midwest Stock Exchange. It is now the *Chicago Stock Exchange.*

MIG('s) for the fighter planes. With a model number: *MIG-21; MIG-21's;* etc.

mile, when not otherwise explained, usually means the *statute mile,* equal to 5,280 feet or about 1,609 meters. A *nautical mile* is about 6,076 feet or 1,852 meters. A *kilometer* (1,000 meters) is about 3,281 feet, roughly 0.6 of a statute mile (about five-eighths of a statute mile). Translations of round or approximate numbers, for distance, should also be rounded. *Also see* KNOT and METRIC SYSTEM.

militant is often an opinionated description, not a neutral one; weigh it with care for the news columns. (Its literal meaning is *at war,* or *ready and willing to fight.*) The related noun is *militancy,* not *militance.*

Military Academy (United States); *the academy; West Point.*

military bases. Follow this style for United States Air Force, Army, Marine Corps and Navy bases: *Edwards Air Force Base; the Air Force base; the base;* or, in this case, *the air base.* In the case of Navy bases, *Naval* is usually the word in the formal name: *Guam Naval Base; Mayport Naval Station.* In later references, use *naval station, Navy station, naval base* or *Navy base.*

The Air Force uses *Air Force base* within the United States and its possessions only; it uses *air base* elsewhere: *Andrews Air Force Base,* in Maryland; *Andersen Air Force Base,* on Guam; *Aviano Air Base,* in Italy. (For installations without landing operations, *Air Force station* and *air station* are used similarly.)

For the handling of articles filed from bases, *see* DATELINE INTEGRITY.

military operations. Capitalize their names, without quotation marks: *Operation Desert Shield.* Some of the names are propagandistic; these should be used only when necessary to identify an action in the news, usually once in an article.

military ranks. See separate entries and AIR FORCE RANKS; ARMY RANKS; COAST GUARD RANKS; MARINE CORPS RANKS; NAVY RANKS AND RATES.

Military Sealift Command; *the command.*

militate, mitigate. *Militate* against something means exert weight or effect against it: *High taxes militate against relocating the plant. Mitigate*, which means ease or soften, is never the word to use with *against: Tax reductions mitigated the financial pressure.*

militia. Lowercase when standing alone; capitalize when part of a name: *Naval Militia.*

mill(-), (-)mill. Most compounds formed with *mill* as a prefix are one word: millowner, millpond, millrace, millstone, millstream, millwork.

Most but not all compounds formed with *mill* as a suffix are two words: coffee mill, diploma mill, flour mill, gristmill, paper mill, pepper mill, sawmill, textile mill, windmill.

millennium. But a spelling exception is the *Millenium* Hilton Hotel in Lower Manhattan.

Technically a millennium, the thousand-year period, begins with an "01" year—1001, 2001, etc.—because there was no year 0. But in the popular consciousness, eras begin with 1000 and 2000. That informal style is suitable for references to celebrations, observances and social or cultural turning points. Articles dealing centrally with the calendar should mention the literal interpretation, but without belittling popular usage.

milli(-). Compounds formed with *milli*, which means one-thousandth, are not hyphenated: millibar, milligram, millimeter.

millimeter. One-thousandth of a meter, or approximately 0.04 inch. The abbreviation *mm.* should not be used in ordinary copy (with weapon caliber, for example), but it may be used in charts, lists and tables. *See* CALIBER and METRIC SYSTEM.

million. *See* DOLLARS AND CENTS and NUMBERS, ROUND.

(-)minded. Hyphenate compounds formed with *minded*: fair-minded, high-minded, money-minded, open-minded.

mind-set.

minefield.

minesweeper.

mini(-). Most but not all compounds formed with *mini* are one word: minibike, minibus, minicomputer, mini-series, miniskirt, minivan.

minister (church position). *Minister* is a suitable description (not ordinarily a title, therefore lowercase) for most Protestant clergy members. For example: *the Rev. Lynn A. Miel, minister of. . . .* Or: *Dr. Miel had served as minister there for 23 years.* Episcopalians' preference must be verified; some prefer *priest.* Most Lutherans and some Baptists prefer *pastor.* Lutherans are also *the Rev.* in first references, but usually use *Pastor* before the name in later references: *Pastor Miel.* For an exception, see PASTOR. *Also see* FATHER; RECTOR; REV.

Minister of Justice (or other department) *Robin P. Agnello; Justice Minister Robin P. Agnello; Justice Minister Agnello; the justice minister* or *the minister of justice; the minister.* Also: *minister without portfolio.*

Minnesota. Abbreviate as *Minn.* after the names of cities, towns and counties.

Minnesota Mining and Manufacturing Company. In later references and in headlines, and even in casual first references, *the 3M Company* or *3M.*

minority. Whether used as a noun or as an adjective, the word means *group* by definition. Its use to mean individuals (*she hired three minorities*) is personnel jargon. Make it *minority applicants* or *minority candidates.* And *minority group(s)* is often redundant. *Members of minorities,* while accurate, may be wooden; in any event, specific ethnic identifications, when relevant, are more useful. *Also see* African-American, black; Asian-American; ethnicity; Hispanic; Latino; Native American.

minority leader. Lowercase the term and separate it from the name with a comma: *Senator Stacy O. Daan, the minority leader;* or *the minority leader, Stacy O. Daan.*

minuscule (not *miniscule*).

mips means million instructions per second, a measure of a computer's speed. Even in technology articles, the term needs explanation.

MIRV('s) for multiple independently targetable re-entry vehicle(s). Ordinarily use the term as a noun; the verb *MIRVed* (meaning equipped with multiple warheads) is military jargon.

mishap. Tempting though it may be for the confines of a headline, *mishap* means only a slight accident with negligible consequences.

mishmash.

Miss. *See* courtesy titles.

missiles are listed separately by their abbreviations.

mission (diplomatic office). Lowercase when standing alone. But: *the United States Mission; the Zambian Mission.*

Mississippi. Abbreviate as *Miss.* after the names of cities, towns and counties.

Missouri. Abbreviate as *Mo.* after the names of cities, towns and counties.

M.I.T. for the Massachusetts Institute of Technology; in later references: *the institute.*

Mitchel Field (former airfield, now an exhibition site and shopping complex, in Uniondale, N.Y.).

mitigate. *See* militate, mitigate.

Mitzi E. Newhouse Theater (at Lincoln Center).

mix-up (n.).

Mlle. *See* courtesy titles.

mm. for millimeter in charts and tables, but not in ordinary copy: *a 105-millimeter gun, 35-millimeter film.*

Mme. *See* COURTESY TITLES.

Mobil Oil Corporation merged with the Exxon Corporation in 1999 to form the EXXON MOBIL CORPORATION.

mockingbird.

modem. It is the device that converts computer data for transmission over telephone lines. The term (a noun only) is a contraction of *modulator-dem*odulator.

moderator (church title). Capitalize only when it is used before a name.

modern (art and architecture). Lowercase when referring generally to the 20th century; for clarity, the word *contemporary* may often be preferable. In art, *Modern* movements include *Dadaism, Surrealism* and *Cubism.* In architecture, the term *Modernist* identifies architecture from 1920 to 1970. *See* ARTS TERMINOLOGY.

Moët & Chandon, the Champagne. But often just *Moët.*

Mohammed. *See* MUHAMMAD.

mold.

molestation. Use the less stilted *molesting* instead.

molt (not *moult*).

mom. Reserve this colloquialism for folksy contexts, and lowercase except when it substitutes for a proper name: *I'll bet Mom was quite a hit in her senior class show; Tracy's mom was in it, too. Also see* MOTHER.

money. Except for dollars and cents and pounds and pence, spell out the names of currencies, and use them with figures: *9 francs; 50 pesos; 30,000 lire;* etc.

Translations of round or approximate amounts should also be rounded. For round sums of dollars in the millions or billions, the style is $2 *million;* $1.65 *billion.* In upper-and-lowercase headlines, capitalize *Million, Billion* and *Trillion. See* DOLLARS AND CENTS; EURO(S); FRANCS AND CENTIMES; NUMBERS; NUMBERS, ROUND; POUNDS AND PENCE.

moneyed (not *monied*).

moneys. As a plural of *money,* the word is stilted. Use *money* instead, or *funds.* Do not use *monies.*

(-)monger. Compounds formed with *monger* are one word: fishmonger, rumormonger, scandalmonger, warmonger.

mongolism, mongoloid. The terms are outmoded. *See* DOWN SYNDROME.

Monmouth University (in West Long Branch, N.J.).

monsignor is an honorary title conferred on some Roman Catholic priests by the pope. Abbreviate it in first references only, and capitalize it only before a name: *Msgr. Tracy X. Berenich; Monsignor Berenich; the monsignor.* In some countries, the title is used in later references to bishops and archbishops (*Bishop Tracy X. Berenich; Monsignor Berenich*). When possible, confine the title to the more familiar American usage; if necessary paraphrase a quotation to avoid the foreign one.

Montana. Abbreviate as *Mont.* after the names of cities, towns and counties.

Mont Blanc (the mountain), **Montblanc** (the pen maker).

Montclair State University (in Upper Montclair, N.J.).

Montenegro. It is a republic in the Yugoslav federation. Also: *Montenegrin(s)*, as a noun for the people, and as an adjective.

Monterey (Calif.), **Monterrey** (Mexico).

Montgomery Ward & Company. In later references: *Montgomery Ward*.

monthlong.

months. Abbreviate the names of months from August through February in datelines and news copy when they are followed by numerals: *Aug. 1*; *Sept. 2*; *Oct. 3*; *Nov. 4*; *Dec. 5*; *Jan. 6*; *Feb. 7*. Do not abbreviate *March, April, May, June* and *July* except as a last resort in a chart or table. *Also see* DATES and YEARS, DECADES, CENTURIES.

months pregnant. No apostrophe: the construction is similar to *years old*.

Moody's Investors Service Inc. *Also see* DEBT RATINGS.

moon. For the rare instances of capitalization, see EARTH, MOON, SUN.

Moonies, for members of the Rev. Sun Myung Moon's Unification Church, is disparaging. Avoid it.

moonlight. Use no quotation marks when the expression is used to mean work at an additional job. Also: *moonlighter; moonlighting*. And: *a moonlit night* (despite the general preference for *lighted*).

moose. The plural is also *moose*.

Moravian Church in America.

more honored in the breach. The passage *more honored in the breach than the observance*, from "Hamlet," refers to a custom that is more *honorably* ignored than followed—not one that is more *often* ignored.

more importantly. See IMPORTANT(LY).

more than. The phrase is useful in many contexts but is sometimes opinionated. *More than $100,000* may seem to suggest that the sum is too large. *About $100,000* is more neutral. *More than* is also imprecise. *More than $100,000* can mean $101,000 or $500,000. Specifics are preferred.

Morgan, J. P. (banking). See J. P. MORGAN CHASE & COMPANY.

Mormon Church. This informal name for the Church of Jesus Christ of Latter-day Saints may be used in first and later references so long as the full title appears in any article that deals centrally with the church. Members of the church are *Mormons*.

The church is headed by a *president*. It also uses the titles *apostle, high priest, seventy, elder, deacon, teacher* and *priest*. A *seventy* (a member of a group of men called a *Seventy*) oversees missionary work and other church activities in a specific part of the world. The term *elder* is appropriate in later references to all except *deacon, teacher* and *priest*. Thus: *President Stacy F. Lamb; Elder Lamb; the president of the church. Mr.* and *Dr.* are also appropriate.

The church has *stakes*, which are the equivalent of dioceses; a stake is headed by a *stake president*. There are also *wards*, which are local congregations. A ward is headed by a *bishop*.

mortician. Except in direct quotations or in the name of a business or organization, use *funeral director* or *undertaker* instead.

Moslem. Use *Muslim* instead in references to Islam. *Also see* BLACK MUSLIM; ISLAM; NATION OF ISLAM.

mosquito(es).

Most Rev., Rt. Rev. Omit these terms before the names of archbishops and bishops in almost all cases. But use *the Most Rev.* before the name of the Anglican prelate who is the archbishop of Canterbury and the names of the superiors general of certain Roman Catholic orders. *See* ARCHBISHOP; BISHOP; CANTERBURY, ARCHBISHOP OF; SUPERIOR GENERAL; REV.; VERY REV.

mother. Describe a woman as a *mother* (or *grandmother*) only when her family status is pertinent and its pertinence is clear to the reader. *Mother* is appropriate where, if the subject were a man, *father* would be used. Lowercase the word except when it substitutes for a proper name: *Ask Mother to lend you her raincoat. See* MEN AND WOMEN and MOM.

mother (religious). Capitalize the term when it serves as a title before the name of a religious superior: *Mother Robin Agneau, Mother Robin* or *Mother Agneau,* depending on her preference. Use the title only for superiors who prefer it; some wish to be known as *Sister.* Except in quotations, do not use *a mother* or *the mother* alone in this sense. But: *the superior; the mother superior. Also see* NUN and SISTER (RELIGIOUS).

mother(-). Some compounds formed with *mother* are one word, some are hyphenated and some are two words: motherboard, motherhood, mother(s)-in-law, motherland, mother lode, mother-of-pearl, mother tongue.

Mothers Against Drunk Driving. Its acronym, *MADD,* is rarely recognizable enough for a headline. Note that the phrasing differs from that of *Students Against Driving Drunk.*

Mother's Day.

motion pictures. Use quotation marks for their titles, and capitalize principal words.

motor(-). Most but not all compounds formed with *motor* are one word: motorbike, motorboat, motorcar, motorcycle, motor home, motorist, motorman, motor pool, motor scooter, motor vehicle.

Mount. Capitalize the word as part of a name and spell it out: *Mount Vernon*. The abbreviation (*Mt. Vernon*) may be used in headlines, charts, tables and maps.

Mountain Daylight Time, Mountain Standard Time (M.D.T., M.S.T.). *See* TIME.

Mount Fuji, Fujiyama. But not *Mount Fujiyama*.

movements (music). Capitalize the names of movements: *the Scherzo*; *the Andante*; etc. Lowercase if the movement is referred to by its place in the sequence: *the second movement*; *the finale*.

movements in the arts. *See* ARTS TERMINOLOGY.

moviemaker.

M.P. for member of Parliament or military police.

m.p.h. for miles per hour or miles an hour. Spell out the first time: *a speed limit of 55 miles per hour*; *a 45-mile-an-hour wind*. In cap-and-lowercase headlines, capitalize: *M.P.H.*

Mr. *See* COURTESY TITLES.

M.R.I. for magnetic resonance imaging.

Mrs. *See* COURTESY TITLES.

Ms. (courtesy title). Use this title in second and later references to a woman unless she prefers *Miss* or *Mrs.* or instead uses a professional, royal, noble, military or religious title. In a direct quotation translated from a foreign language, use the closest English equivalent of the woman's preferred title, or *Ms.* if no preference is known. *See* COURTESY TITLES.

MS. for manuscript in a headline, if the context is clear; *MSS.* for the plural.

M.S. for Master of Science degree. Also: *a master's degree*.

Msgr. *Alex J. Agnello*; *Monsignor Agnello*; *the monsignor*.

M.T.A. *See* METROPOLITAN TRANSPORTATION AUTHORITY.

mugging is a lay expression rather than a legal term for a defined crime. It may be described as an assault in a public place, usually with the intent to rob. Because the term is imprecise, a detailed description of the crime and the legal charges will probably help readers. *See* LARCENY, BURGLARY, ROBBERY, THEFT.

mug shot is police slang.

Muhammad. Use this spelling for the name of the prophet of the Muslim religion and for people who bear his name, except when an individual's preference is known to differ.

multi(-). Compounds formed with *multi* are one word unless another *i* follows immediately or the result would be hard to read: multicolored, multicultural, multidimensional, multiethnic, multifaceted, multifold, multiform, multi-institutional, multilateral, multilevel, multi-line, multimedia, multimillionaire, multinational, multipurpose, multiracial, multispeed.

murder, homicide, killing. Reserve *murder* for a crime that has been so labeled by the authorities in a warrant, a charge or a conviction. A *murder* is the killing of one person by one or more others under conditions specified by law—in a vicious manner, for example, or during another crime. A *homicide* is any killing of one person by another, but *killing* is the simpler word: preferably use it until a legal finding has been made. (*Also see* SLAY, SLAYER, SLAYING.) Someone arrested in a death is not a *murder suspect* unless charges have been filed.

In articles about crime statistics, *murder rate* is an acceptable informal reference. But when counting actual deaths, use *homicides*. The *homicide rate* is a ratio of killings to population: *The national homicide rate rose to 55 per 100,000 population, from 52; The city had a homicide rate of 1 per 1,350 residents.*

Muscle Shoals (in Alabama).

museums. *See* ARTS LOCATIONS.

music. Abbreviation, capitalization and punctuation styles appear in separate listings for various types of composition.

Uppercase the instrumentation when it is integrated into a commonly used title: *Bach's Orchestral Suite No. 1 (BWV 1066); Schubert's Piano Trio in E flat (D. 929).* If the instrumentation is appended and merely adds identification, lowercase it: *Mozart's Sinfonia Concertante in E flat for violin and viola (K. 634).*

When the title includes a nickname, use quotation marks around that part only: *Beethoven's "Eroica" Symphony.* If the literary or fanciful name incorporates the full title, place all of it in quotation marks: *"Symphonie Fantastique"; "Rhapsody in Blue."* In later references without the full title, lowercase *concerto, trio, quartet, symphony, suite,* etc.

Generally follow American capitalization rules for titles of foreign-language works (*"Così Fan Tutte,"* not *"Così fan tutte"*). But European style is widely used, and acceptable, for the names of arias and classical songs. *See* SONGS.

In specifying the key of a work, lowercase *flat, sharp, major* and *minor.* A key is assumed to be major unless labeled minor, so *major* is often omitted (*Minuet in G*). Idiom may warrant an exception if the key precedes the title: *the D major Concerto.*

If a work is mentioned more than in passing, generally cite the opus or catalog number. After a title, abbreviate *Opus* as *Op.* A few composers, notably Bach, Mozart and Schubert, are given specialized catalog citations (and abbreviations) in place of *opus. See* OPUS and SYMPHONY.

Muslim. Use this spelling, not *Moslem,* in references to Islam. *Also see* BLACK MUSLIM; ISLAM; NATION OF ISLAM.

mustache (not *moustache*).

mute may be used in reference to someone who cannot speak. Do not use *dumb*. *Also see* DEAF and DISABILITY, DISABLED.

mutual. In careful writing, the adjective means reciprocal; it describes two people or things acting upon each other: *mutual admiration*. Except in a few established idioms, like *mutual friend* or *mutual fund*, it does not mean merely shared.

Myanmar, formerly Burma. The capital is *Yangon*, formerly Rangoon. Gracefully remind readers of the former names when necessary. For the people, *Burmese* (n. and adj.) remains in informal use and aids comprehension in headlines. The language is *Burmese*.

My Lai (in Vietnam), the site of the massacre by United States troops in 1968.

Mylar is a trademark for sheet polyester.

myself. *See* HERSELF, HIMSELF, MYSELF.

N

N.A.A.C.P. for the National Association for the Advancement of Colored People. But it is *NAACP* (without periods) in the official name of a formerly affiliated civil rights organization: the *NAACP Legal Defense and Educational Fund Inc.* (known familiarly as the *Inc Fund*, pronounced *ink*).

Nabisco for the Nabisco Foods Group, a subsidiary of the RJR Nabisco Holdings Corporation.

Nacogdoches (in Texas).

Nafta in later references and in headlines, for the North American Free Trade Agreement. It took effect in the United States, Canada and Mexico in 1994.

Nags Head (in North Carolina).

naïve, naïveté.

names. *See* PERSONAL NAMES AND NICKNAMES.

names with numbers. Make it *Lee T. Berenich IV* or *Lee T. Berenich 4th*, depending on the bearer's preference. If no preference is known, use Roman numerals. In a listing, if family names are printed before given names, the *IV* or *4th* comes last: *BERENICH, Lee T. IV*, not *BERENICH IV, Lee T. Also see* JUNIOR, SENIOR and PERSONAL NAMES AND NICKNAMES.

nanosecond. One billionth of a second. As a term meaning a very short time, it has become a cliché.

naphtha. The formula includes both *h*'s.

napoleon (the pastry).

Napoleon Bonaparte. But in most cases *Napoleon* will do. Use an accent in *Code Napoléon*.

NASA for the National Aeronautics and Space Administration.

Nascar for the National Association for Stock Car Auto Racing.

N.A.S.D. for the National Association of Securities Dealers, the parent company of two stock markets — NASDAQ and the AMERICAN STOCK EXCHANGE.

Nasdaq, the electronic stock market operated by the National Association of Securities Dealers. It is the second-largest stock market in the United States, after the NEW YORK STOCK EXCHANGE.

national. Use the less bureaucratic *citizen* instead, when that is the intended meaning.

National Academy of Sciences. *See* NATIONAL RESEARCH COUNCIL.

National Airport, in Washington, is now RONALD REAGAN NATIONAL AIRPORT.

national anthem(s). Lowercase the expression. Use quotation marks for titles, with principal words capitalized. *Also see* SONGS.

National Baptist Convention of America. The smaller of two black Baptist groups that split in 1915.

National Baptist Convention, U.S.A. Inc. The larger of two black Baptist groups that split in 1915.

National Broadcasting Company. *See* NBC.

National Capitol (the building).

national chairman (chairwoman). *Lindsay R. Kuzu, Democratic national chairman; the national chairwoman.* The same styles apply to state and county chairman and chairwoman.

national committee. *The Republican National Committee; the national committee; the committee.* The same styles apply to state and county committees.

National Conference of Catholic Bishops.

national conventions. *The Republican National Convention; the national convention; the convention.* The same styles apply to state and county conventions.

National Council of Churches will serve in all references for *the National Council of the Churches of Christ in the United States of America.*

National Geographic Society (publisher of National Geographic).

National Governors' Association.

National Guard; *the Guard.*

National Institutes of Health. Note the plural. In later references, sparingly: *N.I.H.*

nationalist. Capitalize only in references to a political party or movement so named, or to its members.

Nationalist China. The former informal designation of TAIWAN.

nationality. *See* ETHNICITY.

National Labor Relations Board. In later references, *the N.L.R.B.; the board.*

National Oceanic and Atmospheric Administration. In later references, *NOAA.* It is the parent agency of the National Weather Service.

National Organization for Women (NOW), not *of* Women.

National Park Service.

National Public Radio. *See* NPR.

National Research Council. The council, which issues hundreds of reports annually on scientific, medical and technological issues, is the operating arm of the National Academy of Sciences and the National Academy of Engineering.

National Review (without *the*) is the magazine.

National Security Council; *the council.* The abbreviation, *N.S.C.,* may be used sparingly in headlines when the context is clear.

National Weather Service; *the Weather Service; the service.*

nation, national. Lowercase unless it is part of a formal name or title.

Nation of Islam. It is a black nationalist group founded by Elijah Muhammad in the 1920's. Do not use *Black Muslims* to describe its followers. Most black Americans who are Muslim follow traditional Islam or are members of theological splinter groups. They are *black Muslims,* not *Black Muslims.*

NationsBank Corporation merged with the BankAmerica Corporation in 1998 to form what is now the Bank of America Corporation.

nationwide.

native(s). References to *the natives* often give offense. An exception is the term *Alaska Native(s),* used by the Aleuts, Eskimos and Indians of Alaska to describe themselves. Exceptions may be made for similar uses by other ethnic groups. And phrases like *native land* and *native of Chicago* are fully acceptable. *Also see* AMERICAN INDIAN(S).

Native American(s). *See* AMERICAN INDIAN(S).

Nativity. Capitalize when the reference is to the birth of Jesus.

NATO for the North Atlantic Treaty Organization. Also: *the Atlantic alliance; the alliance.* The phrases are preferred to repeated uses of *NATO,* which is typographically intrusive. *Atlantic alliance* may also be used occasionally to streamline a lead sentence provided the full name is given soon afterward. The alliance's members in 1999 were Belgium, Britain, Canada, the Czech Republic, Denmark, France, Germany, Greece, Hungary, Iceland, Italy, Luxembourg, the Netherlands, Norway, Poland, Portugal, Spain, Turkey and the United States. Verify the current makeup, since other countries of the former Soviet bloc have also sought to join.

natural causes. Scientists take the term *death from natural causes* to mean a death brought about by the simultaneous failure of several organs in a person of advanced age. To others, the term has come to mean a death that does not result from murder, suicide or an accident. That interpretation is acceptable if the context is clear.

natural parents. Use *biological parents* instead, to avoid a suggestion that adoptive parenthood is unnatural. (Mention adoptive status only when it is pertinent and its pertinence is clear to the reader.)

Natural Resources Defense Council (not *National* Resources).

Naugahyde is a trademark for plastic-coated fabric.

nauseate, nauseated, nauseous. *Nauseate* means sicken, and *nauseated* means sickened. Use *nauseous* to mean sickening only: people feel *nauseated,* not *nauseous.*

nautical mile. A *nautical mile* equals about 6,076 feet, or 1,852 meters. The term *mile,* without a modifier, usually means the *statute mile,* equal to 5,280 feet or about

1,609 meters. A *kilometer* (1,000 meters) is about 3,281 feet, roughly 0.6 of a statute mile (about five-eighths of a statute mile). In translating round or approximate distances, use round numbers. *Also see* KNOT and METRIC SYSTEM.

Navajo(s). The people and their language.

Naval Academy (United States); *the academy*; *Annapolis*.

Naval Militia (United States). *The New York Naval Militia*; *the militia*. It is a reserve force for the Navy, under state command in peacetime.

naval station. Capitalize only in full names: *Mayport Naval Station*; *the naval station*; *the station*. But: *the Navy station*. See MILITARY BASES.

Navy. Capitalize in *United States Navy, British Navy, French Navy*, etc. It is *the Navy* in later references to that of the United States, but lowercase such references to any foreign navy. It is also *Navy* in references to United States Naval Academy sports teams.

navy blue.

Navy ranks, in descending order, with their abbreviations:

COMMISSIONED OFFICERS

Adm. *Lynn L. Karitsa*; *Admiral Karitsa*; *the admiral*. (An admiral wears four stars.)

Vice Adm. *Alex H. Barany*; *Admiral Barany*; *the admiral*. (A vice admiral wears three stars.)

Rear Adm. *Dale R. Agnello*; *Admiral Agnello*; *the admiral*. (A rear admiral may wear one or two stars.)

Capt. *Hilary M. Daan*; *Captain Daan*; *the captain*.

Cmdr. *Lauren A. Miel*; *Commander Miel*; *the commander*.

Lt. Cmdr. *Morgan T. Bildots*; *Commander Bildots*; *the commander*.

Lt. *Lee D. Kikondoo*; *Lieutenant Kikondoo*; *the lieutenant*.

Lt. j.g. *Stacy M. Milori*; *Lieutenant Milori*; *the lieutenant*.

Ensign *Chris R. Arniotis*; *Ensign Arniotis*; *the ensign*.

WARRANT OFFICERS

(They hold their posts on warrants, or certificates of appointment, rather than commissions. They rank below commissioned officers and above enlisted personnel.)

Chief Warrant Officer *Theo H. Lam*; *Mr. (or Ms., Miss or Mrs.) Lam*; *the chief warrant officer*.

Warrant Officer *Terry A. Daan*; *Mr. (or Ms., Miss or Mrs.) Daan*; *the warrant officer*.

NONCOMMISSIONED OFFICERS

(Enlisted supervisors.)

master chief petty officer of the Navy. Do not use this title before a name, and do not abbreviate or capitalize it. Make it *Hollis S. Yagyonak, the master chief petty officer of the Navy.* Then explain that it is the highest enlisted rank in the service. In later references: *Mr. Yagyonak; Master Chief Yagyonak.*

Master Chief Petty Officer *Hilary T. Baranek; Ms. Baranek; Chief Baranek; the chief.*

Senior Chief Petty Officer *Lauren C. Cordeiro; Mr. Cordeiro; Chief Cordeiro; the chief.*

Chief Petty Officer *Lindsay T. Milori; Ms. Milori; Chief Milori; the chief.*

Petty Officer First Class *Merrill R. Yagyonak; Petty Officer Yagyonak; the petty officer.*

Petty Officer Second Class *Tracy A. Karitsa; Petty Officer Karitsa; the petty officer.*

Petty Officer Third Class *Dale M. Miel; Petty Officer Miel; the petty officer.*

OTHER ENLISTED PERSONNEL

Seaman *Lindsay A. Daan; Seaman Daan; the seaman* (male or female).

Seaman Apprentice *Alex T. Kuzu; Seaman Kuzu; the seaman* (male or female).

Seaman Recruit *Chris M. Lam; Seaman Lam; the seaman* (male or female).

Also see RETIRED.

Navy Seals is the informal name for the Sea-Air-Land units, the Navy's specialists in unconventional warfare. A member is not *a Seal* but an ensign, a seaman, etc., in the Seals. *Also see* SPECIAL OPERATIONS.

Nazi, Nazism.

N.B.A. for the National Basketball Association.

NBC for the National Broadcasting Company, a subsidiary of the General Electric Company. Divisions of NBC include *NBC Entertainment, NBC News, NBC Sports, CNBC* and *WNBC-TV. NBC* or any division name may be used in a first reference, depending on the context, and *NBC* may stand alone in later references. *NBC* may be best, standing alone, when networks are grouped: *ABC, CBS, CNN and NBC will televise the news conference.* (Do not attribute an *NBC News* production to *NBC-TV.) MSNBC* is a joint venture of NBC and the Microsoft Corporation.

N.C.A.A. for the National Collegiate Athletic Association.

N. Carolina. The abbreviation may be used as a last resort in headlines (although more freely in the sports pages) and in charts and tables.

NCO for noncommissioned officer (colloquially a *noncom*). Also: *NCO's*. No periods because the letters do not represent separate words.

NCR Corporation.

N. Dakota. The abbreviation may be used as a last resort in headlines (although more freely in the sports pages) and in charts and tables.

Ndjamena (the capital of Chad).

near(-). Most but not all compounds formed with *near* are separate words: near at hand, nearby (adj. and adv.), near collision, near disaster, near escape, near miss, near riot, nearsighted.

Near East. Do not use this term. *See* MIDDLE EAST.

nearly. This modifier tends to magnify an amount: *nearly $10,000*. And *less than $10,000* tends to minimize the sum. A more neutral approach is *about $10,000*.

Nebraska. Abbreviate as *Neb.* after the names of cities, towns and counties.

Neediest Cases. It is *The New York Times Neediest Cases Fund* for the annual charitable campaign. (Historical references may recall it as the *Hundred Neediest Cases*.) Do not call it *the Neediest Fund*. Capitalize *Neediest Cases* standing alone.

Negro(es) is acceptable only in the name of an organization or in unmistakable historical contexts. In current contexts, use *black* or *African-American*. *See* AFRICAN-AMERICAN, BLACK and ETHNICITY.

Neiman Marcus, the retail chain, no longer uses a hyphen in its name.

neither, neither . . . nor. When *neither* is the subject, the verb is singular: *Neither of the cars is available*. When *neither* and *nor* link singular terms, the verb is singular: *Neither the car nor the truck is available*. When *neither* and *nor* link a singular term and a plural one, put the plural term second and use a plural verb: *Neither the car nor the trucks are available*. If the mixture of terms and verbs gets awkward, recast the sentence: *The car is not available, and neither are the trucks*.

In any *neither/nor* construction, the terms that follow the two words should be parallel in form and purpose: *The chef bakes neither pies nor cakes daily* (not *neither bakes pies nor cakes*). The same principle applies to *either/or* and *both/and*.

neo-Classical (architecture). Use the term *neo-Classical* when referring to an early revival of Greek or Roman style. In reference to 20th-century buildings of similar type, use *neo-Classical style*. *See* ARTS TERMINOLOGY.

Neo-Classicism (music). Capitalize when referring to the movement that originated in the first quarter of the 20th century, using Baroque and Classical forms with 20th-century harmonies and rhythms. *See* ARTS TERMINOLOGY.

neo-Gothic (architecture). The term can be used for buildings constructed during the revival of Gothic style, beginning in the 19th century. *Neo-Gothic* is sometimes referred to as *Gothic Revival*. There is no firm distinction between what can be called neo-Gothic and what came later, and it may be clearer to refer to 19th-century Gothic buildings with the sort of phrase that would be used with a 20th-century example: *an 1880 church in the Gothic style*. See ARTS TERMINOLOGY.

nerve-racking (not *wracking*).

net (v.). Do not use *net* as a verb to mean *earn a profit*.

Netherlands, the. Lowercase *the* in datelines and articles. Confine HOLLAND to historical references (in art, for example). The people are *Dutch*.

net income, also called *profit* or *earnings*, is what a company has left after it has paid its taxes and other expenses. In reference to a company, do not use *income* alone. Make it *income before taxes* or *net income*.

Net, the. This form may be used after a first reference to the INTERNET, or in a headline when the context is clear.

Nevada. Abbreviate as *Nev.* after the names of cities, towns and counties.

new(-). Most but not all compounds formed with *new* are one word: newborn, newcomer, newfangled, newfound, new-mown, new town.

Newark International Airport.

New Brunswick (the New Jersey city and the Canadian province). Do not abbreviate the province name after the names of cities and towns, even in datelines.

Newburgh (in New York). But: *seafood Newburg*, etc.

Newfoundland (Canadian province). Do not abbreviate after the names of cities and towns, even in datelines.

New Hampshire. Abbreviate as *N.H.* after the names of cities, towns and counties.

New Jersey. Abbreviate as *N.J.* after the names of cities, towns and counties. Avoid *Jersey* as a headline expression for the state, except in a few idioms (like *Jersey Shore* and *South Jersey*) shown in this manual.

New Jersey City University (formerly Jersey City State College).

New Jersey Institute of Technology (in Newark).

New Jersey townships. Do not use *township* unless it is needed to differentiate between areas with similar names — Chatham and Chatham Township, for instance, or Princeton and Princeton Township — or unless local idiom favors it, as in Brick Township.

New Jersey Transit operates commuter buses and trains. Do not abbreviate, except in headlines: *N.J. Transit*.

New Left. *Also see* LEFT, LEFTIST, LEFT WING.

New Mexico. Abbreviate as *N.M.* after the names of cities, towns and counties.

New Paltz (in Ulster County, N.Y.).

news(-). Most but not all compounds formed with *news* are one word: news agency, newscast, newsdealer, news gathering, NEWSGROUP, newsletter, newsmagazine, newsmaker, newsman, newswoman, newspaperman, newspaperwoman, newsprint, newsreel, newsroom, newsstand, newsworthy, news writer, news writing.

New School for Social Research; *the New School.* It is part of the *New School University.*

news, editorial. Preserve the distinction. *See* EDITORIAL, NEWS.

newsgroup is the term for an Internet bulletin board dedicated to a single discussion topic. (The global library of newsgroups is known as Usenet.)

New South Wales (in Australia). Do not abbreviate, even after the names of cities and towns.

newspaperman, newspaperwoman. Also: *newsman*; *newswoman.* And *newspeople*, but not the contrived-sounding *newsperson.*

newspaper names. Use them in roman type, without quotation marks. For consistency, capitalize the article in every newspaper name commonly written or spoken with an article: *The Washington Post*; *La Prensa*; *Al Ahram* (but: *Newsday* and *USA Today*). Also capitalize in later references: *The Post.* But lowercase *the* when a newspaper's name serves as a modifier: *the New York Times best-seller list*; *the Times article*; *the Daily News reporter.* (In such a case, *the* actually belongs to the following noun—*reporter*, for example.)

Use or omit hyphens in newspapers' names according to their style: *The International Herald Tribune*, but *The Sarasota Herald-Tribune*, in Florida. Do not append *newspaper* to a title; the device sounds unnatural (*The Guardian newspaper*). If the type of publication is not apparent, convey it subtly: *a newspaper article in The Guardian.*

Names in languages widely understood by Western readers should remain in the original languages: *Le Monde*, not *The World.* So should other well-known names, like *Pravda* and *Izvestia.* But: *People's Daily*, in Beijing. Use *The Times of London*, not *The London Times*; also *The Sunday Times* (in London) and *The Independent on Sunday* (a four-word name).

Major daily newspapers published in the New York metropolitan area include these:

The Asbury Park Press
The Daily News (and *The Sunday News*)
The Hartford Courant
The Journal News
The Journal of Commerce
The New Haven Register
The New York Post
The New York Times
Newsday
The Record
The Star-Ledger

The Staten Island Advance
The Wall Street Journal

If a location is not evident, provide it conversationally: *The Record, in Hackensack, N.J.; The Gainesville Sun, in Florida.* In a listing, or when space is scarce, a locater may be inserted in parentheses: *The Ironton (Ohio) Tribune.* But in a phrase other than a name, use commas: *a Columbus, Ohio, newspaper.*

Also see CAPITALIZATION; COLUMN NAMES; NEW YORK TIMES, THE.

news sources. *See* SOURCES.

New Testament.

New World (Western Hemisphere).

New Year's Day, New Year's Eve. Also: *New Year* (the holiday, not the 12-month period), *Chinese New Year; Jewish New Year; Lunar New Year; Vietnamese New Year;* etc.

New York. Abbreviate as N.Y. after the names of cities, towns and counties.

New York Aquarium. This informal name is acceptable in virtually all references. Occasionally, in an especially detailed article, it may be useful to mention the official name, *the Aquarium for Wildlife Conservation.* The aquarium, in Coney Island, is operated on city property by the WILDLIFE CONSERVATION SOCIETY.

New York Board of Rabbis. It represents Orthodox, Conservative, Reform and Reconstructionist rabbis in New York City, Westchester County, New Jersey and Connecticut.

New York Botanical Garden (in the Bronx). Not *Gardens.* Also: *the Queens Botanical Garden; the Staten Island Botanical Garden.* But: *the Brooklyn Botanic Garden.*

New York City. But: *the city; the city government. See* CITY.

New York City Technical College (part of the CITY UNIVERSITY OF NEW YORK).

New York City Transit; *the transit agency.* Do not abbreviate. A unit of the METROPOLITAN TRANSPORTATION AUTHORITY, it was formerly known as the Transit Authority.

New York Downtown Hospital, once known as Beekman Downtown Hospital, is now known as *NYU Downtown Hospital.* It is associated with New York University but omits periods from its official name.

New York Fire Department; *the Fire Department; the department.* When the local context is clear, *the Fire Department* should generally stand alone in a first reference. In headlines, *Fire Dept.* is acceptable. Do not use *F.D.N.Y.* except in direct quotations.

The *fire commissioner*, a civilian, is the highest authority; the *chief of department* is the top uniformed officer. There is no single *fire chief*; senior officers with *chief* in their titles should be identified by bureau or department: *Chief of Safety Toby A. Bildots; Chief Bildots; the chief of safety.* The department also has several grades within the rank of *chief*; the full designation should be included on first reference: *Deputy Assistant Chief Ashley M. Barany; Chief Barany; the chief.*

Fire stations in New York are informally called *firehouses*; the typical one has both an *engine company* and a *ladder company*. Each borough also has one *rescue company*. Several *squad companies, marine companies* (fireboat units) and *hazardous materials teams* are stationed around the city. (The insider term *Hazmat*, for *hazardous materials*, is too obscure for news articles.) When appropriate, mention the number of the company: *Engine Company 231 in Brooklyn; Ladder Company 17 in the Bronx*. Note that the ladder company and the engine company in the same firehouse are likely to have different numbers.

The rank and file in the department are *firefighters* (not *firemen* or *firewomen*).

The department also includes the *Emergency Medical Service*, though its ambulances are not stationed in firehouses. Generally confine *E.M.S.* to direct quotations, provided the context is clear.

New-York Historical Society. Note the hyphen.

New York Hospital-Cornell Medical Center is now part of New York-Presbyterian Hospital.

New York Police Department; *the Police Department*; *the department.* When the local context is clear, *the Police Department* should generally stand alone in a first reference. In headlines, *Police Dept.* is acceptable. Do not use *N.Y.P.D.* except in direct quotations.

The department includes the former Transit Police Department (now the *Transportation Bureau*) and the Housing Police Department (now the *Housing Bureau*). The *police commissioner*, a civilian, is the highest authority; the top uniformed officer is the *chief of department.* There is no single *police chief*; identify anyone with the title *chief* by bureau or department: *Chief of Patrol Robin L. Milori; Chief Milori; the chief of patrol.*

The department is divided into *precincts, bureaus, divisions* and *units*, with sometimes overlapping responsibilities, so use caution in specifying a member's assignment. Most detectives, for example, are part of bureaus and are assigned to squads, not to precincts, though they may work in a precinct house: *Detective Toby T. Kuzu of the 77th Precinct detective squad*, not just *77th Precinct. Also see* POLICE OFFICER.

New York Power Authority.

New York-Presbyterian Hospital was formed in 1997 by the merger of New York Hospital and Presbyterian Hospital. It has two major locations. One is the former Columbia-Presbyterian Medical Center at 168th Street and Broadway, now called the Columbia-Presbyterian Center and associated with the College of Physicians and Surgeons of Columbia University. The second is the former New York Hospital-Cornell Medical Center at 68th Street and York Avenue, now called the New York Weill Cornell Center and associated with the Weill Medical College of

Cornell University. Each has a separate medical department and staff. When necessary, specify the location.

New York School (art). Capitalize when referring to the ABSTRACT EXPRESSIONIST artists who emerged in New York as an influential group in the 1940's and 1950's. *See* ARTS TERMINOLOGY.

New York State Thruway Authority. It operates the New York State Thruway (formally *the Gov. Thomas E. Dewey Thruway*). In later references: *the Thruway*; *the Thruway Authority*; *the authority*.

New York Stock Exchange; *the New York Exchange*; *the exchange*; *the Big Board.* In tables and charts only: *N.Y.S.E.*

New York Times Company Foundation, The; *the Times Company Foundation*; *the foundation.* A private organization supported solely by the Times Company, it makes grants for educational, environmental, journalistic and cultural programs and for social services. Attribute its projects to the foundation, not to The Times or the Times Company.

New York Times polls. When the newspaper conducts an opinion survey in partnership, the overall designation for the project is *The New York Times/CBS News Poll.* In later references, *the Times/CBS News Poll* (with *the* lowercased) and *the poll.* Some contexts may also call for phrases like *a New York Times/CBS News poll* (lowercased for an individual survey, as opposed to the enterprise) or *a recent New York Times/CBS News poll.*

When the survey is regional, *WCBS-TV News* may substitute for *CBS News* as the partner; the editor in charge of polling will so specify. And occasionally, when The Times conducts a poll without a partner, all of the forms above will apply, with the partner's name omitted.

For statistical terms used in writing about surveys, see OPINION POLLS.

New York Times Regional Newspaper Group, the. Also: *the Times Regional Newspaper Group*; *the regional newspaper group*; *the group.* In print, do not use its acronym, Nytreng. The credit line, when the group's copy appears in The Times, is:

New York Times Regional Newspapers

The group's main office is in Tampa, Fla. Its current makeup is shown in the annual report of The New York Times Company. (The group does not include The New York Times or the company's New England newspapers—The Boston Globe and The Worcester Telegram & Gazette.)

New York Times, The. Use the name in roman type, without quotation marks. Uppercase *The* in the full names of the newspaper and the parent company: *The New York Times*; *The New York Times Company.* In later references, it is *The Times*, but *the Times Company* and *the company.*

When the newspaper name serves as a modifier, lowercase *the*, which actually attaches to the following noun: *the Times reporter*; *the Times editorial*. Note the possessive: *The Times's coverage*.

The preferred source for executives' titles and names (including initials and spelling), and for the names of affiliated companies is the Times Company's corporate Web site:

www.nytco.com

But the writer must verify that the listings there remain current. In reporting business transactions and legal developments, distinguish between the company (which principally operates subsidiaries and takes actions in the financial markets) and the newspaper. Also distinguish between corporate executives and their counterparts in operating units including the newspaper: presidents, vice presidents and chief financial officers exist at various levels.

If an officer holds more than one title, use the one(s) most pertinent to the news: *chairman of The New York Times Company*, for example, or *publisher of The New York Times*, or *president and chief executive of the Times Company*.

Lowercase titles like *executive editor*, *editorial page editor*, *national editor* and *vice president for circulation*. Also *editorial board* and *board of directors*. (Usually, in the latter sense, *board* can stand alone, and *director* should replace the wordier *member of the board of directors*.)

Reserve *editorial* and *editorial staff*, etc., for references to the opinion pages. Use phrases like *news content* and *news staff* for the rest of the journalistic operation.

Do not confuse an *issue* (the full day's output) with an *edition* (a segment of the day's circulation) or a *copy* (a single printed newspaper). Often all three words are unnecessary: *an article in The Times on Tuesday*.

Capitalize *Page 1*; *Page A1*; *Section 8*. Also: *Section 8, Page 1*. Lowercase *front page*.

Names of Times editions and services are capitalized as shown:

the New York edition (known internally as *the metro edition*)
the national edition
the Washington edition
the New England edition
the Northeast editions (comprising Washington and New England)
New York Times Digital (the Times Company's Internet division)
The New York Times on the Web
The New York Times on America Online
New York Today (the local Web service)
The New York Times News Service (a unit of *The New York Times News Services*, which also comprises other syndication and information businesses)

TimesDigest
The New York Times Index (bound volumes of abstracts)
The New York Times Large Type Weekly; the *Large Type Weekly*
City & Suburban Delivery Systems, a wholesale distribution subsidiary of The
    New York Times

FEATURES AND DEPARTMENTS
the Arts & Ideas pages (Saturday)
the editorial page
the Education page
the Health & Fitness pages
the New York Times best-seller list; the *Times best-seller list*
the News Summary
the obituary page(s)
the Op-Ed page (but *op-ed*, for that of any other publication)
the sports pages (in editions that do not carry a separate section)

Also see COLUMN NAMES and NEW YORK TIMES POLLS.

WEEKDAY SECTIONS
The Arts (but *the Arts section*)
Automobiles (or *the Automobile section*)
Business Day
Circuits (or *the Circuits section*)
the Dining section
House & Home
The Living Arts (in the national edition)
The Metro Section
Science Times
SportsMonday (and *SportsTuesday*, etc.)
Weekend

SUNDAY SECTIONS
the Arts & Leisure section
The City (or *the City section*)
the Connecticut section
the Long Island section
the main news section (or *Section 1*)
Money & Business
the New Jersey section
The New York Times Book Review; *The Times Book Review*; the *Book Review*

> *The New York Times Magazine; The Times Magazine; the magazine*
> *Part 2 of The New York Times Magazine; Part 2; the Part 2's* (they are *Home Design, Fashions of The Times, Men's Fashions of The Times, The Sophisticated Traveler*)
> *the Real Estate section*
> *Sunday Styles*
> *the Television section*
> *the Travel section*
> *the Week in Review*
> *the Westchester section*

Times buildings or offices may be identified in any of these ways:

> *The New York Times Building; the Times Building*
> *The New York Times's plant in College Point, Queens* (or *in Edison, N.J.*)
> *the New York Times plant in College Point, Queens* (or *in Edison, N.J.*)
> *The Times's Queens plant, at College Point*
> *the Washington bureau* (similarly, any other bureau)
> *Also see* NEEDIEST CASES.

New York Waterway (the ferry operator).

New York Zoological Society is the former name of the WILDLIFE CONSERVATION SOCIETY.

New Zealand. Do not abbreviate after the names of cities and towns, even in datelines.

N.F.L. for the National Football League.

nicknames. *See* PERSONAL NAMES AND NICKNAMES.

Nielsen Media Research (formerly A. C. Nielsen) is the company that measures television audiences.

Nigerois (sing. and pl.). The people of Niger. The adjective is *Niger.* (Do not confuse with *Nigeria* and *Nigerians*, for the larger country and its people.)

night(-). Some compounds formed with *night* are one word and some are two words: night blindness, nightcap, nightclothes, nightclub, nightdress, nightfall, nightgown, night life, night light, nightlong, nightmare, night owl, night school, night stand, nightstick, nighttime, night watch, night watchman.

N.I.H. for the National Institutes of Health.

1900's, 20th century. In almost all contexts, use numerals for centuries after the ninth. Also: *mid-1900's; mid-20th century.* When unavoidable, at the start of a sentence or for special effect: *nineteen-hundreds. Also see* YEARS, DECADES, CENTURIES.

92nd Street Y (in Manhattan). *The 92nd Street Y.M.-Y.W.H.A.* is always known by the short form of its name.

Niño, El. *See* EL NIÑO, LA NIÑA.

nisei refers to the children of Japanese immigrants, not to all Japanese-Americans.

nitrate, nitrite. They are different salts. Verify the names of compounds when they occur.

nitty-gritty is slang, and overworked.

N.L.R.B. for the National Labor Relations Board.

No. for number. Note the capitalization: *Haste is the No. 1 reason for errors.* Do not use *No.* before the numerical designations of schools, fire companies, lodges and similar units: *Public School 4* (or *P.S. 4*); *Ladder Company 16*; *Engine Company 4. Also see* STREETS AND AVENUES.

NOAA, for the National Oceanic and Atmospheric Administration. It is the parent agency of the National Weather Service.

Nobel Prize. Capitalize in references to the five prizes established under the will of Alfred Nobel, and capitalize the category names: *Nobel Peace Prize*; *Nobel Prize in Chemistry*; *Nobel Prize in Literature*; *Nobel Prize in Physics*; *Nobel Prize in Physiology or Medicine*. Informally, especially in a lead, *Nobel Prize in Medicine* or *Nobel Prize in Physiology* is acceptable, whichever applies; the full name should appear somewhere in an article dealing centrally with the prize.

The Bank of Sweden Prize in Economic Sciences in Memory of Alfred Nobel is not, strictly speaking, a Nobel Prize. It can be called the *Nobel Memorial Prize in Economic Science* or the *Nobel in economic science*.

nolo contendere means "I do not wish to contend," and, by extension, no contest. The criminal defendant who uses that plea is not admitting guilt, but declining to offer a defense. The defendant may then be judged guilty and punished: the effect is the same as with a plea of guilty and a conviction. But the defendant is not prevented from denying the same charge in another proceeding.

no man's land. It is an established idiom, but when the masculine viewpoint is inopportune, *buffer zone* or *neutral zone* may be useful.

non(-). Close up compounds formed with *non* unless the prefix is directly followed by an uppercase letter: nonaggression, nonalcoholic, nonaligned, non-Arab, noncancerous, nonchalance, noncombatant, noncommissioned, noncommittal, noncompliance, nonconducting, nonconformist, nondenominational, nondescript, nonexistent, nonintervention, nonnuclear, nonpareil, nonpartisan, nonplus, nonprescription, nonprofit, nonproliferation, nonresident, non-Russian, nonsectarian, nonskid, nonstick, nonstop, nonunion, nonviolence.

If an unfamiliar or baffling word results, rephrase or make an exception: *non-use.*

Also: *non sequitur* (because it is two Latin words, not a compound; also never hyphenated).

none. Despite a widespread assumption that it stands for *not one*, the word has been construed as a plural (*not any*) in most contexts for centuries. H. W. Fowler's Dictionary of Modern English Usage (1926) endorsed the plural use. Make *none* plural except when emphasizing the idea of *not one* or *no one*—and then consider using those phrases instead.

nonetheless.

no-nonsense (adj.).

nonplused does not mean fazed or unfazed. It means bewildered to the point of speechlessness.

nonprofit is more graceful and natural than *not-for-profit*. Also: *profit-making* or *commercial*, rather than *for-profit*.

no one is singular. The pronouns that refer to it are *he* and *she*, never *they*. *See* ANY-BODY, ANYONE, EVERYBODY, EVERYONE, NO ONE, SOMEONE.

Nordstrom (the retailer).

nor'easter. Use *northeaster* instead for a storm out of the northeast.

Norfolk Southern Railway.

north. Capitalize in references to that region of the United States and to specific regions so known: *North Texas*. Capitalize in later references to any country with *North* in its name: *North Korea, the North*. Also: *Far North*. Lowercase *north* as a point of the compass.

North American Free Trade Agreement. In headlines and in later references, *Nafta*. It took effect in the United States, Canada and Mexico in 1994.

North Atlantic Council (the highest authority of the North Atlantic Treaty Organization); *the council. Also see* NATO.

North Atlantic Treaty Organization. *See* NATO.

North Carolina. Abbreviate as *N.C.* after the names of cities, towns and counties. As a last resort, and somewhat more readily in the sports pages, use *N. Carolina* in a headline.

North Dakota. Abbreviate as *N.D.* after the names of cities, towns and counties. As a last resort, and somewhat more readily in the sports pages, use *N. Dakota* in a headline.

northeast. Capitalize when referring to the geographic region of the United States; lowercase as a point of the compass.

northeaster. A storm out of the northeast.

northern. Capitalize when referring to the North (the region of the United States) and to recognized areas (*Northern California*). But: *northern Ohio*; *northern part of South* (or *North*) *Korea*; *northern half of* Wyoming; etc. *Also see* NORTH.

Northerner. Capitalize when referring to someone from the American North or from a country with *North* in its name, like North Korea.

Northern Hemisphere; *the hemisphere.*

North Jersey. This is an exception to the rule that requires *northern New Jersey, eastern Indiana*, etc. It is exempt, too, from the inhabitants' usual preference for *New* in front of *Jersey*. Similarly: *South Jersey*.

North Pole. But: *the pole; polar.*

North Shore, South Shore (of Long Island).

North Side. Capitalize when regularly used to designate a section of a city.

North Slope (of Alaska).

North Texas.

North Vietnam, North Vietnamese. The terms apply only to the period from 1954 to the reunification of Vietnam in 1975.

northwest. Capitalize when referring to the geographic region of the United States; lowercase as a point of the compass.

Northwest Airlines.

Northwest Territories (in Canada). Do not abbreviate after the names of cities and towns, even in datelines.

Norwegian Cruise Line.

not-for-profit. Use the more natural *nonprofit* instead.

not guilty, innocent. In the American system, a defendant is presumed innocent and therefore never needs to prove innocence; it is guilt that must be proven, by the state. So a defendant's plea (and a successful one's verdict) is *not guilty* rather than *innocent.* The journalistic practice of writing *innocent* arose from a fear of omitting *not* in typesetting. But the distinction is worth preserving, even at the cost of an extra moment to check the copy.

not only . . . but also. Constructions of this type require a balance. The words that follow the first and second parts must be parallel in form (two adjectives, for example, serving comparable purposes): *It would be not only unwieldy but also unworkable.* Note how the symmetry is lost when words are misplaced: *It would not only be unwieldy but also unworkable.*

The *also* in the construction is generally preferred, but may be omitted if something else furnishes the balance or if the second part of the sentence describes an action more sweeping than the first: *She not only invited them to dinner but even paid for the taxi; They not only went but took all their friends.*

Other constructions that require parallel phrasing are *either X or Y, neither X nor Y* and *both X and Y.*

notoriety means more than just fame. Use it only to mean *unfavorable repute.*

Notre Dame, Notre-Dame. It is the *University of Notre Dame,* not *Notre Dame University,* in Indiana. The phrase *Notre-Dame* (meaning Our Lady) is ordinarily hyphenated in the names of French towns, streets and churches (including the *Cathedral of Notre-Dame,* in Paris), but French Canadian usage varies; verify each case. The modifier *Notre* does not take an accent mark, unlike *nôtre,* the pronoun meaning *ours.*

notwithstanding.

Nov. for *November* before numerals (*Nov. 11*), or in charts and tables.

Nova Scotia (Canadian province). Do not abbreviate after the names of cities and towns, even in datelines.

NOW for the National Organization for Women (not *of Women*). A separate but affiliated organization is the NOW *Legal Defense and Education Fund* (not the *National Organization for Women Legal Defense and Education Fund*).

now. Use the word as an adverb (*the film is playing now*) or a noun (*by now, the film must be over*). Dictionaries accept it in compound modifiers also (*the now famous comedian; the now defunct magazine*), but that usage produces unpolished phrasing with the sound of overliteral translation. Replace it with phrases like this: *the comedian, now famous; the magazine, now defunct*.

NPR for National Public Radio. It is a nonprofit network that acquires, distributes and produces programs for public stations.

Nuclear Regulatory Commission. In later references and in headlines: N.R.C.

nucleus (sing.), **nuclei** (pl.).

numbered expressions. A designation consisting of a noun and a numeral is capitalized as a proper name: *Page A1; Act II, Scene 3; Apartment 3B; Column 40; Day 1; Door 12; Flight 424; Gate 27; Phase 2; Room 235; Row 3; Seat 12C; Section 30.* *Also see* CHAPTER NUMBERS and PAGE NUMBERS.

number of subject and verb. After a *neither/nor* construction, if the subjects are both singular, use a singular verb: *Neither Dana nor Dale was happy.* If the subjects are both plural, use a plural verb: *Neither the Yankees nor the Mets were hitting.* If one subject is singular and the other plural, use the number of the one nearer the verb: *Neither the man nor his horses were ever seen again.*

A verb that merely connects two elements in a sentence takes the number of the preceding noun or pronoun, which is the subject: *Her specialty was singing and dancing and playing the violin.* The verb most often used this way is *to be.* Others that can serve as connectors include *appear, become, feel, look, seem, smell* and *taste.* When the subject is the pronoun *what,* the writer must decide whether to construe it as *the thing that* (singular) or *the things that* (plural). Once the decision is made, all affected verbs must conform: *What was remarkable was the errors made on both sides; What were most in demand were language ability and a degree in Russian studies.*

When a verb is far removed from its subject, especially if another noun intervenes, mistakes like this may occur: *The value of Argentina's exports to the United States are 183 million pesos.* The verb should be singular because its subject (*value*) is singular.

Misidentification of the subject also causes trouble: *Terry Cordeiro is one of those people who goes in for striking colors.* The verb should be *go,* since the subject is *who,* which refers to the plural *people.* Test such constructions by reversing them: *Of those people who go in for striking colors, Terry Cordeiro is one.*

Sums of money are usually treated as singular because the focus is on the sum, not on individual bills or coins: *Ten dollars buys less now than five did then.* Similarly: *Five pounds of rice feeds a family of four for a week* (because the pounds are not counted one by one). Use the plural when the focus is on individual items: *Three hundred parcels of food were shipped.*

Total of or *number of* (and a few similar expressions, like *series of*) may take either a plural or a singular verb. In general, when the expression follows *a*, it is plural: *A total of 102 people were injured*; *A number of people were injured.* When the expression follows *the*, it is usually singular: *The total of all department budgets is $187 million*; *The number of passengers injured was later found to be 12.*

If *couple* conveys the idea of two people, treat it as a plural: *The couple were married.* But: *Each couple was asked to give $10.*

numbers. In general, spell out the first nine cardinal and ordinal numbers in ordinary copy: *He walked nine miles*; *There were eight applicants*; *He was the sixth*; *The game ended in the fifth inning.* Use figures for numbers above nine: *The table was set for 10*; *There were 50 in the audience*; *He owns 63 horses*; *The game finally ended in the 15th inning.*

The rule of spelling out below 10 does not apply to these cases:

- AGES OF PEOPLE AND ANIMALS.
- Building numbers: *1 Fifth Avenue*. See ADDRESSES.
- Figures in headlines, charts and tables.
- Figures in some financial contexts: *The stock advanced 3 points.*
- Figures that include decimals: *3.4 inches of snow.* See DECIMALS.
- Results of voting. See VOTES.
- Percentages. See PERCENT, PERCENTAGE.
- Sums of money. See MONEY.
- Times of day. See TIME.
- Days of the month. See DATES.
- LATITUDE AND LONGITUDE.
- Degrees of temperature. See TEMPERATURE.
- Dimensions, measurements, weights and proportion when they consist of two or more elements. See DIMENSIONS, MEASUREMENTS, WEIGHTS AND PROPORTIONS.
- NUMBERED EXPRESSIONS: *Page 1*; *Section 3*; *Chapter V*; *Article 6*; *Room 9.*
- Sports points, scores and times. *Also see* BASEBALL; BASKETBALL; BOXING; FOOTBALL; GOLF; HOCKEY; HORSE RACING; SWIMMING; TENNIS.
- Mentions of the Twelve Apostles and the Ten Commandments.

Round numbers are sometimes rendered in numerals and sometimes in words. In the thousands, it is almost always numerals: *5,000; 2,300th*. But spelling out is sometimes appropriate: *Fifty to sixty thousand voted; They planned to enlist a million workers; He said his opponent was a hundred percent wrong.*

In the millions, this is the usual form: *four million, 10 millionth.* The adjectival form: *four-million-year span; 12-million-year span.* In the case of dollar and sterling sums: *$10 million; £25 million.* When a range is given, repeat the word: *$5 billion to $15 billion* (not *$5 to $15 billion,* except in this modifier form, with hyphens: *$5-to-15-billion program*). Do not hyphenate the simple modifier form: *$10 million loan.*

The rules for spelling and numerals also apply to adjectival forms: *four-mile hike; 11-mile race; three-day trip; 40-hour week; five-ton truck; 9,000-ton ship; two-million-member union; 10-million-vote margin; 3.5-inch snow.*

In ordinary news copy, spell any number that begins a sentence: *Five hundred delegates attended.* In any series of directly parallel items including some numbers that would ordinarily be spelled and some that would ordinarily be figures, use only figures: *4 submarines, 10 destroyers and 15 carriers; the 9th and 10th centuries; 6 of the 12 members.* This consistency rule does not apply to nearby numbers that are outside the related series. Nor does it apply to the pronoun *one* (make it *she was one of 10 children,* not *she was 1 of 10 children*) or to STREETS AND AVENUES.

In ordinary copy, use *to* between numerals in giving the results of voting and rulings by a court with more than one judge: *a vote of 51 to 3; voted 51 to 3; a 51-to-3 vote; ruled 5 to 4; a 5-to-4 ruling.* But the *to* can be dropped in headlines: *a 5-4 vote.*

When paired numbers denote a range, do not use a comma: *Fees will rise by $3 to $20.* Insert a comma when the numbers do not represent a range: *Fees will rise by $3, to $20.* When reporting a rise or a fall, give the *to* figure first (in spite of logic), to prevent misreading as a range: *In a week, the stock rose to $25 from $17.75.* And: *The price fell to $850 from $998.*

In headlines, figures may be used for all cardinal and ordinal numbers, but *1* and *1st* are typographically inelegant and should be a last resort. *One Hurt* is preferred to *1 Hurt* (better yet: *Man Hurt* or *Woman Hurt*). *First Prize* is more readable than *1st Prize.* In an idiom, make it *First Aid* and *Safety First,* not *1st Aid* and *Safety 1st.* But use *1-Cent Tax* (or *1¢ Tax*), *1 percent* and similar constructions.

When using figures, express ordinal numbers this way: *2nd; 3rd; 4th; 11th; 21st; 33rd; 124th.*

To aid comprehension, long numbers may be rounded. Those in which the first omitted digit is 5 or higher are rounded upward; those in which the first omitted digit is 4 or lower are rounded downward. In general, round off figures in the millions to one decimal place (*3.5 million*), those in the billions to two places (*4.56 billion*) and those in the trillions to three (*4.765 trillion*). When highly similar numbers are compared or contrasted, it may be necessary to retain more decimal places.

Use caution, because rounded numbers can be misleading. In an article about a record-breaking $1.95 million contract, for example, a reference to a $2 million deal might be unfair. And any calculation of a percentage change should be based on unrounded numbers because the distortion from rounding can be significant. If, for instance, a company reports that its earnings rose to $1.86 million from $1.23 million, the unrounded numbers yield a change of 51.2 percent. But if the percentage is calculated on rounded figures ($1.9 million and $1.2 million), the change comes to 58.3 percent.

In rounding numbers that are subject to dispute or numbers that may change — estimates of surpluses or budget deficits, for example, and early estimates of damage or deaths in a disaster — use the more conservative figure. But if experience suggests that an earthquake or other disaster is likely to do vast damage because of its location, a general prediction like "hundreds" may be appropriate.

Also see NUMBERS, ROUND.

numbers in names. Make it *Lee T. Berenich IV* or *Lee T. Berenich 4th*, depending on the bearer's preference. If the preference is not known, use Roman numerals. Popes and monarchs use Roman numerals. In a listing, if family names are printed before given names, the number comes last: *BERENICH, Lee T. IV*, not *BERENICH IV, Lee T.* Also: *Jr.* and *Sr.* (without commas) for Junior and Senior in names: *Lee T. Berenich Jr.* (or *Sr.*). *Also see* JUNIOR, SENIOR and PERSONAL NAMES AND NICKNAMES.

numbers, round. Round numbers in the thousands are usually expressed in figures: *She ordered 5,000 cases of beer.* But spelling out is sometimes appropriate: *He said he knew a thousand better ways.*

Round numbers in the millions and billions generally follow the rule of spelling out below 10: *three million people*; *16 million people*. But, with a decimal: *3.5 million people*. Hyphenate the adjectival form: *three-million-year span*; *16-million-year span*. The spelling rule does not apply in the case of money: *$3 million*; *$13-million-a-year job*; *$1.5 billion*; *£7 billion*; *6 million francs*; *4.5 million francs*. Spelling is appropriate in a figure of speech: *I wish I had a million dollars*. And: *He got a million dollars' worth of free publicity*. (Note the apostrophe.)

When two round numbers appear together, one with 10 or a higher figure and the other without, follow this style: *9 million to 11 million people*.

In expressing a range of values, repeat *million* or *billion*, as follows: *60 million to 75 million*; *$5.5 billion to $8 billion*. The repetition is not necessary in this modifier form, with hyphens: *a $5-to-15-billion program*. But do not hyphenate the simple modifier form: *the $10 million loan*.

Here are further examples of the style for round numbers that are not sums of money:

one million tons or (preferably) *a million tons*
two and a half million tons
two million to three million tons (not *two to three million*)
2 million to 11 million tons
1.5 million tons
1.75 million tons
1.5 million to 3 million tons
300,000 to one million
555 billion gallons

In general, do not use *quadrillion, quintillion,* etc., because they are hard to grasp. Instead, express the number in millions or billions (*billion* in the American sense of 1,000 million). The following table shows how very large numbers may be expressed. In each case, the zeros follow the numeral 1.

15 zeros: a million billion (instead of a *quadrillion*)
16 zeros: 10 million billion
17 zeros: 100 million billion
18 zeros: a billion billion (instead of a *quintillion*)

numbskull.

nun. The term (not a title) designates a woman in an organized religious community, most often in the Roman Catholic Church but also in the Anglican (Episcopal) and Orthodox denominations and in Buddhism. Christian nuns generally take vows of poverty, chastity and obedience. *See* MOTHER and SISTER (RELIGIOUS).

Nunavut (in Canada) is a territory, with more limited autonomy and powers than a province. It was created in 1999 from part of the Northwest Territories and is populated largely by INUIT people. Use *Nunavut* after the names of cities and towns. The name, pronounced NOO-na-voot, means "our land."

nuncio. *See* PAPAL NUNCIO and APOSTOLIC DELEGATE.

nursemaid.

nurseryman.

Nynex. The former regional telephone company was succeeded by Bell Atlantic, which became part of VERIZON COMMUNICATIONS in 2000.

N.Y.S.E. *See* NEW YORK STOCK EXCHANGE.

N.Y.U. for New York University.

O

O, oh. The interjection or exclamation *O* is now found mostly in quotations from poetry, in classical references and in religious texts. It is always capitalized, whether at the beginning of a sentence or elsewhere: *For thee, O Lord*. But the modern *oh* is capitalized only at the start of a sentence: *Oh, what a shame! But oh, how glad we were!* Such a construction usually requires an exclamation point.

O.A.S. for the Organization of American States.

obbligato(s).

obituaries. An obituary ordinarily begins with the subject's full name, age, residence, day and place of death and claim to fame or reputation. But the sequence is optional, and the elements need not all appear in the lead; secondary facts (residence and hospital name, for example) should be deferred to avoid clutter. The statement of a subject's accomplishment should fit the prominence or brevity of the obituary; if the statement is unremarkable and the copy is long, broaden the statement or shorten the copy.

For the obituary of a reasonably private person, the reporter should try to learn the cause of death without hectoring the bereaved. If the reporter doubts the truth of the cause given, it should be omitted. If no reasonable doubt arises, the cause should be used with attribution, in a separate sentence or preferably a separate paragraph, to alert careful readers that The Times has not independently verified it. For the very elderly (mid-80's and older) who die of routine illnesses, the cause should usually be omitted. The obituary of a newsworthy public personality, of any age, should reflect energetic reporting on the cause.

If a crime or indiscretion was the subject's main claim to fame, it should of course figure in the lead. But an early indiscretion should be kept in proportion — subordinated or omitted, depending on its ultimate significance in a life. The discovery of a lone article in the newspaper file should not skew the summation of a lifetime.

Education and military service should be given when relevant or interesting, and when space permits. Leadership in civic and volunteer work should be treated comparably with professional achievement. As a service to classmates and early friends of the subject, mention the original name of a woman who used a married name.

Survivors should be listed at the end of a routine obituary. But a fuller one, if artfully constructed, will attend to the basics earlier and end with an anecdote or an otherwise memorable paragraph.

Ordinarily the named survivors include parents, siblings, spouse or companion and children. Give the numbers of grandchildren and great-grandchildren; their names are optional (along with hometowns for all survivors), depending on the length and prominence of the obituary. Those factors, and news value, also determine whether to recall earlier marriages. In obituaries, a man may be survived by *his wife* and a woman by *her husband*. Leave *widow* and *widower* for later articles.

If a survivor's name is likely to be familiar to many readers, include a brief identification: *Mr. Manley is survived by his wife, Joan, and a son, Dana, of Chicago, who is president of XYZ University.*

The Times should not be the arbiter of what makes up a family: if the survivors regard a more distant relative or even a friend as a member of the subject's immediate household, mention the relationship. If survivors disagree about whom to include, refer the question to the news desk, which will weigh the demands of accuracy, news value and compassion. Never write *There are no survivors*, a statement that can cause anguish to anyone overlooked. Instead use *No immediate family members survive.*

Every obituary headline should include the subject's age, directly to the right of the name or of an occupational noun (meaning that the age never begins a line). *John P. Manley, 88, Architect* is fine; so is *Architect, 88*. But *Architect of Churches, 88* is not, because of the momentary incongruity of the notion (even if implausible) that the churches were 88.

The main headline on each obituary page should say *Dies* or *Dead*. Other headlines may omit the word, but if they do, *Dies* or *Dead* is the *implied* verb of the main clause (the clause that begins with the subject's name). Thus a semicolon must come before any other verb occurring in the headline: *John P. Manley, 88; Held Many Titles.* The semicolon may fall anywhere in a single-line head, but should occur at the end of a line in a multiple-line one.

objet(s) d'art.

obscenity, vulgarity, profanity. The Times writes unblushingly about sexual behavior, arts censorship, science, health, crime and similar subjects, opening its columns to any newsworthy detail, however disturbing, provided the approach is dignified and the vocabulary clinical rather than coarse. In these situations, the paper rejects evasiveness and euphemism, which would be a disservice to readers who need to understand issues.

But The Times virtually never prints obscene words, and it maintains a steep threshold for vulgar ones. In part the concern is for the newspaper's welcome in classrooms and on breakfast tables in diverse communities nationwide. But a larger concern is for the newspaper's character. The Times differentiates itself by taking a stand for civility in public discourse, sometimes at an acknowledged cost in the vividness of an article or two, and sometimes at the price of submitting to gibes.

The responsibility for keeping obscenity and vulgarity out of the paper begins with the writer. But if the writer perceives a compelling argument for an exception, a discussion with the department head is mandatory. Finally the question should go to a masthead editor, and judgments about strong vulgarisms will rest with the head of the news department or the editorial page.

The argument that someone's use of a vulgar expression was surprising or politically dramatic, or revealing about art or the intensity of feelings, will not be compelling. Exceptions have been made only a handful of times, and they typify the standard. In 1974 The Times published transcripts of White House conversations that figured in the Watergate scandal. Expressions highly objectionable by Times standards were printed because of the light they shed on a historic matter, the possibility of a presidential impeachment. The paper's top editors judged that in this situation, it was not enough to say merely that an obscenity or a vulgarism had been used. In 1991, the fate of a Supreme Court appointment rested on whether the Senate would believe a complaint of sexual harassment against the nominee. The nationally televised accusation centered on coarse slang, which The Times printed in its articles and hearing transcripts. In 1998 the newspaper retained explicit sexual descriptions and slang in the texts of documents submitted to Congress by an independent counsel recommending impeachment action against President Clinton. (The expressions were omitted from news articles.)

The cases provide this guide for when to print an extreme vulgarism: only when its use will give the reader an essential insight into matters of great moment, an insight that cannot be otherwise conveyed. Such a case would almost certainly involve the use of the term by a figure of commanding influence or in that person's presence, in a situation likely to become momentous.

Discussion about an expletive does not end with the decision against using it. The Times also forgoes offensive or coy hints. An article should not seem to be saying, "Look, I want to use this word, but *they* won't let me." Generally that principle rules out telltale strings of hyphens or dashes (*The prosecutor is full of* – – – –). Editors may sparingly allow paraphrase of a term, if it truly sheds light on a serious question. But a phrase like the legendary *barnyard expletive*, ambiguous about the animal to which it alludes, may raise questions as distracting as those it answers. Finally, editors may permit *[expletive]* or *[epithet]* in a quotation. (Note that the two terms are not synonymous; see EPITHET, EXPLETIVE. And omit *deleted* because it is obvious.)

Profanity in its milder forms (*hells, damns* and, far less acceptable, religious oaths) can sometimes be justified—in combat reporting, for example, to convey the depth of anguish or pain—but those who print it should be aware that it will outrage some readers. Department heads have the discretion to approve profanity (not obscenity or vulgarity) for compelling reasons. But if the paper is peppered with it, the news report is cheapened and the character of the paper tarnished. Rationing must be stringent.

In 1896, Adolph S. Ochs proclaimed that The New York Times would present the news "in language that is parliamentary in good society." Were Mr. Ochs alive today, he could still identify with The Times's passion for its character. But he might simply write, "Keep it clean."

observer(s). Attentive readers have come to suspect *observer(s)* of being a mask for *reporter(s)*. So when *reporter* is not meant, use a more specific and convincing phrase. When reporter *is* meant, say so outright. (The term is suitable, though, in official designations like *election observers* and *truce observers.*)

Occupational Safety and Health Administration. In headlines and in later references, *OSHA.*

o'clock. In cap-and-lowercase headlines and titles, make it *O'Clock.*

Oct. for October before numerals (*Oct. 12*) or in charts and tables.

octet (music). *See* QUARTET and TRIO.

octopus. The plural is *octopuses.*

odd(-), (-)odd. Most compounds formed with *odd* as a prefix are hyphenated, but a few are two words: odd-looking, odd lot (n.), odd-lot (adj.), odd-numbered.

Compounds formed with *odd* as a suffix to a number are hyphenated: 20-odd, 200-odd.

O.E.C.D. for the Organization for Economic Cooperation and Development.

oenophile.

of. Generally, phrases connected by *of* sound most natural when they are intact. *The company completed the conversion to electricity of its heating system* is not nearly so smooth as *The company completed the conversion of its heating system to electricity.* Also: *died of a heart attack yesterday,* not *died yesterday of a heart attack.*

Drop the *of* in constructions like this: *She uses the name of Chris.* The *of* suggests that she is using someone else's actual name. Similarly, replace *of* with a comma in *his hometown of Peoria.*

off(-), (-)off. Most compounds formed with *off* as a prefix are hyphenated, but some are solid and some are two words: offbeat, off-center, off-color (adj., before a noun), offhand, off-key (adj., before a noun), off key (adj., after a noun, and adv.), off-limits (adj., before a noun), off limits (adj., after a noun), off-line (adj.), off-putting, off-road, off-season (n., adj. and adv.), offset, offshoot, offshore, offside, offspring, offstage, off-the-shelf, off-track.

Compounds formed with *off* as a suffix are sometimes solid, sometimes hyphenated and sometimes two words: blastoff (n.), blast off (v.), playoff, runoff, sell-off, send-off, standoff, stop-off, takeoff (all n.). *Also see* LAY OFF, LAYOFF; OFF BROADWAY, OFF OFF BROADWAY.

off again on again. Hyphenate when the phrase precedes a noun: *the off-again-on-again decision*. Otherwise, omit all punctuation: *the plan was off again on again*.

Off Broadway, Off Off Broadway. When *Off* helps to form an adjective or a noun in these terms, it is capitalized: *He is directing an Off Broadway* (or *Off Off Broadway*) *play*; *A survey showed that Off Broadway* (or *Off Off Broadway*) *was flourishing*. But when *off* helps to form an adverb, it is lowercased: *The play was produced off Broadway*; *The play was produced off Off Broadway*.

office(-). Most compounds formed with *office* are one word, but not all. Some examples: officeholder, office hours, officeseeker.

Also: *office boy* and *office girl*, but not in references to adults.

Office of Management and Budget; *the budget office*. And very rarely, mainly in quotations: *O.M.B.*

officer. *See* POLICE OFFICER.

off limits. Hyphenate the phrase when it precedes the noun it modifies, but not otherwise: *an off-limits club near the naval base; the bar was also off limits*.

Off-Track Betting Corporation; *the OTB*.

oh. *See* O, OH.

O. Henry (not *O'Henry*) for the pen name of the short-story writer William Sydney Porter.

Ohio. Do not abbreviate, even after the names of cities, towns and counties.

oil(-). Most but not all compounds formed with *oil* are two words: oil burner, oil can, oilcloth, oil color, oil field, oil painting, oil shale, oilskin, oil slick, oilstove, oil well.

Also: *oilman*, but general references are to *oil executive* or *oil producer*.

O.K., not *okay*. Reserve the term (adv., adj. and interj.) for features or informal contexts. Do not use *O.K.* as a verb except in a direct quotation (*O.K.'s; O.K.'d; O.K.'ing*).

Oklahoma. Abbreviate as *Okla.* after the names of cities, towns and counties.

old(-). Most but not all compounds formed with *old* are hyphenated: old age, old-boy (adj.), old-fashioned, old-school (adj.), Old South, old-timer, Old World.

Old City. The walled part of Jerusalem.

old master(s), lowercased, for the great artists before the 18th century.

Old Testament.

Old World.

Olympic Airways.

Olympic Games; *the Games.*

on again off again. Hyphenate when the phrase precedes a noun: *the on-again-off-again decision.* Otherwise, omit all punctuation: *the plan was on again off again.*

one(-). Some compounds formed with *one* are one word, some are hyphenated and some are two words: one-liner, one-on-one (adj., before a noun) one on one (adv.), one-piece (adj.), oneself, one-shot, one-sided, one-to-one (adj., before a noun), one to one (adv.), one-way. *See* FRACTIONS and ONETIME, ONE-TIME.

one another, each other. Two people look at *each other*; more than two look at *one another.*

one of the. *One of the reasons for her resignation* is wordy. Make it *a reason* (or *one reason*) *for her resignation.* And note the plural verb in a construction like *She is one of the people who love the Yankees.* The test is to reverse the sentence: *Of the people who love the Yankees, she is one.* The subject is *people*, not *one.*

one person one vote. Hyphenate when the phrase serves as a modifier before a noun: *the one-person-one-vote rule.* Otherwise, omit all punctuation: *the principle of one person one vote.* Avoid *one man one vote.*

onetime, one-time. *Onetime* means former, or at some time in the past. *One-time* means just once.

ongoing is bureaucratic. Delete it, or substitute one of its many synonyms: *continuing, developing, proceeding,* etc.

on hold, applied to a delay in anything except a telephone call, is trite.

on line, in line. Few besides New Yorkers stand or wait *on line.* In most of the English-speaking world, people stand *in line.* Use that wording.

online. Make it a solid compound in all references to electronic connections. By extension, the spelling also applies to places like factories (*The plant went online in August*), but that use is usually jargon.

only. Place it next to the word it modifies. *Only she tasted the rutabaga* means that no one else did. *She tasted only the rutabaga* means that she tasted nothing else. *She only tasted the rutabaga* means that she did not devour the rutabaga; she merely nibbled at it.

Idiom demands some exceptions. *It can only get worse,* for example, is smoother and more conversational than *It can get only worse.* And in the compressed language of headlines, the meaning of *only* will probably be unclear if *the* or *a* or *an* has been omitted alongside it (*Court Finds Dann Only Conspirator*). Replace *only* with a word like *mere, sole, lone* or *alone. Also see* NOT ONLY ... BUT ALSO.

onstage (adj. and adv.).

Ontario (Canadian province). Do not abbreviate after the names of cities and towns, even in datelines.

Op Art. Capitalize when referring to the movement in abstract painting, begun in the 1960's, that was characterized by optical illusion or confusion. *See* ARTS TERMINOLOGY.

OPEC for the Organization of the Petroleum Exporting Countries. Also, less often mentioned: *Oapec*, for the Organization of Arab Petroleum Exporting Countries.

Op-Ed. Uppercase for The Times's, lowercase for others'. In all cases, *page* is lowercase.

open(-). Some compounds formed with *open* are one word, some are hyphenated and a few are two words: open admissions, open air (n.), open-air (adj.), open-and-shut, open-door (adj.), open-ended, open-eyed, open-faced, open-field (adj.), openhanded, open-heart surgery, openhearted, open house, open-minded, open shop, open stock, openwork.

operas. Capitalize opera titles and use quotation marks: *"Aida" is an opera by Verdi.* Do not use quotation marks around the names of characters: *Aida, Carmen, Violetta, Mimì,* etc. Also: *opéra bouffe; Opéra-Comique; operagoer.*

opera singer. More specific identification is preferred when available: *tenor; soprano; baritone;* etc.

operations. *See* MILITARY OPERATIONS.

ophthalmologist, ophthalmology. Like eyeglass lenses, the *h*'s and *l*'s in each word come in pairs.

opinion polls. Articles about the findings of a public opinion poll should name the person or group who conducted it, name the sponsor and, if necessary, explain the sponsor's interest in the subject of the poll. The article should also give the number of people surveyed, the dates of the survey and the procedures used (whether interviews were conducted by mail, by telephone or in person). If the poll studied some group other than the general population—registered voters, say, or married adults—the report should say how the respondents were chosen.

The article should give the probable margin of sampling error for a sample of the size used in the poll, and to aid comprehension it should be explained in a sentence like this: *The margin of sampling error for a sample of this size is plus or minus five percentage points, so differences of less than that amount are statistically insignificant.* Both the poll's findings and the margin of error should be rounded to the nearest whole percentage point because results rendered to the tenth of a point suggest an impossible degree of precision.

The terms *opinion poll, poll, survey, opinion sample* and *cross section* should be limited to scientific soundings of opinion. They should not be applied to roundups of comment or interviews of people in the street. Indeed, extensive articles of that kind should include a cautionary note that the interviews are not a scientific sampling and that only limited conclusions can be drawn from them.

Also see NEW YORK TIMES POLLS.

opposition (political). Lowercase, even when referring to a formally designated political faction in a foreign country: *The Labor opposition was divided*; *The opposition party failed again.*

Opus (music). In a title, abbreviate and capitalize *Opus* and enclose the reference in parentheses: *Chopin's Rondo in E flat (Op. 16).* But: *His Opus 16 is moving.* A few composers are given specialized catalog designations in place of *opus.* For Mozart, use the Köchel listing *(K. 145),* for Schubert the Deutsch listing *(D. 93)* and for Bach the Bach Werke Verzeichnis number *(BWV 71). See* MUSIC.

oral, verbal. Use *oral* to mean spoken. *Verbal* applies to spoken or written words.

oratory means skill or eloquence in public speaking, not merely *statements, speeches* or *talks. Also see* RHETORIC.

orbit can be used as a verb with or without a direct object: *The United States orbited a weather satellite*; *The satellite orbited.*

order of magnitude. In mathematics, an *order of magnitude* means multiplication by 10; several *orders of magnitude* means a quantity multiplied by hundreds or thousands. As a way of saying something has increased a great deal, it has become a cliché.

Oregon. Abbreviate as *Ore.* after the names of cities, towns and counties.

organdy.

Organization for Economic Cooperation and Development. In headlines and in later references: *O.E.C.D.*

Organization of American States, *the organization.* In headlines and, sparingly, in later references: *O.A.S.*

Organization of the Petroleum Exporting Countries. In headlines and in later references, *OPEC.* Also, less often mentioned: the Organization of Arab Petroleum Exporting Countries, or *Oapec* (pronounced WAH-peck).

Orient Lines (the cruise line).

Orient, Oriental. Capitalize in references to Asia and the East. Do not use *Oriental* as a noun or adjective for people in or from those regions. (*See* ASIAN-AMERICAN.) Also: *Oriental rug.*

ORT, Women's American. In later references, *ORT*, without *the.* (*ORT* stands for *Organization for Rehabilitation Through Training.*)

orthodontics, not *orthodontia,* for the branch of dentistry that specializes in repairing irregularities of the teeth. And *orthodontic treatment* for its work.

Orthodox Church in America. Originally the Orthodox Diocese in America, it was granted self-government in 1970 by the Orthodox patriarchate in Moscow.

Orthodox Judaism. Its houses of worship are synagogues, not temples.

OSHA for the Occupational Safety and Health Administration.

Oswego, Owego. *Oswego* is in Oswego County, N.Y. *Owego* is in Tioga County, N.Y.

OTB for the Off-Track Betting Corporation.

out(-), (-)out. Most but not all compounds formed with *out* as a prefix are one word: out-and-out, outback, outbid, outboard, outbound, outbuilding, outclass, outclimb, outcry, outdated, outdistance, outdo, outdoor, outfield, outflank, outfox, outgoing, outgrow, outguess, outhouse, outmaneuver, out-of-date, out-of-doors (adj.), out-of-pocket, out-of-the-way, outpatient, outrigger, outrun, outscore, outspoken, outtake(s).

Most but not all compounds formed with *out* as a suffix are one word: dropout, fade-out, fallout, hide-out, pullout, timeout, walkout (all n. only).

outage is jargon and a euphemism for *failure, shutdown* or *cutoff* (of electricity or water, for example). Use the simpler words.

outgoing. For clarity, the modifier is best reserved for a personality trait, meaning genial. In the sense of leaving office, use *departing* instead.

Oval Office (in the White House).

over(-), (-)over. Most but not all compounds formed with *over* as a prefix are one word: overabundant, overact, overarching, overbearing, overcharge, overcompensate, overcrowd, overdose, overdraft, overdrive, overexcitable, overexpand, overextend, overindulgence, overproduction, overprompt, overreach, overreact, overripe, oversensitive, over-the-counter (adj. only), over the counter (adv.), overtime.

Most but not all compounds formed with *over* as a suffix are one word: carry-over, changeover, hangover, holdover, layover, makeover (all n.); make over (v.); takeover (n.); take over (v.); turnover (n.); turn over (v.); walkover. *Also see* OVER ALL, OVERALL, OVERALLS and ROLL OVER, ROLLOVER.

over age, over-age, overage. *Over age* means too old. When it precedes what it modifies, hyphenate it: *over-age applicants*. Use *overage* to mean excess or surplus.

over all, overall, overalls. Use *overall* as an adjective: *overall policy*. But use two words in phrases like these: *Over all, the Democrats made gains; The Senate's political coloration will be little changed over all.* The bibbed trousers with tool pockets are *overalls*.

Overseas National Airways.

overture. Capitalize in a title: *Beethoven's "Egmont" Overture*. But: *a Beethoven overture*. Also capitalize when the overture is designated by its source: *the Overture to* (not *of*) *"La Gazza Ladra," by Rossini*.

oxford. The cloth and the shoes.

oxford blue. The color. (But someone who has, say, rowed for the university is an Oxford Blue.)

oxford gray.

Oxonian(s). The people of Oxford, England, or students and graduates of Oxford University. But phrases using *of Oxford* are usually less stodgy.

P

pablum. Capitalized, *Pablum* is a trademark for infant cereal. Lowercased, *pablum* means anything oversimplified or bland.

Pacific. The actual shoreline of the Pacific Ocean is *the Pacific coast*; the region of the United States lying along the shoreline is *the Pacific Coast* or *the West Coast*. Also: *Pacific Coast States; Pacific States; Pacific Northwest; North Pacific; South Pacific*.

Pacific Daylight Time, Pacific Standard Time (P.D.T., P.S.T.). *See* TIME.

Pacific Stock Exchange.

page numbers. Capitalize them as proper names: *Page A1; Page A14; Page B1; Page 112; Pages A18-20*. Also: *A Page 1 article*, but *the third page* and *the front page*. In charts, diagrams and tables, abbreviations may be used: *P. 5; Pp. 19, 20 and 21; Pp. 19-21*. Also: *321 pp. See* NUMBERED EXPRESSIONS.

PaineWebber Inc. See UBS PAINEWEBBER INC.

paintings. Use quotation marks for their titles and capitalize the principal words.

palate (part of the mouth), **palette** (an artist's paint board), **pallet** (a stacking platform).

Palestine Liberation Organization (P.L.O.). Not *Palestinian*.

Palisade, Palisades. *The Palisades* (overlooking the Hudson River); *Palisades* (New York); *Palisades Interstate Parkway; Palisades Park* (New Jersey); *Palisade Avenue* (in the Bronx and several places in New Jersey); *Pacific Palisades* (California).

pallbearer.

Pan(-). It is generally hyphenated: Pan-African; Pan-American (in the general sense); Pan-German; Pan-Slavic; Pan-American Games; Pan-American Highway.
    But: *the Pan American Union*.

P&O Lines (the ocean carrier).

paneled.

pantsuit.

papal. Lowercase unless it is part of a name or title.

papal nuncio. *Bishop* (or *Archbishop*) *Lee E. Lamm; the papal nuncio; the nuncio.* A nuncio is a Roman Catholic diplomat accredited by the pope to a foreign government with which the Vatican has diplomatic relations. An APOSTOLIC DELE-GATE is the papal envoy to the church or the hierarchy in a country without a treaty.

paparazzi. The singular, pretentious in English writing, is *paparazzo*.

paper(-). Some compounds formed with *paper* are one word, some are hyphenated and some are two words: paperback, paper-backed, paperbound, paper clip, paper cutter, paperhanger, paperweight, paperwork.

Also: *paperboy, papergirl,* but the neutral *paper carrier* is preferred, especially in a reference to an adult.

papier-mâché.

paradox means a statement that seems contradictory or impossible but may in fact be true: *Water, water everywhere, nor any drop to drink. Also see* IRONY.

paragraph numbers. Capitalize them as proper names: *Paragraph 3; Paragraph 16.* But: *the third paragraph. See* NUMBERED EXPRESSIONS.

parallel (latitude). *See* LATITUDE AND LONGITUDE.

paralleled, paralleling.

pardon, amnesty, clemency. A *pardon* is a release from punishment or forgiveness of an offense, granted to an individual. An *amnesty* is a general pardon, usually for political offenses, granted to a group. *Clemency* is leniency or mercy shown by someone in power.

parentheses. In general, parentheses enclose an explanation or clarifying material that was available to the writer, even if the material is actually being provided by an editor: *The painting sold for £100 ($164). Or: Cardinal Agneau cited an encyclical, "Pacem in Terris" ("Peace on Earth").*

Do not use parentheses, though, if the inserted clarification is in a direct quotation or in a verbatim text, transcript or excerpts. In that case, use BRACKETS.

Use parentheses in testimony when describing an action that is not part of the dialogue: *Q. Will you kindly point out the figures. (Handing the witness a list.)*

For special effect, a nickname may appear in parentheses within a full name: *Leslie (Lamb Chops) Arniotis.* But in general resist that device because of its melodramatic gangster-film overtones. *See* PERSONAL NAMES AND NICKNAMES.

In a terse list or table of proper names, locations may be clarified this way: *The Sarasota (Fla.) Herald-Tribune, The Spartanburg (S.C.) Herald-Journal and The Wilmington (N.C.) Morning Star.* But in ordinary copy, fluid phrasing is preferred: *The Wilmington Morning Star, in North Carolina.* Use commas instead of parentheses when the phrase being interrupted is not a proper name: *a Springfield, Mass., hospital.* Smoother: *a hospital in Springfield, Mass. Also see* COMMA and NEWSPAPER NAMES.

PUNCTUATION WITH PARENTHESES

A period (or question mark or exclamation point) may occur inside or outside a closing parenthesis, depending on the surrounding structure.

If the passage in parentheses falls entirely within another sentence, put the sentence-ending punctuation *outside* the parentheses: *She did not identify the college (it could have been Bowdoin).*

When parentheses surround an entire sentence or series of sentences, the sentence-ending punctuation goes *inside* the closing parenthesis: *She did not specify the college. (It was Claremont. Her audience knew that.)*

A comma, a colon or a semicolon never directly precedes an opening or closing parenthesis: *What the agency needs, the mayor said (as he had said before), is $14 million. She cried for help (with no one listening); it was too late. Here is what she shouted (according to witnesses): "I'm falling!"*

Either a dash or parentheses, but not both together, can signify an aside or an abrupt change in the direction of a sentence.

parenthetical attribution. When attribution is inserted in midsentence, it must be truly parenthetical—that is, set off by commas at both ends. Otherwise ambiguity or error results: *In Idaho the Forest Service announced that two hikers were missing.* (The announcing could have taken place anywhere, but *in Idaho* is meant to tell where the hikers are missing.) The phrase *the Forest Service announced* is known as a parenthesis, and it does not modify what follows or govern the tense of the verb later in the sentence. Surround it with punctuation: *In Idaho, the Forest Service announced, two hikers are missing.*

Another example: *While the building was being renovated, the contractor said that the document had been found in a closet.* It should read: *While the building was being renovated, the contractor said, the document was found in a closet.*

Overlooking a parenthesis may result in ambiguity: *In 1973 the witness testified he never saw the defendant.* Note the difference commas can make: *In 1973, the witness testified, he never saw the defendant.*

parenting. Dictionaries accept the term, but it is social service jargon. When possible, use *rearing children* or *parenthood* or *being a parent* instead.

parimutuels (n.), **parimutuel** (adj.).

parkway. Capitalize in names: *Northern State Parkway; Garden State Parkway; Taconic State Parkway.* But: *the parkway.*

parley is a stilted word rarely seen except in headlines. Use conversational alternatives like *talks, meeting* or *conference* instead.

Parliament. Capitalize when referring to a legislature so named or when substituting the term for an equivalent foreign proper name. Also: *member of Parliament. See* LEGISLATIVE BODIES.

parliamentarian. An expert on parliamentary procedure. Do not use to mean a member of a parliament.

parliamentary.

parole, probation. *Parole* is a release, on the condition of good behavior, before a prisoner's sentence is complete. It is granted by a parole board, which can revoke it. *Probation* is the suspension of the sentence of a person who has been convicted but not yet jailed. It is granted by a judge on the condition of good behavior. *Also see* AMNESTY, CLEMENCY, PARDON.

partially. To mean *in part*, use the shorter and simpler *partly*.

participles as nouns. Beware of a present participle (the *ing* form of a verb) when it directly follows a noun or a pronoun. Look twice at the meaning of the phrase, because the participle often plays the role of a noun in such a sentence. And when that happens, the previous word should be possessive (*his, her, their, Ms. Lamm's*). Some examples:

> *The teachers complained about the principal's missing the meeting.* (It was the *missing* they complained about, not the principal. Thus the possessive.)

> *The doctors advise against pregnant women's drinking.* (Their advice is against *drinking*, not against women: so it is not *against pregnant women drinking*.)

Sometimes a sentence works either way: *Terry watched the biplane landing* and *Terry watched the biplane's landing* mean roughly the same thing. And sometimes the change to a possessive is awkward, and the sentence is best rephrased slightly. Thus:

- To be avoided: *The police tried to prevent him jumping.*
- Corrected but stilted: *The police tried to prevent his jumping.*
- Corrected and tidier: *The police tried to prevent him from jumping.*

Participles that play the noun role are known as *gerunds*. When preceded by a noun that ought to be possessive but is not, a gerund is known as a *fused participle*.

To test whether a verb is behaving as a gerund, mentally substitute a noun for it: the principal's *absence*; pregnant women's *health habits*; prevent his *leap*. In each case, the substituted noun fits, meaning that the participle needs to follow a possessive.

particles. For the use of *de, du, di, da, le, la, van, von, ter*, etc., see PERSONAL NAMES AND NICKNAMES.

partner (n.). It is a suitable term for an unmarried companion of the same sex or the opposite one. But if the context allows misreading to mean a business partnership, use COMPANION instead. *Also see* LOVER.

partner (v.). Despite the contrived sound of many nouns forced into service as verbs, *partner* is an established ballet term: *He partnered her in the pas de deux.* And *they* *partnered in "Giselle."* For business and civic alliances, though, use phrases like *teamed up* or *formed a partnership.*

part time (n. and adv.), **part-time** (adj.).

partway.

party (political). Capitalize in names: *Republican Party; Democratic Party; Conservative Party; Liberal Party; Labor Party;* etc. But: *the party; the parties.* Ordinarily translate the names of foreign political parties. (For an exception, see QUEBECER, QUÉBÉCOIS.)

party (social event). A party may be *given, held, organized* or *sponsored.* But avoid the colloquial *thrown;* it is trite. Also resist *party* as a verb except in light or joking contexts (*they partied all night and ached all day*).

party labels, for members of Congress or state legislatures, are given this way: *Senator Lee A. Daan, Republican of New York; Representative Terry E. Bildots, Democrat of Utah; Assemblyman Hilary C. Agnello, Democrat of Buffalo.* Also: *a Utah Democrat.* If a legislator has been elected with the support of two parties: *State Senator Pat J. Miel, Conservative-Republican of Rochester.* For a district in the New York metropolitan area, specify the section or county: *Representative Lindsay R. Baranek, Democrat of Brooklyn* (or *Newark* or *the South Bronx,* etc.).

After a legislator has been mentioned by name, do not use *the Missouri Democrat* as a disconnected form of later reference; instead, relate the identity to the name explicitly (*Ms. Lamm, a Missouri Democrat, added …*). See INDIRECTION.

pass(-). Most but not all compounds formed with *pass* are one word: passbook, pass-fail, passkey, passport, pass-through, password.

passé.

passenger-mile.

passer(s)-by.

Passover.

pastor. This term designates the position of a Roman Catholic priest who leads a parish or of a Lutheran or Baptist minister who leads a congregation. In a first reference, it follows the name.

For a Catholic, it is used this way: *the Rev. Lynn A. Miel, pastor of SS. Peter and Paul Roman Catholic Church; Father Miel; the pastor* or *the priest.*

For a Lutheran, it is *the Rev. Morgan E. Karitsa, pastor of Immanuel Lutheran Church;* then ordinarily *Pastor Karitsa; the pastor;* or *the minister.* (Some Baptists and other Protestants also use that style.) If a Lutheran minister does not have a congregation, serving instead as a seminarian or a denominational executive, later references are to *Mr., Ms., Miss* or *Mrs.,* or to *Dr.,* for a minister with an earned doctorate.

For other churches, use *pastor* the way *minister* or *priest* is used: *the Rev. Hilary T. Dann, pastor of,* etc., or *He had been their pastor.* But the Episcopal Church uses RECTOR. *Also see* FATHER; MINISTER; REV.

Patchin Place (in Greenwich Village), not *Patchen.*

Patchogue (in Suffolk County, N.Y.).

pâté. Also: *pâté de foie gras.* But *pâte* (without the final accent) is the word for pastry or pasta: *pâte à choux; pâte brisée.*

patent. *See* COPYRIGHT, PATENT.

Paterson (N.J.), **Patterson** (N.Y.).

PATH for Port Authority Trans-Hudson, the railroad that connects New Jersey and Manhattan under the Hudson River.

patriarch. In Eastern Orthodox churches and the Ethiopian Orthodox Church, this title is given to some high-ranking bishops. Capitalize it only before a name. (Sometimes an Orthodox prelate is known by a first name only.) *Also see* EASTERN ORTHODOXY and METROPOLITAN.

patrolled, patrolling.

patrolman. For those law enforcement agencies that still use the title: *Patrolman Lee T. Lam; Patrolman Lam; the patrolman; the police officer.* Few agencies use the title *Patrolwoman.* But note that in many law enforcement agencies, the title is now *Patrol Officer.* In New York City, the rank is POLICE OFFICER. *Also see* NEW YORK POLICE DEPARTMENT.

pawn(-). Most but not all compounds formed with *pawn* are one word: pawnbroker, pawnshop, pawn ticket.

pay(-). Most but not all compounds formed with *pay* are one word: pay-as-you-go (n. and adj.), paycheck, payday, payload, paymaster, pay off (v.), payoff (n.), payout, pay phone, payroll.

PBS for the Public Broadcasting Service. It does not produce programs and is not a network. It is a nonprofit membership organization of public television stations, for which it distributes programming and provides other support. The members include WNET, Channel 13, in New York.

PC, for personal computer. The plural is *PC's. See* PLURALS.

P.D.T., P.S.T. for Pacific Daylight Time and Pacific Standard Time. *See* TIME.

peace(-). Most but not all compounds formed with *peace* are one word: peace conference, Peace Corps, peacekeeper, peacekeeping, peacelike, peacemaker, peacemaking, peacetime.

peasant carries differing overtones in various parts of the world. In Asia and parts of rural Europe, subsistence farmers and farm laborers apply the label to themselves matter-of-factly and sometimes with pride; Chinese speak of "rich peasants" and "poor peasants." In articles about industrialized societies, though, the word suggests primitiveness and sounds disparaging; phrases like *poor farmer* or *farm laborer* are preferable.

peccadillo(es).

pedal (what bicyclists and pianists do), **peddle** (what shopkeepers do).

peers. A peer is a member of one of the five degrees of British nobility: BARON; VISCOUNT; EARL; MARQUESS; DUKE. (A baronet or a knight, called SIR, is not a peer.) A peer's son or daughter bears a courtesy title but is not a peer. For example: *the Duke of Marlborough*, a peer; *the Marquess of Blandford*, his son; *the Earl of Sunderland*, his grandson.

To distinguish between peers of the same name, use the full title or territorial designation (capitalized as a full name): *Viscount Alexander of Hillsborough* and *Earl Alexander of Tunis*; *Viscount Alexander* and *Earl Alexander*. When the names are not juxtaposed, each may be called *Lord Alexander* in later references.

A special case: When a peer is well known in a profession, the title may be omitted from a first reference. The famous author, for example, was *Lord Snow* or *C. P. Snow*, but never *Lord C. P. Snow* or *Lord Charles Snow*. And never *Mr. Snow*.

A peer who renounces an inherited title (to serve in the House of Commons, for example) will be known by the family name: *Tony Benn* (formerly Viscount Stansgate); *Mr. Benn*.

Some Britons are designated life peers, with the title *baron* or *baroness*. A life peer sits in the House of Lords, but the title is not inheritable. An example was Baroness Spencer-Churchill, the widow of Sir Winston Churchill.

Pekingese (the dog).

Peking man (anthropological); not changed to *Beijing*.

PEN is an international association of editors and writers devoted to defending freedom of expression. The name is an acronym for *poets, playwrights, essayists, editors and novelists*. The PEN American Center is one of 130 national groups that compose International PEN.

penal code.

pence. *See* POUNDS AND PENCE.

pendant (n.), **pendent** (adj.).

Pennsylvania. Abbreviate as *Pa.* after the names of cities, towns and counties.

Pennsylvania Station (in New York and in Newark); *Penn Station; the station.*

pennywhistle.

Pentecostal churches are Protestant denominations. Many stress visible manifestations of the Holy Spirit, like speaking in tongues or healing. Note the spelling: not *Pentacostal*.

people, person. Use *people* as the plural of *person*. Allow *persons* in letters to the editor, in untranslated texts, in direct quotations and in a few established idioms like *displaced persons* and *missing persons bureau*.

people of color. Except in direct quotations, the expression is too self-conscious for the news columns. Substitute a term like *minorities* or, better, refer to specific ethnic groups—*black and Hispanic authors*, for example. *Also see* ETHNICITY.

people's democracy, people's republic. Because these expressions convey political judgments, use the shorter forms of country names instead: *China*, for example, rather than *People's Republic of China*. In lowercase contexts, avoid the phrases except in direct quotations or in citing countries' official characterizations of themselves.

PepsiCo Inc. (the multinational conglomerate).

percent, percentage. *Percent* is one word. The preceding number is always expressed in figures (except when it begins a sentence): *80 percent; 8 percent; one-half of 1 percent; four-fifths of 1 percent; 0.5 percent*. But: *five percentage points; 12 percentage points*. The symbol % may be used with a figure in headlines, tables and charts: *5% Raise; 93%*. Do not use the abbreviation *pct*.

Do not confuse *percent* and *percentage point*: If an interest rate rises to 11 percent from 10 percent, the increase is one *percentage point*, but 10 *percent*. Similarly, a decline in rates to 7.5 percent from 10 percent is a drop of two and a half *percentage points*, but 25 *percent*. Ordinarily spell out the number of *percentage points*, up to nine, except if it appears in a series with figures above nine.

No drop or decline can exceed 100 percent: once 100 percent is gone, nothing remains to fall.

Be wary of false precision in calculating percentages. Taking a percentage beyond the decimal point is misleading if one number in the calculation is an estimate or padded with many zeros. For example, when a company reports that its net income rose to $685 million from $545 million, describing the increase as 25.7 percent implies a precision that cannot be realized because both of the original numbers are approximations.

Note how the change in income is expressed in the previous sentence: Despite the apparent illogic, give the "to" figure before the "from" figure, to prevent hasty misreading of the difference as a range (that is, as *an increase somewhere between $545 million and $685 million*).

Successive percentage changes cannot simply be added together to determine an overall change. For example, a three-year labor contract that specifies annual pay increases of 3 percent, 3 percent and 4 percent will produce a cumulative increase (that is, a compounded one) greater than 10 percent. If the original base pay is $100 a week, the first increase will be $3, creating a base of $103. The second increase will be $3.09 (3 percent of $103), bringing the base to $106.09. The last increase will be $4.24 (4 percent of $106.09), bringing the base to $110.33 and the cumulative change to 10.3 percent.

perigee. The lowest altitude of an orbiting space vehicle or other object in relation to the Earth. *Perigee* also has the general meaning of the lowest or nearest point. Its opposite is *apogee*, the highest or farthest point.

period. The best thing about a period is that it ends a sentence. A period can often mean two readable sentences instead of a single cumbersome one, especially in a lead paragraph.

Uses of the period are shown in entries throughout this manual. See especially ABBREVIATIONS. For the placement of a period alongside other punctuation, see PARENTHESES and QUOTATION MARKS.

Do not use a period after a sum of money in dollars without cents ($50, not $50.), except at the end of a sentence, and do not use a period with parentheses in a sequence designation like *(1)* or *(a)*.

periodical names. Use them in roman type, without quotation marks. For consistency, capitalize the article in every magazine or journal name commonly written or spoken with an article: *The Atlantic Monthly, The Nation, The New Republic, The New Yorker, L'Express, Der Spiegel, The Journal of the American Medical Association* (but: *Fortune, National Review, Newsweek, New York, Time, Reader's Digest, Stern, Vanity Fair*). Also capitalize in later references: *The Journal.* But lowercase *the* when a periodical's name serves as a modifier: *the New Republic article; the Journal editorial; the New Yorker writer.* (In such a case, *the* actually attaches to the following noun — *writer*, for example.) Append the word *magazine*, lowercased, if it is needed for clarity or euphony: *Time magazine; New York magazine.* But: *Harper's Magazine.*

Use roman type and quotation marks for periodical article names, and capitalize the principal words: *"10 Days to a Healthier Diet."* Also see CAPITALIZATION and COLUMN NAMES.

periodontics (not *periodontia*), for the branch of dentistry that specializes in the bone and tissue around the teeth. And *periodontal treatment* for the work performed by periodontists.

permanent representative. That is the official phrase for a delegation chief at an international organization or conference, but it defies conversational usage because "permanent" representatives inevitably prove impermanent. Use DELEGATE and CHIEF DELEGATE instead (with the preposition *to*) for those attending temporary or periodic meetings. Use REPRESENTATIVE and CHIEF REPRESENTATIVE (with the preposition *at*) for those assigned to permanent bodies. Also use AMBASSADOR when a delegate or representative holds that personal rank.

permissible.

persecution (oppression), **prosecution** (legal effort toward a criminal conviction).

Persia is the former name of Iran. Use it only in historical or biblical references.

Persian lamb, Persian rug.

(-)person. Find conversational substitutes for self-conscious coinages like *assemblyperson, chairperson, councilperson, foreperson, newsperson* and *salesperson*. *See* ASSEMBLYMAN, ASSEMBLYWOMAN; BUSINESSMAN, BUSINESSWOMAN; CHAIRMAN, CHAIRWOMAN; CONGRESSMAN, CONGRESSWOMAN; COUNCILMAN, COUNCILWOMAN; MEN AND WOMEN.

personal names and nicknames. The normal first reference is a first name, middle initial and surname, with a title if warranted (but not *Ms., Miss, Mrs.* or *Mr.,* until later references). If a name serves unavoidably as a modifier, fluid style favors omitting the middle initial and, when possible without confusion, omitting *Jr., Sr.,* etc.: *the Leslie Anyell faction.* And in a breezy conversational passage, a reference to well-known personalities should not bog down in middle initials or *Jr.* or *Sr.*

Use a nickname as the principal reference if a well-known figure wishes to be identified that way (*Jimmy Durante; Bill Clinton*). In such a case, the nickname takes no quotation marks or parentheses. But if the nickname is provided only as a background or occasional reference, find a graceful way to introduce it: *Mr. Lamm was known to his classmates as Dutch.* Resist this form: *Leigh (Dutch) Lamm.*

An exception may be made for organized-crime figures, whose nicknames are customarily shown this way: *Leslie (Racko) Lamm.* Note that this style means the bearer is popularly called *Racko Lamm.* If the surname is not spoken as part of the nickname, do not use the parenthetical style, which would be misleading. In other words, if Toby Agneau is known simply as Toby the Nose, do not write *Toby (the Nose) Agneau.* And since the style clearly implies unsavory ties, use these nicknames only when such ties are well established.

Except for unusual effect, do not use famous initials (*J.F.K., L.B.J., F.D.R.,* etc.) as a substitute for a name, even in a headline. Do not use abbreviations for given names (*Wm.* or *Thos.,* for example), even if the bearers do.

The particles *de, du, di, da, le, la, van, von, ter,* etc., when used, are usually lowercased in foreign names (*Charles de Gaulle*) and capitalized in the names of United States citizens (*Martin Van Buren*). But follow individual preferences. (*See* DU PONT, DUPONT, DUPONT.) A lowercase particle remains lowercase when it appears in midsentence without a first name or title: *the de Gaulle legend.* Capitalize the particle when it begins a sentence or a headline.

Use *Jr.* and *Sr.* (without commas) for Junior and Senior in names: *Lee C. Berenich Jr.* (or *Sr.*). In bylines: **By LEE C. BERENICH Jr.** Also: *Lee C. Berenich*

IV or *Lee C. Berenich 4th*, depending on individual preference. If the preference is not known, use Roman numerals.

In a listing with surnames printed first, the *Jr.* (or *Sr.*, or *IV*, etc.) comes last: *BERENICH, Lee C. Jr.*, not *BERENICH Jr., Lee C.*

Titles and ranks used with personal names are listed separately. *Also see* COURTESY TITLES and INITIALS IN NAMES.

persona non grata. If the expression is used, a translation is unnecessary and probably intrusive. But it is usually possible to substitute the less stuffy *declared unwelcome.*

personnel.

person, people. *See* PEOPLE, PERSON.

persuade, convince. *Convince* should be followed by an *of* phrase or a *that* clause: *She convinced the teacher of her ability; She convinced her sister that it was too late.* But *convince* cannot be followed by a *to* phrase; in such a case, *persuade* is required: *He persuaded his sister to take the day off.* (*Persuade* is more versatile than *convince* and can be followed by any of the three constructions.)

Pesach (the Hebrew for Passover). Use the English, except for special effect.

petit larceny, petty larceny. Use *petit* in direct quotations only; otherwise, make it *petty larceny.*

Petty Officer. *Petty Officer First Class* (or *Second* or *Third Class*) *Merrill S. Yagyonak; Petty Officer Yagyonak; the petty officer.* Also (capitalized only before a name): *Chief Petty Officer; Master Chief Petty Officer; Senior Chief Petty Officer.*

Pfc. *Chris R. Agneau; Private Agneau; the private.*

P.G.A. for the Professional Golfers Association (which uses no apostrophe in its name).

pharmacopoeia.

phases (numbered). Capitalize the names of phases in a program or course of action and use Arabic numerals: *Phase 1; Phase 2.*

Ph.D. for Doctor of Philosophy. *Also see* DR.

phenomenon (sing.), **phenomena** (pl. only).

Philip Morris Companies.

Philippine (adj.), **Philippine Islands** (pl.), **the Philippines** (n. for the country, always singular). *Also see* FILIPINO(S) and FILIPINO NAMES.

Phillips Petroleum Company.

Phnom Penh (the capital of Cambodia).

phony (adj. and n.). It is colloquial. These synonyms, among many others, are standard English: *counterfeit, fake, false, forged, forgery, fraud* and *sham.*

Photostat is a trademark, but *photocopy* (n. and v.) is not.

physician assistant, not *physician's assistant,* for a person licensed to practice medicine under the supervision of a physician.

pick(-). Most but not all compounds formed with *pick* are one word: pick-me-up, pickpocket, pickup (n. and adj.), pick up (v.).

picket (n. and v.), never *picketer*.

picnic, picnicking.

pièce de résistance.

piecemeal.

pied(s)-à-terre.

Pietà, without quotation marks, for an image or sculpture of the grieving Mary with the body of Jesus. *Also see* SCULPTURES.

Pikes Peak.

Pilsener, for the beer or its glass.

PIN for personal identification number. Thus *PIN number* is redundant.

pinch-hitter, pinch-runner.

Ping-Pong is a trademark. The generic term is *table tennis*.

pinstripe(s).

pint. A pint equals 16 ounces, or half a quart.

pistols. *See* HANDGUNS.

Pittsburg (Kan.), **Pittsburgh** (Pa.).

pizazz.

Place. Spell out and capitalize in ordinary text when part of a name: *Agnello Place.* The abbreviation (*Agnello Pl.*) may be used in headlines, charts, tables and maps.

place-kick (n., v., adj.), **place-kicker.**

place names. *See* GEOGRAPHIC NAMES.

plainclothesman(men), in a reference to a man or men. But in general references, avoid implying maleness: use *plainclothes officer, officer in plain clothes* or *officer in civilian clothes.*

plaque.

plaster of paris.

Plattsburgh (in New York).

play(-). Most but not all compounds formed with *play* are one word: playback, playbill (and *Playbill,* magazine title), playbook, playboy, play-by-play (adj.), playgoer, playground, playhouse, playmaker, playmate, playoff (n.), playpen, playroom, playwright.

plays and revues. In news and review copy, use quotation marks for their titles and capitalize the principal words.

P.L.C. for public limited company. *See* COMPANY AND CORPORATION NAMES.

plea bargain (n.), **plea-bargain** (v.), **plea bargaining** (n.), **plea-bargaining** (adj.). The verb takes no direct object: *The lawyer advised her client to plea-bargain.* But never *The lawyer plea-bargained the case.*

plead. The past tense is *pleaded,* not *plead* or *pled.*

plebeian.

plethora means not just a lot but an excess, too much or too many.

Plexiglas is a trademark, but *plexiglass* is not.

P.L.O. for the Palestine Liberation Organization (not Palestinian).

plow (not *plough*).

ploy. Use this word with caution; it often suggests deviousness.

plurals. Form the plurals of most common nouns by adding *s: hammers; saws; pencils; pens.* Form the plural of a word ending in a soft *ch* by adding *es: churches.* But after a hard *ch,* add only *s: monarchs.*

For some words ending in *f,* simply add *s: briefs; goofs; reefs; roofs.* But other words ending in *f* have irregular plurals, with *ves: hooves; leaves; lives; shelves.* The dictionary is the best guide.

When a word ends in *is,* change the *is* to *es: oases; parentheses; theses;* and *basis* becomes *bases.*

Words ending in *o,* directly after a vowel, take the *s: folios; radios.* Words ending in *o,* directly after a consonant, usually take *es: echoes; embargoes; mosquitoes; noes; potatoes.* But *pianos* is an exception.

Form the plural of words ending in *s, sh, ss, x* or *z* by adding *es: gases; dishes; dresses; boxes; buzzes.*

Common nouns ending in *y* preceded by a vowel take only the *s: alloys; attorneys; days.* But if *y* is preceded by a consonant or by *qu,* change the *y* to *i* and add *es: armies; ladies; skies; soliloquies.*

The plurals of most proper names are formed by adding *s: Cadillacs; Harolds; Websters.* But if the name ends in *s* or *z,* form the plural by adding *es: Borderses; Charleses; Mercedeses; Rodriguezes.* In forming the plurals of proper names ending in *y,* ordinarily keep the *y: Harrys; Kennedys; Kansas Citys.* There are some exceptions, like *Alleghenies, Rockies* and *Sicilies.*

Some words are the same in the plural as in the singular: *chassis; corps; deer; sheep; swine; fowl;* etc. The collective plural of *fish* is the same as the singular, but *fishes* may be used in referring to different species: *Many fishes, including trout and bass, are native to North America.*

Nouns derived from foreign languages form plurals in different ways. Some use the original, foreign plurals: *alumnae; alumni; data; media; phenomena.* But form the plurals of others simply by adding *s: curriculums; formulas; memorandums; stadiums.* For a word not in this manual, consult the dictionary.

Use apostrophes in the plurals of abbreviations and in plurals formed from letters and figures: *M.D.'s; C.P.A.'s; TV's; VCR's; p's and q's; 747's; size 7's.* (Many publications omit such apostrophes, but they are needed to make The Times's all-cap headlines intelligible and are therefore used throughout the paper for consistency.) Unlike abbreviations, shortened word forms do not take the apostrophe in the plural: *co-ops*; *condos*. Also omit apostrophes in the plurals of "words as words" (that is, words that are themselves under discussion): *ifs, ands or buts*; *dos and don'ts*.

Form the plurals of most compound terms by adding *s* to the more important element: *adjutants general*; *commanders in chief*; *courts-martial*; *daughters-in-law*; *delegates at large*; *deputy attorneys general*; *lieutenant colonels*; *major generals*; *passers-by*; *postmasters general*; *rights of way*; *sergeants major*. When compounds are written as one word, the plurals are formed in the normal way: *breakthroughs*; *cupfuls*; *handfuls*; *tablespoonfuls*.

Some words that are plural in form have singular meanings: *measles*; *news*. They take singular verbs. But others—*scissors*, for example—take plural verbs. And still others (*ethics, politics*) can be singular or plural. Use a singular verb when these words refer to an art or science: *Ethics is a branch of philosophy, while politics is the study of government*. But use a plural verb in reference to practices: *Her ethics are beyond reproach, but his politics are contemptible*.

plus. Do not use *plus* as a substitute for *and*: *He was an experienced gandy dancer, plus a smooth talker*. Use *plus* as a preposition (*five plus one*), as a noun (*Her knowledge of hematite was a plus*) or as an adjective (*a plus factor*). Because *plus* is not a conjunction, use a singular verb in a sentence like *Five plus two is seven*.

p.m. (time). Lowercase: *10:30 p.m. yesterday*. In a headline, uppercase both letters. Avoid this redundancy: *10:30 p.m. last night*. Also: *10 p.m.*, never *10:00*. See TIME.

pocket(-). Most but not all compounds formed with *pocket* are two words: pocket book (a small book), pocketbook (a purse), pocketknife, pocket money, pocket-size, pocket veto.

podium, lectern. A speaker stands *on* a podium and *at* or *behind* a lectern.

poetry. In news articles, use quotation marks around a poem title, with the principal words capitalized. Omit quotation marks from the title when the poem or a section is reproduced bodily. Normally, verse incorporated in an article is set in full-size italics, without quotation marks, and indented on both sides. A very short verse passage may be treated as an ordinary quotation, with slashes (/) to denote line breaks. A free-standing poem is ordinarily in roman type or as specified by a page designer. The copyright owner should be consulted on the wording of a credit, either in agate type at the bottom or in an italic introduction.

Point. Spell out and capitalize when it is part of a name: *Montauk Point*. The abbreviation (*Montauk Pt.*) may be used in headlines, charts, maps and tables.

point. See PERIOD.

point-blank.

pointillism (art). Capitalize in reference to the art of Seurat and others who applied dots individually to cover a surface so that when viewed from a distance, the dots blend to appear as a representation of an object or scene. Lowercase in more general references to the technique itself: *Toby Kikondoo paints in a pointillistic style.* *See* ARTS TERMINOLOGY and POST-IMPRESSIONISM.

points of the compass. Spell out *north, northeast, north-northeast,* etc. Abbreviations (without periods) may be used in addresses (*I Street* NW), in yachting articles and in charts, tables and maps: *N; NE; NNE.* *See* LATITUDE AND LONGITUDE.

Polaroid is a trademark for instant cameras and film and for light-polarizing lenses. Also: *the Polaroid Corporation.*

pole vault (n.), **pole-vault** (v.), **pole-vaulter.**

police. Use the word the way *army* is used—as a collective term for an organization, not for individuals. Make it plural, and precede it with *the*: *The police say* (not *police say*) *crime rates are down* and *Seven police officers* (not *seven police*) *were injured.*

Police Commissioner *Lauren B. Miel; Commissioner Miel; the commissioner.*

Police Department; *the department.* In headlines, *Police Dept.* is acceptable. *Also see* NEW YORK POLICE DEPARTMENT.

Police Headquarters; *headquarters.*

policeman, policewoman. *Police officer* is preferred in most references.

Police Officer *Merrill E. Anyell; Officer Anyell; the police officer; the officer.* This is the rank in the NEW YORK POLICE DEPARTMENT. In references to the police elsewhere, use their official designations. *Also see* PATROLMAN.

police ranks are listed separately. Capitalize a title only when it precedes a name.

police stations. Lowercase, even when referring to a specific station: *47th Street station* or *station house.* Use PRECINCT to mean a command, not a building.

policyholder.

Polish National Catholic Church of America.

politic (v.), **politicked, politicking.**

political correctness (or *politically correct*) is a term of ironic disparagement, connoting excesses committed in the name of sensitivity. In impartial news copy, avoid applying the label, though it can be used in discussion of the term itself.

political parties. Capitalize *Party* in names: *Democratic Party; Republican Party; Communist Party; Labor Party;* etc. Also capitalize designations of members: *Democrats; Republicans; Communists; Laborites.*

politics can be singular or plural. Use a singular verb when the word refers to an art or science: *Politics is the study of government.* But use a plural verb in reference to practices: *His politics are contemptible.*

polls. *See* NEW YORK TIMES POLLS and OPINION POLLS.

pollster. Use this word rather than *poll taker.*

pompom, pom-pom, pompon. *Pompoms* are decorative fabric balls or clusters of streamers waved by cheerleaders. *Pom-poms* are rapid-firing automatic cannons. *Pompons* are flowers — chrysanthemums, for example — with small round heads.

pontiff, pontifical. Lowercase unless the word is part of a name or title. And most of the time, a repeated reference to *the pope* will be more conversational than variation for its own sake. *See* TITLES.

Pop Art. Capitalize in reference to the style and movement dating from the late 1950's and 1960's. In general, capitalize *Pop* in reference to fine art, and lowercase *pop* in references to more general aspects of mass culture. *See* ARTS TERMINOLOGY.

pope. Capitalize the title when it precedes a name: *Pope John Paul II*; *the pope*; *a pope*; *popes*. *See* TITLES.

Popsicle is a trademark.

pore (study intently), **pour** (spill from a container).

porn, porno. Both words are slang, however useful they might otherwise be in headlines. In a narrow headline, *sex* may sometimes serve. *Smut* is acceptable as a last resort, but is old-fashioned. Do not use *adult* in this context.

Port-au-Prince (the capital of Haiti).

Port Authority of New York and New Jersey; *the Port Authority*; *the authority*. Its operations include the three major airports in the New York metropolitan area; Teterboro Airport; port, marine and helicopter terminals; buses and bus terminals; bridges and tunnels; and the PATH train. It also owns the World Trade Center.

Port Chester (in New York).

Port Elizabeth (in New Jersey). Use ELIZABETH MARINE TERMINAL instead.

portland cement.

Port of Spain (the capital of Trinidad and Tobago).

Portuguese (sing. and pl.).

posh words. Unless the aim is to caricature a gushing style, avoid trite words like *chichi, glitz, glitzy, posh, swank, swanky* and *tony*. Substitute concrete detail.

possessives. Ordinarily form a possessive by adding *'s* to a singular noun (*the boy's boots*; *the girl's coat*), even if the noun already ends in an *s* (*The Times's article*). If the word ends in two sibilant sounds (*ch, j, s, sh* or *z*) separated only by a vowel sound, drop the *s* after the apostrophe (*Kansas' climate*; *the sizes' range*). But keep the *s* after the apostrophe when a name ends in a silent sibilant letter (*Arkansas's*; *Malraux's*).

Omit the *s* after the apostrophe in certain common expressions that consist of a possessive followed by a word starting with *s* (*for appearance' sake*; *for goodness' sake*) and when a singular idea is expressed in words that are technically plural (*General Motors' trucks*; *the United States' laws*). By custom, the possessive of an ancient classical name also omits the final *s* (*Achilles' heel*; *Euripides' dramas*).

For most plural words, the possessive form is *s'* (*girls' coats*; *boys' boots*). But for a plural word that does not end in *s* (*women*; *children*), the possessive is formed by adding *'s* (*women's*; *children's*). And when a plural is formed with *es* (on a proper name and a common noun equally), the apostrophe follows that ending: *the Joneses' house*; *the buses' routes*; *the Mercedeses' doors.*

Proper names that are possessive in form often omit the apostrophe (*Doctors Hospital*; *Teachers College*); the owners' preferences can often be checked on Web sites. But if the basic word is an irregular plural, keep the apostrophe when forming a possessive (*Children's Court*; *Ladies' Home Journal*).

A "double possessive" occurs when ownership is shown twice—first by *of* and then by *'s* or the equivalent: *a friend of hers*; *a student of Mr. Dann's.* While sometimes unnecessary, the construction is proper. Note, for example, the difference between *a picture of Matisse* and *a picture of Matisse's.*

Also see APOSTROPHE; PARTICIPLES AS NOUNS; PLURALS; POSSESSIVES WITH PROPER NOUNS.

possessives with proper nouns. When an expression (typically a proper name) is fully specific, modifying it with a possessive sounds redundant, because the purpose of a possessive is to answer the question "Which one?" Thus avoid *Paris's Eiffel Tower*, because there is only one Eiffel Tower; make it, if necessary, *the Eiffel Tower, in Paris.* Similarly: *Bill Gates of Microsoft*, not *Microsoft's Bill Gates.* Usage sanctions a few exceptions. In sportswriting, a team name may be used this way: *the Yankees' Mickey Mantle.* In the arts, an author or composer may be credited possessively: *Verdi's "Aida"*; *Hardy's "Jude the Obscure."* Finally, this rare situation is entirely logical: *Zubin Mehta's New York Philharmonic was different from Kurt Masur's.*

post(-). Most but not all compounds formed with *post* are one word: post-bellum (adj.), postclassic, post-Columbian, postcard, postdate, postdoctoral, postgraduate, posthaste, postindustrial, postman, postmark, postmaster, postmaster(s) general, POSTMODERN, post-mortem, postnasal, postnuptial, post office, postpaid, post road, postscript, post time, postwar (but *post-cold-war*, when the phrase precedes a noun).

Postal Service, capitalized, may be used in first references to the United States Postal Service. In later references, *the service* or *the post office.*

Post-Impressionism (art). Capitalize in reference to the diverse styles (also known as Neo-Impressionism) initiated by Seurat, van Gogh, Cézanne and others emerging from Impressionism. *See* ARTS TERMINOLOGY.

Post-it is a trademark for removable memo stickers and other office products.

postmaster. Whether a woman or a man, the Postal Service says, the person in charge of a post office is a *postmaster.*

postmodern (architecture). In the absence of agreement on what constitutes postmodernism, use the term lowercased, and with caution. In general, it describes two movements in late 20th-century architecture: buildings that make eclectic use of past historical styles and those inspired by contemporary French philosophy. *See* ARTS TERMINOLOGY.

potter's field.

poundcake.

pounds and pence. The symbol £ is usually used with figures: £15,000; £3 *million*; £74 *million*; £23.6 *billion*. In a simple modifier, do not use a hyphen: *a £2.5 million lawsuit*. But use hyphens in a modifier like this: *a £10-to-11-million increase* (though the repetition of *million* is clearer and preferred). As with dollars, indefinite and round sums may be spelled out conversationally, without the symbol: *half a million pounds* or, in cases of ambiguity, *pounds sterling*. Spell out *penny* and *pence* when they appear alone in sums: *a halfpenny* (never *a half-pence* or *one-half pence*); *1 penny* (never *1 pence*); *3 pence*; *98 pence*. Detailed sums of pounds and pence are set thus: £8.75; £9.40. The expressions *cent* and *cents* are not used in the British system. *Also see* DOLLARS AND CENTS; MONEY; NUMBERS, ROUND.

pour (spill from a container), **pore** (study intently).

power(-). Most but not all compounds formed with *power* are two words: powerboat, power brake, power broker, power dive (n.), power-dive (v.), powerhouse, power mower, power pack, power plant, power play, power station, power structure.

Prairie States.

prayer services. Uppercase the designations of formally named services: *Divine Eucharist*; *Divine Liturgy*; *Eucharist*; *Friday Prayer* (Islam); *high Mass*; *Holy Communion*; *Mass*; etc.

pre(-). Ordinarily close up compounds formed with *pre* unless the prefix is directly followed by an *e* or an uppercase letter: preadolescent, preamplifier, precancerous, pre-Columbian, preconcert, precondition, preconvention, predate, predecease, predestination, predetermined, pre-election, pre-eminent, pre-empt, pre-emptive, pre-emptory (not to be confused with peremptory, meaning arbitrary), pre-existing, prefabricated, preflight, pregame, preheat, prehistoric, prejudge, premarital, PRE-MED, prenatal, prenuptial, prepackage, prepaid, prerelease, pre-Roman, preschool, preshrink, pretax, pretest, pretrial, preview, prewar.

When *pre-* attaches to a compound, hyphens are usually necessary for clarity: *pre-cold-war alliances*; *pre-school-age children*.

precede is newsroom jargon for the introductory paragraph, usually in italics, explaining the source of an article, a text or a transcript. *See* BYLINES and TEXTS AND EXCERPTS.

precinct. Spell out numbers through *ninth*, and capitalize: *Fourth Precinct*. But: *40th Precinct*. Also: *the Central Park Precinct*. Use *precinct* to mean the command or its territory; use *police station* or *station house*, or just *station*, to mean the building. *Also see* NEW YORK POLICE DEPARTMENT.

precipitate (adj., sudden), **precipitous** (steep). A memory aid: The *a* in *precipitate* stands for *action*; the *s* in *precipitous* stands for *steep*.

predominant (adj.), **predominantly** (adv.), **predominate** (v., never adj.).

pre-existing is a long way of saying *existing*.

preferences, in the vocabulary of affirmative action programs, are advantages allotted to one class of candidate (minority applicants or women, for example), among those equally qualified, for benefits like employment, education or government contracts. As a way of rectifying discrimination, preferences are legal, but limited by law. Articles dealing with the debate over such programs should detail the provisions and avoid polemical terms like *reverse discrimination*. *Also see* AFFIRMATIVE ACTION; QUOTAS; SET-ASIDES.

prefixes and suffixes. See separate listings for various prefixes, suffixes and other combining words. Avoid prefix pileups like *nonbipartisan*.

pregnant. Use no apostrophe in an expression like *three months pregnant*; it is a short form of *pregnant for three months*, not a possessive.

prelude (music). Capitalize in a title: *Chopin's Prelude in C sharp minor*. Also: *the Prelude to the third act of "Die Meistersinger."*

pre-med for the course leading to medical school and for the student taking it.

premier. Use PRIME MINISTER instead for the first minister of a national government (except in countries, like Germany and Austria, that use *chancellor*). Use *premier*, though, for the heads of some nonsovereign governments, including those of the Canadian provinces, the Australian states, associated states in the Caribbean, etc.: *Premier Tracy B. Kikondoo; Premier Kikondoo; the premier*. And in a headline, *Premier* may substitute for *Prime Minister*.

premier, premiere. *Premier* means first in rank or importance, or earliest. *Premiere* means first performance or showing. As a verb (*the show premiered* or *the orchestra premiered the piece*), the word is jargon, to be avoided.

preposition pileups. Ordinarily use prepositions one at a time, each immediately before a noun or a pronoun. When prepositions are doubled, they create cumbersome phrases: *It was priced at below market value* and *It was owned by between 50 and 100 people*. In the first case, delete *at*. In the second (and in most cases involving *between* with numbers), use this construction instead: *by 50 to 100 people*.

prepositions, missing. Avoid constructions like these, which are dialect at best: *wait tables, baby-sit children* and *graduate college*. They should be *wait on tables, baby-sit for children* and *graduate from college*.

prerecorded. Normally *recorded* alone does the job.

Presbyterian Church (U.S.A.).

prescribe (order or command), **proscribe** (forbid).

presently. Use it to mean *soon*. The alternative meaning, *now*, is out of favor with many precise writers, and for that meaning, *now* is more direct in any case.

presidency, presidential. Always lowercase.

president. It is *President Lamm* (without a given name) in a first reference to the current president of the United States. In later references: *President Lamm*; *the president*; *Mr.* (or *Ms.* or *Miss* or *Mrs.*) *Lamm*. In first references to presidents of other countries, use given names and ordinarily middle initials. For other presidents — of companies, associations, clubs, universities and organizations — lowercase the title and separate it from the name (before or after) with a comma. *See* TITLES.

President-elect *Stacy E. Kikondoo*; *President-elect Kikondoo*; *the president-elect*. In cap-and-lowercase headlines, capitalize *-Elect*.

president pro tem (of the Senate). Do not use this title capitalized before a name. Make it *Tracy M. Baranek, the president pro tem*.

Presidents' Day is the popular name for *Washington's Birthday*, the federal holiday celebrated on the third Monday of February. The name reflects the decision by some states to use the holiday to honor both Washington and Lincoln. Other states (among them New York, New Jersey and Connecticut) have designated Feb. 12, *Lincoln's Birthday*, as a separate holiday.

press secretary. Always lowercase and always separated from the name by a comma: *Chris T. Kuzu, the White House press secretary*.

preventive (n. and adj.). Not *preventative* except in a quotation.

price fixing (n.), **price-fixing** (adj.).

PricewaterhouseCoopers L.L.P. is an accounting firm formed in 1998 by the merger of Price Waterhouse and Coopers & Lybrand.

priest. It is a position, not a title, so it is always lowercased and separated from the name by a comma. The term applies to Roman Catholic and Orthodox clergymen and to some men and women in the Episcopal clergy who choose it in place of *minister*.

prima facie (adj.), never hyphenated.

Primary Day.

primate. It is a religious position, not a title, therefore lowercased and always separated from the name by a comma. A *primate* is a bishop (possibly an archbishop, possibly a cardinal) who heads an original see of a rite or church — the first diocese organized in a nation.

Prime Minister *Robin E. Cordeiro*; *Prime Minister Cordeiro*; *the prime minister*. Use this title instead of *premier* for the first minister of a national government unless, as in Germany and Austria, the country uses CHANCELLOR. Also use *prime minis-ter* if the first minister is formally called something like *chairman of the Council of Ministers*. Accept PREMIER for such an official if it occurs in an untranslated direct quotation or a text. It may also substitute for *Prime Minister* in a headline. Other-wise *premier* is the title to use for the heads of some nonsovereign governments, including those of the Canadian provinces.

Prince *Ashley; the prince.* Also capitalize with a territorial phrase: *the Prince of Wales.*

Prince Edward Island (Canadian province). Do not abbreviate after the names of cities and towns, even in datelines.

Princes Bay (a section of Staten Island).

Princess *Ashley; the princess.* For a princess with a territorial title, or the wife of a prince with one, capitalize as a full name: *the Princess of Wales; the princess.* Never use a given name in those cases. But upon being widowed or divorced, she may be awarded the right to append it to her former title: *Diana, Princess of Wales; the princess;* and on occasion just *Diana.*

Princess Cruises.

Princeton Theological Seminary, in Princeton, N.J., is an institution of the Presby-terian Church and not part of Princeton University.

Princeton University. In many casual references, *Princeton* can stand alone, for the university or for its undergraduate college. Note that the Institute for Advanced Study and the Princeton Theological Seminary, although in Princeton, N.J., are not part of the university.

principal (head of school; chief or main thing; sum drawing interest). When it is used as a title, lowercase it and put it after the name: *Pat U. Agneau, principal of,* etc.; *the principal.*

principle (doctrine or precept).

prior to is stilted. Use *before.*

private (military). *See* PVT.

private first class. *See* PFC.

prix fixe. No accent, and never *fixed.* Also never hyphenated. The phrase means *set price,* or the meal that is sold complete for a set price.

prizefight.

pro(-). Latin terms are two words (even when they precede what they modify): pro bono, pro forma, pro rata, pro tem.

    Terms that mean "in favor" are hyphenated: pro-Arab, pro-French, pro-slavery. Other compounds using *pro* are solid: proactive, prorate, prorated.

    Except in quotations, do not use the polemical terms *pro-choice* and *pro-life.* *See* ABORTION.

probation. *See* PAROLE, PROBATION.

probe (n. and v.). Do not use as a synonym for *inquiry, investigation* or *investigate*; the effect is journalese.

Procter & Gamble Company. In later references, sparingly: *P.&G.*

products and purposes. When the name of a company or organization does not indicate what it makes or does, the article should. What does the National Manufacturing Company manufacture? What is the purpose of a group of analysts that puts out a report on oil prices? Who are its clients or sponsors? Does it have any regular connection with the oil industry? What do the Friends of Amity hope to accomplish? How and for whom?

Prof. *Ashley T. Berenich; Professor Berenich; the professor.* Also: *Ashley T. Berenich, professor of history* (or *chairwoman of the history department* or *distinguished professor of history*). And if the professor holds a special chair: *Ashley T. Berenich, the Terry B. Yagyonak professor of history.* Also see EMERITUS.

profanity. *See* OBSCENITY, VULGARITY, PROFANITY.

Professional Golfers Association (P.G.A.), without an apostrophe.

program is a specialized term in architecture. It refers to the set of functions, spaces and other requirements to be accommodated by an architect: *The program called for a 60-story residential tower surrounded by 10 stories of retail outlets and a small park.*

programmed, programmer, programming.

programs (computer). *See* SOFTWARE.

Prohibition. Capitalize in references to the period (1920-33) when alcoholic beverages were outlawed in the United States under the 18th Amendment and the Volstead Act. The 18th Amendment may be referred to informally as the *Prohibition amendment.*

prone means lying face down; **supine** means lying face up.

pronouns and antecedents. In precise writing, a pronoun (*he, she, it, they, them,* etc.) refers back to a specific noun, and only one (the antecedent). Thus avoid writing *The Berenich plan has enraged her critics* because *Berenich* is used here as a modifier, not a pure noun, and *her* is left without an antecedent. Make it *Ms. Berenich's plan has enraged her critics.* (As a last resort, a tightly confined headline may have to settle for *Berenich Plan Enrages Her Critics.*)

   Also rework a sentence like *Chris told Dana that he had a strange foible,* because *he* could refer to either Chris or Dana.

pronouns for countries and ships. Use *it* and *its* in references to countries, ships and boats. In such contexts, *she, her* and *hers* evoke dated stereotypes of the roles of women and men.

pronunciation keys. When an unfamiliar and hard-to-pronounce term appears prominently in the news, provide a pronunciation guide at a graceful point early in the article, with uppercasing to denote the stressed syllable: *Moesha (pronounced moe-EE-shah)*; *Skaneateles (pronounced skinny-AT-las)*.

(-)proof. Compounds with *proof* as a suffix are usually solid: blastproof, bulletproof, childproof, fireproof, foolproof, rustproof, waterproof, weatherproof. But hyphenate a coined or unusual term: recession-proof, Democrat-proof.

Also: *60-proof liquor*.

propeller.

prophecy (n.), **prophesy** (v.).

proscribe (forbid), **prescribe** (order or command).

prosecutor. When the title is official, as in New Jersey, capitalize it before a name: *Prosecutor Ashley N. Daan*; *Prosecutor Daan*. But: *the prosecutor*; *a prosecutor*; *prosecutors*.

Prospect Park Zoo. Use this informal name in virtually all references. Occasionally, in a detailed article about the zoo, it may be useful to mention the official name, *the Prospect Park Wildlife Center*. The zoo is operated on city property by the Wildlife Conservation Society.

protagonist, antagonist. A *protagonist* is the central character in a drama or novel. One drama or novel can have only one protagonist. An *antagonist* is an adversary, competitor or opponent. One person can have many antagonists.

protégé (masc.), **protégée** (fem.).

prototype means the *first of a kind*—the original model, not a copy.

proved, proven. In general, *proved* is preferred: *The prosecutor had proved the defendant's guilt*. But as an adjective before a noun, *proven* is better: *a proven remedy*; *proven oil reserves*.

provided. Use *provided*, not *providing*, in the sense of *if*: *He will make the trip, provided he gets a week off*.

proviso(s).

provost marshal(s).

P.S. for Public School in most later references: *P.S. 105*. In first references (except anecdotal or colloquial ones), spell out *Public School 105* (without *No.* before the numeral).

p's and q's. Use the apostrophe in this phrase and in the plurals of other letters and numerals (*size 7's*; *B-52's*). For the rationale, see PLURALS.

P.S.A.T. is no longer an abbreviation for preliminary college entrance tests. *See* COLLEGE BOARD.

P.S.C. for the Public Service Commission.

pseudo(-). Dictionaries tend to solidify almost all compounds formed with *pseudo*. But to avoid awkwardness use a hyphen between vowels: pseudoclassic; pseudo-intellectual; pseudo-official; pseudoscience; pseudosophisticated.

psych, psyched. The verbs are slang and best confined to quotations.

PTA. The National Congress of Parents and Teachers is informally called *the National PTA* (no periods). There is no *National Parent-Teachers Association*.

PT boat for motor torpedo boat.

Public Broadcasting Service. *See* PBS.

Public School. In first references (except anecdotal or colloquial ones), use *Public School 105* (without *No.* before the numeral). In most later references: *P.S. 105*.

Puerto Rico. Use *P.R.* after the names of cities and towns.

Puerto Rico, Puerto Rican. Puerto Rico is a commonwealth of the United States; do not describe it as a territory, possession or colony. Puerto Ricans are not immigrants or foreign-born. *Puerto Rican* describes ethnic or cultural heritage, not nationality; the nationality of Puerto Ricans is American. Puerto Ricans are United States citizens with a special status: they do not pay federal taxes or vote in presidential elections, but they send one nonvoting representative to Congress. *Also see* ETHNICITY.

Pulitzer Prize(s). Capitalize the two-word expression but not the names of categories: *Pulitzer Prize for international reporting*; *Pulitzer Prize for biography*; etc. Entries are submitted by news organizations or members of the public, and finalists are chosen by panels of *nominating judges*. The winners are selected by *the Pulitzer Prize Board* (*the board*). Articles dealing centrally with the prizes should mention that they are administered by Columbia University. Detailed rules and lists of winners are available on the World Wide Web:

http://www.pulitzer.org

punctuation is discussed in these separate entries: BRACKETS; COLON; COMMA; DASH; ELLIPSIS; EXCLAMATION POINT; HYPHEN; PARENTHESES; PERIOD; QUESTION MARK; QUOTATION MARKS; SEMICOLON.

puns have a place in the newspaper, but as a trace element rather than a staple. A pun should be a surprise encounter, evoking a sly smile rather than a groan and flattering the intelligence of a reader who gets the joke. Plays on personal names never qualify: no one will be flattered to read, say, that a pitcher named Butcher *carved up* the opposing team. The successful pun pivots on a word that fits effortlessly into two contexts, as in this example from an opinion piece in the arts pages: *Elected Bodies With Hardly a Cultured Bone*. The more obvious kind of wordplay (*Rubber Industry Bounces Back*) should be tested on a trusted colleague the way mine shaft air is tested on a canary. When no song ensues, start rewriting.

Punxsutawney (Pa.). It is so spelled. And *groundhog* is so spelled. And *overexposed publicity stunt* is so spelled.

Purim, the Jewish feast celebrating deliverance from a massacre planned by Haman (in the biblical Book of Esther), falls in late winter or early spring.

purport means seem (often questionably) or intend: *The letter purports to be signed by Washington. She purports to be leaving for China.* But never *the purported letter* or *the purported mobster*; this verb cannot be used in the passive voice. Grammatically, *purport* behaves in sentences the way *seem* does: if one word will not fit in a construction, neither will the other.

push(-). Most but not all compounds formed with *push* are one word: push button (n.), push-button (adj.), pushcart, pushover, pushpin, push-up (n.), push up (v.).

putout (n.).

putsch. Lowercase except in the name of a specific uprising that has become known in history: *the Beer Hall Putsch* (Hitler's, in 1923).

Pvt. *Alex D. Cordero; Private Cordero; the private.*

PX for post exchange.

Q

Q. and A. *See* TESTIMONY.

Qantas Airways.

QE2 may be used in later references to the ocean liner Queen Elizabeth 2. The queen on the throne is *Elizabeth II*.

Q-Tips is a trademark for cotton swabs.

Quai d'Orsay. The riverfront street on the Left Bank of the Seine and, by extension, the French Foreign Ministry headquarters there.

Quakers. This informal term is fully acceptable for members of the Religious Society of Friends. In the Eastern United States, most Quakers belong to *monthly meetings*. These are the equivalent of local congregations; they hold monthly business meetings in addition to Sunday worship services. Members of monthly meetings in a local area are organized into *quarterly meetings*; there are also *yearly meetings*, roughly comparable to other churches' dioceses. In a reference to a specific body, capitalize *Monthly Meeting, Quarterly Meeting, Yearly Meeting* (example: *the Philadelphia Yearly Meeting*).

In the East, most Quakers attend "unprogrammed" services, sitting in silence until a worshiper is moved to speak. In the Midwest and elsewhere, most Quakers belong to churches rather than monthly meetings and hold "programmed" services, with clergy members, music and other elements of traditional Protestant worship. The *Friends General Conference* and the *Friends United Meeting* are respectively the principal national organizations of unprogrammed and programmed Quakers.

quart. A quart equals 32 ounces or two pints or a quarter of a gallon. It is slightly less than a liter.

quarter(-). Most but not all compounds formed with *quarter* are one word: quarterback, quarterdeck, quarterfinal, quarterfinalist, quarter horse, quarter-hour (n. and adj.), quarterly, quartermaster, quarter note, quarterstretch.

quartet. Capitalize in the title of a musical work: *Brahms's String Quartet No. 3 in B flat (Op. 67); Beethoven's "Ghost" Quartet*. Capitalize in the name of an ensemble: *the Budapest String Quartet*. But: *a new quartet*. See MUSIC.

Do not use *quartet* in copy or headlines as a nonmusical synonym for *four* (*Quartet of New Plays Opens on Broadway*).

quarto(s).

quasi(-). *Quasi* is a separate word when used with a noun: *quasi comfort*; *quasi contract*; *quasi scholar*. But hyphenate when using it with an adjective: *quasi-judicial*; *quasi-stellar*.

Quebec (Canadian province). Do not abbreviate after the names of cities and towns, even in datelines.

Quebecer(s), Québécois. In general, use *Quebecer(s)* in news articles, but *Québécois* (sing. and pl.) may be used in references to the French Canadian culture of Quebec: *a Québécois novelist* or *"Above all," the separatist leader said, "I am proud to be a Québécois."* Also: *Parti Québécois*, an exception to the general practice of translating the names of political parties.

Queen *Elizabeth* or *Queen Elizabeth II*. Also, *the queen* and sometimes *Elizabeth*. Capitalize *Her Majesty*, but use it only in direct quotations or for special effect.

Queen Elizabeth 2 for the ocean liner. *QE2* (without spaces or periods) may be used in later references and in headlines.

queen mother. On first reference, capitalize as a full name: *Queen Elizabeth the Queen Mother* (her official designation, without a comma). In later references: *the queen mother* or *the queen*.

Queensboro Bridge. But: *Triborough Bridge*.

Queensborough Community College (part of the City University of New York).

Queens Borough Public Library. It is independent of the New York Public Library.

Queens Botanical Garden (not *Gardens*).

Queens College is part of the City University of New York. But *Queen's College* is part of Oxford University and *Queens' College* is part of Cambridge University.

Queens-Midtown Tunnel.

Queens Zoo. Use the informal name in virtually all references. Occasionally, in a detailed article, it may be useful to mention the official name, *the Queens Wildlife Center*. The zoo is operated on city property by the Wildlife Conservation Society.

queer, in the sense of homosexual, should be treated as an offensive slur, but with a limited exception. Some gay men and lesbians have rehabilitated the term as an ironic badge of pride. In that sense, it may be used when the viewpoint is unmistakable. The term is acceptable in references to the emerging academic field of *queer studies*.

questionnaire.

question mark. For the placement of a question mark alongside other punctuation, *see* PARENTHESES and QUOTATION MARKS.

A question mark denotes a direct query: *What problems face the country?* Indirect questions and requests cast in the form of questions do not require the mark: *They asked if he could attend. Will you please register at the desk. May I take your beret.*

Do not use the question mark as headline shorthand for speculation: *Court Seat Next for Karitsa?* Readers rely on the news columns to answer or discuss questions rather than dangle them.

queue. In the sense of waiting in line, the word, mainly British, should usually be replaced by an American synonym.

quick(-). Some compounds formed with *quick* are one word and some are hyphenated: quick-fire (adj.), quick-freeze, quicklime, quicksand, quicksilver, quickstep, quick-tempered, quick-witted.

quincentenary, noun or adjective, refers to a 500th anniversary. If an alternative is required, use *quincentennial.* Or say *500th anniversary.*

Quinnipiac University (in Hamden, Conn.) was formerly Quinnipiac College.

quintet (music). *See* QUARTET and TRIO.

quip. As a verb of attribution, *quip* is usually a small slight to the reader's intelligence. If a quoted remark is truly funny, the reader will notice. If the remark is less than amusing, the label makes it worse.

quotas, as a technique in government-backed programs of affirmative action, were outlawed by the Supreme Court in 1978. Articles about a debate over any such program to rectify discrimination should specify the provisions explicitly; if the argument includes an assertion that it includes quotas (numerical minimums, maximums or percentages), the contention must be attributed. *Also see* AFFIRMATIVE ACTION; PREFERENCES; SET-ASIDES.

quotation marks. Use double marks in news copy for direct quotation of speech or writing. A quotation within a quotation takes single marks: *"I do not know the meaning of 'collegial,' "* he said. *"Please tell me."* If the inner quotation enclosed yet another quotation, that third level would require another set of double marks. But a newspaper, edited for rapid comprehension, should rarely exceed two levels of nested quotations. When a single and a double quotation mark fall side by side, separate them with a thin space, to prevent a line break from occurring between them.

Picture captions and news summary entries use the same marks as news copy. So do the large initial letters that begin articles in many feature sections.

In a headline, a bank, a subheading, a chart heading, a caption overline or a "blurb" floating in a news article, use the single mark: *Governor Regrets 'Partisan Squabbling.'*

If an expression in a foreign language carries quotation marks, so should any parenthetical translation: *the papal blessing "Urbi et Orbi" ("To the City and to the World").*

When a direct quotation is longer than one paragraph, begin each paragraph with quotation marks, but use closing marks after the last paragraph only. In such a case, place attribution ahead of the entire quotation or within the first paragraph only. *See* QUOTATIONS.

Do not use quotation marks to enclose dialogue labeled with *Q.* and *A.* or passages in which each paragraph begins with the speaker's name or a label like *The Judge* and *The Witness*. Verbatim TEXTS AND EXCERPTS (including transcripts) and TESTIMONY do not take quotation marks, except for any direct quotations within the textual material.

In general, do not use quotation marks around slang or jargon words; the marks convey condescension. If the terms are used, the context should be justification enough. But use the marks with words or phrases that are used in an ironic or opposite sense: *That sad day was the only "happy" one he could recall.*

PUNCTUATION WITH QUOTATION MARKS
Periods and commas, in American usage, always go inside the closing quotation marks, regardless of grammatical logic. If inner and outer quotations are closing side by side, the period or comma precedes all the marks: *"While you're there," he said, "buy me a copy of 'Treasure Island.' "*

Colons and semicolons go outside all closing quotation marks, whether single or double: *He defined "zymurgy": the branch of chemistry that deals with fermentation.*

Question marks and exclamation points may come before or after quotation marks, depending on whether the symbol applies to the entire sentence or just to the quoted material: *The crowd shouted, "Long live the king!" Just imagine: he was afraid of "elephants without trunks"! She shouted, "What are we waiting for?" Have you read "The Color Purple"? "Did I say, 'I don't agree with you'?" "She asked, 'Do you agree with me?' "*

Also see references to quotation marks in these separate entries: ANTHEMS; DICTIONARIES; MAGAZINES; MUSIC; OPERA; PAINTINGS; PLAYS AND REVUES; POETRY.

quotations. Readers have a right to assume that *every word* between quotation marks is what the speaker or writer said. The Times does not "clean up" quotations. If a subject's grammar or taste is unsuitable, quotation marks should be removed and the awkward passage paraphrased. Unless the writer has detailed notes or a recording, it is usually wise to paraphrase long comments, since they may turn up worded differently on television or in other publications. "Approximate" quotations can undermine readers' trust in The Times.

The writer should, of course, omit extraneous syllables like "um" and may judiciously delete false starts. If any further omission is necessary, close the quotation, insert new attribution and begin another quotation. (The Times does adjust spelling, punctuation, capitalization and abbreviations within a quotation for consistent style.) In every case, writer and editor must both be satisfied that the intent of the speaker has been preserved. Except in verbatim TEXTS AND EXCERPTS, do not add material in brackets or use ellipses (. . .) to clarify or abridge the quoted material; those devices divert attention to the editing process. *See* BRACKETS and ELLIPSIS.

When two people are quoted in a row, the second quotation should begin a new paragraph, preceded by the identification of the speaker, to make it immediately clear that the voice has changed. If a quotation begins with a sentence fragment, do not go on to quote one or more full sentences. Instead, close the quotation at the end of the fragment and introduce the full sentences as a separate, further quotation, preferably as a new paragraph: *The president said the ceremony represented "the beginning of the difficult task of administering clemency."*

"Instead of signing these decisions in a routine way," he continued, "I want to underline my commitment to an evenhanded policy of clemency."

If a quotation consists of several sentences, the attribution should either precede the quotation or follow the first sentence; if the first sentence is long, the attribution may be inserted between phrases (at a natural breathing point). In other words, a quotation should not go beyond a phrase or a brief sentence before the reader learns who is speaking.

A long quotation should not hang from a stubby or abrupt introduction, like *He said*, at the beginning of the paragraph. Instead, the attribution should be expanded and run into the preceding paragraph or should be moved down to follow the first phrase or sentence of the quotation.

When attribution introduces a quoted sentence fragment or a single quoted sentence, use a comma before the quotation marks; if the quotation is longer than one sentence, introduce it with a colon.

An abrupt interruption in dialogue or Q. and A. should be marked by a two-em dash (twice the length of a normal dash):

"Your Honor," she said, *"please let me finish my* —— *"*

"Overruled!" the judge shot back.

A quotation that trails off inaudibly or indecisively should end with a period and then an ellipsis: *"I wonder,"* the philosopher mused. *"What if, right at this moment, on another planet. . . ."*

Also see ATTRIBUTION; DIALECT; PARENTHETICAL ATTRIBUTION; QUOTATION MARKS.

quote. While standard as a verb, it is colloquial as a noun. Ordinarily use *quotation* as the noun.

R

Rabbi *Merrill J. Baranek; Rabbi Baranek; the rabbi.* (Do not use *Mr., Ms., Mrs.* or *Miss.*) The title may be moved after a name to replace the ponderous *spiritual leader*: *Merrill J. Baranek, rabbi of Congregation Beth Shalom.* Or: *Rabbi Merrill J. Baranek of Congregation Beth Shalom.* The Yiddish equivalent, *rebbe,* may be used for special effect in an article about a Yiddish-speaking sect or community (for example, *the Lubavitcher rebbe*). *Also see* CHIEF RABBI.

Rabbinical Assembly. A Conservative group.

Rabbinical Council of America. An Orthodox group.

race should be cited only when it is pertinent and its pertinence is clear to the reader. The race of a victim of a hate crime or the subject of a police search is clearly germane, an essential part of the person's description. But the race of a person convicted of a crime is not pertinent unless the case has racial overtones; if it does, the overtones should be explained. *Also see* AFRICAN-AMERICAN, BLACK; (-)AMERICAN; AMERICAN INDIAN(S); ASIAN-AMERICAN; HISPANIC.

race(-). Compounds formed with *race* are one word: racecourse, racegoer, racehorse, racetrack, raceway. But it is *Race Course* in some proper names.

racial slurs. *See* SLURS.

rack, wrack. *Rack* means stretch, strain or torture. *Wrack,* which is archaic, means wreck, ruin or destroy; substitute a modern synonym. Something that strains the nerves is *nerve-racking.*

racket (not *racquet*) for the equipment in tennis, badminton and similar games. But the game is *racquetball.*

radio(-). Most but not all compounds formed with *radio* are one word: radioactive, radioactivity, radio astronomy, radiobiology, radio control, radiogram, radioisotope, radioman, radiophone, radiotelephone, radio telescope, radiotherapy.

radio stations. The style is *WQXR* or, if the context requires it, *radio station WNYC* or *WQXR-FM.* When citing a program that readers may wish to hear, give the frequency: *WNYC-AM (820). Also see* CHANNELS.

R.A.F. for the Royal Air Force.

railroads. Principal railroads in the United States and Canada are listed separately.

rain(-). Some compounds formed with *rain* are one word, some are two and a few are hyphenated: rainbow, rain check, raincoat, raindrop, rainfall, rain forest, rain gauge, rainmaker, rainproof, rain-soaked, rainstorm, rainwater, rainwear.

raise. Use this word, not *rise*, for an increase in pay: *He received a $50 raise.* But *$50 pay raise* is redundant.

raison d'être.

RAM for random access memory.

Ramadan, the ninth month of the Islamic calendar, a period of daytime fasting.

Ramapo College (in Mahwah, N.J.).

Randalls Island (at the confluence of the East and Harlem Rivers).

RAND Corporation.

rank and file. But hyphenate the modifier: *rank-and-file* opinion.

rap. Rhythmic verse spoken over music. Performers are *rappers*, not *rap singers. Also see* HIP-HOP.

rape. Though some states, notably New Jersey and Connecticut, have adopted *sexual assault* as the common term for felony sexual offenses, use *rape* to mean forced intercourse, or intercourse with a child below the age of consent. Avoid *criminal attack, criminal assault* and other euphemisms. Do not write that a rape victim was "uninjured" or "otherwise uninjured"; those phrases slight the gravity of the crime.

　　Most often The Times shields the identity of a sex crime complainant, but rare circumstances may warrant an exception. *Every* decision to divulge such an identity or to withhold it should be discussed with a masthead editor or with the head of the news desk.

rapid-fire (adj.).

rapprochement. A diplomatic term for warming of relations, it often seems overelegant. A more conversational word is *reconciliation. Also see* DÉTENTE.

(-)rate. Most but not all compounds formed with *rate* are two words: birthrate, cut-rate (adj.), death rate, first-rate (adj.), insurance rate, interest rate, tax rate.

ratios. Spell out numbers used in a ratio if both are nine or below: *The ratio of men to women was three to one.* But: *In New York City, 29 of every 1,000 apartments are covered by rent regulations.*

re(-). Ordinarily close up compounds formed with *re* unless the prefix is directly followed by an *e* or an uppercase letter: realign, reappear, reapportion, reappraise, rearm, reborn, rebroadcast, re-Christianize, reconstruct, redeploy, redistrict, re-educate, re-elect, re-election, re-enter, re-entry, refinance, refit, regroup, reimburse, reinforce, remake, reopen, reorder, rerun, resale, reunion, reusable, reuse (n. and v.).

　　But when two *re* words with differing meanings are spelled identically, hyphenate the less familiar one to avoid ambiguity. Thus: *recover* (retrieve or get well), but *re-cover* (cover again); *reform* (change for the better), but *re-form* (form again). Similarly, *recreation/re-creation* (but always *recreate*, not *re-create*), *redress/re-dress*, *relay/re-lay*, *release/re-lease*, *repose/re-pose*, *repress/re-press*, *resent/re-sent*, *reserve/re-serve*, *resign/re-sign*, *resort/re-sort*, *resound/re-sound*, *restore/re-store* and *restrain/re-strain*. Often, rephrasing is a better solution than a cumbersome word like *re-dress* or *re-sound*.

Reader's Digest (without *the*). It is published by the Reader's Digest Association.

ready. Though a recognized verb, the word can be stilted and artificial in a headline (*Congress Readies Energy Plan*). More natural synonyms include *shape* and *prepare*.

ready(-). Most but not all compounds formed with *ready* are hyphenated: ready-made (n. and adj.), ready-mix (adj.), ready room, ready-to-wear (n. and adj.).

real time (n.), **real-time** (adj.).

Realtor, a trademark, designates an affiliate of the National Association of Realtors. The preferred generic terms are *real estate agent* and *real estate broker*.

Rear Adm. *Dale N. Agnello; Admiral Agnello; the admiral.*

rear guard (n.), **rear-guard** (adj.).

reason (n). Both *because* and *why* are built into the meaning of *reason*. So avoid *the reason is because* and *the reason why*. Write *The reason is that the mayor got more votes* and *She found out the reason the mayor won*. Usually a phrase like *reason why the decision was made* can be shortened to *reason for the decision*.

rebut, refute. *Rebut*, a neutral word, means reply and take issue. *Refute* goes further and often beyond what a writer intends: it means disprove, and successfully. Unless that is the intention, use *rebut, dispute, deny* or *reject*.

recherché (adj.).

reconnaissance.

Reconstruction. Capitalize in references to the reorganization of the Southern states of the United States after the Civil War. The period is usually given as 1867-77.

Reconstructionist Judaism. This young movement in Judaism stresses intellectual searching to adjust to modern times rather than close interpretations of traditional observances and teachings. *Also see* CONSERVATIVE JUDAISM; ORTHODOX JUDAISM; REFORM, REFORMED.

record(-). Most but not all compounds formed with *record* are two words: record-breaking, record changer, record-holder (a person), record player.

record, new. This phrase is redundant: *He set a new record in the high jump.* But this is acceptable: *The new record exceeded the old by two inches.*

Some careful writers also avoid *all-time record*, believing that "all time" includes the unknowable future. Whether or not that is true, the phrase is needlessly breathless.

rector is the position of an Episcopal clergy member in charge of a parish: *the Rev. Chris Lamb, rector of*, etc. *Also see* MINISTER and PASTOR.

Red. Except for special effect, do not use *Red* as a noun or adjective to mean Communist; the tone is too polemical for the news columns.

Red China. The phrase, now rarely seen, is too polemical for news copy. *See* CHINA.

redneck, for an ignorant rustic, is slang and pejorative.

refer. *See* ALLUDE, REFER.

reference is business jargon when used as a verb: *She referenced the new transmission standards*. More natural substitutes include *cite, mention* and *refer to*. But *cross-reference* (n. and v.) is conversational English.

reference works. Capitalize the principal words in titles of almanacs, dictionaries, encyclopedias and similar reference works, without quotation marks.

referendums (not *referenda*).

reform suggests not just change but improvement. *Change* and *overhaul* can be more neutral synonyms in the news columns.

Reform, Reformed (religion). *Reform* (never *Reformed*) denotes the branch of Judaism that emphasizes ethics and observes modernized rituals. Its organizations include *the New York Federation of Reform Synagogues*. Many of its congregations refer to their houses of worship as *temples*, though *synagogue* is also correct; preferences should be verified.

Reformed denotes Protestant churches of the Dutch and Calvinist traditions, like the Reformed Church in America and the Presbyterian Church (U.S.A.).

Reformed Church in America, a Protestant body.

refute, rebut. The words are not interchangeable. *See* REBUT, REFUTE.

Regents, Board of. It is *the Regents* or *the board* in later references to any state board so named, including New York's, and in all references to the Regents examinations.

regime, as an alternative to *government* or *leadership*, can imply at least faint disapproval. Use it with caution.

regiment (military). Do not abbreviate: *Fifth Regiment; 13th Regiment; the regiment*. In the United States Army, most regiments have been eliminated, though individual battalions (formerly parts of those regiments) bear their old numbers for the sake of tradition. In such cases, the word *regiment* is omitted: *First Battalion, 21st Infantry*. National Guard armories often bear traditional regimental names: *Seventh Regiment Armory; 69th Regiment Armory*.

regional names. Uppercase the names of recognized regions: *East Texas; North Jersey; West Bank; New England; Middle Atlantic States; Gulf Coast States; Mountain States; Pacific States;* etc.

Regular Army (of the United States).

relative (not *relation*), for a family member.

relativity theories. Do not capitalize the designation of either Einstein theory—the *special theory of relativity* or *the general theory of relativity*.

religion. Churches, religions and clerical titles are listed separately. The religion of a person in the news should be mentioned only when it is pertinent and its pertinence is clear to the reader.

religious (n.). As a term for a member or members of a religious order, it has a specialized flavor and is best confined to religion columns and similar copy.

religious slurs. *See* SLURS.

relinquish. While the word is valid, it is also stodgy. Relaxed writing uses *give up* or *yield* instead.

Renaissance. Capitalize when referring to the movement and the period that followed the medieval period. Lowercase in its general meaning: *a renaissance of poetry*.

Reorganized Church of Jesus Christ of Latter Day Saints is the largest of several groups that split from the Mormons. Do not use *Mormon* in reference to this church or its members. In this name *Latter Day* is two words, without a hyphen.

repellent (n. and adj.), not *repellant*.

repertory. Not *repertoire*, except for special effect.

replica. Strictly speaking, a *replica* is an exact copy or reproduction by the maker of the original, usually a copy of a work of art. Less strictly speaking, *replica* has also come to mean any close reproduction, not necessarily by the original maker. But *a spun sugar replica of Notre-Dame* is absurd. Use *model, copy, imitation* or another more general word. *Also see* FAKE, FORGERY, COPY.

reports. An article about the significant findings of a commission or study group should tell readers how to get copies of the report. Give the title of the document, the name and address of the issuing agency (including its Internet address), the number of pages and the price.

Representative *Lauren J. Miel, Democrat of Utah*; *the representative* (for members of Congress and state legislatures). Do not abbreviate, except in headlines, charts or tables: *Rep. Miel.* When necessary for clarity, use *State Representative* or *United States Representative* in a first reference. *Also see* DISTRICT.

representative (diplomatic). Lowercase and use the preposition *at*: *Dana E. Cordero, United States representative at the World Health Organization; Dr. Cordero; the representative.* Confine *representative* and *chief representative* to assignments to permanent bodies, like the United Nations. (But do not ordinarily use *permanent representative*, a bit of diplomatic jargon that overstates the tenure.) For temporary or periodic meetings, use CHIEF DELEGATE, DELEGATE and, when appropriate, AMBASSADOR.

representative at large. No hyphens. Lowercase except when used as a title before a name: *Representative at Large Lynn U. Bildots*; *the representative at large.*

Representative-elect *Hilary H. Arniotis*; *Representative-elect Arniotis*; *the representative-elect.* In cap-and-lowercase headlines: *Rep.-Elect Arniotis.*

Republic. Capitalize *Republic* when it is used alone to mean the United States.

Republican national chairman (or chairwoman), or state or county chairman or chairwoman. *Merrill Y. Barany, Republican national* (or *state* or *county*) *chairman*; *the national* (or *state* or *county*) *chairwoman.*

Republican National Committee (or *State* or *County Committee*); *the national* (or *state* or *county*) *committee*; *the committee.*

Republican National Convention (or *State* or *County Convention*); *the national* (or *state*) *convention*; *the convention.*

Republican Party. *Also see* G.O.P.

Reserve(s). Capitalize *Air Force Reserve, Army Reserve, Naval Reserve*, etc. Also: *the Reserve*; *the Reserves*; *Reserve officer.* But: *a reservist*; *the reserves* (meaning people rather than organizations).

resin, rosin. Use *resin* for the organic or synthetic substance used in varnishes, lacquers, inks and plastics. Use *rosin* for the turpentine derivative that is rubbed on violin bows and on athletes' hands to prevent slipping.

respectively is often superfluous, and it can force a reader to retrace steps to grasp a sentence. Omit it when possible.

rest(-). Most but not all compounds formed with *rest* are two words: rest cure, rest home, rest house, rest period, restroom, rest stop.

restaurateur (not *restauranteur*).

restructure. As a verb, although bureaucratic-sounding, the term is unavoidable in the sense of altering the terms of public or corporate debt. In other meanings, more natural replacements include *overhaul, rebuild, recast, reconstruct, reorganize, revamp* or *revise.*

result. Since virtually everything has more than one result, make it *as a result*, rather than *as the result.*

résumé.

Resurrection. Capitalize when the reference is to Jesus or to the rising of the dead at the Last Judgment.

retail (n.). Use the noun to mean a type of sale (*He bought it at retail*). But as a short form of *the retail business*, the term is jargon (*This is a good year for retail*). Make it *retailing.*

reticent. It means silent or taciturn. For hesitancy to act, use *reluctant* instead.

retired. Do not abbreviate or capitalize in denoting military status: *Col. Morgan E. Lamm, retired.* Often, retirement status may be noted more gracefully, not necessarily in the first reference: *Colonel Lamm, who retired from the Army in 1989, became president of the company two years ago.* Unless they choose otherwise, retired generals and admirals keep their military titles in place of civilian ones. On request, other retired senior officers (colonels, majors and their naval counterparts, for example) may also keep military titles.

Reuters (not *Reuter*) is the news agency. In datelines: CARACAS, *Venezuela, June 10 (Reuters)* — etc. Use this credit line on undatelined Reuters articles:

By Reuters

Rev. *The Rev. Lee A. Bildots.* For most Protestants the later reference is *Mr., Ms., Mrs.* or *Miss.* For Roman Catholics, Orthodox Christians and those Episcopalians who prefer it, use *Father* in later references: *Father Bildots.* Lutheran ministers, in later references, are normally called *Pastor: Pastor Bildots.* (For an exception, see PASTOR.) Never use *the Rev.* (or just *Reverend*) with a surname alone, as in *Reverend Bildots is coming to dinner.*

Do not omit *the* in front of *Rev.*, except in a headline. And whenever *Rev.* is used, even in a headline, it must be followed by a given name or initials: *Rev. Lee A. Bildots. Also see* MINISTER and RECTOR.

Rev. Dr. *The Rev. Dr. Stacy T. Miel; Dr. Miel.* Ordinarily use *Dr.* to reflect an earned doctorate only. Doctor of Divinity (D.D.) is not an earned degree.

reveille (meaning the signal or the assembly) is lowercased.

reverse discrimination is a pejorative term for programs that seek to rectify discrimination; it should be confined to quotations from opponents or descriptions of their view. *Also see* AFFIRMATIVE ACTION; PREFERENCES; QUOTAS; SET-ASIDES.

Revolutionary War (the American one). Also: *the American Revolution; the Revolution.*

revolver. *See* HANDGUNS.

rhapsody. Capitalize it in a title: *Brahms's Rhapsody in E flat (Op. 119).* Use quotation marks if it is part of a title affixed by the composer and goes beyond a mere description: *Gershwin's "Rhapsody in Blue."*

rhetoric. The classic meaning of the term is the art of using language persuasively or effectively. In a looser sense, now accepted by many dictionaries, *rhetoric* means bombast or verbiage, but that usage is trite. In either sense, *rhetoric* is not simply a synonym for *speech* or *talk. Also see* ORATORY.

rhinoceros(es).

Rhode Island. Abbreviate as *R.I.* after the names of cities, towns and counties.

Rhone for the river in Switzerland and France. But in a foreign name or phrase: *Côtes du Rhône.*

Richter scale. A means of measuring earthquake magnitudes now rarely used by seismologists. *See* EARTHQUAKES.

RICO, sparingly, in later references to the Racketeer Influenced and Corrupt Organizations Act, the federal statute enacted in 1970 as a way to combat organized crime.

Rider University (in Lawrenceville, N.J.).

riffle (to leaf or shuffle), **rifle** (v., to ransack or pillage).

riffraff.

rifles are weapons fired from the shoulder using two hands. Spiral grooves (called *rifling*) are cut into the interior of a rifle barrel. The grooves make bullets spin as they move along the barrel, and the spinning creates a stability that increases accuracy. *Cartridges* (also called *rounds*) are the ammunition for rifles. Part of the cartridge is the *bullet*, the projectile (usually lead) that is discharged when the cartridge explodes. The casing, another part of the cartridge, remains behind. Automatic rifles keep shooting as long as their triggers are depressed. Semiautomatic rifles fire one round each time the trigger is pulled. The discharge of a rifle is called a shot. *Also see* CALIBER; CARTRIDGE; HANDGUNS; SHOTGUNS.

right(-). Most but not all compounds formed with *right* are hyphenated: right field, right-hand (adj.), right-handed, right-hander, right-minded, right(s) of way, right wing (n.), right-wing (adj.).

Right Bank (of the Seine, in Paris).

right, rightist, right wing. Lowercase *right* unless the political divisions in a country are formally designated as *the Right, the Right Wing,* etc., or the word appears in a party name. Lowercase *rightist* unless the reference is to such a division or party or to a member of it. Lowercase *right wing* or *right-wing* (adj.) unless the reference is to such a division or party.

right-to-work laws is a partisan term for state laws that forbid union shops (workplaces with compulsory union membership). More neutral phrases include *states that outlaw union shops*.

Rikers Island (in New York).

Ringling Brothers and Barnum & Bailey is the full name of the circus. In later references: *Ringling Brothers*. Since 1996 its parent company has been known as Feld Entertainment Inc.

Rio Grande (not *Rio Grande River*).

riot is a powerful word that can inflame a community during or after a disturbance. Reserve the term for a wild or violent outbreak, usually one involving deaths, major injuries or heavy property damage.

rip-off (n.), **rip off** (v.). In references to theft or cheating, these words are slang, rarely suitable for news copy.

rise. Use *raise* instead for an increase in pay.

Road. Spell it out and capitalize it in articles as part of a name: *Fordham Road*. The abbreviation (*Fordham Rd.*) may be used in headlines, charts, tables and maps.

robbery. *See* LARCENY, BURGLARY, ROBBERY, THEFT and MUGGING.

Robert's Rules of Order (not *Roberts'*); no quotation marks.

Rockefeller Center, Rockefeller Plaza. The complex of buildings is *Rockefeller Center*; the central square, which figures in the addresses of several buildings, is *Rockefeller Plaza*.

Rockefeller University (in New York City).

rockets. Use Arabic numerals in designations: *Titan 4*.

rock 'n' roll. Use this spelling or simply *rock* (not *rock-and-roll*). Also: *folk-rock*.

Rockville Centre (an exception to the *Center* spelling usually preferred), in Nassau County, N.Y.

rococo (art, music, architecture and decorative arts). Capitalize in reference to the 18th-century style derived from BAROQUE but characterized by lighter, more decorative forms. Lowercase *rococo* as an adjective meaning florid. *See* ARTS TERMINOLOGY.

roll call (n.), **roll-call** (adj.).

Rollerblade is a trademark for in-line skates. Use *in-line skating* (and *skater*, etc.) rather than suffixes on the trademark.

roller coaster.

roll over (v.), **rollover** (n. and adj.).

Rolls-Royce. *Rolls-Royce Motor Cars Ltd.*, which makes Bentley and Rolls-Royce automobiles, was purchased by Volkswagen A.G. in 1998. A different company, *Rolls-Royce P.L.C.*, makes aircraft engines.

ROM for read-only memory.

roman. Lowercase when the reference is to upright typefaces. But capitalize *Roman alphabet* (the set of letters originated by the Romans) and ROMAN NUMERALS (or *Arabic numerals*).

roman à clef, a novel based on real characters with identities veiled.

Roman Catholic Church. In first references, it is *the Roman Catholic Church*, not *the Catholic Church*. Also: *a Roman Catholic*; *a Roman Catholic church*. In later references: *the Catholic Church* (the institution); *the Catholic church* (a building); *a Catholic church*; *a Catholic*; *the church* (always lowercase). Use *Roman* in later references too if the context is ambiguous.

Romania (not *Rumania*). The capital is Bucharest and the people are *Romanians*.

Roman numerals are used in the names of popes, monarchs, Army corps, annual Super Bowl games and people who prefer the numerals (*Lee H. Berenich IV*). *See* NUMBERS IN NAMES.

The numeral system uses seven letters, shown here with their Arabic number equivalents: *I (1)*; *V (5)*; *X (10)*; *L (50)*; *C (100)*; *D (500)* and *M (1,000)*. When a letter follows one of equal or greater value, it is added; thus *CX* equals *110*. When a smaller number immediately precedes a larger one, the smaller value is subtracted from the larger; thus *IV* equals *4*. A bar printed above a letter multiplies its value by 1,000. Details appear in the dictionary.

Romanticism (music, art and literature). Capitalize when referring to the movements that were the dominant force from the early 19th century through the early 20th century. In music, Chopin, Liszt, Schumann, Berlioz and Wagner are considered the principal composers of *Romanticism*; the creations of the last decades of the period and the music of composers like Mahler and Richard Strauss are often called *Late Romanticism* and *Post-Romanticism*. *See* ARTS TERMINOLOGY.

Ronald Reagan National Airport (in Washington). In later references, and in headlines when the context is clear: *Reagan Airport* or *National Airport*.

room(-), (-)room. Most but not all compounds formed with *room* as a prefix are two words: room and board, room clerk, roomful, roommate, room temperature.

Most but not all compounds formed with *room* as a suffix are one word: bedroom, classroom, dining room, family room, living room, reading room, schoolroom, stateroom, stockroom, storeroom, workroom.

room names. Capitalize the names of specially designated rooms: *Oak Room*; *Oval Office*; *Pump Room*. Also: *Room 235*. *See* BUILDING NAMES.

Roosevelt Island in New York City was formerly Welfare Island and, before that, Blackwells Island. It is part of Manhattan.

Rosh Hashana, the Jewish New Year. Rosh Hashana and Yom Kippur are Judaism's *High Holy Days* (preferred, rather than *High Holidays*).

rosin. *See* RESIN, ROSIN.

R.O.T.C. for the Reserve Officers Training Corps.

round is used without an apostrophe in expressions like *round-the-clock negotiations, round-the-world voyage, the year round*. Do not use hyphens in adverbial phrases: *He sailed round the world in a dinghy*.

round(-). Some compounds formed with *round* are one word, some are two words and some are hyphenated: roundabout, round-bottomed, roundhouse, round robin (n.), round-robin (adj.), round-the-clock (adj.), round trip (n.), round-trip (adj.), roundup (n.), round up (v.).

round numbers. *See* NUMBERS, ROUND.

round table (n.), **round-table** (adj.).

Route. Capitalize in the names of roads: *Route 22*. The abbreviation may be used in headlines, charts, tables and maps: *Rte. 22*. Also: *Route 9W*; *Rte. 9W*. *Also see* INTERSTATE SYSTEM.

Rowan University (in Glassboro, N.J., formerly Glassboro State College).

row house, or *town house*. It is usually a narrow building that shares common walls with those on both sides. Only those with facades of reddish-brown sandstone are *brownstones*.

row to hoe. The idiom is *a hard* (or *long* or *tough*) *row to hoe* (not *road*).

Royal Caribbean Cruises.

Royal Dutch/Shell Group. Its major United States affiliate is the Shell Oil Company.

r.p.m. for revolutions per minute.

Rte. The abbreviation for *Route* may be used with a number in headlines, charts, tables and maps: *Rte.* 22; *Rte.* 9W; etc.

Rt. Rev., Most Rev. Omit these terms before the names of almost all Episcopal and Roman Catholic bishops and archbishops. But *the Most Rev.* is used with the name of the Anglican prelate who is the archbishop of Canterbury and with the names of the superiors general of certain Catholic orders. *Also see* ARCHBISHOP; BISHOP; CANTERBURY, ARCHBISHOP OF; REV.; SUPERIOR GENERAL; VERY REV.

rubber stamp (n.), **rubber-stamp** (v. and adj.).

ruble.

run(-). Most but not all compounds formed with *run* are one word: runaround (n.), runaway (n. and adj.), rundown (n.), run-down (adj.), runoff (n.), run-of-the-mill, run-through, runway.

runner(s)-up.

running mate.

Russian names. Names that have become well known in English should keep their familiar forms: *Peter the Great*, not *Pyotr*; *Tchaikovsky*, not *Chaikovsky*; *Khrushchev*, not *Khrushchyov*; *Rachmaninoff*, not *Rahkmaninov*. (Another exception: *czar*, not *tsar*.)

Women's names in Slavic languages have feminine endings. Use such an ending when a woman has a reputation under her own name: the ballerina *Maya Plisetskaya*, for example, not *Plisetsky*. But *Naina Yeltsin* (not *Yeltsina*), the wife of President Boris N. Yeltsin.

Generally Russian surnames with the *sky* ending (*Zhirinovsky*) are so spelled, unlike similar-sounding names in Polish, which end with *ski* (*Jaruzelski*). Russian surnames will end with *ov* or *ev* (*Fyodorov* or *Lebedev*), not *off* or *eff*. But follow the spelling preferences of émigré Russians: *Nicholas Kalashnikoff*, for example, not *Nikolai Kalashnikov*. And if a Russian cultural figure appears or records often in the West and is extensively publicized or advertised, use the artist's preferred spelling. The goal is to avoid inconsistency between highly visible publicity materials and the news columns.

Typically names are rendered erratically when they enter English through other languages—those of athletes, for example, at a meet in Germany or France.

Check any Russian name obtained from a non-Russian source. When time permits, consult a Russian-speaking editor or reporter.

Use this system for converting Russian names into Roman characters: Where an exact equivalent exists for a single Cyrillic character, use it. (This means, for example, *ks* rather than *x* in a name like Aleksandr or Aleksei.) For other letters and symbols, use phonetic renderings: *zh*, as in Zhukov; *kh*, as in Kharkov; *ts*, as in Trotsky; *ch*, as in Chernyshevsky; *sh*, as in Shostakovich; *shch*, as in the middle of Khrushchev; *ya*, as in Yalta. Choose the most economical spelling to produce the desired English sound: the *u* in Yuri, for example, rather than a French-influenced *ou*. And *ch* rather than a German-influenced *tsch*.

А а	a		У у	u
Б б	b		Ф ф	f
В в	v		Х х	kh
Г г	g		Ц ц	ts
Д д	d		Ч ч	ch
Е е	e[1]		Ш ш	sh
″	ye[2]		Щ щ	shch
″	yo[3]		Ъ	—
Ж ж	zh		Ы	y
З з	z		Ь	—
И и	i		Э э	e
Й й	i		Ю ю	yu
К к	k		Я я	ya
Л л	l			
М м	m		ADJECTIVAL ENDINGS	
Н н	n		ый	y
О о	o		ий	i
П п	p		ая	aya
Р р	r		яя	yaya
С с	s		ое	oye
Т т	t		ее	eye

[1]Use *e* after consonants.
[2]Use *ye* after vowels and after the "soft sign," and in the initial position.
[3]Use *yo* in certain special cases. See the next paragraph.

Russian uses two forms of *e* with three sounds: *ye*, as in Yevgeny; *yo*, as in Pyotr; *eh*, as in Edda. In written Russian, *ye* and *yo* look the same; only the pronunciation is different. Where the pronunciation is known to be *yo*, use it. Example: *Semyon* (spelled *Semen* in Russian). If in doubt, use *ye* or *e*.

Since the breakup of the Soviet Union, some countries with Cyrillic alphabets (Ukraine and Bulgaria, for example) have departed from the Russian conversion system. Their spellings of personal and place names should be followed.

Russian(s). Apply the term to people of Russia only, even in historical references to the Soviet period. The broader term, embracing all nationalities that made up the Soviet Union, is *Soviets*.

Russian Orthodox Church. It was once the established church of Russia and is, like the Greek Orthodox Church, one of the autonomous Eastern Orthodox churches. *See* EASTERN ORTHODOXY; METROPOLITAN; PATRIARCH.

Russian Revolution. Also: *the Bolshevik Revolution; the revolution. October Revolution*, while also correct, may be confusing because calendar changes have since moved its anniversary into November.

Russo-. In references to Russia, use the more conversational *Russian-Chinese, Russian-American*, etc.

Rutgers University, the New Jersey state university, has campuses in Camden, Newark and New Brunswick.

S

SA for Sturmabteilung, the Nazi storm troopers. No periods because the letters are drawn from a single word.

Sabena Belgian World Airlines. Usually just use *Sabena*.

SAC for the Strategic Air Command.

saccharin (n.), **saccharine** (adj.).

sacrilegious does not contain the word *religious*.

safe(-). Most but not all compounds formed with *safe* are one word: safe-conduct (n.), safecracker, safe-deposit (adj.), safeguard (n. and v.), safe house, safekeeping.

safe deposit box (not *safety deposit*).

safe sex is usually an overstatement, and *safer sex*, preferred by some health organizations, is imprecise. Use more specific phrasing, like *protected sex*.

saga. It is a long story of adventure or heroism, not just any story.

Sahara means desert, so *Sahara Desert* is redundant. Make it *the Sahara*. Also: *the sub-Saharan region*. *Sub-Sahara* is not the name of a place; use it only in the adjectival form.

Sahel. This term, absorbed into the French language from Arabic, refers to a coastal or border strip and designates the belt of African countries immediately south of the Sahara. Except in a quotation, it is best replaced by a more familiar phrase, like *the sub-Saharan region*. Also see SAHARA.

Saigon, Vietnam, was renamed *Ho Chi Minh City* after the Communist takeover in 1975. The old name remains in popular use.

sail(-). Compounds formed with *sail* are one word: sailboat, sailcloth, sailfish, sailmaker, sailplane.

Saint Laurent, Yves.

Saint, Sainte. *See* ST., STE.

Saks Fifth Avenue.

salable.

salesgirl. Use *saleswoman* instead, for an adult. The general term is *salesclerk* or *sales representative*, not *salesperson*. *See* MEN AND WOMEN.

Sallie Mae for the Student Loan Marketing Association, the government-chartered company that makes low-cost student loans available through private lenders.

Salomon Smith Barney Inc., the brokerage firm formed in the 1997 merger of Salomon Inc. and Smith Barney, is a subsidiary of Citigroup Inc.

Salonika (not *Thessaloniki*). Also: *Gulf of Salonika*.

saloonkeeper.

SALT is acceptable in later references to the *strategic arms limitation treaties*: *SALT I*, signed in 1972, and *SALT II*, signed in 1979. *SALT treaty* is redundant, and *SALT agreement* only slightly less so.

Saltaire (on Fire Island, in Suffolk County, N.Y.).

Salvadoran(s). The people of El Salvador.

salvo(s).

SAM('s) for surface-to-air missile(s). Also: *SAM-2*; *SAM-6*; *SAM-6's*; etc.

sanction. As a noun, *sanction* can mean either approval or penalty, so the context must make the meaning clear. As a verb, *sanction* should be used only to mean approve or permit. A newer usage, to mean penalize (*they sanctioned the company for breaking an embargo*), is jargon.

S.&L. for savings and loan association, but sparingly. Also: *S.&L.'s*. Except in direct quotations, do not use *thrift* as a synonym for savings and loan association.

S-and-M, for sadism and masochism, or sadomasochism. *S-M* is also acceptable, in a clear context.

Sands Point (in Nassau County, N.Y.).

sanitarium(s) (not *sanatorium*), for rest home(s) or resort(s).

Santa Ana wind. The hot, dry wind that blows from the north, northeast or east into Southern California.

São Paulo (in Brazil).

Sarajevo is the capital of BOSNIA AND HERZEGOVINA.

Sardinia. Use the name instead of *Italy* after the name of a city or town, in a dateline or when a locating phrase is needed.

Saskatchewan (Canadian province). Do not abbreviate after the names of cities and towns, even in datelines.

SAT is a trademark but no longer an abbreviation for the name of a college entrance examination. *See* COLLEGE BOARD.

Satan. Also capitalize *Devil* if Satan is meant. Lowercase *a devil* and *devils*.

satellites. *See* EARTH SATELLITES.

saturnalian.

sauté, sautéed, sautéing.

savings. Do not use it as a singular noun: *The cuts produced a savings of $50,000.* Delete *a* or make it *saving*. Also: *daylight saving time*.

savings and loan associations are not banks. They collect deposits from consumers and make mortgage loans. After the first reference and in headlines, *S.&L.* and

S.&L.'s are acceptable, but sparingly. Do not use *thrift* as a synonym for savings and loan association.

Savior in references to Jesus or to God. Lowercase for other meanings.

saw (v.) is a journalese mannerism in this kind of sentence: *The scandal saw 33 officers arrested*; *The day saw 11 people injured*. Neither scandals nor days can see.

SBC Communications (the regional telephone company). It is the parent of Pacific Bell, Southwestern Bell and the Southern New England Telecommunications Corporation, the dominant telephone company in Connecticut. In 1998, it announced an agreement to merge with Ameritech.

scaloppine.

scam. The term is slang, for fraud or swindle.

Scandinavian Airlines System (S.A.S.).

scant means not just small but inadequate.

Scarborough (in Westchester County, N.Y.).

scarf, scarves.

S. Carolina. The abbreviation may be used as a last resort in headlines (although more freely in the sports pages) and in charts and tables.

scenario means a synopsis of a play or film. As a synonym for *chain of events, plan* or *situation*, it is a cliché.

scheme. The British use the term to mean plan or project (*highway construction scheme*). But in American usage, *scheme* connotes a devious plot.

schizophrenia is a mental illness often characterized by episodic disorientation, delusions and hallucinations. It is not characterized by a split personality, and the word *schizophrenic* does not mean two-faced, of two minds or self-contradictory.

schnauzer (the dog).

Scholastic Assessment Tests. *See* COLLEGE BOARD.

school(-). Most but not all compounds formed with *school* are one word: school age (n.), school-age (adj.), school board, schoolbook, schoolboy, school bus, schoolchildren, school day, school district, schoolgirl, schoolhouse, schoolmate, schoolroom, school ship, schoolteacher, schoolwork, schoolyard, school year.

school colors. Capitalize when referring to a school or a school athletic team by its colors: *the Blue and White*; *the Crimson*; etc. Also: *The Crimson strategy paid off.* But: *Columbia's colors are blue and white.*

school names. Use *Public School 4* (not *No. 4*); *P.S. 4*; *Intermediate School 9*; *I.S. 9*; *Junior High School 113*; *J.H.S. 113*. Capitalize full names: *Cordeiro High School*; *Milori Junior High School*.

Schools Chancellor *Lee H. Milori* (in the New York City system); *Chancellor Milori*; *the chancellor*; *Mr.* (or *Ms., Miss, Mrs.* or *Dr.*) *Milori*. Elsewhere, *Chancellor* may be capitalized as a governmental title before a name, but it is lowercased for non-governmental officials and separated from the name by a comma.

schools in the arts. *See* ARTS TERMINOLOGY.

Schubert (the composer), **Shubert** (the theatrical organization and its founders).

Schuylkill, the. Do not use *River* after the name; *kill* means stream.

Schwarz, F. A. O. (the toy store).

score (v.). *Score,* when used as a verb to mean *criticize* or *denounce,* is stilted and sounds archaic.

scoreboard, scorecard.

Scot(s), Scotsman(men), Scotswoman(women) for the people of Scotland. The preferred adjective is *Scottish* except in special cases where *Scotch* is established, as in *Scotch whiskey. Scot* and *Scots* are also acceptable as adjectives, but for consistency are best restricted to quotations.

scotch plaid, but *a Scottish tartan.*

Scotch tape is a trademark.

Scotch whiskey. *Scotch* can stand alone when the context is clear.

scot-free.

Scottie (not *Scotty*), for the Scottish terrier (when the context is clear).

screen(-). Most but not all compounds formed with *screen* are two words: screen door, screen pass (football), screenplay, screen test, screenwriter.

Scripture(s). Capitalize the noun in singular and plural when referring to books of the Old and New Testaments. Lowercase the adjective *scriptural.* Give scriptural citations as follows: *II Corinthians 4:3; Mark 9.* Typical citations might read: *He took as his text II Corinthians 4:3; He read from Psalm 4; He quoted Isaiah 12.* But in some contexts a reference to a psalm may be better this way: *the Sixth Psalm; the 23rd Psalm.* Lowercase *a psalm.*

sculpture (v. as well as n.). Do not use *sculpt, sculpted* or *sculpting.*

sculptures. Capitalize the principal words in their names. And use quotation marks, except for generic titles like *Pietà.*

S. Dakota. The abbreviation may be used as a last resort in headlines (although more freely in the sports pages) and in charts and tables.

sea(-). Most but not all compounds formed with *sea* are one word: seabed, seaboard, sea breeze, sea change, seacoast, seafarer, seafood, seagoer, seagoing, sea gull, sea lane, sea level, sea lion, seaman, seaplane, seaport, seascape, seashell, seashore, seasick, sea wall, seaway, seaweed.

Sea-Land Service, the ocean carrier, was sold to the Maersk Line in 1999 to form Maersk Sealand.

Seaman *Lindsay J. Daan* (of the Navy); *Seaman Daan; the seaman.* Also: *Seaman Apprentice Daan; Seaman Recruit Daan.*

Sears, Roebuck & Company. In later references: *Sears, Roebuck* or *Sears.*

seasons. Do not capitalize *spring, summer, autumn, fall* or *winter.*

S.E.C. for the Securities and Exchange Commission.

second, secondly. In enumerating causes, factors, etc., use *second*, not *secondly.* The phrase is a short form of *what is second.*

second(-). Compounds formed with *second* are usually two words or hyphenated: second base, second baseman, second best (n.), second-best (adj.), second-class (adj.), second cousin, second-degree (adj.), second grader, second growth (n.), second-guess, secondhand (adj. and adv.), second hand (on a clock), second mortgage, second nature, second-rate (adj. and adv.), second sight, second-string, second thought, second wind.

Second Lt. *Alex E. Karitsa; Lieutenant Karitsa; the lieutenant.*

Second Vatican Council. It was an assembly of the bishops of the Roman Catholic Church (1962-65). In later references, use *Vatican II.* Follow the same style for the First Vatican Council (1869-70) and *Vatican I.*

Secretary of Labor (or *Foreign Secretary*, etc.) *Tracy B. Lam; Secretary Lam; the secretary.* When used as a nongovernmental title, it is separated from the name by a comma: *Tracy B. Lam, secretary of the company* (or *club*, etc.). See TITLES.

Secretary General *Dana P. Kikondoo* (of the United Nations, for example); *Secretary General Kikondoo; the secretary general.* No hyphen in this or similar titles, like *director general.*

secretary-treasurer. Hyphenate the kind of title that joins two nouns of equal importance (but not *secretary general*, etc.).

Securities and Exchange Commission; *the commission; the S.E.C.*

Securities Investor Protection Corporation. It is a nonprofit corporation that insures the securities and cash in investors' brokerage accounts. In later references, and in headlines when the context is clear: *SIPC*, without periods because it is pronounced as a word, SIP-ick.

Security Council (United Nations); *the Council.* But: *the National Security Council; the council.*

Seder. The ritual Passover supper, at which Jews recite from the Haggadah to retell the story of the Exodus. Use the plural *Seders* rather than the Hebrew *Sedarim.*

Seeing Eye is a trademark for guide dogs trained by Seeing Eye Inc. of Morristown, N.J.

seesaw.

self. Do not use the word as a headline synonym for *himself* or *herself*, as in *Man Kills Self.*

self(-). In general, terms with the prefix *self* are hyphenated: self-adulation, self-conscious (also: *un-self-conscious*), self-governing, self-made, self-respect, self-service.

But: *selfhood, selfless, selfsame, selfward.* Avoid the redundant *self-confessed. Confessed* should stand alone. *Also see* SELF-STYLED.

(-)self. The *self* words—*herself, himself* and *myself*—are used for emphasis (*She will do* *it herself*) and to turn the action in a sentence back on the subject (*He composed himself quickly*). Do not use these words as substitutes for *her*, *him* and *me* in sentences like *He gave the book to my brother and myself*. Make it *me*.

self-styled. The modifier is journalese. Use a more conversational expression, like *professed*, or *who calls herself a psychic*.

semi(-). Most but not all compounds formed with *semi* are one word: semiautomatic, semiclassical, semiconductor, semidarkness, semifinal(s), semifinalist, semi-invalid, semiofficial, semiprecious, semiprivate, semiprofessional, semisweet. Hyphenate unfamiliar or coined compounds. *Also see* SEMIANNUAL, SEMIYEARLY; SEMIMONTHLY; SEMIWEEKLY.

semiannual, semiyearly. These words mean twice a year, as does *biannual*. *Biennial* means every two years. For comprehension, avoid the prefix forms when possible and use *twice a year*.

semicolon. For the placement of a semicolon alongside other punctuation, see PARENTHESES and QUOTATION MARKS.

The semicolon can mark a division in a sentence made up of statements that are closely related but require a separation more emphatic than a comma: *The contestants were ready*; *the timekeeper was not. The assignment was hard*; *still, he carried it out.* When the separation is even more emphatic, or reflects cause and effect, a COLON may be used.

If three or more items form a series in a sentence and any item includes a comma, use semicolons between items: *Those present were Ashley T. Miel, a banker; Hilary F. Cordeiro, a lawyer; Lauren J. Baranek, a tax consultant; and Lindsay Lamb, a principal stockholder.* Retain the semicolon even before the final *and*.

Use semicolons in the tops of headlines, in single-line banks and in "panel" banks (multiple lines, uniformly indented). In cone-shaped banks, most often used on the front page, a dash replaces the semicolon. A semicolon may appear anywhere in a single-line head, but in a multiple-line head the logical break in phrasing, marked by a semicolon, should occur at the end of a line.

semimonthly means twice a month. Every two months is *bimonthly*. To minimize confusion, avoid the prefix forms whenever possible and use *twice a month* or *every two months*.

semiweekly means twice a week. Every two weeks is *biweekly* (which can also, but rarely, mean twice a week). To minimize confusion, avoid the prefix forms whenever possible. Use *twice a week* or *every two weeks*.

Senate. Capitalize specific references, domestic and foreign.

Senator *Dale B. Cordero, Republican of Arizona*; *Senator Cordero*; *the senator*. Do not abbreviate, even in headlines. When necessary for clarity, use *State Senator* or *United States Senator* on first reference. *See* TITLES.

Senator-elect *Chris P. Agneau; the senator-elect.* In cap-and-lowercase headlines: *Senator-Elect.*

senatorial.

send-off (n.), **send off** (v.).

Senhor, Senhora, Senhorita (Portuguese). *See* COURTESY TITLES.

senior for the class or a member of the class.

Senior, Junior. Use *Jr.* and *Sr.* (without commas) for Junior and Senior in names: *Lee D. Berenich Jr.* (or *Sr.*). In bylines: **By LEE D. BERENICH Jr.** Also: *Lee D. Berenich IV* or *Lee D. Berenich 4th*, depending on individual preference. If the preference is not known, use Roman numerals.

In a listing, if family names are printed before given names, the expression *Jr.* (or *Sr.*, or *IV*, etc.) comes last: *BERENICH, Lee D. Jr.*, not *BERENICH Jr., Lee D.*

Senior Airman *Hilary D. Agnello; Airman Agnello; the airman.*

Senior Chief Petty Officer *Lauren Z. Cordeiro; Chief Cordeiro; the chief.*

senior citizen. It is a euphemism, to be avoided except in quotations or organization names.

Senior Master Sgt. *Lee F. Miel; Sergeant Miel; the sergeant.*

Señor, Señora, Señorita. *See* COURTESY TITLES.

sensitive means easily hurt or having keen sensibilities. Its use to mean secret, important or diplomatically fragile is jargon.

separate.

Sephardi is the term for a Jew who lived in Spain or Portugal before the Inquisition, or that Jew's descendant. The plural is *Sephardim*, and the adjective is *Sephardic. Also see* ASHKENAZI and JEW(S).

Sept. for *September* before numerals (*Sept. 17*), or in charts and tables.

septet (music). *See* QUARTET and TRIO.

sepulcher (not *sepulchre*). Example: *Church of the Holy Sepulcher.*

sequence of tenses. In a newspaper, the prime verb in a sentence is generally in the past tense because newspapers tend to report recent history. For precision, the other verbs in a sentence should relate logically to the tense of that governing verb. This helps the reader keep track of the chronology. Consider, for example, the difference between *They dined when the countess arrived* and *They had dined when the countess arrived.*

With such a governing verb, events in the immediate past should ordinarily be reported in the past tense. *She said she was ecstatic* means she was ecstatic when she spoke. Not *She said she is ecstatic.*

Events more distant in the past are generally reported in the past perfect tense. *He said he had been delirious* means that he was delirious at some time before he spoke.

Events in the future are ordinarily reported in the conditional tense. *She said she would be cooperative* means that she promised to be cooperative at some point after she spoke.

When the sentence specifies a time element, the special tenses are unneeded: *She said she was ebullient on Wednesday.* Her ebullience preceded the speaking, but *on Wednesday* makes that clear. Sentences may also be simplified when they describe a continuing, eternal truth: *He said that the earth is round.* Use *is* because the earth is forever round.

To choose tenses, first identify the governing verb; in each example above, it is *said.* The governing verb appears at the beginning of the sentence; if it moves, it ceases to govern.

Ms. Lamm has a sprained ankle, Dr. Baranek said, and cannot play means that Ms. Lamm had the sprained ankle when Dr. Baranek spoke. *Said* is not the governing verb, but merely part of a parenthetical phrase; thus *has* and *cannot* are correct. If the sentence began with *Dr. Baranek said,* etc., the verbs would change to *had* and *could not.*

Ms. Lamm had a sprained ankle, Dr. Baranek said, and could not play. Here the meaning is that Ms. Lamm was injured at some time before Dr. Baranek spoke.

Similar rules apply to headlines, though the starting point is usually different because the governing verb is most often in the present tense. *See* HEADLINES.

Also see CONDITIONAL TENSES and SUBJUNCTIVE.

Serbia is a republic in Yugoslavia. Use *Serb(s)* as the noun for its people, and *Serbian* as the adjective. Distinguish Serbia from the *Serbian Republic,* one of the two political entities that make up BOSNIA AND HERZEGOVINA; its people are *Bosnian Serbs.*

serenade. Capitalize in a title: *Beethoven's Serenade for Flute, Violin and Viola (Op. 25).* But: *a Mozart serenade.*

sergeant. *Sgt. Dale L. Kuzu; Sergeant Kuzu; the sergeant. Also see* SGT. MAJ. and SERGEANT MAJOR OF THE ARMY.

sergeant(s)-at-arms.

sergeant first class. *Sgt. First Class Leslie T. Karitsa; Sergeant Karitsa; the sergeant.*

sergeant major. *Sgt. Maj. Lindsay N. Daan; Sergeant Major Daan; the sergeant major.* The plural is *sergeants major.*

sergeant major of the Army. Lowercase the full title and use it after the name, without abbreviation: *Lindsay E. Bildots, the sergeant major of the Army; Sergeant Major Bildots; the sergeant major.* The title is held by only one person at a time, the highest-ranking enlisted member of the Army. It usually requires explanation.

serialism (music). Do not capitalize the name of this composing technique, which originated in the first quarter of the 20th century and is also called "the 12-tone system." *See* ARTS TERMINOLOGY.

Sermon on the Mount. Also: *the Beatitudes.*

serviceable.

serviceman, servicewoman.

service mark. *See* TRADEMARK, SERVICE MARK.

set(-). Compounds formed with *set* can be one word, hyphenated or two words: setback (n.), set piece (n.), set-piece (adj.), setscrew, set shot, set-to (n.), setup (n.).

set-asides are funds or contracts reserved for minority bidders or women. The verb is *set aside. Also see* AFFIRMATIVE ACTION.

Seton Hall University (in South Orange, N.J.).

7-Eleven, the name of the convenience store chain, is a trademark.

1700's, 18th century. In almost all contexts, use numerals for centuries after the ninth. Also: *mid-1800's; mid-19th century.* When unavoidable, at the start of a sentence or for special effect: *seventeen-hundreds. Also see* YEARS, DECADES, CENTURIES.

Seventh-day Adventists.

7Up is a trademark for the soft drink.

severe thunderstorm. The National Weather Service classifies a thunderstorm as severe when it produces damaging winds of at least 58 miles an hour, hail at least three quarters of an inch in diameter or a tornado.

Sèvres.

sewage is waste matter; *sewerage* is the drainage system that removes it.

sex. *See* GENDER, SEX.

sex crimes. *See* RAPE.

sextet (music). *See* QUARTET and TRIO.

sexual assault. *See* RAPE.

sexual orientation, never *sexual preference,* which carries the disputed implication that sexuality is a matter of choice. Cite a person's sexual orientation only when it is pertinent and its pertinence is clear to the reader. *Also see* BISEXUAL; GAY; LESBIAN; STRAIGHT.

sexual preference. Use SEXUAL ORIENTATION instead.

sexual slurs. *See* SLURS.

Sgt. *Terry F. Agnello; Sergeant Agnello; the sergeant.*

Sgt. First Class *Pat C. Karitsa; Sergeant Karitsa; the sergeant.*

Sgt. Maj. *Stacy A. Kuzu; Sergeant Major Kuzu; the sergeant major.* The plural is *sergeants major.* Also, for the senior enlisted member of a uniformed service: *the sergeant major of the Army; the sergeant major of the Air Force.*

shake-up (n.), **shake up** (v.).

Shakespearean.

shantung (cloth).

shape-up (n.), **shape up** (v.).

shareholder, share owner.

Shariah, the legal code of Islam based on the Koran.

shar-pei (the dog).

Shavuot, the Jewish Feast of Weeks. It occurs in the spring.

she. In references to countries or ships, except for special literary effect, use *it* instead.

sheepdog.

Sheetrock is a trademark for wallboard.

sheik, sheikdom. *Also see* ARAB NAMES AND TITLES.

shell. In weaponry, it is the ammunition for a shotgun, a naval gun or an artillery piece. The shell of a big gun is the projectile that leaves the barrel when the gun is fired. The shell may contain high explosives, shrapnel or chemicals. A shotgun shell consists of a casing, a primer, powder and some sort of projectile—multiple pellets or slugs. When a shotgun is fired, only the projectile leaves the barrel; the shell remains behind. *Also see* BULLET and CARTRIDGE.

shell shock (n.), **shellshocked** (adj.).

Shemini Atzeret, a Jewish festival, follows the seventh day of SUKKOT and is observed with a service for the dead and a prayer for autumn rain.

sherbet (not *sherbert*).

Sheriff *Terry P. Yagyonak*; *Sheriff Yagyonak*; *the sheriff.*

Sherman Antitrust Act; *the antitrust act.*

Shetland (the wool and the pony).

shh.

Shiite Muslims are members of the Shia branch of Islam, which regards Ali, the son-in-law of Muhammad, as Muhammad's legitimate successor. *Also see* SUNNI MUSLIMS.

shine, shined, shone. When *shine* has an object, the past tense is *shined: He shined the light at the boat.* But when it has no object, the past tense is *shone: The sun shone yesterday.*

ship(-), (-)ship. Most but not all compounds formed with *ship* as a prefix are solid: shipboard, shipbuilding, ship canal, shipmate, shipowner, ship-rigged, shipwreck.

Most but not all compounds formed with *ship* as a suffix are solid: fire ship, flagship, friendship, lightship, slave ship, steamship, tight ship, transship.

ship lines are listed separately.

shippers are the owners of freight being transported. *Carriers* are the transporters.

ships. Use their names without quotation marks. Refer to them as *it* and *its*—not *she* and *her*—except for literary effect.

shish kebab.

shofar. The ram's horn, sounded as a trumpet at Jewish High Holy Day services. Plural: *shofars.*

shootdown (n.). Use *shooting down* instead as the noun form. In a narrow headline: *downing.* The verb form, entirely acceptable, is *shoot down.*

shooter is recognized by dictionaries, but in criminal contexts it has a flavor of police jargon. *Gunman*, when accurate, is more conversational. (*Sharpshooter*, curiously, does not have the problem.)

shop(-), (-)shop. Most but not all compounds formed with *shop* as a prefix are one word: shopkeeper, shoplifter, shop steward, shoptalk, shopworn.

Compounds formed with *shop* as a suffix are usually one word: barbershop, bookshop, machine shop, pawnshop, repair shop, sweatshop, toyshop.

ShopRite Supermarkets Inc., a subsidiary of the Wakefern Food Corporation.

short(-). Most but not all compounds formed with *short* are one word: shortchange, short circuit (n.), short-circuit (v.), shortcut (n.), shortfall, shorthand, short-lived, shortsighted, shortstop, short-tempered, shortwave (n. and adj.).

short ton. See TON.

shotguns are weapons that are fired from the shoulder using two hands. The inner surfaces of their barrels are smooth. *Shells* are the ammunition for shotguns. A shotgun shell consists of a casing, a primer, powder and some sort of projectile — pellets or a slug. Only the projectile is discharged when the shotgun is fired. The discharge of a shotgun is called a *blast*. Shotgun sizes are usually given in gauges: 10 gauge, 12 gauge, 16, 20 and 28 gauge (the bigger the number, the smaller the shotgun). The one exception is the .410 bore shotgun, which is of limited use. *Also see* CALIBER; HANDGUNS; RIFLES.

shot-put, shot-putter, shot-putting.

show(-). Most but not all compounds formed with *show* are one word: showboat, show business, showcase, showdown, showman, show-off (n.), showroom.

Shubert (the theatrical organization and its founders), **Schubert** (the composer).

shut(-). Most but not all compounds formed with *shut* are one word: shutdown (n.), shut-in (n.), shutout (n.).

S.I., for Staten Island, may be used only in headlines for editions confined to the New York metropolitan area. Do not use *Staten I.* When necessary, insert a reference to Staten Island after the name of a locale there: *Tottenville, Staten Island.*

Sichuan (not *Szechwan* or *Szechuan*), for the province in China. Its capital is Chengdu. Also use *Sichuan* in a reference to the cuisine, but not necessarily in the name of a restaurant. See CHINESE NAMES.

Sicily. Use this name instead of *Italy* after the names of Sicilian cities and towns in datelines or when a locater is needed.

sick(-). Most but not all compounds formed with *sick* are two words: sick bay, sickbed, sick call, sick leave, sick list, sickout, sickroom.

side(-). Most but not all compounds formed with *side* are one word: side arm (weapon), sidearm (style of pitching), sideboard, sideburns, sidelight, sideline, sidelong, sidesaddle, sideshow, sidestep, sidestroke, sideswipe, sidewalk, sideways.

Sierra Nevada; *the Sierra* (not *Sierra Nevada Mountains* or *the Sierras*).

sightseeing, sightseer.

Signal Corps (United States Army); *the corps*.

signaled.

signatory. Except in quotations or texts, use a simpler word, *signer*, for a person or a country that has subscribed to a treaty or other agreement.

signature, signing. Use *signing* for the act or ceremony of endorsing a treaty or document. Reserve *signature* for the name written at the end of a document.

signatures may be used in place of bylines on brief opinion articles (arts reviews, for example) and in feature sections, but not ordinarily in news reporting. Such signatures should be set in italic capitals, flush right. Unless otherwise designed in a special section, the signature should be tucked into the last line of copy when room exists for at least two em spaces of separation: *HILARY T. KARITSA*

The signature on a letter to the editor, or on a letter printed as a verbatim text, should ordinarily be set in capitals and small capitals, flush right, and tucked into the last line when room exists for at least two em spaces: LINDSAY J. DAAN

Signor, Signora, Signorina. *See* COURTESY TITLES.

Simhat Torah is the Jewish autumn festival celebrating the end of the yearlong cycle of Torah readings. The name means Rejoicing in the Law.

Simon & Schuster Inc.

Sinai (not *the Sinai*) for the peninsula in northeast Egypt. But: *the Sinai Desert*; *the Sinai Peninsula*.

singles, as in *singles bar* and *singles scene*, has no apostrophe.

Sino(-). In references to China, use the more conversational *Chinese-American, Chinese-Russian*, etc. But: *Sinologist*.

SIPC for the Securities Investor Protection Corporation, which insures the securities and cash in investors' brokerage accounts. No periods, because the term is pronounced SIP-ick.

Sir *Leslie Agneau*; *Sir Leslie*. In headlines: *Agneau*. In the British system, the title designates baronets and knights; they are not PEERS. (When it is relevant, specify whether Sir Leslie is a knight or a baronet.) *Sir* is always followed by a given name, without a middle initial (never *Mr. Agneau*). If the title is awarded to a figure who is independently known by a full name—a musician, for example—the famous name may stand without the title on first reference: *the conductor Leslie Agneau*; *Sir Leslie*.

sister (religious). A title for a woman in a religious order (a nun) in the Roman Catholic, Anglican (Episcopal) and Orthodox Churches. Do not abbreviate *sister*, and except in quotations, use it only with a name: *Sister Robin Agneau* and *Sister*

Robin or *Sister Agneau*, according to her preference. Lowercase *nun. Also see* MOTHER (RELIGIOUS) and NUN.

sit-down (n. and adj.), **sit down** (v.).

sit-in (n.), **sit in** (v.).

situated is often an excess word, as in *The town is situated in Klopstock County.*

situp (n.), **sit up** (v.).

Sixth Avenue (in Manhattan). *See* AVENUE OF THE AMERICAS.

sizable.

(-)size. Most but not all compounds formed with *size* are hyphenated: king-size, life-size, medium-size, midsize, outsize, pint-size.

> Ordinarily use *-size*, not *-sized*, for the suffix.

sizes. Express in numerals: *size 8 dress; size 44 long; 11½B shoes; 15½ collar.*

skeptical.

ski, skied, skier, skiing, ski jumping.

skillful.

skin-dive (v.), **skin diving** (n.).

sky boxes, for the luxurious suites in sports stadiums.

slang. Words bearing this label, in the dictionary or in this manual, are highly informal, usually flippant and often coined as a badge of membership in an in-group (for example, teenagers, the military, the underworld or the police). When used unmistakably for special effect—*perp*, say, to evoke the flavor of byplay in a feature about a police station—they are welcome, without quotation marks or other signs of self-consciousness. Do not use slang, though, in straightforward copy or headlines, where it would *hit a clinker*—that is, undermine the seriousness of the reporting. No one would be likely to write that negotiators *snookered* a diplomat or celebrated afterward by getting *smashed*. But the writer's ear should be attuned to the infiltration of more current slang, like *in-your-face* and *rip-off*; it can create the embarrassing spectacle of a grown-up who tries to pass for an adolescent. Some slang expressions will evolve into standard English. Others, like *crunch* (for showdown) and *edgy* (on the cutting edge), show up so relentlessly that they vault overnight from the novel to the hackneyed.

> *Also see* COLLOQUIALISMS.

slash, in the sense of budget cutting, can be a partisan word. One politician's *slashes* are another politician's prudent *trims*.

slate, as a verb meaning *plan* or *schedule* (*The vote was slated for Thursday*), is journalese and trite.

slave state, free state. Lowercase in references to the situation before the Civil War.

slay, slayer, slaying. Archaic, almost biblical, the words are best replaced by more modern synonyms (usually *kill*, etc.). If an exception is warranted, *slay* remains a

verb only; even in headlines, the noun and the adjective are *slaying. Also see* MUR-
DER, HOMICIDE, KILLING.

slew, as a noun meaning a lot, is colloquial, too informal for news reporting.

Slovakia. Its capital is Bratislava.

Slovenia (the country), **Slovene(s)** as a noun for the people and as an adjective.

slowdown (n.), **slow down** (v.).

slurs (ethnic, racial, religious and sexual). The epithets of bigotry ordinarily have no
place in the newspaper. Even in ironic or self-mocking quotations about a speaker's
own group (in rap lyrics, for example), their use erodes the worthy inhibition against
brutality in public discourse. If an exception is essential to readers' understanding of
a highly newsworthy crime, conflict or personality, the decision should first be discussed thoroughly by senior editors. For one limited exception, see QUEER.

small-business man, small-business woman. Also: *business owner; small-business
owner; business people; small-business people.*

Smith Barney is now part of Salomon Smith Barney Inc., a subsidiary of Citigroup
Inc.

SmithKline Beecham Corporation.

Smithsonian Institution (not *Institute*).

smoke screen.

Smokey Bear (not *Smokey the Bear*).

smolder.

smut. *See* PORN, PORNO.

Smyrna. Use *Izmir* in all but historical references to the Turkish seaport.

sneak, sneaked, sneaking. Never *snuck.*

S.N.E.T. for the Southern New England Telecommunications Corporation, the dominant local telephone company in Connecticut. It is a subsidiary of SBC Communications.

snow(-). Most but not all compounds formed with snow are one word: snowball,
snowbank, snow-blind, snow blower, snowboard, snowbound, snowcapped,
snowdrift, snowfall, snow fence, snowflake, snowman, snowmobile, snowpack,
snowplow, snowshoe, snowstorm, snowsuit, snow tire.

Snow Belt.

so-called (adj.), **so called** (adv.). With this phrase, quotation marks are redundant: *the
so-called "poison-pill defense."*

soccer is what the rest of the world calls *football.* Its international championship every
four years is the World Cup.

socialism, socialist. Capitalize if the reference is to a political party or movement that
professes socialism, or to its members. Lowercase in a general sense: *He said the
plan smacked of socialism.*

Social Security. Also: *the Social Security Act.*

Society of Friends. *See* QUAKERS.

software. Capitalize the principal words in program names, and use no quotation marks if a name is simple and descriptive. But use the marks for a fanciful name that is more like a book title: *"Where in the World Is Carmen Sandiego?"* When the title consists of a common word, the context should make the meaning clear, perhaps by identifying the manufacturer or appending a release number: *Microsoft Word; Word 7; Word for Windows 98; Borland Paradox.*

Soho, SoHo. Soho is the district in central London. *SoHo* (from *South of Houston Street*) is in Manhattan.

solo(s).

somber.

some(-). Compounds formed with *some* are one word: somebody, someday (adv.), someone, sometimes (adv.). But: *30-some years.*

someone. Always singular. *See* ANYBODY, ANYONE, EVERYBODY, EVERYONE, NO ONE, SOMEONE.

somewhere is often superfluous, as in this sentence: *He is somewhere between 55 and 60.*

sonata. Capitalize in a title: *Beethoven's "Moonlight" Sonata; Beethoven's Sonata in E flat, "Les Adieux."*

songs. Use quotation marks with the titles of songs, popular or classical, including national anthems. If the title is in English, capitalize all the principal words: *"Get Me to the Church on Time."* If the title of a classical song (or aria) is in French, Spanish or Italian, generally capitalize only the first word: *"Nuit d'étoiles"; "Il bacio."* If the title is in German, capitalize the first word and all the nouns: *"An den Frühling."*

sophomore for the class or a member of the class.

S O S (with thin spaces between letters). The distress call.

Sotheby's Inc. (a subsidiary of Sotheby's Holdings Inc.).

sound bite can be a cliché and can be partisan, suggesting that a comment is empty or meaningless. Use it with care.

soundtrack. But: *sound truck.*

source documents. *See* REPORTS.

sources. Standing by itself, the word is too vague to serve as attribution in a news article: *a source said* or *sources said* means no more than *somebody said.* And *informed* or *reliable,* as a modifier, is no improvement. *See* ATTRIBUTION.

sous-chef (a chef's assistant).

south. Capitalize in all references to the region of the United States and in first references to other specific regions: *South Texas.* Capitalize in later references to a country with *South* in its name, like South Korea. Lowercase *south* as a point of the compass.

Southampton, in Suffolk County, N.Y. (Spellings for nearby towns differ: *East Hampton, Bridgehampton, Westhampton.*)

South Carolina. Abbreviate as *S.C.* after the names of cities, towns and counties. As a last resort, and somewhat more readily in the sports pages, use *S. Carolina* in a headline.

South Dakota. Abbreviate as *S.D.* after the names of cities, towns and counties. As a last resort, and somewhat more readily in the sports pages, use *S. Dakota* in a headline.

southeast. Capitalize when referring to that geographic region of the United States; lowercase as a point of the compass.

Southeast Asia comprises Cambodia, Indonesia, Laos, Malaysia, Myanmar, the Philippines, Singapore, Thailand and Vietnam.

southern. Capitalize when used in reference to the South, the geographic region of the United States, or to recognized areas (*Southern California*). But: *southern Utah; southern Italy; southern part of North Korea; southern half,* etc. *Also see* SOUTH.

Southern Baptist Convention. Now the largest Baptist group in the United States, it split from an even larger group in 1845 over the issue of whether a slaveholder could be a missionary.

Southerner. Capitalize when referring to someone from the American South or from a country with *South* in its name, like South Korea.

Southern Connecticut State University (in New Haven).

Southern New England Telecommunications Corporation (S.N.E.T.) is the dominant local telephone company in Connecticut. It is a subsidiary of SBC Communications.

Southern Hemisphere; *the hemisphere.*

Southern Tier. Capitalize in reference to the row of counties in New York State that are directly north of Pennsylvania.

South Jersey. An exception to the rule that requires *southern New Jersey, southern Ohio, southern France,* etc. And an exception to the preference for keeping the *New* in front of *Jersey.* Also: *North Jersey.*

South Pole. But: *the pole; polar.*

South Shore, North Shore (of Long Island).

South Side. Capitalize when regularly used to designate a section of a city.

South Texas.

South Vietnam, South Vietnamese. The terms apply only to the period from 1954 to the reunification of Vietnam in 1975.

southwest. Capitalize when referring to the region of the United States; lowercase as a point of the compass.

Southwest Airlines.

Soviet, Soviets, Soviet Union. In historical references, use *Soviet Union* for the name of the country (which dissolved in 1991), *Soviet* as an adjective and *Soviets* as a noun for the people or, informally, for the country. Also, in rare formal contexts: *Union of Soviet Socialist Republics* and *U.S.S.R.*

space(-). Most but not all compounds formed with *space* are one word: space age, space bar, spacecraft, spaceflight, spaceman, space platform, spaceport, spaceship, space shuttle, space station, spacesuit, spacewalk.

space vehicles. Use their names without quotation marks and with Arabic numerals: *Enterprise*; *Apollo 13*; *Titan 4*.

span. It is the part of a bridge between piers or supports. Do not use the word, even in a headline, to mean *bridge*.

spandex is a generic term for elasticized fabric. One well-known brand is Lycra.

Spanish-American War.

Spanish Civil War; *the civil war.*

Spanish names usually consist of the father's family name followed by the mother's family name. Thus in a later reference *José Molina Valente* ordinarily becomes *Mr. Molina,* not *Mr. Valente.* But some people choose to keep both family names in repeated references. Names may include *y* (for *and*): *José Molina y Valente.* A married woman may use her own family name in the middle position: *Isabel Martínez de Perón,* the widow of *Juan Perón.*

　　In the name of a United States resident, use or omit accents as the bearer does; when in doubt, omit them. (Exception: Use accents in Spanish names of Puerto Rico residents.) *See* ACCENT MARKS.

spark, as a verb meaning *incite*, is journalese.

spartan. Lowercase except in references to ancient Greece.

speaker of the Assembly, speaker of the House. Capitalize *Speaker* when it serves as a title before a name, without the separation of a comma. Elsewhere it is always lowercase, but the context must make the term recognizable as a title.

speakeasy.

spearfishing.

Special Forces. Capitalize in reference to the Army's unconventional-warfare units. Their nickname, *the Green Berets,* may stand alone in casual references. *Also see* SPECIAL OPERATIONS.

Specialist *Leslie M. Berenich* (Army rank); *Specialist Berenich*; *the specialist.*

Special Operations. Capitalize in a reference to the unified military command that trains and equips unconventional-warfare units for three branches of the armed forces. The troops are the Army's SPECIAL FORCES, Rangers and Special Operations Airborne Regiment; the NAVY SEALS and Special Boat Units; and the Air

Force Combat Controllers and Pararescue units. The Marines train their own guerrilla unit, known as Marine Force Recon.

species. *See* GENUS AND SPECIES.

specter.

speeches and lectures. Use quotation marks for their titles and capitalize the principal words.

speechwriter.

speed(-). Most but not all compounds formed with *speed* are one word: speedboat, speed bump, speed demon, speed trap, speedup (n.), speedway.

spelling. Words listed in this manual without explanation should be spelled and capitalized or lowercased as shown. For words not listed, spelling is governed by the latest edition of Webster's New World College Dictionary (IDG Books Worldwide). If that dictionary shows more than one spelling of a word, use the one that is given with a full definition. If a word appears neither in this manual nor in the New World, consult the latest printing of Webster's Third New International Dictionary (G.& C. Merriam Company), but only for spelling, not for usage.

This manual is also the first authority for the spelling of place names. Different reference sources—one group for foreign names and one for domestic— govern place names not shown here. *See* GEOGRAPHIC NAMES.

spelling checker. Not *spellcheck, spell check,* etc.

spell out, in the sense of explaining or detailing, is overused. Try *detail, enumerate, explain, list* or *specify. Spell out in detail* is redundant. In the sense of rendering letter by letter, preferably use *spell.*

spilled (not *spilt*).

spinoff (n. and adj.), **spin off** (v.). In a *spinoff,* a company transforms a division or a subsidiary into a separate entity and distributes the shares to holders of the original corporation's stock. A sale is not a spinoff.

spiral (n. and v.) can suggest movement in any direction, not automatically upward or downward. It does not add much in references to things like *costs, prices* and *wages.*

spit. Use the word as both present and past tense (rather than *spat*).

spit and image (not *spitting image*) is the idiom for an exact likeness.

split infinitives are accepted by grammarians but irritate many readers. When a graceful alternative exists, avoid the construction: *to show the difference clearly* is better than *to clearly show the difference.* (Do not use the artificial *clearly to show the difference.*) When the split is unavoidable, accept it: *He was obliged to more than double the price.* Note, however, that compound verbs are an unrelated issue: they should usually be separated (as this one was) when used with an adverb. *See* ADVERB PLACEMENT.

split-up (n.), **split up** (v.).

spokesman, spokeswoman. But not *spokesperson*; in a general reference, use a term like *press officer*. *See* MEN AND WOMEN.

sport (v.) does not mean merely wear; it means wear ostentatiously or flamboyantly: *Even at a dinner for pinstriped Wall Street bankers, the senator sported an iridescent flamingo necktie.*

sports(-). Most but not all compounds formed with *sports* are one word: sports car, sportscast, sports editor, sportsman, sports medicine, sports page, sportswear, sportswoman, sportswriter.

sports sponsorship. If an event has an established name that does not publicize a commercial sponsor, use that name: *the Fiesta Bowl.* But when the sponsor's identity is part of an event's only name, use it: *the Buick Open.* Also use the official name of an arena (*Continental Airlines Arena*), but remind the reader of recent name changes: *Brendan Byrne Arena.*

spring, springtime.

sputnik. Lowercase except in the name of a specific satellite: *Sputnik 5.* Use Arabic numerals.

Spuyten Duyvil (the strait between Manhattan and the Bronx).

squad (police). Lowercase: *sex crime squad; safe, loft and truck squad;* etc.

Squadron Leader *Lee M. Agneau* (British military and others); *Squadron Leader Agneau; the squadron leader.*

Square. Spell out and capitalize in articles as part of a name: *Washington Square.* The abbreviation (*Washington Sq.*) may be used in headlines, charts, tables and maps.

Sr., Jr. *See* SENIOR, JUNIOR.

SS. for Saints, as in the names of churches: *the Church of SS. Peter and Paul.*

SS for Schutzstaffel, the Nazi special police. No periods because the letters are drawn from a single word.

S.S., for steamship, is an appropriate designation for only a relative handful of very old vessels. Except in datelines, write *the liner Queen Elizabeth 2* or *the tanker Exxon Valdez.* In a shipboard dateline, use a locating phrase (but not an imprecise one, like *at Sea*): *ABOARD QUEEN ELIZABETH 2, off Bermuda, July 16*—etc.

SST for a supersonic transport plane.

St. for Street, but only in headlines and charts, maps and tables.

St., Ste. Abbreviate *Saint* and *Sainte* in almost all place names. In references to the saints themselves, generally use *St.* with men's and women's names alike: *St. Agnes; St. George.* The feminine *Ste.* occurs in place names and occasionally in the name of a building or a church. The plural abbreviation is *SS.,* as in *SS. Peter and Paul.*

stable(-). Compounds formed with *stable* are one word: stableboy, stablehand, stableman, stablemate.

stadiums (not *stadia*). Capitalize the names of stadiums, playing fields and indoor sports arenas: *Shea Stadium; Yankee Stadium; the Yale Bowl; Franklin Field; Madison Square Garden* (*the Garden*). *Also see* SPORTS SPONSORSHIP.

staff, staffer. Like *army*, the noun *staff* is collective, referring not to individuals but to the group. For individuals, use *staff members*. References to *three staff* or *many staff*, or to *training staff*, are jargon. Confine *staffer(s)* to informal contexts.

Staff Sgt. *Ashley K. Lam; Sergeant Lam; the sergeant.*

stage(-), (-)stage. Most but not all compounds beginning with *stage* are two words: stage door, stage fright, stagehand, stage-manage, stage manager, stage-struck, stage whisper.

And when *stage* is a suffix: center stage, offstage, onstage.

stalactites hang from cave roofs like icicles; **stalagmites** rise from cave floors. A handy reminder: The *c* in one word stands for *ceiling*; the *g* in the other stands for *ground*.

stanch, staunch. Use *stanch* to mean stop a flow— of blood, for example. Use *staunch* to mean steadfast or resolute.

stand(-). Compounds formed with *stand* can be one word or hyphenated: stand-alone, standby (n. and adj.), standee, stand-in (n.), standoff (n.), standout (n. and adj.), standstill.

Standard & Poor's. In later references: *S.&P. Also see* DEBT RATINGS.

standard-bearer.

standard time. Lowercase the expression standing alone: *9 a.m., standard time.* But *Eastern Standard Time* (and *Central, Mountain* or *Pacific*). Abbreviations: *E.S.T.; C.S.T.; M.S.T.; P.S.T. Also see* TIME.

Star-Ledger, The. The newspaper's office is still in Newark, but *Newark* is no longer part of the name.

"Star-Spangled Banner, The." Use quotation marks for the titles of anthems, as with other songs. *See* SONGS.

Start is acceptable on later references to the *strategic arms reduction treaties: Start I,* signed in 1991, and *Start II,* signed in 1993. *Start treaty* is redundant, and *Start agreement* only slightly less so.

Star Wars. The nickname for the Strategic Defense Initiative, the missile-based defense system advocated by President Ronald Reagan, is acceptable in casual references. A detailed discussion should include the full term at some point.

state. Capitalize *New York State, Washington State* and formal references to any state government: *The State of Ohio brought the suit.* Lowercase *state* in references to a geographic area (*They drove through the state of Illinois*) and when it stands alone (*The state sued the city*). Capitalize when *State* appears with the name of an official agency or with an official title that is capitalized: *the State Education De-*

partment; *State Treasurer Pat Y. Berenich*. Use *State* in references to New York and Washington when necessary to distinguish them from the cities, but omit *State* if the context is unmistakable: *The governors of California and New York have similar powers. Nebraska's population is smaller than Washington's.* Lowercase in the general sense: *affairs of state.*

Do not use *State* in a headline, standing alone, to mean New York State except in a locally distributed section or under a label that makes the meaning clear.

state abbreviations. The abbreviation to be used for each state, after the names of cities, towns and counties, is listed separately, under the full name. Use no spaces between initials like *N.H.* Do not abbreviate *Alaska, Hawaii, Idaho, Iowa, Ohio* and *Utah.* (Do not ordinarily use the Postal Service's two-letter abbreviations; some are hard to tell apart on quick reading.) For a list of cities that do not routinely require state names, see DATELINES. But in articles, omit state names even more freely, so long as no ambiguity results. In particular, when a sentence mentions a series of cities and some carry no state abbreviations, the states should be omitted for all, if clarity permits.

Do not use a state abbreviation after a geographic name that does not designate a specific locality: *Martha's Vineyard, in Massachusetts,* not *Martha's Vineyard, Mass.* (Or use the name of a town on the island: *Edgartown, Mass.*) Other such expressions include *Cape Cod, Nantucket* and *Block Island.*

Abbreviations like *N. Dakota, S. Dakota, N. Carolina, S. Carolina* and *W. Virginia* may be used in headlines when unavoidable (especially for sports teams) and in tables or charts.

State Assembly; *the Assembly.*

State Capitol (the building); *the Capitol.*

state chairman or **chairwoman** of a political party. *Merrill N. Milori, Democratic state chairwoman; the state chairwoman; the chairwoman.*

State Commission of Investigation. The abbreviation, *S.C.I.,* is rarely familiar enough for headlines.

state groupings. Capitalize designations like *New England States, Middle Atlantic States, Middle Western States, Southern States, Gulf Coast States, Mountain States, Pacific States,* etc., when referring to complete groupings.

Statehouse. Capitalize in specific references. In New Jersey it is the *State House.*

Staten Island. The abbreviation *S.I.* may be used only in headlines for editions confined to the New York metropolitan area. Do not use *Staten I.* When necessary, insert a reference to Staten Island after the name of a locale there: *Tottenville, Staten Island.*

Staten Island Botanical Garden.

State of the State Message. For a governor's written report, if it is formally so called. But a related speech is the *State of the State address.*

State of the Union Message. For the president's written report to Congress. But the related speech is the *State of the Union address*.

State Senate; *the Senate.*

states' rights.

State University of New York. A system of more than 60 two-year and four-year colleges and graduate programs supported by the state. The acronym *SUNY* is acceptable on later references and in headlines. Units include the State University at Albany, the State University at Binghamton, the State University at Buffalo and the State University at Stony Brook. Other campuses use the word *college*, but their formal names (*State University of New York College at Brockport*, for example) are often cumbersome. In most cases, a more familiar name, *SUNY College at Brockport*, for example, or *Oneonta College*, can be used, with a graceful notation elsewhere that the school is part of the State University system. The system's Web site provides information about SUNY and its campuses:

http://www.suny.edu

The State University has its own board and should not be confused with the University of the State of New York. *Also see* City University of New York.

statewide.

stationary (unmoving), **stationery** (office supplies).

station house.

statute mile. *See* MILE.

staunch, stanch. Use *staunch* as an adjective to mean steadfast or resolute. Use *stanch* as a verb to mean stop the flow of a liquid—blood, for instance.

St. Bernard (the dog).

St. Catharines (in Ontario).

stealth. Lowercase this term, without quotation marks, for the technology that makes airplanes harder to detect by radar. Though the word is often coupled with a model number, it is not part of the name. *See* AIRCRAFT NAMES.

steam(-). Most but not all compounds formed with *steam* are one word: steam bath, steamboat, steam boiler, steam engine, steamfitter, steam heat, steamroller, steam room, steamship, steam shovel, steam table.

step(-). Nearly all compounds formed with *step* are one word: stepbrother, stepchild, stepdaughter, stepfather, stepladder, stepmother, stepsister, stepson, step-up (adj. and n.).

steppingstone.

stereotypes. Avoid sweeping characterizations of ethnic, racial or religious groups or of the sexes and sexual orientations. And take care to detect stereotypes that are indirect, sometimes known as code words. References to *qualified minority* applicants will fall on some ears as an implication that unqualified is the norm. Calling a black man *articulate* or *well dressed* will strike some readers as a suggestion that these qualities are exceptional. Other readers may find similar overtones in the observation that an Asian-American speaks unaccented English, that religious people are *devout* or that a woman is *decisive*. The best protection is for writers and editors to satisfy themselves that descriptions are relevant, and preferably to demonstrate how. *Also see* ETHNICITY.

sterling. *See* POUNDS AND PENCE.

stevedore. A *stevedore* can be either a waterfront cargo loading company or the company's laborer. *Longshoreman* is another word for the laborer.

Stevens Institute of Technology (in Hoboken, N.J.).

St.-Germain-des-Prés (not *Près*), the Left Bank church and neighborhood in Paris.

St. James's Palace. *Also see* AMBASSADOR TO BRITAIN and COURT OF ST. JAMES'S.

St. John the Divine, Cathedral Church of.

St. Luke's-Roosevelt Hospital, in New York. It has two main centers, at 114th Street and Amsterdam Avenue (formerly St. Luke's Hospital) and at 59th Street and 10th Avenue (formerly Roosevelt Hospital). When either figures in the news, specify the location.

St. Mark's Church in-the-Bowery. The full name has just two hyphens. On later reference, make it *St. Mark's* or *St. Mark's in-the-Bowery*.

St. Marks Place (in Manhattan).

St. Mary Hospital (not *St. Mary's*), in Hoboken, N.J.

stock(-). Most but not all compounds formed with *stock* are one word: stockbroker, stock car, stock certificate, stockholder, stockman, stock market, stockpot, stockroom, stock split, stock-still, stockyard.

stock prices are reported in dollars and cents (or other currencies, when appropriate), rounded to two decimal places.

stone. As a unit of weight used in Britain, it is equal to 14 pounds.

Stone Age.

stop(-). Most but not all compounds formed with *stop* are one word: stopgap, stoplight, stop-off (n.), stopover (n.), stoppage, stopwatch.

store(-), (-)store. Most compounds formed with *store* as a prefix are one word: storefront, storehouse, storekeeper, storeroom.

    Most but not all compounds formed with *store* as a suffix are two words: bookstore, cigar store, department store, drugstore, grocery store.

storms. The National Weather Service defines a storm as having winds of 55 to 74 miles an hour—between gale force and hurricane force. When the service issues a *storm warning*, it foresees sustained winds of those speeds. The word *storm*, though, need not be restricted by this definition: *dust storm, hailstorm, ice storm,* *rainstorm, snowstorm, thunderstorm, windstorm,* etc. *Also see* BLIZZARD; CYCLONE; GALE; HURRICANE; SEVERE THUNDERSTORM; TORNADO; TYPHOON.

story. The preferred word for a newspaper or magazine report is ARTICLE(S).

St. Peter's College (in Jersey City).

straight, meaning heterosexual, is classed as slang by some dictionaries and standard by others. Avoid any use that conveys an in-group flavor. But use the term freely (adj. only) in phrases drawing a contrast with GAY: *The film attracted gay and straight audiences alike.*

strait (passage) is almost always singular: *Bering Strait; Strait of Gibraltar; Strait of Malacca.* An exception is the *Straits of Florida,* though some authorities make that singular, too.

straitjacket (n. and v.).

strait-laced.

strangle. It means not merely choke, but choke to death. Also: *stranglehold.*

strapped, meaning short of cash, is colloquial and trite. And *cash-strapped* is redundant.

stratagem, with two *a*'s, unlike *strategy.*

strategic arms agreements. *See* SALT and START.

stratum, strata. In nonscientific contexts, *layer(s)* is less stodgy.

streetcar.

street-length (adj.).

streets and avenues. In routine references to streets, avenues, etc., spell out and capitalize ordinal numbers through *Ninth.* Also spell out and capitalize *Avenue, Street, West, East,* etc.: *First Avenue; Fifth Avenue; Park Avenue; East Ninth Street.* Use figures for *10th* and above: *10th Avenue; West 14th Street; 42nd Street; West 113th Street.*

Use the plural (*Streets* or *Avenues*) when *and* occurs in a location: *between 43rd and 44th Streets.* But use the singular in a *to* phrase: *along Fifth Avenue, from 43rd to 44th Street.*

Also see ADDRESSES.

stricken. In mentioning the onset of an illness, avoid terms that overstate the patient's disability. Make it *she contracted tuberculosis,* not the dramatic *she was stricken with tuberculosis. Also see* AFFLICTED; SUFFER; VICTIM.

strikebreaker.

strikeout (n. and adj.), **strike out** (v.).

strongman, for a dictator or dominant political figure. Otherwise: *strong man.*

Stroock & Stroock & Lavan, the New York law firm.

structure. As a verb, although bureaucratic-sounding, the term is unavoidable in the sense of setting the terms of public or corporate debt. In other meanings, conversational replacements include *arrange, build, construct* and *organize.*

Students Against Driving Drunk. Its acronym, *SADD*, will rarely be familiar enough for a headline. Note that the phrasing differs from that of *Mothers Against Drunk Driving.*

St. Vincents Hospital and Medical Center (without an apostrophe), in Manhattan.

styles and schools in the arts are listed separately. *See* ARTS TERMINOLOGY.

Styrofoam is a trademark of the Dow Chemical Company for a polystyrene used in insulation and boat construction. It is not used in cups or food containers; for those, write *plastic foam.*

sub(-). Except before a proper noun or in Latin expressions that have migrated into English, compounds formed with *sub* are one word: subassembly, subatomic, subbasement, subcommittee, subcompact, subcontinent, subculture, subdivision, subfloor, subfreezing, sublet, submachine gun, subnormal, subplot, sub rosa (never hyphenated), sub-Saharan, subsoil, substandard, subtext, subtitle, subtotal, subzero.

subcommittees. *See* CONGRESSIONAL COMMITTEES AND SUBCOMMITTEES.

subject-verb agreement. *See* NUMBER OF SUBJECT AND VERB.

subjunctive. Use this form of verb to express a wishful notion or a proposition contrary to fact:

- *The mayor wishes the commissioner were retiring this year* (not *was retiring,* because the commissioner is staying on).
- *If the commissioner were rich, she could retire* (not *was rich,* because she needs the salary).
- *If the bill were passed, taxes could go down* (not *was passed,* because it is still just a hope).

Do not use the subjunctive form (even with a tantalizing *if* in the sentence) when the intent is merely to convert an *is* idea to the past tense:

- *The mayor asked if the commissioner was rich* (the past version of *asks if she is rich*).
- *Secretary Kuzu asked if the bill was going to pass this year* (simply the past version of *asks if it is*).
- But: *If the bill were going to pass, Secretary Kuzu would know by now* (not *was going to pass,* but *were,* because the hypothesis is untrue: the bill is unlikely to pass).

One cue to use the subjunctive is the phrase *as though* or (preferred) *as if.* Either phrase signifies that what follows is contrary to fact: *Secretary Kuzu acts as if she were* (not *was*) *in the White House. The actor looked as if he were sick.*

subpoena, subpoenaed.

sub-Saharan. Use this adjectival form: *sub-Saharan region.* There is no place called the sub-Sahara. *Also see* SAHARA and SAHEL.

subway lines. New York City once had three systems: the BMT (Brooklyn-Manhattan Transit), the IND (Independent Subway System) and the IRT (Interborough

Rapid Transit). While the abbreviations survive in local idiom, they are confusing to visitors and newcomers. Except in direct quotations, use *the A train* (or *line*), *the N train*, *the No. 9 train*, *the No. 4 line*.

such. It is used as an adjective (*such men exist*) and as an adverb to indicate degree (*such big pears*).

such as. In introducing an example (*multinational companies such as Coca-Cola*), the phrase is stilted and should usually be replaced by *like*. The phrase is slightly less stiff when a noun falls between the words (*such companies as PepsiCo*), but *like* remains more fluid. (Some writers believe that *like*, in this sense, can be used only to compare a group to an example *outside* the group: in other words, that *Coca-Cola*, in the illustration above, should not be introduced by *like* because it *is* one of the multinational companies. Usage authorities dispute that rule.)

Sudan (not *the Sudan*).

suffer. Avoid this pitying term in references to people with disabilities. Make it *he has AIDS*, not *he suffers from AIDS*. *Also see* AFFLICTED; STRICKEN; VICTIM.

suffixes and prefixes, with the words they form, are listed separately.

suffocate. Its primary meaning is not merely stop breathing, but do so fatally.

suffragan bishop. *See* BISHOP.

suffragette. Use *suffragist* instead. The *-ette* ending is often considered belittling.

suite (music). Capitalize in a title: *Bach's Suite No. 1 for Orchestra*; *Ravel's "Daphnis et Chloé" Suite No. 2*.

sukkah. The tabernacle, or hut, that symbolizes the Jewish autumn harvest festival of Sukkot.

Sukkot, the Jewish Feast of Tabernacles, celebrates the autumn harvest.

sulfate, sulfite. They are different salts. Verify compounds' names when they occur.

sulfur, not *sulphur*, in all its lowercase forms. Use *Sulphur* in proper names only. Also: *sulfa*, a class of antibacterial drug.

summer, summertime. But: *summer time* for the British equivalent of daylight time.

summit is used as a modifier in phrases like *summit meeting* or *summit conference*, but preferably only when the participants are top leaders of powerful countries. As a noun, *summit* may designate the level or format of a meeting (*the issue will go to the summit*) but is jargon when used as a synonym for *meeting* (*they held a summit*). Resist devices like *minisummit*.

sun. For rare instances of capitalization, see EARTH, MOON, SUN.

Sun Belt.

Sunni Muslims, one of the two major branches of Islam, accept the first four caliphs as the rightful successors to Muhammad. *Also see* SHIITE MUSLIMS.

SUNY, on later reference or in headlines, for the STATE UNIVERSITY OF NEW YORK.

super(-). Most compounds formed with *super* are one word, except before a proper name: superabundant, superagency, supercarrier, supercharge, supereloquent, Superfund (the fund devoted to cleaning up toxic waste), superheated, superhighway, superhuman, superindifference, superman, supermarket, supernatural, superpowers, superrefined, super-Republican, supersaturated, supersonic, superstar, superstate, superstructure, supertanker.

Do not use *super* by itself unless it appears in a name (*Super Bowl*, for instance) or in direct quotations or texts.

Super Bowl is two words, capitalized, and takes Roman numerals: *Super Bowl XXXII.*

Superintendent of Schools *Dale K. Arniotis*; *Superintendent Arniotis*; *the superintendent of schools* or *the superintendent.*

superior general (religious). *The Very Rev.* (or, in certain orders, *the Most Rev.*) *Lindsay X. Baranek, superior general of the Jesuit order* (or *of the Society of Jesus*); *the superior general*; *Father Baranek.* Plural: *superiors general.* Also see ARCHBISHOP; BISHOP; MOST REV., RT. REV.; REV.; VERY REV.

supersede, without a *c.*

supine means lying face up; **prone** means lying face down.

Supreme Court of the United States; *United States Supreme Court; the Supreme Court.* In later references: *the court.* Avoid *High Court*; in a narrow headline, *Justices* will serve. In reporting decisions, include case names and docket numbers (*Burlington Industries Inc. v. Ellerth,* No. 97-569). Note that the title is *chief justice of the United States,* not *of the Supreme Court. Also see* ASSOCIATE JUSTICE and CHIEF JUSTICE.

Surgeon General *Tracy R. Lamm; the surgeon general.* The full title is *surgeon general of the Public Health Service,* not *surgeon general of the United States.* Plural: *surgeons general.*

Suriname, Surinamese (sing. and pl.). Suriname was formerly Surinam and, before that, Dutch Guiana. The adjective is *Surinamese* or *Suriname.* The capital is Paramaribo.

Surrealism. Capitalize in reference to the movement in art and literature that developed in Europe in the late 1910's and early 1920's. Lowercase *surreal* to mean merely bizarre or grotesque. *See* ARTS TERMINOLOGY.

Surrogate *Hilary H. Kikondoo; Surrogate Kikondoo; Judge Kikondoo; the surrogate.*

Surrogate's Court, Surrogates' Courts.

suspect. Fairness calls for *suspect* in referring to people accused of crimes; that reflects the presumption of innocence. But when no one has yet been accused, *suspect* is the wrong word for the person sought or involved. Use *robber, rapist* or a similarly specific term.

suspected. If a *suspected* architect is an architect, then a *suspected* rustler is a rustler. In other words, avoid constructions implying that someone merely *accused* or *charged* has been convicted. Make it *suspected of rustling*. *Also see* ALLEGEDLY.

swath (n., a cleared strip, like a mower's), **swathe** (v., to wrap or bind).

sweatshirt, sweatsuit. But: *sweat pants*.

swimming. Times of races are given in figures: *57.6 seconds*; *0:57.6*. Competitions involve four strokes: breaststroke, backstroke, freestyle and the butterfly. A race with all four strokes is called a *medley*.

Swissair.

syllabus(es), not *syllabi*.

symbolism (art and literature). Capitalize in reference to the European movement of the late 19th and early 20th centuries. Lowercase in more general references. *See* ARTS TERMINOLOGY.

symphonies. Capitalize the designation of a symphony without a nickname or a special title, and use no quotation marks: *Brahms's Symphony No. 1*, or *Brahms's First Symphony*. A literary or fanciful title goes in quotation marks: *Beethoven's "Eroica" Symphony*; *Berlioz's "Symphonie Fantastique."* Capitalize the name of a movement: *the Scherzo*; *the Andante*. Lowercase if the movement is merely numbered or located: *the third movement*; *the finale*. When a work is mentioned more than in passing, the opus or other catalog number follows, in parentheses: *Tchaikovsky's Symphony No. 4 in F minor (Op. 36)*. *See* MUSIC and OPUS.

sync (n. and v.), for *synchronize* or *synchronization*, is colloquial: *in sync*; *out of sync*; *lip-sync*. When a vowel follows the *c*, insert an *h*: *synched*; *synching*.

Synod of Bishops (Roman Catholic).

Syrian Arab Airlines.

Syrian Catholic Church. A Roman Catholic church of the EASTERN RITE.

Szechwan. Use *Sichuan* instead for the province in China. *See* CHINESE NAMES.

T

Tabasco is the name of a Mexican state and a trademark for hot sauce.

table (v.). Do not use *table* as a verb. Its meanings conflict in British and American English. In the United States, it means *set aside* (or *shelve*) a topic on the agenda. In Britain and at the United Nations, it means *bring up for discussion*.

tableau(s).

table d'hôte.

tablespoonful(s). A tablespoonful is equal to three teaspoonfuls.

Taft-Hartley Act.

tailor-made (adj., before a noun).

Taipei (the capital of Taiwan).

Taiwan should be used in datelines after city and town names; the island's capital is Taipei. Either name can serve, in headlines and articles, as a synonym for the entity that calls itself the Republic of China. Because the governments in Beijing and Taipei both claim to speak for all of China, phrasing (except in quotations) should remain neutral on the island's status. While many of Taiwan's people are Chinese (émigrés from the mainland, or descendants of émigrés), the people native to the island are *Taiwanese*.

Tajik(s) for the people of Tajikistan.

take, bring. Use *bring* to mean movement toward the speaker or writer; *take* means movement away from the speaker or writer (in fact, any movement that is not toward the speaker or writer). So the Canadian prime minister cannot be *bringing* a group of industrialists to a conference in Detroit, except in an article written from Detroit. Since datelines do not govern headlines, *bring* in a Times headline usually refers to movement toward New York or toward the United States.

takeoff, takeover (n. and adj.). But as verbs: *take off* and *take over*.

Taliban. The movement of militant Sunni Muslims in Afghanistan, and its members. Ordinarily use the term as a plural: *The Taliban are seeking allies abroad.*

Talmud. The overall term (literally, *study*) for the body of Jewish oral law and tradition. It consists of the *Mishna*, which is the written version of the oral tradition, and the *Gemara*, which is commentaries on the Mishna by later scholars.

tanks (military). Use Arabic numerals in designations: *M-60; M-60's.*

TAP-Air Portugal.

tape (v.), **tape-record** (v.), **tape recording** (n.) Also: *videotape* (n. and v.).

tapping (of a telephone). Distinguish it from *bugging. See* BUG.

taps, the name of the bugle call, is lowercase and takes no quotation marks. It is construed as a singular.

target. As a verb, *target* is military and governmental jargon. Synonyms include *concentrate on, single out* and *take aim at.*

Tass is acceptable in all references to the Russian government's press agency, officially known as Itar-Tass. *Itar* stands for Information Telegraph Agency of Russia. *Tass* was formed from the Russian initials for Telegraph Agency of the Soviet Union.

TB for tuberculosis.

Tbilisi (formerly Tiflis) is the capital of Georgia, the country on the Black Sea.

tchotchke(s), the Yiddish for *knickknack(s)* or *trinket(s),* is also colloquial English, to be used sparingly.

tea(-). Most but not all compounds formed with *tea* are two words: tea bag, tea biscuit, tea cart, teacup, tea dance, teahouse, teakettle, tea party, teapot, tearoom, tea set, teaspoon, tea table, tea taster, teatime, tea tray, tea wagon. *See* TEASPOONFUL(S).

Teachers College (at Columbia University).

team(-). Most but not all compounds formed with *team* are one word: teammate, team play, team teaching, teamwork.

Teamster. Ordinarily use *Teamsters union* in first references to the International Brotherhood of Teamsters (formally, the International Brotherhood of Teamsters, Chauffeurs, Warehousemen and Helpers of America). Also: *the Teamsters.* An individual union member is a *Teamster,* but lowercase *teamster* as a job title.

tear gas (n.), **tear-gas** (v.).

teaspoonful(s). A teaspoonful is one-third of a tablespoonful.

Technicolor is a trademark for color motion picture film and processes. Dictionaries accept a lowercase variation in the general sense of *varicolored* or *brightly colored,* but use those expressions instead, or *multicolored.*

Tech. Sgt. *Dana J. Kuzu; Sergeant Kuzu; the sergeant.*

teenage, teenager. Without a hyphen. Before a noun, use *teenage* (not *teenaged,* except in a quotation): *teenage daughter.* And do not use *teen* as a separate word, even in headlines, unless the reference is to a span of dates or ages (*inventions during the teens and 20's; sons in their teens;* but not *teen smoking*).

Tehran (the capital of Iran).

telecommuter, telecommuting.

telephone calls, telephone messages. Calls are *returned.* Messages are *answered* or *responded to,* but not *returned.*

telephone numbers. For United States, Canadian and similar numbers, including toll-free numbers, enclose the area code in parentheses and use a hyphen after the exchange: *(920) 448-0050.* Use a thin space after the area code, to prevent a line break from occurring there in typesetting. When a business renders its number in words, remove the parentheses around the area code, use hyphens and provide a translation for callers with all-number keypads: *1-800-NYTIMES (1-800-698-4637).* If a number is toll-free, say so; if it is "pay per call" (a "900" number), give the price: *75 cents a minute,* for example.

For telephones in other countries, give the international access code, *011,* followed by the country code, the city code (if any) and the number. Group the numerals with periods or hyphens according to local practice: *011-999-00-555-0123.*

teleprompter is a generic term for a prompting device in a television studio; *prompter* is a briefer synonym. (A company called TelePrompTer stopped making the devices in 1963 and was absorbed by Westinghouse Broadcasting in 1981.)

televangelist has a disparaging tone. Use a neutral term like *religious broadcaster.*

television networks. Omit periods in abbreviations for networks and network subsidiaries, for consistency with the appearance of station call letters, which often adjoin them in news articles. *See* ABC; BBC; CBC; CBS; CNN; NBC; PBS. *Also see* CHANNELS.

television programs. In news articles, use quotation marks around their titles and capitalize the principal words: *"Issues and Answers"*; NBC's *"Tonight"* show; *"The CBS Evening News."* Show applies to entertainment, but *program* or *broadcast* is preferred for news and public affairs except in the expression *talk show.*

television ratings. In audience estimates for television programs, a *rating point* is 1 percent of the number of households that can be reached by a given station or network. NIELSEN MEDIA RESEARCH adjusts the basic audience figure annually. In 1998, it put the number of homes in the broadcast television audience at 99.4 million, so one rating point—for a show sent over the air—was equal to 994,000 households. For cable, however, the number of households in the potential audience differs from one service or network to another, and so does the size of a cable rating point. A *share* is the percentage of the sets in use in a station's or network's audience that were tuned to a given program.

telltale.

temblor (not *tremblor*) for EARTHQUAKES.

temperature-humidity index. The National Weather Service no longer uses this term. *See* HEAT INDEX.

temperatures. Spell out *degrees*, and use figures for a reading: *The temperature was 9 at midnight*; *Heat of 92.5 degrees was reported*; *It was 10 below (or minus 10) at 3 a.m. His temperature was 101.9.* Use figures for a "decade" of degrees: *The tem-*

perature stayed in the 90's for three hours. But spell out a number of degrees (as distinct from a thermometer reading) below 10: *The temperature dropped nine degrees overnight.*

In headlines and tables or charts, use the minus sign and the degree mark: *−10°; 60°.* (The minus sign is an en dash, half as wide as a normal dash.)

Do not write *He had a temperature.* Everyone alive always has a temperature. Make it either *He had a high temperature* or *He had a fever.* Better: *His temperature was 104.*

Also see CELSIUS, CENTIGRADE; FAHRENHEIT; HEAT INDEX; KELVIN.

tempo(s), not *tempi.*

Ten Commandments (the Decalogue). Do not abbreviate or use figures: *First Commandment; Third Commandment.* Also *Tenth Commandment* (an exception to the style of using figures above ninth).

tendinitis (not tendonitis).

Tennessee. Abbreviate as *Tenn.* after the names of cities, towns and counties.

tennis. Give a result this way, using the scores of the sets that made up the match: *Ashley Karitsa won by 7-5, 3-6, 6-4.* (The winner of two sets out of three or three sets out of five wins the match.)

The score of a set (7-5, for example) represents the numbers of games won by the sides. To win a set, the side must normally take six games and hold a two-game lead. If the score of a set is 6-6, the winner is usually determined in an additional game, a *tie breaker.*

A side's score in an individual game ordinarily progresses from *love* (meaning zero) to *15,* then *30* and *40,* which represent one, two and three points respectively. At least four points are needed to win a game. If each side has three points, the score is *deuce,* and one side must then score two consecutive points to win. The side that scores the point after deuce has the *advantage.*

Players hitting the ball back and forth are *rallying,* not *volleying. Volley* means hit the ball before it strikes the ground. The Grand Slam of tennis comprises the Australian Open, the French Open, Wimbledon and the United States Open.

tenpins. Also: *ninepins.* When referring to the game, use a singular verb; when referring to the pins, use a plural.

tenses. *See* CONDITIONAL TENSES; SEQUENCE OF TENSES; SUBJUNCTIVE.

terror-. Compounds formed with *terror* are hyphenated: terror-ridden, terror-stricken, terror-struck.

testimony. Extensive passages of legal or legislative testimony printed verbatim in the body of a news article should be separately paragraphed, in normal body type, full column width, and without quotation marks. Use the attribution labels *Q.* and *A.* (punctuated with periods), but replace them with names entirely in capitals when the speakers are first identified or when the speaker changes. Page designers will specify the typography for the names, depending on the length of the passage. Use parentheses when describing an action that is not part of the dialogue: *Q. Will you kindly point out the figures. (Handing the witness a list.) Also see* TEXTS AND EX-CERPTS. And for the punctuation of a sentence that trails off or is interrupted abruptly, see QUOTATIONS.

Tet (the Lunar New Year).

tête-à-tête.

Texas. Abbreviate as *Tex.* after the names of cities, towns and counties.

Texas A&M University.

texts and excerpts. A verbatim text or transcript, or an extract, begins with an italic introduction explaining the material's nature and source. The introduction specifies any excerpting (and attributes it, unless it is by The Times) and credits the translation, if any, specifying the original language. If the full document is available on the World Wide Web (on The Times's site especially), readers will welcome a Web address.

Transcript denotes a literal rendering of speech. It is *a* transcript, not *the*, because punctuation and paragraphing vary according to the ear of the listener; the introduction should therefore credit the transcribing. *Text* (always *the*) denotes reproduction of a written document. *Excerpts* (always *from*, never *of*) may apply to written or spoken material. (Those distinctions govern headlines as well as introductions.) *Excerpts from the text* is redundant; delete the last two words.

A formal introduction (for a document in current news) normally begins *Following is a transcript of* or *Following is the text of* or *Following are excerpts from.* But if the material is chosen more for flavor than for content, or is drawn from history as a refresher, introduce it with a narrative lead instead, and use a feature headline, possibly a vivid phrase from the document. A one-sentence introduction ends with a colon. A longer introduction may end with a period.

When excerpts are used, editors should select one or a few substantial, coherent sections rather than a larger number of short bites too fragmented to convey the tone of the whole.

If the newspaper goes to press with a speech text issued before the event, the introduction should refer to a *prepared text* or to one *prepared for delivery*; the headline may say simply *text.* In editions that close after the event, *prepared* is deleted, and ideally an actual transcript replaces the text.

Self-contained texts, transcripts and excerpts are not enclosed in quotation marks. Spelling, punctuation and indentions in a verbatim document (though not grammar or word usage) should conform to The Times's style unless literal reproduction is necessary to convey the significance. If the text of a judge's opinion uses italics to designate court cases, substitute quotation marks in any instance that might otherwise be cryptic: *as we learn from "Nixon,"* or *the lesson that "Nixon" teaches us.* In a transcript of a speech, paragraphing should be adjusted for ease of reading.

(Exception: In a long or complex text, occupying at least a full page in the newspaper, the document's own style may be retained literally, to simplify production.)

For the punctuation of an abrupt interruption in a transcript, or of a comment that trails off, see QUOTATIONS. For the treatment of Q. and A. labels, see TESTIMONY.

In verbatim documents—though usually not in news articles—ellipses are used to signal omissions, whether by the newspaper or by the supplier: three dots within a sentence, or three dots after the period at the end of a sentence or paragraph. (For the spacing style, see ELLIPSIS.) Explanations by The Times or the supplier, when the intrusion is unavoidable, are set off by square brackets: *The bomber crashed 40 kilometers [about 25 miles] from the Chinese border.*

Ideally, in a long text, typographical color is provided by the document's own headings. Consult a page designer on the choice of faces and sizes to reflect the relative importance of text sections. If the original document includes numbered or lettered paragraphs, the labels may be detached, enclosed in brackets and boldfaced as headings for eye relief:

[III]
He has kept among us, in times of peace, standing armies, without the consent of our legislatures.

[IV]
He has affected to render the military independent of and superior to the civil power.

[V]
He has combined with others to subject us to a jurisdiction foreign to our constitution and unacknowledged by our laws, giving his assent to their acts of pretended legislation.

[A]
For protecting them by a mock trial from punishment for any murders which they should commit on the inhabitants of these states.

[1]
For imposing taxes on us without our consent.

[a]
For depriving us in many cases of the benefits of trial by jury.

In excerpts, if a heading is omitted in the midst of a lettered or numbered sequence, avoid a jarring effect by deleting the letters or numbers of all parallel headings in that sequence.

text, transcript. A *text* is a reproduction of a written document. A *transcript* is a rendition of a spoken statement or exchange. For the many conventions that govern the printing of verbatim material, see TEXTS AND EXCERPTS.

T, fit to a (not *fit to a tee*).

T formation.

Thai names. Nearly every Thai uses a given name followed by a surname. But in later references, the given name is used with the courtesy title: *Foreign Minister Surin Pitsuwan; Mr. Surin.*

Thanksgiving, Thanksgiving Day. The fourth Thursday in November.

that (conj.). After a verb like *said, disclosed* or *announced,* it is often possible to omit *that* for conciseness: *He said he felt peaked.* But if the words after *said* or any other verb can be mistaken for its direct object, the reader may be momentarily led down a false trail, and *that* must be retained: *The mayor disclosed that her plan for the rhubarb festival would cost $3 million.*

   When a time element follows the verb, *that* is always needed to make quickly clear whether the time element applies to the material before or after it: *The governor announced today that he would organize a knackwurst fiesta.*

   Often a sentence with two parallel clauses requires the expression *and that* in the second part; in such a case, keep *that* in the first part also, for balance: *The mayor said that she might run again and that if she did, her brother would be her campaign manager.*

that, which. Use *that,* not *which,* in a restrictive clause—a clause necessary to the reader's understanding of the sentence: *The town that the pitcher calls home is tiny Hawley, Pa.* (The sentence serves no purpose without *that the pitcher calls home.*) Note that there are no commas around the clause. In a nonrestrictive clause—one providing added information, not essential to understand the sentence—use *which,* preceded by a comma: *Hawley, Pa., which the pitcher calls home, is tiny.* (The sentence is understandable without *which the pitcher calls home.*)

that, who. Use *who* or *whom* to refer to people. Use *that* or *which* to refer to objects and plants. As for animals, use *who* if the animal's sex is known or if it has been personalized with a name. Otherwise, use *that* or *which.*

the. Capitalize uniformly in the names of newspapers, journals and magazines: *The New York Times, The Times; The Daily News, The News.* But lowercase *the* when using a publication title as a modifier (*the Daily News reporter*), because in such a case, *the* is grammatically attached to the noun (*reporter*). Some publication names do not include *the*, even in conversation: *Newsday*; *National Review*; *Reader's Digest*; *Congressional Quarterly*.

Lowercase *the* in names of organizations, companies, schools, restaurants, hotels, etc. And the country is *the Netherlands*, though its capital is *The Hague*. Also see A, AN, THE.

theater, theatergoer. Capitalize *Theater* in names: *the Shubert Theater*. For a consistent appearance in the news columns, where numerous theater names occur side by side daily, use the *er* spelling of *theater* uniformly. Also see ARTS LOCATIONS.

The Dalles (in Oregon). An exception to the usual preference for lowercasing *the*.

thee, thou, he, him, his, who, whom. Do not capitalize, even in references to God, Jesus, the Holy Ghost (or the Holy Spirit) or Allah.

theft. *See* LARCENY, BURGLARY, ROBBERY, THEFT; *also see* MUGGING.

The Hague, an exception to the usual preference for lowercasing *the*.

their, theirs, them, they. These pronouns are plural. Do not apply them to singular antecedents (like *anyone* or *someone*) even when the aim is to avoid assuming maleness or femaleness; other solutions exist. *See* ANYBODY, ANYONE, EVERYBODY, EVERYONE, NO ONE, SOMEONE.

then. Use the word as an adverb (*they were married then*) or a noun (*by then, the game was over*). Dictionaries accept it as an adjective also (*her then husband*; *then-President Carter*; *Mr. Carter, the then president*), but that usage produces clumsy phrasing with the sound of overliteral translation from a foreign language. Replace it with phrases using *then* as an adverb: *Mr. Carter, then the president*; *Leslie T. Lamb, who was then her husband*.

thereby. A musty word, redolent of old lawbooks. Try *that way* or *in that way* instead.

theretofore. *See* HERETOFORE, HITHERTO.

thermos (n. and adj.) for a vacuum bottle or flask. The term is no longer a trademark.

thesauruses (not *thesauri*).

think tank is slang.

third(-). Compounds formed with *third* can be one word, hyphenated or two words: third base, third baseman, third-class (adj.), third degree (n.), third-degree (adj.), third dimension, third grader, thirdhand (adj. and adv.), third rail. Also see THIRD WORLD.

third, thirdly. Use *third*, not *thirdly*, in enumerations. The phrase is a short form of *what is third*.

third world. Lowercase, without quotation marks. The phrase was coined in 1952 to denote countries outside the Western and Soviet political spheres. It has come to mean the economically underdeveloped or emerging nations. Do not use it as a term of disparagement for primitive conditions.

Thirty Years' War.

Thomas Edison State College (in Trenton).

thoroughgoing.

thrash (flog or flail), **thresh** (remove grain husks). In the idioms for grappling with a problem, use the spellings *thrash out* and *thrash over.*

3M. *See* MINNESOTA MINING AND MANUFACTURING COMPANY.

thrift. Use this jargon word as a last resort, in headlines only and as an adjective only, in reference to SAVINGS AND LOAN ASSOCIATIONS and their regulators (*thrift agency*). Do not use *thrifts* or *thrift units* in this context.

Throgs Neck (the bridge and the neighborhood).

throw. Coined as a witty synonym for *give a party*, the colloquial *throw a party* has grown trite. Use *give*. Parties are also *held, organized* or *sponsored*, but never *hosted.*

Thruway. This spelling may be used in names of roads. In New York, it is officially the *Gov. Thomas E. Dewey Thruway* (formerly the New York State Thruway), operated by the New York State Thruway Authority. *Dewey Thruway* or *New York Thruway* can serve as a first reference. In later references: *the Thruway.*

thunder(-). Compounds formed with *thunder* are one word: thunderbolt, thunderclap, thundercloud, thunderhead, thundershower, thunderstorm, thunderstruck. *Also see* SEVERE THUNDERSTORM.

ticket. Use it as a noun only. As a verb (*ticketing a double-parked car* or *stadium ticketing*) it has a bureaucratic sound.

tidal wave is restricted in scientific terminology to a sea wave that is due chiefly to the effects of lunar gravity. For the wave induced by an earthquake or submarine landslide, *tsunami* is the correct scientific term. Because it is relatively obscure, *tsunami* should be explained.

tidelands. The area between the high-tide and low-tide marks.

tie-up (n.), **tie up** (v.).

Tiffany & Company.

tightrope.

'til. Do not use except in quoting a written or printed source. But *till* is largely interchangeable with *until.*

tilde. *See* ACCENT MARKS.

time. Use numerals in giving clock time: *10:30 a.m.; 10:30*. Do not use *half-past 10* except in a direct quotation. Also avoid the redundant *10:30 a.m. yesterday morning* and *Monday afternoon at 2 p.m.*

   Midnight refers to the end of one day, not the beginning of the next. Do not say, *The bomb went off at midnight today.* In a morning newspaper, that should be *last midnight.* References to coming midnight deadlines should elaborate on which day is meant. Avoid *12 a.m.* and *12 p.m.*, which are confusing. Use *noon* and *midnight* instead.

Styles and abbreviations for the principal time zones in the United States are:

Eastern Standard Time, E.S.T.   *Eastern Daylight Time, E.D.T.*
Central Standard Time, C.S.T.   *Central Daylight Time, C.D.T.*
Mountain Standard Time, M.S.T.   *Mountain Daylight Time, M.D.T.*
Pacific Standard Time, P.S.T.   *Pacific Daylight Time, P.D.T.*

Include the time zone when it is pertinent: *10 a.m. yesterday, Central Standard Time* (or just *Central time*). Use *summer time* for the British equivalent of daylight time.

By act of Congress, the legislatures in states that straddle time zones may choose to observe daylight time or not. For those that do, the law sets the changeover times as 2 a.m. on the first Sunday in April, when clocks are set forward one hour, and 2 a.m. on the last Sunday in October, when they are set back an hour.

Greenwich Mean Time (G.M.T.) has been replaced as the world standard by *Coordinated Universal Time*, which is the equivalent but is corrected by atomic clocks to take account of the earth's rotation. The abbreviation for Coordinated Universal Time, chosen as a compromise that would favor neither English nor French, is U.T.C.

Clock times outside the Eastern zone may be translated parenthetically, but only if the conversion is truly useful to readers or if the news event is momentous: *The shooting erupted in the Middle East at 10 a.m. (3 a.m. Friday, Eastern Standard Time). Eastern time* is an acceptable short form of Eastern Standard or Daylight Time, but *New York time* is too parochial. In translations, name the day rather than write *yesterday, today* or *tomorrow.*

An event is dated by the zone where it occurs. If, for example, an earthquake strikes California at 11 p.m. on May 1 (when it is already May 2 in New York), later articles should give May 1 as the date of the quake.

In giving elapsed times of voyages, races, etc., do not use commas: *4 days 16 hours 13 minutes.*

Also see DATES *and* YEARS, DECADES, CENTURIES.

time(-), (-)time. Most but not all compounds formed with *time* as a prefix are two words: time bomb, timecard, time clock, time-honored (adj.), timekeeper, timeless, time limit, time lock, timeout, time sheet, time warp, time zone.

Most but not all compounds formed with *time* as a suffix are one word: all-time (adj.), daytime, drive time, full time (adv.), full-time (adj.), lifetime, longtime, nighttime, overtime, part time (adv.), part-time (adj.), real time. *Also see* ONETIME, ONE-TIME.

Time & Life Building.

time elements in leads. The lead of a morning newspaper article is most often in the past tense. In that kind of lead, the main clause must include a time element—typically *yesterday* or (in a datelined article) *today*. Example: *President Dann signed the fisheries employment bill yesterday, hailing "a new and lasting era of opportunity on both coasts."* (But not: *Signing the fisheries employment bill yesterday, President Dann hailed*, etc.; the time element should not be sidelined in a parenthetical or secondary clause.)

In fluid writing, the best place for the time element is after the verb—immediately after, if the verb has no direct object: *The dean of Cordero University announced yesterday that undergraduates would be required to perform four hours of community service a week.* But if there is a direct object, the object should immediately follow the verb, and the time element should ideally follow both: *Mayor Leslie T. Baranek ordered the police yesterday to arrest jaywalkers.*

When the direct object is long or cumbersome, *yesterday* or *today* must come before the verb, though smoothness will usually suffer: *Mayor Leslie T. Baranek yesterday ordered the police, already complaining of overwork and threatening a slowdown, to arrest jaywalkers.*

Occasionally, if the news is not quite fresh or a direct object is impossibly long, the lead may be written without a time element. In that case, the verb must change to *has ordered* (the present perfect tense). And of course the timing of the action should be specified early in the article.

In a datelined article, use *today* for the day named in the dateline. But do not use *yesterday* and *tomorrow*, which can be confusing under the dateline; instead, spell out the day of the week (*arrives here on Tuesday*). Note that the dateline does not govern the headline. So while *today*, in the article, means the day of writing, the same word in the headline means the day of publication; thus it is often helpful to omit the time element from the headline.

TimesDigest (formerly *TimesFax*).

times less, times more. Writers who speak of *three times more* or *three times faster* often mean "multiplied by 3," but precise readers are likely to understand the meaning as "multiplied by 4": the original quantity or speed, plus three *more times*. For clarity, avoid *times more, times faster, times bigger*, etc. Write *four times as much* (or *as fast*, etc.). And do not write *times less* or *times smaller* (or things like *times as thin* or *times as short*). A quantity can *decrease* only one time before disappearing, and then there is nothing left to decrease further. Make it *one-third as much* (or *as tall*, or *as fast*).

Time Warner Inc.

titleholder.

titles. Personal titles of all sorts — academic, business, foreign, governmental, military, religious, etc. — are listed separately, with abbreviation styles. Lowercase titles except when they appear before full names, and place long titles after names: *Lee P. Milori, minister of internal affairs*. Only official titles — not mere descriptions — should be affixed to names. Do not, for example, write *pianist Lynn C. Arniotis* or *political scientist Tracy F. Baranek*. But in a reference to someone well known, a descriptive phrase preceded by *the* is acceptable: *the sociologist Merrill H. Cordero*. In identifying officials of cities, states or countries, do not make the place name part of the title: *Mayor Stacy K. Bildots of Chicago*, not *Chicago Mayor Stacy K. Bildots*. As an exception, for clarity, *city* and *state* are acceptable in titles: *State Senator Morgan R. Daan*; *City Comptroller Pat C. Berenich*. (Standing without a name, expressions like *the French president* or *the California governor* are proper.) *Also see* FLOOR LEADER; MAJORITY LEADER; MINORITY LEADER.

By tradition, sports positions are a limited exception. Uppercased, an elective or appointive sports title (with a team name) may precede a proper name: *Giants Coach Chris Miel*; *Red Sox Manager Pat Agneau*. Team names and lowercased playing positions may also precede names: *Mets outfielder Terry Lamb*; *Nets forward Chris Cordeiro*; *jockey Lynn Yagyonak*. But do not string other kinds of phrases together as titles; avoid, for example, *suspended Braves pitcher Leigh Dann*.

In the titles of books, plays, speeches, etc., capitalize the principal words (as defined in the entry on CAPITALIZATION): *"Dust Tracks on a Road"*; *The World Almanac*; *"A Taste of Honey"*; *"American Prospects and Foreign Trade"*; etc. For specific styles, see ALMANACS; ARTICLES; BOOKS; CONCERTO; COURTESY TITLES; DICTIONARIES; ENCYCLOPEDIAS; GAZETTEERS; MAGAZINES; NEWSPAPER NAMES; OPERAS; PAINTINGS; PLAYS AND REVUES; POETRY; SCULPTURES; SONATA; SONGS; SPEECHES AND LECTURES; SYMPHONIES.

TNT for trinitrotoluene, the explosive, and for Turner Network Television.

tobacco(s).

to-do (n.).

toe the line, toe the mark (not *tow*). The allusion is to the starting position in a footrace.

toll(-). Some compounds formed with *toll* are one word and some are two words: tollbooth, toll bridge, toll call, toll collector, tollgate, tollhouse cookie, tollkeeper, toll road.

Tolstoy.

Tomb of the Unknowns, in Arlington National Cemetery, was formerly the Tomb of the Unknown Soldier.

Toms River (in New Jersey).

ton. This unit of weight in the United States and some other countries, called a *short ton*, is equal to 2,000 pounds. The *long ton*, used in Britain, is equal to 2,240 pounds. The *metric ton* is equal to 1,000 kilograms, or 2,204.62 pounds. *See* MET-RIC SYSTEM.

Tontons Macoute. The Haitian Creole name (always plural) for a militia that terrorized the population under the Duvalier dictatorship is still sometimes applied to similar gangs. The name, from the singular *Uncle Knapsack*, alludes to the boogeyman of folklore.

Tony Award(s); *the award(s); the Tony(s).* Articles dealing centrally with the awards should mention their formal name, the *Antoinette Perry Awards*, and note that they are presented by the American Theater Wing.

top(-). Most but not all compounds formed with *top* are one word: topcoat, top dollar, top-drawer, top-flight, Top 40 (n. and adj.), top hat, top-heavy, topknot, topless, top-level, topmast, topmost, topsail, top secret, topsoil.

topsy-turvy.

Torah refers to the Five Books of Moses, the first five books of the Bible, inscribed on a scroll (a Torah) kept in the ark of a synagogue. *Torah* in a generic sense refers to all of Jewish learning. Thus: *The rabbi is a renowned Torah scholar.*

torch. Use it as a noun. As a verb it is slang.

tornado. A violent whirlwind. The National Weather Service uses the Fujita scale of intensity to classify tornadoes. Category descriptions are on the World Wide Web:

http://www.crh.noaa.gov/lmk/fujita.htm

The marine equivalent of a tornado is a *waterspout*. (CYCLONE is too ambiguous for routine use.)

tortuous, torturous. *Tortuous* means winding or twisting: *a tortuous road to legislation. Torturous* means tormenting or anguishing: *a torturous ordeal.*

Tory (sing.), **Tories** (pl.). The terms are acceptable in later references and in headlines for the Conservative Party or its members in Britain, and in some other countries; local usage should be verified.

totaled, totaling.

touch(-). Many compounds formed with *touch* are one word and many are hyphenated: touch and go (but: *a touch-and-go situation*), touchback, touchdown, touch-me-not (n.), touch-typing.

touch-tone, for push-button telephone calling, is no longer a trademark.

Tourette's syndrome (the neurological disorder).

toward (not *towards*).

towboat.

towheaded means pale blond.

town house. A *town house* or *row house* is ordinarily a two-story or three-story dwelling that shares walls with the adjacent homes. Not every town house is a *brownstone*.

toxin, toxic. A toxin is a poison produced by a plant or an animal. Do not use the noun to mean any other kind of poison (mineral, for example). The adjective *toxic* applies more broadly, to any poison, and may be useful in a headline about a substance that is not a toxin: *Toxic Spill*, for example.

Toys "R" Us Inc. In headlines, use single quotation marks: 'R.'

tractor-trailer.

trademark, service mark. Trademarks and service marks should be capitalized in news articles and treated as modifiers when idiom permits: *She bought a Minolta camera* but not *He swigged a 7Up brand soft drink*. Though generic terms—*bandage*, for example, instead of *Band-Aid*—are sometimes preferable, brand names can add to precision and enrich detail. They are uppercased as a caution to readers who might inadvertently adopt a name owned by someone else. A *trademark* is a name, symbol or slogan (*Coca-Cola*; *Coke*; *Kodak*; *Mercedes-Benz*; etc.) used by a manufacturer or dealer to distinguish its products from those of competitors. A *service mark* is a name, symbol or slogan (*Blue Cross*; *Century 21*; *Planned Parenthood*; etc.) used by the supplier of a service to distinguish it from the offerings of competitors. In the news columns, do not use registration symbols (® and ™).

To verify ownership, call the International Trademark Association at (212) 768-9886 or consult its electronic Trademark Checklist:

http://www.inta.org/tmcklst1.htm

The checklist is fast and easy to use. But it is not as complete as the database of the United States Patent and Trademark Office:

http://www.uspto.gov/

In using the Trademark Office database, choose "Trademarks," then "Trademark Electronic Search System," then "Structured Form Search."

traffic (v.), **traffics.** But: *trafficked*; *trafficking*. Also: *trafficker*.

tragedy. A *tragedy* is a calamitous or disastrous event. Do not use it for a relatively minor incident, even if sad.

tranquil, tranquilize, tranquilizer, tranquilizing. But: *tranquillity*.

Tranquillity, Sea of.

trans(-). Except before a proper noun, compounds formed with *trans* are one word: trans-Atlantic, transcontinental, transmigrate, transoceanic, trans-Pacific, transsexual, transship, transshipment, trans-Siberian.

transcripts. *See* TEXTS AND EXCERPTS.

transpire. In careful writing, *transpire* means leak out or become known, not simply happen.

Trans World Airlines (T.W.A.).

trapshooting (n.). But: *skeet shooting.*

trash. As a verb meaning destroy or denounce, *trash* is slang—both coarse and trite.

traveled, traveler, traveling.

traveler's check (not *cheque*); *traveler's* is always singular.

treaties, pacts and plans. Capitalize specific names: *Treaty of Ghent; Treaty of Versailles; Pact of Paris; Warsaw Pact.* But: *nine-power treaty; United States-Canadian trade treaty.* Capitalize *Monroe Doctrine, Marshall Plan* and similar designations that acquire official or semiofficial stature. *Also see* NAFTA; SALT; START.

tremblor. Do not use; an earthquake is a *temblor.*

Trenton State College is now the College of New Jersey.

tri(-). Compounds formed with *tri* are one word: triangular, triathlon, tricentennial, tricolor, trifecta, trifocals, trilateral, trilingual, trimester, trimonthly, tripartite, tristate, triweekly. *Also see* TRIMONTHLY, TRIWEEKLY and TRISTATE AREA, TRISTATE REGION.

TriBeCa (*tri*angle *be*low *Ca*nal Street) for the Manhattan area south of Greenwich Village, between Broadway and the Hudson River.

Triborough Bridge. But: *Queensboro Bridge.*

Triborough Bridge and Tunnel Authority; *the authority.* It is a unit of the METROPOLITAN TRANSPORTATION AUTHORITY.

trickle down, in reference to an economic policy, is a polemical term, not for use outside direct quotations.

trigger. As a verb, the word is trite and makes for overheated writing, except in contexts like alarms and weaponry. Calmer alternatives include *incite* and *set off.*

trillion is used in the American sense of one million million. *Also see* DOLLARS AND CENTS; NUMBERS; NUMBERS, ROUND.

trimonthly, triweekly. *Trimonthly* means every three months, and *triweekly* means every three weeks (though some authorities also accept it to mean three times a week). For comprehension, avoid the form when possible and use *every three months* or *every three weeks* or *three times a week.*

Trinity College (in Hartford).

trio. Capitalize in the title of a musical work: *Mozart's Piano Trio in B flat* (K. 254); *Beethoven's "Archduke" Trio.* Also capitalize *trio* in the name of an ensemble: *Vienna Trio.* Do not use *trio* in copy or headlines as a nonmusical synonym for *three* (*Trio Held in Bank Robbery*). See MUSIC.

Triple Crown (horse racing). It is the feat of winning the Kentucky Derby, the Preakness and the Belmont Stakes in a single year; also, informally, the overall name for the three races.

tristate area, tristate region. In a newspaper with nationwide readership, do not use the terms in first references to New York, New Jersey and Connecticut. Instead, name the states. And in later references, *the states* will usually serve.

Trooping the Color (British ceremony). Not *Trooping of the Color*.

troop(s). In its singular form, *troop* means a group of people, often military: *a cavalry troop*. In conjunction with a small number, the plural form means several groups of people: *three Girl Scout troops*. But when the plural appears with a large number, it is understood to mean individuals. *The president sent 3,000 troops to Bosnia* is fine. *Four troops were injured* is not. And whatever the number, the modifier is always singular: *troop movements*.

tropical storms have maximum sustained winds of 39 to 73 miles an hour. Use the assigned names of these storms sparingly, for necessary identification. But do not personalize them with pronouns like *his* or *her*, and do not attribute human traits to them. *Also see* HURRICANE.

Truman, Harry S. He used the period, though he had no legal middle name.

tryout (n.), **try out** (v.).

tsar. Use the more familiar *czar*. *See* CZAR, CZARIST.

T-shirt.

tsunami (sea wave). *See* TIDAL WAVE.

tugboat.

tug(s) of war.

tune up (v.), **tuneup** (n.).

turbid, turgid. *Turbid* means muddy, cloudy or confused. *Turgid* means swollen, distended or bombastic.

turboprop may be used, as adjective or noun, in reference to a plane with propellers driven by turbine engines.

turn(-). Most but not all compounds formed with *turn* are one word: turnabout (n.), turnaround, turnbuckle, turncoat, turndown (n.), turnkey (n.), turnoff, turn-on, turnout (n.), turnover (n.), turnpike, turnstile, turntable.

turnpike. Capitalize in names: *New Jersey Turnpike*; *Pennsylvania Turnpike*. But: *the turnpike*.

Tuskegee University (formerly Tuskegee Institute).

Tutankhamen was the Egyptian king, now popularly known as *King Tut*.

TV for television. Like all abbreviations, it should be used sparingly in articles, to avoid speckling the column of type. The plural, in a reference to sets, is *TV's*.

T.V.A. for the Tennessee Valley Authority.

Twelve Apostles. An exception to the rule of using figures for numbers above nine.

20th Century Fox Film Corporation. No hyphens.

"21" Club (not *Twenty-One Club*), for the restaurant. In headlines, provided the context is clear: '*21*.'

21-gun salute. The ritual often performed at a military funeral is not a 21-gun salute. That honor, fired by cannons, is reserved for a few national holidays and for salutes to a national flag, the sovereign or head of state of a foreign country, a member of a reigning royal family or a president, former president or president-elect of the United States. Lesser dignitaries receive similar honors but with fewer volleys. Graveside ceremonies for military people typically involve three rifle volleys fired by an honor guard.

two-by-four. So spelled and punctuated in a reference to the piece of lumber, despite the usual style for DIMENSIONS.

tying.

type(-), (-)type. Most but not all compounds formed with *type* as a prefix are one word: typecast, typeface, type foundry, typescript, typesetter, typewriter.

Most but not all compounds formed with *type* as a suffix are one word: antitype, blood type, stereotype, tintype.

Avoid the faddish use of *type* to form compound modifiers (*theater-type seating*; *soda-type drinks*). Write *theater seating* or *drinks like soda*.

typhoon. The term is used in the western Pacific region to describe a violent storm of the type called a hurricane in the United States. It is often helpful to explain the similarity. *Also see* CYCLONE and HURRICANE.

tyro(s).

Tyrol (not *the Tyrol* and not *Tirol*).

U

U. for *University* may be used in headlines when the context is clear (*U. of Michigan*; *Boston U.*) and in tables or charts. Do not use *U.* for padding with a name that is otherwise unmistakable (*Princeton U.*).

U.A.W. for the United Automobile Workers.

UBS PaineWebber Inc. is the investment firm formed in 2000 by a merger between UBS and Paine Webber Group Inc. The company's investment banking arm in the United States is UBS Warburg.

U.F.O.('s) for unidentified flying object(s).

UHF for ultrahigh frequency, and *VHF* for very high frequency.

UJA-Federation of New York is the local affiliate of UNITED JEWISH COMMUNITIES, a national organization formed in 1999 through the merger of the United Jewish Appeal, the Council of Jewish Federations and the United Israel Appeal. In later references: *UJA-Federation* (without *the*).

Ukraine, Ukrainian (not *the Ukraine*).

ukulele.

Ulan Bator (in Mongolia).

ultra(-). Ordinarily close up compounds formed with *ultra* unless the prefix directly precedes an *a* or an uppercase letter: ultra-atomic, ultra-German, ultrahigh frequency, ultramodern, ultranationalistic, ultrasonic, Ultrasuede (a trademark), ultraviolet.

In applying *ultra* to a person or a belief, beware of a pejorative suggestion of excess. *Ultraconservative*, for example, can seem to mean *too* conservative. And a faction described as ultra-Orthodox may consider itself merely Orthodox. *Also see* ARCH(-).

umlaut. *See* ACCENT MARKS.

un(-). Nearly all compounds formed with *un* are one word except when the prefix occurs before an uppercase letter: unaffected, un-American, unbiased, uncalled-for, undo, unforgettable, unheard-of, unneeded, un-self-conscious, unselfish, unsolved, untraveled, unused, unwed.

U.N. for the United Nations, but only in direct quotations, headlines, tables and charts and when unavoidable in picture captions.

uncharted waters (meaning unmapped territory), not *unchartered.*

unctuous.

under(-). Most but not all compounds formed with *under* are one word: underachieve, underbid, underbrush, undercharge, underclothes, underconsumption, undercount, undercover (adj.), under cover (adv.), underdeveloped, underdog, underdone, underemployed, underestimate, undergraduate, underground, underhand, underripe, undersheriff, understudy, under-the-counter (adj.), under way (adv.), underworld, underwrite.

    Also see UNDER SECRETARY and UNDERTAKER.

under age, underage. Use *under age* to mean too young and *underage* to mean short-fall. Also: *under-age drinking.*

Under Secretary *of State* (and other agencies) *Toby C. Dann; Under Secretary Dann; the under secretary.* The same styles apply, in international organizations, to *under secretaries general.*

undertaker may be used interchangeably with *funeral director.* Do not use *mortician.*

undocumented. It is a euphemism in references to people who have entered a country in violation of the law. *Illegal immigrant(s)* is preferred.

Unesco for the United Nations Educational, Scientific and Cultural Organization.

unflappable. This British-flavored colloquialism for imperturbable is overused.

unheard-of. A rare exception, this modifier keeps its hyphen even when it follows the noun. In a headline, uppercase the *O.*

Uniate. Do not use the term, which is sometimes applied to Eastern Rite churches in union with the Roman Catholic Church. The word is often regarded as offensive.

Unicef for the United Nations Children's Fund, even though *international* and *emergency* were long ago dropped from the name.

Unification Church is appropriate in all references to the Holy Spirit Association for the Unification of World Christianity, which was founded by the Rev. Sun Myung Moon. Do not use the disparaging *Moonie(s).*

Uniform Code of Military Justice. The first word refers to standardization among the armed forces.

union names may be shortened in later references or in headlines: *the United Brotherhood of Carpenters and Joiners of America, the Brotherhood of Carpenters, the carpenters' union; the United Mine Workers of America, the United Mine Workers, the Mine Workers, the miners' union.* Capitalize references to individual union members (*two Mine Workers, a Teamster*), but lowercase the terms when they serve as job titles. *Also see* TEAMSTER.

Union of American Hebrew Congregations. A Reform group.

Union of Needletrades, Industrial and Textile Employees. In later references, and in headlines when the context is clear: *Unite.* It was formed in 1995 by a merger of the Amalgamated Clothing and Textile Workers Union and the International Ladies Garment Workers Union.

Union of Orthodox Jewish Congregations. Commonly known as the *Orthodox Union,* it represents about 850 Orthodox synagogues in the United States, Canada and Israel.

Union of Soviet Socialist Republics is the full version of the former country name. But *Soviet Union* served in nearly all references and (for historical ones) still does. In headlines: *U.S.S.R.*

Union Pacific Railroad, a subsidiary of the Union Pacific Corporation.

Union Theological Seminary. In later references: *Union* or *Union Seminary* or *the seminary,* but never *Union Theological.*

unique means having no equal, unparalleled. Do not modify the word with a term like *very* or *rather* or *almost*; either something is unique or it is not. On the rare occasion when an innovation fits the description, carefully specify the aspect that does.

Uniroyal Chemical Corporation.

Unitarian Universalist Association. *Unitarian(s)* is acceptable in headlines and in later references to individual members or churches. So is the somewhat rarer *Universalist(s),* but the longer combined form is always accurate. The denomination is theologically diverse and would not call itself Christian, though a significant minority of Unitarian Universalists think of themselves as Christian.

Unite, the Union of Needletrades, Industrial and Textile Employees. It was formed in 1995 by the merger of the Amalgamated Clothing and Textile Workers Union and the International Ladies Garment Workers Union. *Unite* may be used in a headline if the garment context is clear.

United Airlines is a subsidiary of UAL Corporation.

United Arab Emirates. It is a country incorporating seven emirates: Abu Dhabi, Dubai, Sharjah, Ajman, Al Fujayrah, Umm al Qaywayn and Ras al Khaymah. A member emirate is not a country or a nation. The country name, unlike *United States,* is treated as a plural.

United Automobile Workers; *the U.A.W.* Formally, the United Automobile, Aerospace and Agricultural Implement Workers of America.

United Church of Christ. A merger of the Evangelical and Reformed Church and the Congregational Christian Churches. Although the name *Congregational* is technically incorrect, it is still used by many individual churches.

United Jewish Communities was formed in 1999 through the merger of the United Jewish Appeal, the Council of Jewish Federations and the United Israel Appeal.

Its affiliate in the metropolitan area is UJA-FEDERATION OF NEW YORK (singular and with a hyphen).

United Kingdom. This formal name, a shortened version of *United Kingdom of Great Britain and Northern Ireland*, is not ordinarily used except in quotations or in contexts requiring emphasis on Northern Ireland's status. Otherwise use BRITAIN.

United Methodist Church. It is a denomination formed in 1968 by the merger of the Methodist Church and the Evangelical United Brethren Church.

United Nations Charter; *the Charter*. Also: *Chapter IV, Article 9.*

United Nations dateline. This is the style:

UNITED NATIONS, Dec. 4—

United Nations Economic and Social Council; *the Council*. Its acronym, *Ecosoc*, is too obscure for articles or headlines. Do not confuse the Council with UNESCO.

United Nations General Assembly; *the Assembly.*

United Nations Secretariat; *the Secretariat.*

United Nations Security Council; *the Security Council; the Council.*

United Negro College Fund. Informally, it advertises itself as *the College Fund.*

United Press International; *U.P.I.* Always without *the.*

United States. Do not abbreviate, except in quotations, highway designations, texts and organization names that officially include the abbreviation, and in headlines, charts, tables or maps. Use a singular verb with the country name, but form the possessive as if it were plural: *United States'.*

United States Air Force; *the Air Force*. But lowercase *air force* in later references to a foreign air force. *Also see* AIR FORCE RANKS.

United States Army; *the Army*. But lowercase *army* in later references to a foreign army. *Also see* ARMY RANKS.

United States Attorney *Lindsay V. Arniotis; the United States attorney*. Also: *the United States attorney for the Southern District* (or *Eastern District*) *of New York.*

United States Catholic Conference.

United States Coast Guard; *the Coast Guard. Also see* COAST GUARD RANKS.

United States Marine Corps; *the Marine Corps; the Marines; the corps*. Capitalize *Marine(s)* as a synonym for the Marine Corps: *He enlisted in the Marines. A Marine landing*. But: *three marines; a company of marines; the corps*. If the word *soldier* or *soldiers* would fit logically in place of *marine* or *marines*, lowercase the *m*. If *Army* or *Air Force* can be substituted logically for *Marine* or *Marines*, uppercase the *M. Also see* MARINE CORPS RANKS.

United States Navy; *the Navy*. But lowercase *navy* in later references to a foreign navy. *Also see* NAVY RANKS AND RATES.

United States Postal Service. It may be called *the Postal Service* in all references, and in later references *the service* or *the post office.*

United Synagogue of Conservative Judaism. It represents about 800 Conservative congregations.

university. Carefully verify the placement in names; Web sites are often the best source. It is, for instance, *Indiana University*, not the *University of Indiana*; it is the *University of Notre Dame*, not *Notre Dame University*. For consistency in the news columns, lowercase *the* in a university name, regardless of individual styles. Omit *College* or *University* freely in a mention of a well-known institution: *She graduated from Purdue*. Do not use *school* as a synonym for *university*.

University of Connecticut (in Storrs).

University of Medicine and Dentistry of New Jersey (in Newark).

University of the State of New York. It consists of all public and private elementary, secondary and higher educational institutions, libraries, museums and all other institutions chartered and overseen by the Board of Regents. The president of the University of the State of New York is the state commissioner of education. Do not confuse this legal entity with one of its components, the STATE UNIVERSITY OF NEW YORK.

unlike. *Unlike* can be used as a preposition meaning *different from*. The items contrasted by *unlike* must be parallel and therefore comparable. Do not write *Unlike Miami, winter is cold in New York*. That sentence contrasts winter with Miami, not what its author meant. Make it *Unlike Miami, New York is cold in winter*.

As a preposition, *unlike* requires a noun or a pronoun as its object. Revise any construction (*unlike in recent years*, for example) that omits an object.

unprecedented means for the first time. Do not modify the word with a term like *very*, *rather* or *almost*; either something is unprecedented or (far more likely) it is not. Use the term rarely and only after verifying the history. Then carefully specify the aspect that qualifies.

up. As a verb, *up* is colloquial. Accept it in idioms like *up the ante*, but avoid *up the price of sugar* and the like.

up(-), (-)up. Compounds with *up* as a prefix are usually not hyphenated: up-and-coming (adj.), up-and-down (adj.), upbeat, updraft, upgrade, uphill, upload, upscale, upstage, upstairs, upstate, up-tempo, up-to-date (adj.), uptown, upward (not *upwards*).

But: avoid the telegraphic *upcoming*.

Compounds with *up* as a suffix are sometimes hyphenated and sometimes solid: backup, blowup, breakup, buildup, flare-up, grown-up, holdup, hookup, letup, makeup (n. and adj.), pickup, pinup, push-up, runner(s)-up, setup (n.), situp (n.), stand-up, tie-up, tossup, wake-up, walk-up (n. and adj.), warm-up, windup, wrap-up.

upcoming is a staccato holdover from the age of penny-a-word telegram economies. Use straightforward alternatives like *coming, planned* and *scheduled,* if indeed a modifier is needed.

upper(-). Most but not all compounds formed with *upper* are one word: uppercase (adj, n. and v.), upper class, upperclassman, uppercut, upper hand, uppermost.

Upper East Side, Upper West Side (of Manhattan).

U.R.L., for uniform resource locator, is the technical term for an address on the WORLD WIDE WEB. Ordinarily write *Web address* instead. *See* INTERNET ADDRESSES.

U.S. for United States, but only in headlines, tables and charts, and when unavoidable in picture captions. If an organization's name officially includes the abbreviation, use it: *the U.S. Trust Company.* Also, in highway designations: *U.S. 40.*

usage, use. *Usage* refers to habitual or preferred practice in fields like grammar, law, etiquette and diplomacy. *Use* is the less stilted term for employment or consumption: *the use of energy; gasoline use; automobile use; drug use.*

US Airways (formerly USAir).

USA Today. *See* NEWSPAPER NAMES.

user-friendly. It can be reader-tiresome.

U.S.O. for United Service Organizations Inc.

U.S.S. for a United States ship in government service: *the U.S.S. Harry S. Truman.* In articles, however, the vessel type, spelled out, is preferred: *the aircraft carrier Harry S. Truman.* In datelines: *ABOARD U.S.S. HARRY S. TRUMAN, off California* (or a similar locating phrase).

U.S.S.R. (mainly in headlines) or *Soviet Union* in historical references to the Union of Soviet Socialist Republics.

US West Inc. (the regional telephone company). Use a thin space between *U* and *S.*

Utah. Do not abbreviate after the names of cities, towns and counties, even in datelines.

U.T.C. is the abbreviation for COORDINATED UNIVERSAL TIME.

utilize is a fancy word for *use.* Use *use.*

utopia. Uppercase the name of the place in Sir Thomas More's book, but lowercase *a utopia; a utopian enterprise; a utopian* (for a believer in a utopia); *utopianism.*

V

v., vs. for versus. Reserve *v.* for the names of court cases and proceedings. In cap-and-lowercase headlines, lowercase both abbreviations. *Also see* VERSUS.

V.A. for the Department of Veterans Affairs, formerly the Veterans Administration. *See* VETERANS AFFAIRS, DEPARTMENT OF.

Vale of Kashmir.

Valium is a trademark.

Valley. Capitalize when part of a name: *Mississippi Valley*. But: *the valley*.

ValuJet Airlines is now AirTran Airlines.

van (the particle). *See* PERSONAL NAMES AND NICKNAMES.

Van Cortlandt Park (in the Bronx).

variations (music). Capitalize in a title: *Brahms's Variations on a Theme by Haydn*; *Elgar's "Enigma Variations." Also see* MUSIC.

Varig Brazilian Airlines. In most references, *Varig* can stand alone.

Vaseline is a trademark for petroleum jelly.

Vatican I, Vatican II. Use these terms in later references to the First Vatican Council (1869-70) and the Second Vatican Council (1962-65).

VC (without periods) for VIETCONG.

VCR for videocassette recorder. The plural is *VCR's*.

V.D. for venereal disease.

V-E Day, the Allied designation for the date of victory in Europe in World War II (May 8, 1945).

veejay. *See* V.J.

V8, V-8. The vegetable juice is *V8* (a trademark). The engine is a *V-8*.

Velcro is a trademark for fabric fasteners made of tiny hooks and loops.

vendor.

venue. As a synonym for *place* or *site*, the word is sports jargon or show business jargon, best replaced by a less pretentious term. *Venue* is appropriate, though, in the legal expression *change of venue*.

verbal, oral. Use *oral* to convey the idea of spoken words. *Verbal* is less precise; it applies to words used in any manner—spoken, written or printed.

verdict. In legal matters, reserve *verdict* for decisions in criminal cases. For a civil suit, use *award*, *decision* or *judgment*.

vérité (French for *truth*) is a short form of CINÉMA VÉRITÉ or an allusion to it.

Verizon Communications was formed in 2000 by a merger of the Bell Atlantic Corporation and the GTE Corporation.

vermilion.

Vermont. Abbreviate as *Vt.* after the names of cities, towns and counties.

Verrazano is the preferred spelling of the name of the explorer: *Giovanni da Verrazano*.

Verrazano-Narrows Bridge.

verse style. *See* POETRY.

versus. Spell out in ordinary contexts: *It was cowboy versus steer, and the steer won.* The abbreviation *vs.* may be used in most headlines, and for special effect in articles. But in legal contexts use *v.* for the names of court cases. In cap-and-lowercase headlines, lowercase the abbreviations.

Very Rev. The expression is used in the Episcopal Church before the name of a dean of a cathedral or, in some instances, the head of a seminary: *the Very Rev. Lynn J. Cordero, dean of the Cathedral Church of St. John the Divine*; *Dean Cordero*; *the dean.* In the Roman Catholic Church it is *the Very Rev. Lindsay Q. Baranek, superior general of the Jesuit order* (or *of the Society of Jesus*); *the superior general*; *Father Baranek. See* ARCHBISHOP; BISHOP; MOST REV., RT. REV.; REV.; SUPERIOR GENERAL.

vest pocket (n.), **vest-pocket** (adj.).

vet. Do not use for *veteran* except in an organization name like Amvets.

Veterans Affairs, Department of. This federal department succeeded the Veterans Administration in 1989. It operates hospitals and clinics and guarantees mortgages for qualified veterans. In most later references, *the department*; in headlines, V.A.

Veterans Day, Nov. 11, is a federal holiday. Use no apostrophe in the name.

VHF for very high frequency, and *UHF* for ultrahigh frequency.

VHS for the videocassette recording technology.

Viacom Inc. agreed in 1999 to merge with the CBS Corporation. *Also see* CBS.

Viagra is a trademark.

Vice Adm. *Alex T. Barany*; *Admiral Barany*; *the admiral.*

Vice Consul *Ashley C. Kikondoo*; *Vice Consul Kikondoo*; *the vice consul.*

vice president. A government official is *Vice President Ashley N. Cordeiro* on first reference; in later references, *Vice President Cordeiro*; *the vice president*; *Mr.* (or *Ms.* or *Miss* or *Mrs.*) *Cordeiro.* When serving as a nongovernmental title, *vice president* is lowercase, always separated from the name by a comma. The bearers are officers *of* their organizations and *for* specialized duties (regardless of the organizations' usage): *Morgan J. Baranek, a vice president of the Bildots Corporation; Dale E. Lamm, vice president for operations. See* TITLES.

Vice President-elect *Lauren D. Karitsa; Vice President-elect Karitsa; the vice president-elect.* In cap-and-lowercase headlines: *Vice President-Elect.*

vice-presidential, vice presidency. Lowercase.

vice versa.

vichyssoise.

victim. Applied to people with serious illnesses or disabilities, the term conveys an undesired tone of pity, and slights the aspects of their lives that may be unimpaired. Make it *she has multiple sclerosis,* not *she is a victim of multiple sclerosis. Also see* AFFLICTED; STRICKEN; SUFFER.

victorias are the four-wheeled carriages commonly seen in New York. *Hansoms* are covered, two-wheeled carriages with the drivers' seats above and behind the cabs.

Victrola (a trademark). It will usually be found only in historical references, but it is still a trademark and still capitalized.

video(-). Most but not all compounds formed with *video* are one word: video (n. and adj.), videocassette, videoconference (n.), videodisc, video game, videophone, videotape (n. and v.), videotex (not *videotext,* for online data retrieval services).

Vietcong (sing. and pl.). The pro-Hanoi guerrilla movement in South Vietnam during the war of 1954 to 1975, or a member or members of that movement. Also, colloquially, *VC.*

Vietminh (sing. and pl.). The movement of Communists and nationalists in Vietnam in the 1940's and 50's, or a member or members of that movement.

Vietnamese names. A Vietnamese name usually consists of the family name followed by two given names. But Western practice, accepted by the Vietnamese, treats the last part of the name in later references as if it were a surname. So a Vietnamese man named *Nguyen Van Hai* would later be referred to as *Mr. Hai* and in headlines as *Hai.* A woman named *Ngo Phuong Lan* would be *Ms.* (or *Miss* or *Mrs.*) *Lan,* and in a headline *Lan.* If Mr. Hai's wife figured in the news in that role only, she might properly be called *Mrs. Nguyen Van Hai,* and in later references *Mrs. Hai.*

    An exception was Ho Chi Minh, who used his assumed name in Chinese fashion; in later references, he was *Mr. Ho.*

Vietnam War (not *Vietnamese War*).

Village. Capitalize the word when it stands alone to mean Greenwich Village. Do not use quotation marks, which look old-fashioned; if the context in a headline is not clear, find a different reference (*Washington Sq.; Bleecker St.;* etc.).

vilify.

V.I.P.

Virgin Atlantic Airways.

Virginia. Abbreviate as *Va.* after the names of cities, towns and counties.

Virgin Islands. Abbreviate as *V.I.* (with no space) after the names of cities and towns in news articles or datelines: *CHARLOTTE AMALIE, V.I., March 18.* The name of the individual island (St. Thomas, in this case) should be omitted from the dateline but mentioned in the article when it is useful.

Virgin Mary; *the Virgin.*

virtuoso(s).

vis-à-vis.

viscount. Capitalize the first reference as a full name: *Viscount Lamb of Kent; Lord Lamb; the viscount. Also see* PEERS.

viscountess. Capitalize the first reference as a full name: *Viscountess Lamb of Kent; Lady Lamb; the viscountess. Also see* PEERS.

visitation. Except in religious or supernatural contexts (*visitations of angels*), the word is a pompous synonym for *visit* or *visiting.* Use the simpler word: *visiting rights; visiting privileges.*

vitamin A (or *B* or *E*, etc.). Also: *vitamin A2; vitamin B12;* etc.

Vivian Beaumont Theater (at Lincoln Center).

V.J. (not *veejay*) for the host of a television program built around music videos. But use *V.J.* only when a colloquial flavor is in order.

V-J Day, the Allied designation for the date of victory over Japan in World War II.

voice mail. Also: *a voice mail message,* but not *a voice mail.*

Voice of America. Capitalize, without quotation marks.

voilà.

Volkswagen A.G., the German company, can often be referred to simply as *Volkswagen* or, in later references, *VW.* Its subsidiary in the United States is *Volkswagen of America Inc.* In headlines and in colloquial references, *VW* may be used when the context is clear.

von (the particle). *See* PERSONAL NAMES AND NICKNAMES.

voodoo is a religion with many followers in Africa and the West Indies, not to mention the United States. They are offended by disparaging uses of *voodoo* to mean irrational beliefs.

votes. In articles, use numerals for pairs of vote figures or the division of judges in a court decision: *The vote was 51 to 3; The justices ruled 9 to 5 in his favor.* Also: *a 51-to-3 vote; a 9-to-5 ruling.* In such constructions, spell out *to,* but a hyphen may replace it in a headline: *9-5 Decision.* Except when figures are paired, ordinarily spell out nine and below: *She had a majority of nine; He received six votes, four of them invalid.* (But for consistency, in a series that also includes a figure above nine: *She had a majority of 11 votes, 4 of them invalid.* And: *The vote was 51 to 3, with 3 abstentions.*)

voting district. *See* DISTRICT.

vulgarity. *See* OBSCENITY, VULGARITY, PROFANITY.

VW for Volkswagen (the car or the company) in colloquial references, and in headlines when the context is clear.

W

WAC for the Women's Army Corps, but only in historical references; it no longer exists. A member of the corps was a *Wac*.

WAF for Women in the Air Force, but only in historical references; the designation is no longer used. A member of the group was a *Waf*.

Wailing Wall (in Jerusalem). It is now the WESTERN WALL.

wait on. Use *wait in line*, not *on*, which is regional dialect. Also avoid *wait on*, another dialect phrase (from a different region), meaning *await*; make it *wait for* or *await*. (But servers *wait on tables*—never *wait tables*.)

waiter, waitress. *Waiter* and *server* can apply to a woman or a man. While most words with grafted feminine endings (*executrix, aviatrix, poetess*) have virtually disappeared, *waitress* remains in wide use and seems exempt from most objections. Do not use self-conscious coinages like *waitperson, waitron* or *waitstaff*.

wake-up call, except in an instruction to a hotel switchboard operator, is a cliché.

Waldenbooks (the store chain).

Waldorf-Astoria. With a hyphen.

walk(-). Most but not all compounds formed with *walk* are hyphenated: walk-in (adj.), Walkman (a trademark), walk-on (n. and adj.), walkout (n.), walkover (n.), walk-through, walk-up (n. and adj.), walkway.

Wal-Mart Stores Inc. (the national retail chain).

wannabe is the faddish slang of adults who, well, want to be teenagers.

war(-). Most but not all compounds formed with *war* are one word: war chest, war crime, warfare, war game, warhead, war horse, warlike, warlord, warpath, warplane, warship, wartime.

War Between the States. Use only for special effect; otherwise it is *the Civil War*.

Wards Island (in New York City).

War of 1812.

Warrant Officer *Terry B. Daan; Mr.* (or *Ms., Miss* or *Mrs.*) *Daan; the warrant officer*.

warranty, warrantee. A *warranty* is a guarantee or assurance. A *warrantee* is the person who gets one.

wash(-). Most but not all compounds formed with *wash* are one word: washable, wash-and-wear, washbowl, washcloth, washed-out (adj.), washout (n.), washroom.

Washington. Abbreviate the state name as *Wash.* after the names of cities, towns and counties. When *Washington State* is needed for clarity, uppercase *State.* And when there is no likelihood of confusion in references to the national capital, omit *D.C. Also see* DISTRICT.

Washington Arch (not the *Washington Square Arch*) is the monument in Washington Square.

Washington Heights; *the Heights.* In first references, do not use *the* before *Washington.* In headlines, charts, tables and maps: *Washington Hts.*

Washington's Birthday is the official name of the federal holiday observed on the third Monday in February. Because some states use the holiday to honor both Washington and Lincoln, it is popularly known as *Presidents' Day.* But other states (including New York, New Jersey and Connecticut) have designated Feb. 12, *Lincoln's Birthday,* as a separate holiday.

WASP, for white Anglo-Saxon Protestant, is usually disparaging to a segment of the population wrongly thought to be impervious to slurs.

water(-). Most but not all compounds formed with *water* are one word: water bed, watercolor, water-cooled, water cooler, watercress, waterfall, waterfront, waterline, waterlogged, water main, watermark, watermelon, water meter, water mill, water pipe, waterproof, water-repellent, water-resistant, watershed, waterside, water ski (n.), water-ski (v.), waterspout, water table, watertight, waterway, waterworks.

waterspout. A violent whirlwind that occurs over water. *Also see* TORNADO.

wavelength(s).

Waves for Women Accepted for Volunteer Emergency Service, a term once used by the Navy but now discontinued. A *Wave* was a member of that group.

W.C.T.U. for the National Women's Christian Temperance Union.

weapons. Terms for many types of weapon, from pistols and rifles to missiles, appear in separate listings.

weapons plant (not *weapon plant*) is the idiom.

(-)wear. Most but not all compounds formed with *wear* are one word: children's wear, eyewear, footwear, formal wear, headwear, men's wear, rainwear, sportswear, swimwear, women's wear.

weather. *See* BLIZZARD; CYCLONE; GALE; HEAT INDEX; HURRICANE; NORTHEASTER; SEVERE THUNDERSTORM; STORM; TORNADO; TYPHOON; WIND CHILL.

Weather Service. Capitalize in later references to the *National Weather Service.*

Web site, for a collection of documents offered for access on the WORLD WIDE WEB.

Web, the. This form may be used after a first reference to the WORLD WIDE WEB.

week(-). Compounds formed with *week* are one word: weekday, weekend, weekender, weeklong, weekly, weeknight.

weeks. Capitalize officially designated weeks: *Parsnip Week; Mildew Week;* etc.

weight lifter, weight lifting.

weights and measures. Many common units of weight and measure used in the English-speaking countries, as well as many metric units, are listed separately. *Also see* MET- RIC SYSTEM.

Weill Medical College of Cornell University was formerly Cornell University Medical College, in New York. Its full name, rarely necessary, is the *Joan and Sanford I. Weill Medical College and Graduate School of Medical Sciences of Cornell University.*

Weimaraner (the dog).

weird.

well(-). Nearly all modifiers formed with *well* are hyphenated when they occur before nouns: well-advised, well-behaved, well-bred, well-done, well-founded, well-groomed, well-intentioned, well-known, well-mannered, well-nigh, well-read, well-rounded, well-spoken, well-thought-of, well-timed, well-to-do, well-worn.

Thus: *He is a well-read man.* But omit the hyphen when such a compound follows the word it modifies: *He is well read.*

Also: well-being, wellhead, well-wisher.

welsh, meaning renege on an obligation, is slang and an ethnic slur (even if often un- recognized by the user).

Wesleyan University (in Middletown, Conn.).

west. Capitalize when referring to the region of the United States, to Europe and the Americas, to the group of nations that opposed the Communists or to a specific re- gion so named: *West Texas.* Lowercase as a point of the compass.

West Bank, East Bank (of the Jordan River). Because its status is evolving, do not treat the West Bank as a sovereign territory or as an official part of Israel or Jordan; use the territory name in a dateline after the name of a city or town.

West Berlin, East Berlin. *See* BERLIN.

Westchester (N.Y.), **West Chester** (Pa.).

west coast. Capitalize when referring to the region of the United States along the Pa- cific, but lowercase when referring to the actual shoreline. Do not use *Coast* standing alone as a reference to the West Coast.

West End (of London).

western. Capitalize when referring to the region of the United States, to Europe and the Americas or to the group of nations that opposed the Communists. But: *western Ohio; western France; western half;* etc. And: *western movie; a television western.*

Westerner, for a person of the Western United States or, in an Asian context, of Europe or the Americas. But: *westernize(d)*.

Western Front, the battlefront in World War I.

Western Hemisphere; *the hemisphere.*

Western Wall is the name that replaced Wailing Wall, in Jerusalem. The change was intended to symbolize modern Israel's emergence from despair.

West Germany. *See* GERMANY.

Westhampton (in Suffolk County, N.Y.). Spellings for nearby towns differ: *East Hampton, Bridgehampton, Southampton.*

West Indian. This term applies to people from the former British colonies in the Caribbean. It does not refer to people from Cuba, Puerto Rico or Central or South America.

West Indies. Do not abbreviate after the names of cities and towns, even in datelines. In most datelines, provided an island is specified, *West Indies* may be omitted.

Westinghouse Electric Corporation changed its name in 1997. *See* CBS.

West Side. Capitalize when the term regularly designates a section of a city. But in London it is the *West End.*

West Side Highway. At least in formal references, it is now *Joe DiMaggio Highway.*

West Texas.

West Virginia. Abbreviate as W.Va. (without a space) after the names of cities, towns and counties. As a last resort, and somewhat more readily in the sports pages, use *W. Virginia* in a headline.

Weyerhaeuser Company.

wharf (sing.), **wharves** (pl.).

Wharton School (of the University of Pennsylvania). It is no longer the Wharton School of Finance and Commerce.

wheelchair. People *use wheelchairs* or *are in wheelchairs.* Do not write *confined to a wheelchair*, a phrase that may exaggerate the user's immobility. When possible, say why the person uses a chair: *He has used a wheelchair since he lost both legs in Vietnam.*

whence means *from where.* So *from whence* is redundant.

whereabouts. Construe it as a singular: *Her whereabouts was unknown.*

whether. Often *or not* is redundant after *whether*, but not always. The phrase may ordinarily be omitted in these cases:

- When the *whether* clause is the object of a verb: *She wonders whether the teacher will attend.* (The clause is the object of *wonders.*)
- When the clause is the object of a preposition: *The teacher will base his decision on whether the car has been repaired.* (The clause is the object of *on.*)

- When the clause is the subject of the sentence: *Whether the car will be ready depends on the mechanic.* (The clause is the subject of *depends.*)

But when a *whether* clause modifies a verb, *or not* is needed: *They will play tomorrow whether or not it rains.* (The clause modifies *play.*)

Some sentences require a choice between *whether* and *if.* Often both are correct: *Leslie wonders whether* (or *if*) *she should take algebra.* But when the sentence explicitly describes a choice, *whether* is preferred: *Toby wonders whether she should take chemistry or physics.* (The clue is *or.*) Sometimes an *if* sentence, although correct, is ambiguous while *whether* would be unmistakable. *Tell Leslie if she should take algebra* could mean talk to her regardless of your recommendation. But it could also mean *If Leslie should take algebra, tell her*—that is, talk to her only if your recommendation is yes.

which, that. In introducing clauses, the words are not interchangeable. *See* THAT, WHICH.

whimsy, whimsies.

whip (legislative title). Lowercase: *Merrill J. Lam, the Republican whip in the House.*

whiskey(s). The general term covers bourbon, rye, Scotch and other liquors distilled from a mash of grain. For consistency, use this spelling even for liquors (typically Scotch) labeled *whisky. Also see* ALCOHOLIC BEVERAGES.

white. Lowercase this racial designation and all others derived from skin color (*black, brown, yellow, red*). Use racial designations only when they are pertinent and their pertinence is clear to the reader.

white(-). Most but not all compounds formed with *white* are hyphenated: whitecap, white-collar (adj.), white-faced, whitefish, white-haired, white-hot, white paper, white room, white sale, white sauce, white-shoe (adj.), whitewall, whitewash.

wholehearted.

W.H.O. for the World Health Organization.

who, whom. Many dictionaries have relaxed the distinction between these words, abandoning *whom* unless it directly follows a preposition. But in deference to a grammar-conscious readership and a large classroom circulation, The Times observes the traditional standard:

Use *who* in the sense of *he, she* or *they*: *Pat L. Milori, who was appointed to fill the vacancy, resigned.* (*He* or *she* was appointed.) Use *whom* in the sense of *him, her* or *them*: *Pat L. Milori, whom the board recommended, finally got the job.* (The board recommended *her* or *him.*) The same test applies to *whoever* and *whomever*: *Whoever wins will collect $64.* (*He* or *she* wins.) *Whomever you ask will provide directions.* (You ask *her* or *him.*)

Sometimes *whoever* or *whomever* will occur, confusingly, in a clause that is part of a larger sentence. In that case, disregard the overall sentence, and choose the pronoun according to its function inside the clause: *Give the book to whoever answers the door.* (*He* or *she* answers.) *Hand the package to whomever you see first.* (You see *her* or *him*.)

Do not be distracted by a verb that occurs in a parenthetical phrase between the pronoun and its verb, in a construction like this: *Pat L. Milori, who the police said was the mastermind, was arrested yesterday.* Mentally remove *the police said*, and the need for *who* becomes clear. But in this sentence, *whom* is correct: *Pat L. Milori, whom the police described as the mastermind, was arrested today.* (They described *him* or *her*.)

Occasionally the traditional use of *whom* may sound stilted, especially in large type: *Whom Should They Blame?* Do not simply substitute *who*; instead, rephrase the passage: *Who Gets the Blame?* or *Whose Fault Is It?*

wide(-), (-)wide. Compounds with *wide* as a prefix are almost always hyphenated when they precede the nouns they modify (and are two words otherwise): wide-angle, wide-awake, wide-brimmed, wide-eyed, wide-open, wide-screen; widespread.

As a simple adjective or as part of a noun, *wide* is usually a separate word: a wide angle, a wide receiver.

Compounds with *wide* as a suffix are solid: boroughwide, citywide, continentwide, countrywide, industrywide, nationwide, statewide, worldwide. But: *World Wide Web.*

wide-body (n. and adj.) for large planes like the DC-10, L-1011, 767, 777, A330 and A340.

widow, widower. Identify a woman by her marital status only when it is clear that a man would be identified that way in the same context. And cite marital status only when it is pertinent. *Also see* MEN AND WOMEN and OBITUARIES.

wife. Use the word only in ways that *husband* would be used. In particular, avoid *his wife* in contexts that imply an unequal relationship. *See* MEN AND WOMEN.

Wildlife Conservation Society. Formerly called the New York Zoological Society, it operates the BRONX ZOO, the CENTRAL PARK ZOO, the PROSPECT PARK ZOO, the QUEENS ZOO and the NEW YORK AQUARIUM, all on city property. It is based at the Bronx Zoo.

Wilkes-Barre (in Pennsylvania).

William Paterson University (in Wayne, N.J.).

Williamsburg for the New York bridge, the Brooklyn neighborhood and the Virginia city (*Colonial Williamsburg*). But: *the Dime Savings Bank of Williamsburgh.*

wind chill is a measurement devised by the National Weather Service to describe the combined effects of sustained winds and low air temperatures on exposed skin. It is expressed in degrees Fahrenheit. For example, if the air temperature is minus 20 and the wind speed is 10 miles an hour, the wind chill, according to the Weather

Service chart, is minus 46. (In those conditions, the human body loses heat as fast as it would if the temperature were 46 below and there were no wind.) Wind chill begins to become dangerous around minus 25, the point at which exposed flesh may freeze in a minute. The Weather Service's wind chill chart is on the World Wide Web:

http://www.nws.noaa.gov/er/box/tables/windchill.html

windfall. A windfall is not just any gain or stroke of good luck but a sudden or unexpected one.

Windows is Microsoft's trademark for its series of operating systems, the programs that perform the central functions in a personal computer. Windows (and later Windows 95 and 98) added "look and feel" features to simplify the entry of commands to the predecessor system, DOS. *Also see* DOS.

wind up (v.), **windup** (n. and adj.).

wine(-). Most but not all compounds formed with *wine* are one word: wine cellar, wine-colored, wine cooler, wineglass, winegrower, winemaker, wineskin, wine steward.

wines and spirits. When a wine is named for the town or region that produces it, uppercase the name, as noun or adjective: *Beaujolais*; *Bordeaux*; *Burgundy*; *Champagne*; *Chianti*; *Mosel*; *Rhine wine*; *Rioja*; *Sauternes*; etc. The same is true of a distilled liquor, or brandy: *Armagnac*; *Cognac*. When using such a term loosely or generically, also uppercase: *Wall Street is enjoying a season of caviar and Champagne*; *The couple received Champagne glasses*; *The senator favors a sip of Cognac*. But lowercase a regional name when applying it specifically to a wine or spirit produced elsewhere: *a California burgundy*; *Russian cognac*; *an Australian champagne*. (It is often more precise to write *Russian brandy* or *an Australian sparkling wine*.)

Lowercase *sherry* and *port* because they are not place names although derived from them.

Lowercase varietal names (the names of grape types) serving as wine designations: *cabernet sauvignon*; *pinot noir*; *chardonnay*; *gewürztraminer*; *merlot*; *riesling*; *sémillon*; *sylvaner*; *zinfandel*. An exception is *Müller-Thurgau*, a German varietal named for its developer. Consult a wine guide to distinguish between varietal and regional names.

Uppercase a name used as a brand or trademark, regardless of where the wine is produced: *Gallo Hearty Burgundy*; *Napa Ridge Zinfandel*.

Also see ALCOHOLIC BEVERAGES.

Wing Cmdr. *Dana L. Lamb* (in British and other foreign air forces); *Wing Commander Lamb*; *the wing commander*.

wingspan, wingspread.

winter, wintertime. The adjective is *wintry*.

wiretapping. Do not confuse with bugging. *See* BUG.

Wisconsin. Abbreviate as *Wis.* after the names of cities, towns and counties.

(-)wise. Use this suffix with care. It forms standard compounds like *clockwise, lengthwise, otherwise, penny-wise* and *slantwise*. It is also commonly accepted in *streetwise* and in *weather-wise*, meaning informed about weather: *He was a weather-wise old mariner*. But avoid faddish uses that seem to parody Madison Avenue: *Weather-wise, it was a terrible day*.

within, without. Ordinarily use *in* rather than the pretentious *within*, in sentences like this: *Ms. Karitsa had no enemies within the party*. And *without* is often unclear or unconversational: *Ms. Kikondoo's critics within and without the industry were seldom silent*. Make it *in and out of the industry* or *inside and outside the industry*. The fancier phrase may be justified (sparingly), though, when the two words act as adverbs, without an object: *They defended the country from enemies within and without*.

witness protection program is acceptable in nearly all references to the federal Witness Security Program and to similar state programs.

woebegone.

women and men. *See* MEN AND WOMEN.

women's wear.

Woodbridge, Wood-Ridge (N.J.). Woodbridge is in Middlesex County. Wood-Ridge is in Bergen County.

Woods Hole (in Massachusetts).

woolen, woolly.

word division. When a word must be divided at the end of a line of type, use the breaks shown in the latest printing of Webster's New World College Dictionary, which are generally programmed into The Times's computers. Under deadline pressure, editors are not expected to verify word breaks, but they should know a few principles.

Because its columns are narrow, unlike those of books, The Times permits a break before or after a two-letter syllable, provided it is pronounceable (*in-tend, want-ed*, but not *hop-ed*). In the American system, pronunciation governs division (*photog-raphy*, for example), while the British system relies on word origins (*photo-graphy*). For some words spelled identically, division depends on the sense (*pro-duce* for the verb, *prod-uce* for the noun meaning fruits and vegetables). Such words are called homographs, and The Times's computers are ordinarily programmed to keep them intact rather than risk error.

Editors should be alert to names that the computer may mishandle, especially in foreign news and the arts. Consonant combinations like *gn* in French or Italian, *sz* and *cz* in Polish and *kh, zh* and *shch* in Russian should not be broken and usually belong at the start of a syllable. When it is necessary to override the computer, insert a "discretionary hyphen" symbol (shown here as "··") at the preferred break point: *Ti··khon*. Used at the start of a word, the symbol will prevent any break: *··vignes*.

wordplays. *See* PUNS.

work(-). Most but not all compounds formed with *work* are one word: workaday, workaholic, workbench, work camp, workday, work ethic, workfare, work force, workhorse, workhouse, workload, workman (or workingman), workmanlike, workmanship, workout (n.), workplace, work-release (adj.), workshop, workstation, work-study (adj.), workweek.

workers' compensation. Always a plural possessive for the insurance system, formerly known as workmen's compensation.

World Airways.

World Bank may be used in most references to the International Bank for Reconstruction and Development; the official name should appear somewhere in any article dealing centrally with the institution. In later references: *the bank*.

world-class. But do not hyphenate when it follows what it modifies: *The boat was world class*.

World Council of Churches. An organization of Protestant and Orthodox churches, including most major ones. Its members are denominations, not countries. Its headquarters are in Geneva, and its chief executive is a general secretary (not secretary general). The highest policy-making body is the general assembly, which meets every six or seven years. Interim policy is set by the central committee, which has more than 100 members and meets at intervals of about 18 months.

World Court may be used in most first and later references to the International Court of Justice, in The Hague. Also, in later references: *the court*. The formal name should appear somewhere in any article dealing centrally with the court.

World Cup. The most prominent event bearing this name is the international soccer championship.

World Financial Center (in Manhattan).

World Series. In later references: *the Series*. Also: *Little League World Series*.

World Trade Center (in Manhattan). In later references: *the trade center*.

worldview.

World War I, World War II. *First World War* and *Second World War* may also be used, but the Roman numeral forms are preferred. Also: *a world war; a third world war; the world wars*.

worldwide. But: *World Wide Web*.

World-Wide Shipping, the ocean carrier.

World Wide Web, the global library of multimedia documents (text, sound and images) shared over the INTERNET. In later references: *the Web*. Also, acceptable even on first references: *Web site(s)*. Note that in all other contexts, *worldwide* is a solid word. *See* INTERNET ADDRESSES.

worshiped, worshiper, worshiping.

worth. Use the apostrophe in expressions like *a year's worth, five days' worth, money's worth, million dollars' worth*. But with the currency symbol: $5 *million worth*.

wrack. *See* RACK, WRACK.

W. Virginia. The abbreviation may be used as a last resort in headlines (although more freely in the sports pages) and in charts and tables.

www, in INTERNET ADDRESSES, for the World Wide Web.

Wyoming. Abbreviate as *Wyo.* after the names of cities, towns and counties.

X

Xerox is a trademark for a photocopying process. Do not use it as a verb or as a generic term for a photocopy.

Xmas. Do not use; spell out *Christmas*.

X-rated. In headlines: *X-Rated*.

X-ray. (n., adj., v.). In headlines: *X-Ray*.

Y

Yale University. In many casual references, *Yale* can stand alone, for the university or for its undergraduate college.

Yangon, formerly Rangoon, is the capital of Myanmar, formerly Burma.

Yangtze River.

yard(-), (-)yard. Most but not all compounds formed with *yard* as a prefix are one word: yardage, yardarm, yard goods, yardmaster, yard sale, yardstick.

Compounds formed with *yard* as a suffix are one word: backyard, barnyard, churchyard, graveyard, lumberyard, schoolyard, shipyard, steelyard. An exception: *front yard.*

yarmulke. Yiddish for *skullcap*. Because American Jews increasingly use the Hebrew term *kipa* instead of *yarmulke, skullcap* is often preferable in print.

year(-). Most but not all compounds formed with *year* are one word: yearbook, year-end, yearling, yearlong (adj.), year-round (adj.).

years, decades, centuries. Use numerals for specific years (*1492, 1995, mid-1997*) and decades and centuries (*the 1990's, the 1800's, the mid-1700's*). Use an apostrophe when reducing a year to two digits: *the class of '93; mid-'75.* Omit the apostrophe before a two-digit designation of a decade: *the 90's.* First references in articles should usually give all four digits (*1990, the 1980's*), but the shorter forms (*'90 or 90's or mid-90's*) are acceptable in later references and in headlines. Nicknames of decades should be spelled out and capitalized: *the Gay Nineties; the Roaring Twenties.*

Give spans of years this way: *1861-65; 1880-95; 1895-1900; 1903-4* (not *1903-04*). Spell out and lowercase the numbers of centuries from first through ninth: *the first century; the eighth century.* Use numerals from 10th on: *the 12th century; the 19th century.* Hyphenate the modifier form: *eighth-century ruins; 17th-century house.*

If, rarely, a year or a decade must begin a sentence, spell and capitalize the numbers: *Nineteen sixty-seven was not his lucky year; Nineteen-eighties answers are no longer valid.* More often, in such a case, the sentence can be rephrased: *The answers of the 1960's . . .* or *The year 1967 was not. . . .*

Omit commas when a year is used with a month alone: *the January 1995 issue of Gristle, the magazine of meat cutting.* But punctuation is essential before and after the year when it follows a specific date: *the March 5, 1994, proclamation.*

Technically a century begins with the "01" year—1901, 2001, etc.—because there was no year 0. But in the popular consciousness, "turn of the century" means 1900, 2000, etc. That informal style is acceptable in references to celebrations, observances and social or cultural turning points. Articles dealing centrally with the calendar should mention the literal interpretation, but without belittling popular usage.

Also see DATES and MONTHS.

Yerevan, formerly Erivan, is the capital of Armenia.

yeses and noes.

Y.M.C.A., Y.M.H.A., Y.W.C.A., Y.W.H.A. But the 92*nd Street* Y in Manhattan (actually a Y.M.-Y.W.H.A.) is always known by the short form of its name.

yogurt.

yoke (n. and v.), never *yolk*, for a tight or burdensome bond. The allusion is to a shoulder harness, of an ox team or a bucket carrier.

Yoknapatawpha County.

Yom Kippur, the Day of Atonement. Yom Kippur and Rosh Hashana are the High Holy Days (preferred, rather than *High Holidays*) of Judaism.

York College (part of the CITY UNIVERSITY OF NEW YORK).

Young Turk(s). Uppercase only in a reference to insurgents in a political group or other organization.

Yucatán (in Mexico).

Yugoslavia. The name applies to the central government in Belgrade and its federal apparatus, most prominently the Yugoslav National Army. In a dateline specify the republic instead: *BELGRADE, Serbia, Sept. 22* or *PODGORICA, Montenegro, Feb. 11.* In articles it is often necessary to distinguish between Serbian republic and Yugoslav federation officials, armed forces, legislatures, etc., though Serbs dominate throughout. The noun and adjective are *Yugoslav(s)*, not *Yugoslavian(s)*.

The country consists only of the republics of Serbia and Montenegro, which in turn comprise provinces. After the collapse of Communism, four republics in the Yugoslav federation became independent: Bosnia and Herzegovina (1992); Croatia (1991); Macedonia (1992, generally recognized in 1995); and Slovenia (1991).

Yukon Territory (of Canada). Do not abbreviate after the names of cities and towns, even in datelines. In later references: *the Yukon.*

Yule, Yuletide. They are trite. Just write *Christmas.*

yuppie. The colloquial term is derived from *y*oung *u*rban *p*rofessional, and it is graying fast. So are its many offspring, like *buppie* (*b*lack *u*rban *p*rofessional) and *ouppie* (*o*ld *u*rban *p*rofessional).

Z

Zaire. The central African country has gone back to an older name. *See* CONGO.

zeitgeist. When it appears in an English phrase, lowercase the German noun meaning "spirit of the age." Still better, resist it, as pretentious.

zero(s).

zigzag (adj., n., v.).

Zim Israel Lines (the ocean carrier).

zine. The colloquial term for a small magazine (usually amateur and often online) takes no apostrophe.

ZIP code. The first word is all uppercase, the second all lowercase. Do not use a comma between the name of the state and the ZIP code. When giving the nine-digit version, use a hyphen after the first five digits: *New York, N.Y. 10036-3959.*

zoom. In the sense of rapid movement, the word describes only upward motion. *Zooming sounds* and *zoom lenses* are another matter.

STANDARD PROOFREADING MARKS

∧	Make correction indicated in margin.	WF	Wrong font.
STET	Retain crossed-out material.	CAP	Uppercase.
RUN IN	No new paragraph.	≡	Uppercase.
NO ¶	No new paragraph.	ROM	Change to roman.
OUT; SEE COPY	Some material dropped; see copy.	ITAL	Change to italic.
¶	Begin a new paragraph.	___	Change to italic.
⊔⊓	Transpose words or characters.	∿	Change to bold.
TR	Transpose words or characters.	BF	Change to bold.
ℓ	Delete.	⌃	Insert comma.
ℓ̃	Delete character(s); remove space.	⌃	Insert semicolon.
ℓ̶	Lowercase.	⌃	Insert colon.
LC	Lowercase.	⊙	Insert period.
⌒	Close up; no space.	⌄	Insert apostrophe.
#	Insert a space.	⌄⌄	Insert quotation marks.
[	Move to the left.	=	Insert hyphen.
]	Move to the right.	⊢⊣	Insert dash.

A MARKED PROOF

By CHRIS CORDERO

ST. LOUIS, Sept. 8 Mark McGwire of the St. Louis Cardinals set Major league Baseball's home run record tonight by hitting his 62d and shortest home run of the season.

With two outs in the fourth inning, McGwire lined a shot that just cleared the left-field fence near the foul line. The drive was estimated at 341 feet, six feet shorter than his previous shortest this year.

McGwire, a 34-year-old right-hander, has hit five home runs that sailed more than 500 feet, the longest, his 16th estimated at 545 feet. The hit that made McGwire the greatest single-season home run hitter of all time broke the tie that he created only a day erlier. In 1961, Maris hit his 61st home run in the Yankees' 163d and last game. In 1927, Babe Ruth hit his 60th home run in the Yankees 154th and last game. This game, against the Chicago Cubs, was the Cardinals' 145th of th season. Thwey won, 6-3.

McGwire beat Sammy Sosa of the Cubs to the record home run. They had conducted a spirited race that captivated the nation and brought back to baseball many fans who became disenchanted in the labor dispute of 1994-95. McGwire leads Sosa, 62 homers to 58, but the man who will enter the record book will be the one who has the most home runs at the end of the season.

But for now, Sosa recounted a coversation with McGwire after the historic home run that summed it up: "I told him, You're the Man. You did it.

(Proofreader's marks in margins:)
BOLD ROM
n
#
e
i
Roger
r
e/e
STET
a
though/n
L.C. ITAL
Tonight's
TR